Thomas Terrell

The Law and Practice Relating to Letters Patent for Inventions

Thomas Terrell

The Law and Practice Relating to Letters Patent for Inventions

ISBN/EAN: 9783743394841

Manufactured in Europe, USA, Canada, Australia, Japa

Cover: Foto ©Suzi / pixelio.de

Manufactured and distributed by brebook publishing software (www.brebook.com)

Thomas Terrell

The Law and Practice Relating to Letters Patent for Inventions

Letters Patent for Inventions.

THE LAW AND PRACTICE

RELATING TO

LETTERS PATENT FOR INVENTIONS.

With Appendix

CONTAINING THE

PATENTS, DESIGNS AND TRADE MARKS ACT, 1883,

AND THE

PATENT, TRADE MARKS, DESIGNS

AND PRIVY COUNCIL

RULES.

BY

THOMAS TERRELL, F.C.S.,

BARRISTER-AT-LAW.

LONDON:
HENRY SWEET, 3, CHANCERY LANE,
Law Publisher.

1884

PREFACE.

I am aware that in the following pages I have ventured to express strongly my views as to the effect of some of the most important provisions of the new Patent Act, and that the conclusions I have come to are at variance with the opinions of some of the leading living authorities on patent law. I regret that on carefully reconsidering what I have written, I am unable to so alter the opinions which I have given as to place myself in accord with those to whose exposition of the law it is evident far greater weight should be given than to my own.

The principal section as to the effect of which this difference of opinion has arisen is section 5, and the question is, does that section abolish patents for communications from abroad? The history of the grant of letters patent for communicated inventions may be thus shortly stated. The Common Law consideration for the grant of letters patent was the *introduction of a new manufacture within this realm.* The consideration was certainly not the invention of a new manufacture, except in so far that a man who *invented* and put in practice an invention might be said with justice to *introduce* the new manufacture. (See *In re Hastings' Patent, In re Malling's Patent*, and *Darcy* v. *Allen*.) The Statute of Monopolies defined the royal prerogative to grant patents, limiting it by section 6 to the grant for fourteen years or under " of the sole working or making of any manner of new manufactures within this realm, to the true and first inventor and inventors of such manufactures, which others at the time of making such letters patent and grants shall not use, &c." This was intended to be nothing more or less than a declaration of the Common Law; and so it was held in *Edgeberry* v. *Stephens* and in a great number of cases which are hereinafter cited; and thus it was that after the Statute of Monopolies the introduction of a new manufacture was still the primary consideration for the grant. Afterwards came the Patent Law Amendment Act, 1852, which left the law as regards communicated inventions in precisely the same position that it was before, except that the applicant had to declare whether he claimed for an original invention or for a communicated invention. In the Act of 1852 it is not required that the inventor should declare that " he is the true and first inventor." In *Milligan* v. *Marsh*, Vice-Chancellor Wood, afterwards Lord Hatherley, held that a person declaring himself a true inventor, when, in truth, the invention was communicated to him from abroad, made a false suggestion, and that the patent was void; and this, indeed, is mere common sense. The strict view with which this subject should be regarded may be gathered from the decision of Sir George Jessel in the Court of Appeal in *Marsden* v. *The Saville Street Co.* (L. R., 3 Ex. D. at p. 205.)

When the Act of 1883 was passed, some totally new provisions were adopted, and it was enacted by sect. 5, sub-sect. 2, that in every case the applicant must declare *that he is the first and true inventor of an invention.* This may have been an oversight, or it may have been intentional. I am rather inclined to think it was designed to abolish imported inventions; because we find only one form of declaration provided in the Act, which will clearly not do for an imported invention. Sect. 46 defines the word "invention" as meaning any manner of new manufacture within sect. 6 of the Statute of Monopolies. As soon as the Act was passed, a great deal of discussion arose as to whether or not communicated inventions were abolished by sect. 5. The opinion seemed to prevail that this form of patent could not thenceforth be granted, and that the definition of the word "invention" did not empower a man in possession of a communicated invention to make a declaration (equivalent to an affidavit) that he was the true and first inventor. Of course, patent agents, who were vitally interested, strongly objected to the change which was supposed to have been made in the law; and Mr. Chamberlain, I imagine, must have yielded to their representations, for we find in the Board of Trade Rules, which were issued late in December, a form of declaration which is very remarkable. It runs as follows:—"I, ——, do solemnly and sincerely declare that I am in possession of an invention for ——, which invention has been communicated to me from abroad by ——, *that I claim to be the true and first inventor thereof*, &c., &c." In other words, "I am not the inventor, but still, it being necessary under the Act to declare that I am the inventor, I make the necessary declaration." All must regret that Sir George Jessel is not now on the Bench to construe this document, and to give his judgment as to the power of the Board of Trade to institute any such form of declaration. I can only say that, in my opinion (worthy of very little consideration, no doubt), this form of declaration is nonsense, and that I believe the Courts will hold that it is altogether *ultra vires*. It bases its existence upon the construction given in the Act of the word "invention" and an endeavour to apply thereto the judicial decisions on the words "first and true inventor within this realm" in the Statute of Monopolies. If the definition had been, "the words 'first and true inventor' shall have the meaning which has been applied to the same words under the Statute of Monopolies," the matter might have been different; but even then it is difficult to see how, without overruling it, the decision in *Milligan* v. *Marsh* would have been got over. It is to be hoped that before long the point will have received judicial decision, as otherwise a vast number of patents will be in some jeopardy of being at any moment held to be invalid. I trust that I shall be pardoned for having perhaps too boldly expressed myself. I respectfully submit these my opinions, and I admit that it is very probable that in many instances they are erroneous.

I have to thank my friend Mr. H. G. Watts, of 3, Harcourt Buildings, Temple, for many valuable suggestions in the preparation of this work, and especially for the Index to it.

THOMAS TERRELL.

New Court, Temple,
    8th Jan. 1884.

CONTENTS.

	PAGE
PREFACE	v
TABLE OF CASES	xvii

THE LAW OF PATENTS.

INTRODUCTION 1

CHAPTER I.
THE PATENTEE 5
    (First Inventor; First Importer.)

CHAPTER II.
THE CONSIDERATION 9
    (The Actual Inventor; the First Introducer.)

CHAPTER III.
THE CONSIDERATION (*continued*) 22
    (A New and Useful Invention.)

CHAPTER IV.
THE CONSIDERATION (*continued*) 52
    (The Specification; the Title; the Provisional Specifications; the Complete Specification; the Claims.)

CONTENTS.

CHAPTER V.

AMENDMENT OF SPECIFICATIONS 90
    (Memorandum of Alteration; Disclaimer.)

CHAPTER VI.

OPPOSITION TO THE GRANT 99

CHAPTER VII.

THE GRANT 102
    (The Address; the Recitals; the Grant; the Prohibition; the Conditions; the Construction of the Grant.)

CHAPTER VIII.

THE DEVOLUTION OF A PATENT 112
    (By Operation of Law; by Assignments; by the Grant of Licences.)

CHAPTER IX.

EXTENSION OF TERM OF PATENT 123
    (Jurisdiction of the Privy Council.)

CHAPTER X.

CONFIRMATION 140

CHAPTER XI.

REMEDIES OF THE PATENTEE AND OF THE PUBLIC 141
    (Action for Infringement; Parties.)

CHAPTER XII.

THE CAUSE OF ACTION 145
    (Infringement; by Making; by Using; by Selling.)

CHAPTER XIII.

THE REMEDY 167
    (Injunction; Damages; Account of Sales and Profits.)

CHAPTER XIV.

REVOCATION 181

CHAPTER XV.

INTERNATIONAL AND COLONIAL ARRANGEMENTS 185

PRACTICE.

CHAPTER I.

ACTION FOR INFRINGEMENT 187

CHAPTER II.

PARTIES 188

CHAPTER III.

INTERLOCUTORY INJUNCTION 190

CHAPTER IV.

STATEMENT OF CLAIM 193

CHAPTER V.
PARTICULARS OF BREACHES 194

CHAPTER VI.
STATEMENT OF DEFENCE 199

CHAPTER VII.
PARTICULARS OF OBJECTIONS 201

CHAPTER VIII.
INTERROGATORIES 210

CHAPTER IX.
INSPECTION 216

CHAPTER X.
THE TRIAL 221

CHAPTER XI.
QUESTIONS FOR COURT AND JURY 234

CHAPTER XII.
CERTIFICATES 239

CHAPTER XIII.
PRACTICE ON PETITION FOR REVOCATION 246

CHAPTER XIV.
ACTION FOR INJUNCTION TO RESTRAIN THREATS 249

FORMS OF PRACTICAL PROCEDURE 251

APPENDIX.

Patents, Designs and Trade Marks Act, 1883...............	269
Patents Rules...	302
Trade Marks Rules	325
Designs Rules...	348
Privy Council Rules.....................................	358

INDEX... 361

TABLE OF CASES.

A.

	PAGE
ADAIR's Patent, In re (1881), L. R. 6 App. Cas. 176......128,	133
Adair v. Young (1879), L. R. 12 Ch. D. 13..............162,	174
Adams v. North British Rail. Co. (1873), 29 L. T. R. N. S. 367..	189
Adamson's Patent, In re (1856), 6 De G. M. & G. 420; 25 L. J. Ch. 456; 4 W. R. 473	99
Alcock v. Cook (1829), 5 Bing. 340	104
Allan's Patent, In re (1867), L. R. 1 P. C. 507; 4 Moo. P. C. C. N. S. 443	127
Allen v. Rawson (1845), 1 C. B. 551 (at p. 574)............13,	33
Arkwright v. Nightingale (1785), 1 Web. P. C. 60 (at p. 61); Dav. P. C. 37	72
Aube's Patent, In re (1854), 9 Moo. P. C. C. 43	135
Aveling v. Maclaren (1881), L. R. 17 Ch. D. 139, n.	206
Axmann v. Lund (1874), 22 W. R. 789; L. R. 18 Eq. 330; 43 L. J. Ch. 655; 3 L. T. Rep. N. S. 119	117

B.

Bacon v. Jones (1839), 4 My. & Cr. 433 (at p. 438)	175
——— v. Spottiswood (1839), 1 Beav. 382 (at p. 387)	180
Bailey v. Roberton (1878), L. R. 3 App. Cas. 1055; 38 L. T. Rep. N. S. 854; 27 W. R. 477......................63,	155
Bainbridge v. Wigley (1810), Higgins' Digest, 155; Par. Rep. Pat. 1829, p. 197; 18 Rep. Arts. 127; 1 Carp. P. C. 270; Higgins' Digest, 340....................................59,	105
Baird v. Moules' Patent Earth Closet Co. (1881), L. R. 17 Ch. D. 139, n.	206
Bancroft v. Warden (1873), Romilly's Notes to Cases, 103	147
Barber v. Walduck (1823), 1 Carp. P. C. 438; 1 C. & P. 567, reported under name of Barber v. Shaw; Holroyd Pat. 60; 1 Web. P. C. 126	10
Barker v. Grace (1847), 1 Ex. 339; 17 L. J. Ex. 122	71
Barrett v. Vernon (1876), 45 L. T. Rep. N. S. 755; 25 W. R. 343	155
Bateman v. Gray (1853), Mac. P. C. 93 (at p. 102)	156
Bate's Patent, In re (1836), 1 Web. P. C. 739, n.	130
Bates & Redgate, Ex parte (1869), L. R. 4 Ch. 577; 38 L. J. Ch. 501; 17 W. R. 900; 21 L. T. Rep. N. S. 410........16,	17
Batley v. Kynock (1874), L. R. 19 Eq. 91 (at p. 231) 194,	218
Beard v. Egerton (1846), 3 C. B. 97; 10 Jur. 643; 15 L. J. C. P. 270	20

T.   *b*

	PAGE
Beard v. Egerton (1819), 19 L. J. C. P. 36 (at p. 38); M. Dis. 75; 8 C. B. 165; 13 Jur. 1004	67, 237
Bentley v. Keighley (1844), 7 M. & G. 652; 1 D. & L. 944; 8 Scott, N. R. 372; 13 L. J. C. P. 167	196, 204
Besseman v. Wright (1858), 6 W. R. 719	116
Betts' Patents, In re (1862), 1 Moo. P. C. C. N. S. 49; 9 Jur. N. S. 137; 11 W. R. 221; 7 L. T. Rep. N. S. 577; 1 N. R. 137	127, 129, 132, 135
Betts v. De Vitre (1864), 11 L. T. Rep. N. S. 533; 11 Jur. N. S. 9; 5 N. R. 165; 34 L. J. Ch. 289 ..	178, 187, 244
—————————— V.-C. W. (1864), A. 119	176
—————————— (1865), 12 L. T. Rep. N. S. 51; 34 L. J. Ch. 291	176, 177
—————————— (1868), L. R. 3 Ch. 441; 37 L. J. Ch. 325; 18 L. T. Rep. N. S. 165; 16 W. R. 529 ..	43, 144, 189
—————————— (1873), L. R. 6 H. L. 319 (at p. 321); 21 W. R. 705	177, 187
——— v. Gallais (1870), L. R. 10 Eq. 392; 18 W. R. 945; 22 L. T. R. N. S. 841	180
——— v. Menzies (1857), 3 Jur. N. S. 357 (at p. 358) ..	41, 42, 169
—————————— (1859), 1 Ell. & Ell. 990; 28 L. J. Q. B. 361; 5 Jur. N. S. 1164	36
—————————— (1862), 10 H. L. Cas. 117; 31 L. J. Q. B. 233; 9 Jur. N. S. 29; 11 W. R. 1; 7 L. T. Rep. N. S. 110	42, 43, 44, 69, 72
——— v. Neilson (1868), L. R. 3 Ch. 429; 37 L. J. Ch. 321; 18 L. T. Rep. N. S. 159; 16 W. R. 524..	40, 43, 77
—————————— (1865), 6 N. R. 221; 12 L. T. Rep. N. S. 489; 13 W. R. 804	189
—————————— (1871), L. R. 5 H. L. 1; 40 L. J. Ch. 317; 19 W. R. 1121	226
——— v. Wilmott (1871), L. R. 6 Ch. 239; 19 W. R. 369; 25 L. T. Rep. N. S. 188	120, 148, 165, 166, 174, 191, 227
Bowley v. Hancock (1856), 6 De G. M. & G. 391 (at p. 402); 2 Jur. N. S. 289; 4 W. R. 334	26
Bickford v. Skewes (1837), 1 Web. P. C. 211 (1838), 1 Web. P. C. 211 } (at p. 213)	170
—————————————— (1841), 1 Q. B. 938; 1 G. & D. 736; 6 Jur. 167; 10 L. J. Q. B. 302; 1 Web. P. C. 214 (at p. 218) ..	66, 83, 237
Bircot's case (15 Eliz.), 3 Inst. 184; 1 Web. P. C. 31, n.	27
Blake's Patent, In re (1873), L. R. 4 P. C. 535; 9 Moo. P. C. C. N. S. 373	135
Bloxham v. Elsee (1825), 1 C. & P. 558 (at p. 565); Ry. & Moo. 187; 1 Carp. P. C. 434	51, 237
—————————— (1827), 1 Web. P. C. 132, n.; 6 B. & C. 169; 9 Dow. & Ry. 215; 1 Carp. P. C. 440	10, 56, 113, 143, 188
Bodmer's Patent, In re (1853), 8 Moo. P. C. C. 282; 6 M. D. 114	135, 136
Booth v. Kennard (1856), 1 Hurl. & Norm. 527; 26 L. J. Ex. 23; 3 Jur. N. S. 21; 28 L. T. Rep. 160; 5 W. R. 85	25

                                                                PAGE
Booth *v.* Kennard (1857), 2 Hurl. & Norm. 84 ; 26 L. J. Ex.
 305 ; 5 W. R. 607 ; 29 L. T. Rep. 163 72
Boulton *v.* Bull (1795), 2 H. Blac. 463 (at p. 491) ; Dav. P. C.
 162 ; 1 Carp. P. C. 117..........19, 22, 23, 39, 49, 76
—— *v.* Watt (1795), 2 H. Bl. 468 26
—— *v.* Keyworth (1857), 7 Ell. & Bl. 725 ; 3 Jur. N. S. 817 ;
 5 W. R. 686 ; 29 L. T. Rep. 194 33
—— *v.* Moore (1815), 2 Coop. C. P. 56, n. 216, 217
——————— (1816), Dav. P. C. 361 (at p. 400) 81, 84, 155
—— *v.* Pimm (1856), 11 Ex. 718 (at p. 739)............27, 234
Bovill *v.* Crate (1865), L. R. 1 Eq. 388 (at p. 391) 176
—— *v.* Smith (1866), L. R. 2 Eq. 459 212
—— *v.* Goodier (1866), L. R. 2 Eq. 195 ; 35 Beav. 427 ; 35
 L. J. Ch. 432 233
—— *v.* Hadley (1864), 17 C. B. N. S. 435 ; 10 L. T. Rep. N. S.
 650 ; 4 N. R. 464 240
Bower *v.* Hodges (1853), 22 L. J. C. P. 194 (at p. 198) ; 13
 C. B. 765 ; 17 Jur. 1057 ; 1 Ch. R. 807 119
Bowman *v.* Taylor (1834), 2 A. & E. 278 ; 4 N. & M. 264 114
Braham *v.* Hardcastle (1789), Holroyd, 81 ; 1 Carp. P. C. 168 ;
 1 Web. P. C. 44, n. 47, 48
Bridson's Patent, In re (1852), 7 Moo. P. C. C. 499.......... 138
—— *v.* Benecke, 12 Beav. 1 ; 34 Lond. Jour. 295........175, 191
—— *v.* M'Alpine (1845), 8 Beav. 229 ; L. R. 4 Ch. 289..170, 191
Brook *v.* Aston (1857), 8 El. & Bl. 478 (at p. 485) ; 4 Jur. N. S.
 279 ; 27 L. J. Q. B. 145 ; 6 W. R. 42 ....30, 31
Brooks *v.* Ripley (1831), 2 Lond. Jour. C. S. 35 ; Web. P. C. 102.. 228
Brunton *v.* Hawkes (1821), 4 B. & Ald. 541 (at p. 550) ; 1 Carp.
 P. C. 405 ....33, 48, 56, 57, 104
Bulnois *v.* Mackenzie (1837), 4 Bing. N. C. 432 203
Butler's case (about 1680), Vent. 344 183
Bush *v.* Fox (1852), Macrory's P. C. 152 (at p. 164) ; 23 L. J.
 Ex. 257 30
——————— (1856), 5 H. L. Cas. 707 ; 2 Jur. N. S. 1029 ;
 25 L. J. Ex. 251 ; Macrory's P. C. 178 ....30, 72

C.

Caldwell *v.* Vanvlissingen (1851), 9 Ha. 415 ; 16 Jur. 115 ;
 21 L. J. Ch. 97 ....144, 148, 161, 165
Campion *v.* Benyon (1821), 6 B. Mo. 71 ; 3 B. & B. 5 55
Canham *v.* Jones (1813), 2 Ves. & B. 218 107
Cannington *v.* Nuttall (1871), L. R. 5 H. L. 205 ; 40 L. J.
 Ch. 739..33, 153
Cardwell's Patent, In re (1856), 10 Moo. P. C. C. 488 (at p. 490). 126
Carpenter *v.* Smith (1841), 1 Web. P. C. 530 (at p. 538)..33, 36, 47
——————— (1842), 1 Web. P. C. 268, n. 203
—— *v.* Walker (1842), 1 Web. P. C. 268, n. 205
Carr's Patent, In re (1873), L. R. 4 P. C. 539 130
Chambers *v.* Crichley (1864), 33 Beav. 374 117
Chanter *v.* Dewhurst (1844), 12 M. & W. 828 ; 13 L. J. Ex. 198
                                                      113, 119

TABLE OF CASES.

	PAGE
Chanter *v.* Johnson (1845), 14 M. & W. 408 (at p. 411); 14 L. J. Ex. 289	114
—— *v.* Leese (1838), 1 Web. 295; 4 M. & W. 295; 1 H. & H. 224	116, 119
Chollett *v.* Hoffman (1857), 7 Ell. & B. 686; 26 L. J. Q. B. 249; 3 Jur. N. S. 935; 5 W. R. 573; 29 L. T. Rep. 158	121, 122
Clarke's Patent, In re (1870), 7 Moo. P. C. C. N. S. 255; L. R. 3 P. C. 421	132
Clarke *v.* Adie (1875), L. R. 10 Ch. App. Cas. 667 (at p. 674); 45 L. J. Ch. 228	149
—————— (first appeal), 33 L. T. Rep. N. S. 295	149
—————— (1877), L. R. 2 App. Cas. 315; 46 L. J. Ch. 585; 36 L. T. Rep. N. S. 923; 26 W. R. 45	72, 88, 151, 227
—————— (second appeal) (1876), L. R. 3 Ch. D. 134 (at p. 144); 24 W. R. 1007	116
—————— (1877), L. R. 2 App. Cas. 423; 46 L. J. Ch. 598; 37 L. T. Rep. N. S. 1; 46 W. R. 47	68
—— *v.* Ferguson (1859), 1 Giff. 184	191
Clothworkers of Ipswich case (1615), Godbolt R. 252 (at p. 253); 1 Roll. R. 4; 1 Web. P. C. 6	7, 18
Cochrane *v.* Smethurst (1816), Davy's P. C. 354; 1 Stark. 205	55
Collard *v.* Allison (1839), 4 My. & Cr. 433	191
Cook *v.* Pearce (1844), 8 Q. B. 1054; 8 Jur. 499; 13 L. J. Q. B. 189	56
Cornish *v.* Keene (1835), 1 Web. P. C. 501 (at p. 507); 2 Carp. P. C. 314	11, 13, 36, 47, 51, 237
—————— (1837), 2 Bing. N. C. 570; 4 Scott, 337; 2 Hodges, 281; 6 L. J. C. P. 225; 1 Web. P. C. 513; 2 Carp. P. C. 371; 6 Rep. Arts. 4th Series, 102	37, 237
Crane *v.* Price (1842), 1 Web. P. C. 393 (at p. 411); 4 Y. & G. 580; 5 Scott, N. R. 338; 12 L. J. C. P. 81; 2 Carp. P. C. 669; 18 Rep. Arts. 4th Series, 102	33, 50
Croll *v.* Edge (1850), 9 C. B. 479; 14 Jur. 553; 19 L. J. C. P. 261; M. Dig. 194	59, 148
Crompton *v.* Ibbertson (1828), 1 Web. P. C. 83; Dan. & Lloyd, 33; 1 Carp. P. C. 460	83
Crosskill *v.* Evory (1848), 10 L. T. R. 459	169
Crossly *v.* Beverley (1829), 9 B. & C. 62; 1 Web. P. C. 106, 112, 119; 3 C. & P. 513; Mo. & Mal. 283; 1 Russ. & My. 166	65, 73, 81, 176
—— *v.* Derby Gas Co. (1834), 4 L. J. Ch. 25; 1 Web. P. C. 119 (at p. 120)	176, 179
—— *v.* Dixon (1863), 10 H. L. Cas. 293; 9 Jur. N. S. 607; 11 W. R. 716; 8 L. T. Rep. N. S. 260; 1 N. R. 540; 32 L. J. Ch. 617	117, 120
—— *v.* Potter (1853), Macrory, P. C. 240	22, 58, 77
—— *v.* Stewart (1863), 1 N. R. 426	210
—— *v.* Tomey (1876), L. R. 2 Ch. D. 533; 34 L. T. R. N. S. 476	211
Curtis *v.* Platt (1863), 3 Ch. D. 135 n.; 19 Newt. Lond. Jour. N. S. 44; 8 L. T. Rep. N. S. 657	32
—— (1864), 11 L. T. Rep. N. S. 245	147
—— (1866), 35 L. J. Ch. 852; L. R. 1 H. L. 337	146, 153, 155, 238

Cutler v. Bower (1848), 11 Q. B. 973; 12 Jur. 721; 17 L. J. Q. B. 217 117

D.

Daines' Patent, In re (1856), 4 A. & E. 949; 26 L. J. Ch. 298; 4 W. R. 455 110
Dangerfield v. Jones (1865), 13 L. T. Rep. N. S. 142 33
Darcy v. Allin (1602), 1 Web. P. C. (at p. 6); Noy R. 173 (at p. 182) 6, 19, 35, 49
Davenport v. Goldberg (1865), 2 Hem. & N. 282; 5 N. R. 584.. 169
——————————— (1865), 2 H. & M. 725 .... 212, 214
——————————— (1865), L. R. 1 Eq. 38; 13 L. T. R. N. S. 399; 14 W. R. 48 207
——————— v. Jepson (1862)), 1 N. R. 73, 307 .... 169, 219
——————— v. Richards (1860), 3 L. T. Rep. N. S. 503...... 188, 226
Daw v. Eley (1867), L. R. 3 Eq. 496; 36 L. J. Ch. 482; 15 L. T. Rep. N. S. 559 176
Deering's Patent, In re (1880), 13 Ch. D. 393 16
De la Rue v. Dickenson (1857), 7 E. & B. 738; 3 Jur. N. S. 841; 5 W. R. 704; 29 L. T. R. 194 .... 145, 237
Denley v. Blore (1851), 38 Lond. Jour. 224...... 143, 144, 189, 244
Dent v. Turpin (1861), 2 J. & H. 139 142
Derosne's Patent, In re (1844), 2 Web. P. C. 1 (at p. 4); 4 Moo. P. C. C. 416 .... 126, 128
Derosne v. Fairie (1835), 1 Web. P. C. 154 (at p. 155); 1 Mo. & Rob. 457 142
De Vitre v. Betts (1873), L. R. 6 H. L. 319; 21 W. R. 705 ..177, 187
Dircks v. Mellor (1845), 26 Lond. Jour. 268 191
Dixon v. London Small Arms Co. (1875), L. R. 10 Q. B. 130; L. R. 1 App. Cas. 641; 31 L. T. Rep. N. S. 830; L. R. 1 Q. B. D. 384.................... 110, 111, 159
——————————— (1876) L. R. 1 App. Cas. 632; 46 L. J. Q. B. 617; 35 L. T. R. N. S. 559; 25 W. R. 142.................... 159
Dollond's Patent (1758), 1 Web. P. C. 43; 2 H. Bl. 469, 470, 487; Dav. P. C. 170, 171, 172, 199; 1 Carp. P. C. 28 ....10, 39
Downton's Patent, In re (1839), 1 Web. P. C. 565 (at p. 567).. 138
Dudgeon v. Thompson (1874), L. R. 3 App. Cas. 53; 22 W. R. 464; 30 L. T. Rep. N. S. 244 ....68, 97, 154, 169, 191
Dunnicliff v. Mallett (1859), 7 C. B. N. S. 209; 1 L. T. Rep. N. S. 514; 6 Jur. N. S. 252; 29 L. J. C. P. 70; 8 W. R. 260 ..141, 188

E.

East India Co. v. Kynaston (1820), 3 Bl. App. Cas. 153 217
——————— v. Sandys (1728), Skin. 225.................. 102
Edgeberry v. Stevens (1691), 1 Web. P. C. 35; 2 Salk. 447; Comb. 84; Dav. P. C. 36; 1 Carp. P. C. 35 ....7, 19, 49
Edison Telephone Co. v. India Rubber Co. (1881), L. R. 17 Ch. D. 137 206
——————————— v. Nott (1847), 4 C. B. 462; 11 Jur. 590; 16 L. J. C. P. 174; 2 Coop. 41 ....174, 197

TABLE OF CASES.

	PAGE
Electric Telegraph Co. v. Brett (1851), 10 C. B. 838 ; 20 L. J. C. P. 123 ; 15 Jur. 579	141, 156, 188
Elliott v. Aston (1840), 1 Web. P. C. 222	237
Ellwood v. Christy (1864), 10 Jur. N. S. 1079 ; 17 C. B. N. S. 754 ; 34 L. J. C. P. 130 ; 13 W. R. 54 ; 11 L. T. Rep. N. S. 342 ; 5 N. R. 12	118
Elmslie v. Boursier (1869), L. R. 9 Eq. 217 (at p. 222); 39 L. J. Ch. 328 ; 18 W. R. 665	164
Erard's Patent, In re (1835), 1 Web. P. C. 557 (at p. 559); 5 Rep. Arts. N. S. 58	125
Evans v. Rees (1842), 2 Q. B. 334	143

F.

Feather v. R. (1865), 8 B. & S. 257 ; 35 L. J. Q. B. 200 ; 12 L. T. N. S. 114	110, 159
Felton v. Greaves (1829), 3 C. & P. 611	56, 58, 105
Finnigan v. James (1875), L. R. 19 Eq. 72	212
Fisher v. Dewick (1838), 1 Web. P. C. 267 ; 1 Web. P. C. 551, n.	195, 203, 204, 205
Flower v. Lloyd (1876), W. N. 1876, 169, 230 ; 20 Sol. Journ. 1876, 860	196, 207, 217
———— (1877), W. N. 1877, 132 ; Johnson's P. M. 245	155
Forsyth v. Riviere (1819), 1 Web. P. C. 97 ; Chit. Prerog. Ca. 182 ; 1 Carp. P. C. 401	155
Fox v. Dollestable (1866), 15 W. R. 194 (at p. 195)	28
Foxwell v. Bostock (1864), 12 W. R. 723 (at p. 725) ; 10 L. T. R. N. S. 144 ; 4 De G. J. & S. 298	32, 36, 61, 87, 88, 96, 150, 152
———— v. Webster (1863), 3 N. R. 103, 180 ; 4 De G. J. & S. 77 ; 9 L. T. N. S. 528 ; 12 W. R. 186 ; 10 Jur. N. S. 137	175
Frearson v. Loe (1878), L. R. 9 Ch. D. 48 (at pp. 58 and 64); 27 W. R. 183	47, 51, 158, 172, 176

G.

Galloway v. Bleaden (1839), 1 Web. P. C. 268, n.; 1 Web. P. C. 521 (at p. 525)	47, 203, 204
Galloway's Patent, In re (1843), 1 Web. P. C. 724 (at p. 729) ; 7 Jur. 453	130, 133
Gamble v. Kurtz (1846), 3 C. B. 425	155
Gardner v. Broadbent (1856), 2 Jur. N. S. 1041 ; 4 W. R. 767	169, 190, 192
Gillett v. Green (1841), 7 M. & W. 347 ; 9 Dowl. 219 ; 1 Web. P. C. 271 ; 10 L. J. Ex. 124	239
———— v. Wilby (1839), 9 C. & P. 334 (at p. 336); 1 Web. P. C. 270	149
Gibson v. Brand (1841), 1 Web. P. C. 627 (at p. 628)	13, 47
———— (1842), 4 M. & G. 179 ; 4 Scott, N. R. 844 ; 1 Web. P. C. 631 ; 11 L. J. C. P. 177	26, 84, 144
Goucher v. Clayton, 11 Jur. N. S. 107 and 462	117
Goucher's Patent, In re (1865), 2 Moo. P. C. C. N. S. 532	139
Graham v. Campbell (1878), L. R. 7 Ch. D. 490	190

TABLE OF CASES. xxiii

	PAGE
Granger, Ex parte (1812), Godson on Patents, 2nd ed. p. 225..	113
Greaves v. Eastern Counties Rail. Co. (1859), 1 E. & E. 961; 28 L. J. Q. B. 290; 5 Jur. N. S. 733	242
Grover and Baker Sewing Machine Co. v. Millard (1862), 8 Jur. N. S. 713 (at p. 714)	117

H.

Hall v. Jarvis (1822), 1 Web. P. C. 100	25
Hallett v. Hague (1831), 2 B. & Ad. 370 (at p. 377)	67
Hancock v. Moulton (1852), Johnson's Patentees' Manual, 3rd ed. p. 208; M. Dig. 506	156, 173, 176
—— v. Somervell (1851), 39 Newton's Lond. Jour. 158	38
Hardy's Patent, In re (1849), 6 Moo. P. C. C. 441; 13 Jur. 177	131
Harmar v. Playne (1809), Dav. P. C. 311 (at p. 316); 11 East, 101	65, 73, 76
Harrison v. The Anderston Foundry Co. (1876), L. R. 1 App. Ca. 574 (at p. 581); 2 S. C. L. R. 4th series, 857	68, 86
Harwood v. Great Northern Rail. Co. (1860), 29 L. J. Q. B. 193; 6 Jur. N. S. 993	31, 36
—— (1865), 11 H. L. Cas. 654; 35 L. J. Q. B. 27; 12 L. T. Rep. N. S. 771; 14 W. R. 1	32
Hassall v. Wright (1870), 40 L. J. Ch. 145; L. R. 10 Eq. 509; 18 W. R. 821	122, 188
Hasting's Patent (1567), 1 Web. P. C. 6; Noy, R. 182	18, 35
Haworth v. Hardcastle (1834), 1 Web. P. C. 480 (at p. 483); 4 M. & Sc. 720; 1 Bing. N. C. 182; 3 L. J. C. P. 311	51, 67, 105
Hayne v. Maltby (1789), 3 T. R. 438; Dav. P. C. 156	114, 115, 116
Heath's Patent, In re (1853), 8 Moo. P. C. C. 217; 2 Web. P. C. 247; M. Dig. 114	132, 136
Heath v. Smith (1854), 2 Ell. & Bl. 256; 2 C. L. R. 1584; 18 Jur. 601; 23 L. J. Q. B. 166; 2 Web. P. C. 268	39, 47
—— v. Unwin (1842), 15 Sim. 553; 10 M. & W. 684 (at p. 687)	146, 204, 208
—————— (1845), 14 L. J. Ex. 153 (at p. 156); 2 Web. P. C. 221; 13 M. & W. 583	146, 156
—————— (1852), 22 L. J. C. P. 7; 2 Web. P. C. 236; 12 C. B. 522; 25 L. J. C. P. 19	72, 74, 82, 146
Henderson v. Mostyn Copper Co., L. R. 3 Ch. 202	120
Herbert's Patent, In re, L. R. 1 P. C. 399; 4 Moo. P. C. C. N. S. 300	127
Hesse v. Stevenson (1803), 3 B. & P. 565	113
Heugh v. Chamberlain (1877), 25 W. R. 742	118
Higgs v. Godwin (1858), 27 L. J. Q. B. 421; 5 Jur. N. S. 97; Ell. Bl. & Ell. 529	25, 158
Hills' Patent, In re (1863), 1 Moo. P. C. C. N. S. 258 (at p. 265); 9 Jur. N. S. 1209; 12 W. R. 25; 9 L. T. Rep. N. S. 101	128, 129, 130, 134, 138
Hill v. Thompson (1817), 1 Web. P. C. 235 (at p. 237), 229; 3 Mer. 622, 626	32, 51, 66, 67, 191, 192, 237
—————— (1818), 2 B. Moo. 424; 8 Taunt. 375; 1 Web. P. C. 239	39, 48, 59, 104, 105, 154

Hills *v.* Evans (1862), 31 L. J. Ch. 457 (at p. 463); 8 Jur. N. S. 525; 6 L. T. Rep. N. S. 90; 4 De G. F. & J. 288 .. 44, 67, 72, 169, 178, 187, 234
—— *v.* London Gaslight Co. (1857), 27 L. J. Ex. 60.......... 71
—————— (1860), 29 L. J. Ex. 409; 5 H. & N. 312 (at p. 336) 25, 40, 44, 47
Hinks *v.* Safety Lighting Co. (1876), L. R. 4 Ch. D. 607 (at p. 612); 46 L. J. Ch. 185; 36 L. T. Rep. N. S. 391 ......67, 72
Hoffman *v.* Posthill (1869), L. R. 4 Ch. App. Cas. 673; 17 W. R. 901; 20 L. T. Rep. N. S. 893 ....213, 214
Holland *v.* Fox (1853), 1 C. L. R. 440; 1 W. R. 448 .. 195, 204, 205
Holmes *v.* London and North Western Rail. Co. (1852), 22 L. J. C. P. 57; Macrory's P. C. 13; 12 C. B. 831 71
Honiball *v.* Bloomer (1854), 2 Web. P. C. 199 (at p. 200); 10 Ex. 538; 1 Jur. N. S. 188; 24 L. J. Ex. 11; 3 W. R. 71; 3 C. L. R. 167; M. Dig. 46 ....47, 242
Hornblower *v.* Boulton (1799), 8 T. R. 95 (at p. 101); Dav. P. C. 221; 1 Carp. P. C. 156 ....22, 23, 27, 65, 73
Houghton's Patent, In re (1871), 7 Moo. P. C. C. N. S. 309; L. R. 3 P. C. 461 132
Househill Iron Co. *v.* Neilson (1842), 1 Web. P. C. 673, 676, 718, n.; 9 C. & F. 788.....................22, 41, 47, 55, 73
How *v.* McKernan (1862), 30 Beav. 546.................... 210
Huddart *v.* Grimshaw (1803), Dav. P. C. 265 (at p. 267); 1 Web. P. C. 85; Carp. P. C. 200 ....32, 226
Hughes' Patent, In re (1879), L. R. 4 App. Cas. 174; 48 L. J. P. C. 20; 27 W. R. 493....................................... 127
Hull *v.* Bolland (1856), 25 L. J. Ex. 304; 1 H. & N. 134 ......196, 205, 231
Hutchinson's Patent, In re (1861), 14 Moo. P. C. C. 364...... 132

J.

Jackson *v.* Duke of Newcastle (1864), 33 L. J. Ch. 698 220
Jessop's case (before 1795), Cit. 2 H. Bl. 490; Dav. P. C. 182, 203; 1 Web. P. C. 42, n. 105
Johnson's Patent, In re (1871), 8 Moo. P. C. C. N. S. 282 (at p. 291); L. R. 4 P. C. 75 ....129, 135
—————— (1877), 8 Moo. P. C. C. N. S. 291; L. R. 5 Ch. D. 503; 46 L. J. Ch. 555............ 129, 136
—————— and Atkinson's Patent, In re (1873), L. R. 5 P. C. 87.. 131
Jones's Patent, In re (1854), 9 Moo. P. C. C. 41 138
Jones *v.* Berger (1843), 1 Web. P. C. 504 (at p. 549); 5 M. & G. 208; 6 Scott, N. R. 208; 7 Jur. 883; 12 L. J. C. P. 179 ....195, 204, 207, 208
—— *v.* Lees (1856), 1 H. & N. 189; 2 Jur. N. S. 645; 26 L. J. Ex. 9 120
—— *v.* Pearce (1831), 2 Coop. 58 191
—————— (1832), 1 Web. P. C. 122; 1 Carp. P. C. 524; 1 Lon. Jour. C. S. 215............................25, 47, 158
Jordan *v.* Moore (1866), L. R. 1 C. P. 624; 12 Jur. N. S. 766; 35 L. J. C. P. 268; 14 W. R. 769 31
Jupe *v.* Pratt (1837), 1 Web. P. C. 145 (at p. 146) 22, 156

K.

	PAGE
Kay's Patent, In re (1839), 1 Web. P. C. 568 (at p. 572); 3 Moo. P. C. C. 24	130
Keynaston v. East India Co. (1819), 3 Swan. 248	217
Knowles v. Bovill (1870), 22 L. T. Rep. N. S. 70	119
Kynock v. National Arms Co. Limited (1877), 37 L. J. Rep. N. S. 31; 26 W. R. 22	98

L.

Lang v. Gisborne (1862), 31 Beav. 133 (at p. 135); 8 Jur. N. S. 736; 31 L.J.Ch.769; 10 W. R. 638; 6 L. T. Rep. N. S. 771	45
Lea v. Saxby (1875), 32 L. T. R. N. S. 731	211
Lewin v. Brown (1866), 14 W. R. 640	118
Lewis v. Davis (1829), 1 Web. P. C. 488; 3 C. & P. 502; 1 Carp. P. C. 471	33
—— v. Marling (1829), 10 B. & C. 22; 4 C. & P. 56; 5 M. & R. 66; 1 Web. P. C. 493; 1 Carp. P. C. 478	11, 36, 51, 77, 83, 104, 105
Liardet v. Johnson (1778), 1 Web. P. C. 52; Bull. N. P. 78; 1 Carp. P. C. 35	35, 82
Lister v. Eastwood (1864), 9 L. T. R. N. S. 766	153
—— v. Leather (1857), 8 E. & B. 1004 (at p. 1017); 3 Jur. N. S. 433, 811; 5 W. R. 603; 29 L. T. Rep. 142	28, 86, 150, 151, 152
—————— (1858), 27 L. J. Q. B. 295; 4 Jur. N. S. 947; 4 K. & J. 425; 8 E. & B. 1031	33
Losh v. Hague (1837), 1 Web. P. C. 200 (at p. 205)	47, 51, 173, 175
—————— (1839), 7 D. P. C. 495; 5 M. & W. 387; 3 Jur. 409; 8 L. J. Ex. 251; 7 Dowl. 495	242
Lovell v. Hicks (1836), 2 Y. & C. 46; 5 L.J. Ex. 101	118
Lowe's Patent, In re (1846), 10 Jur. 363	131

M.

M'Alpine v. Mangnall (1846), 15 L. J. C. P. 298; 3 C. B. 496	113
M'Cormick v. Gray (1861), 5 H. & N. 25; 31 L. J. Ex. 42; 9 W. R. 809; 4 L. T. Rep. N. S. 832	48, 147
M'Dougal's Patent, In re (1867), L. R. 2 P. C. 1; 37 L. J. P. C. 17; 5 Moo. P. C. C. N. S. 1	127
M'Innes' Patent, In re (1868), 5 Moo. P. C. C. N. S. 72 (at p. 78; L. R. 2 P. C. 54; 37 L. J. P. C. 23	134
Macfarlane v. Price (1816), 1 Web. P. C. 74; 1 Stark. 199	76
Macnamara v. Hales (1842), C. & M. 471; 2 Web. P. C. 128, n.	237, 238
Manceaux's Patent, In re (1870), L. R. 6 Ch. 272	100
Manton v. Manton (1815), Dav. P. C. 333 (at p. 350); 1 Carp. P. C. 278	229
Marsden v. Savill Street Foundry and Engineering Co. Limited (1878), L. R. 3 Ex. D. 203; 39 L. T. Rep. N. S. 97, 100; 26 W. R. 784	19, 21, 109

	PAGE

Medlock's Patent, In re (1865), 22 Newt. Lond. Jour. N. S. 69..97, 101
Mercier *v.* Cotton (1876), L. R. 1 Q. B. D. 442.............. 210
Milligan *v.* Marsh (1856), 2 Jur. N. S. 1083 21
Milner's Patent, In re (1854), 9 Moo. P. C. C. 39............ 138
Minter *v.* Mower (1835), 1 Web. P. C. 138.................. 36
—— *v.* Wells (1834), 1 Web. P. C. 127, 134; 1 Carp. P. C. 622, 639; 1 C. M. & R. 505; 5 Tyr. 163; 4 L. J. Ex. 2 ....11, 155
—— *v.* Williams (1835), 1 Web. P. C. 135; 4 A. & E. 251; 5 N. & M. 657; 1 H. & N. 585; 5 L. J. K. B. 60.......... 163
Mitchell *v.* Barker (1851), 39 Lond. Jour. 531 191
—— *v.* Reynolds (1713), 19 Mod. R. 130; 1 P. Wms. 181.. 35
Morewood *v.* Tupper (1855), 3 C. L. Rep. 718 151
Morey's Patent, In re (1858), 25 Beav. 581; Higgins' Dig. 339; 6 W. R. 612 122
Morgan's Patent, In re (1843), 24 W. R. 245; 1 Web. P. C. 737 (at p. 739)............122, 125, 137
———————— (1876), 24 W. R. 245; 1 Web. P. C. 739..121, 125, 138
Morgan *v.* Fuller (1866), L. R. 2 Eq. 296 (at p. 297) 195
—— *v.* Seaward (1837), 2 M. & W. 544; Mur. & H. 55; 1 Jur. 527; 1 Web. P. C. 167, 170, 187, 196; 1 Carp. P. C. 37, 96; 6 L. J. Ex. 153..36, 46, 58, 65, 77, 82, 103, 155, 217, 237
Mullins *v.* Hart (1852), 5 Car. & K. 297.................... 47
Muntz' Patent, In re (1846), 2 Web. P. C. 113 (at p. 119)..127, 129, 130
—— *v* Foster (1843—4), 2 Web. P. C. 93 (at p. 103), 1 Dowl. & Low, 942..28, 41, 48, 72, 145, 155, 158, 163—169, 223, 237
—— *v.* Grenfell (1842), 2 Coop. 61 n.; 7 Jur. 121.......... 191
Murray *v.* Clayton (1872), L. R. 7 Ch. 570 (at p. 584); 20 W. R. 649; 27 L. T. Rep. N. S. 100; 21 W. R. 118; 42 L. J. Ch. 191; L. R. 15 Eq. 115; 27 L. T. Rep. N. S. 644; 21 W. R. 498..33, 155, 179, 213

N.

Napier's Patent, In re (1861), 13 Moo. P. C. C. 543; 9 W. R. 390 126
Needham *v.* Oxley (1863), 11 W. R. 852; 8 L. T. Rep. N. S. 604; 2 N. R. 388................ 177, 187
———————— (1863), 1 H. & M. 248 194
Neilson *v.* Betts (1871), L. R. 3 Ch. 429; L. R. 5 H. L. 1; 40 L. J. Ch. 317; 19 W. R. 1121......43, 160, 177, 187
—— *v.* Forman (1841), 2 Coop, 6 n. 170
—— *v.* Fothergill (1841), 1 Web. P. C. 287 116
—— *v.* Harford (1841), 1 Web. P. C. 295 (at p. 310)..73, 155, 236, 237
———————— (1841), 1 Web. P. C. 331 (at p. 342), 295, 324, 373; 8 M. & W. 806; 11 L. J. Ex. 20; 10 L. J. Ex. 493; 2 Coop. C. C. 61, n... 22, 58, 67, 83, 205, 231, 235
—— *v.* Thompson (1841), 1 Web. P. C. 278; 2 Coop. 61, n. 65, 170

TABLE OF CASES. xxvii

PAGE

Newall *v.* Elliott (1858), 4 C. B. N. S. 269; 4 Jur. N. S. 562; 27 L. J. C. P. 537 .... 47, 61, 62
——— (1864), 13 W. R. 11; 10 Jur. N. S. 954; 10 L. T. Rep. N. S. 792; 4 N. R. 429 .... 25, 60, 147, 162
——— *v.* Wilkins (1851), 17 L. T. Rep. 20 240
——— *v.* Wilson (1852), 2 De G. M. & G. 282; 19 L. T. Rep. 161 191
Newbery *v.* James (1817), 2 Mer. 446 (at p. 451); 1 Carp. P. C. 367 .... 66, 107
Newton's Patent, In re (1861), 14 Moo. P. C. C. 156 .... 128, 135
Newton *v.* Grand Junction Rail. Co. (1846), 5 Ex. 331 (at p. 334); 20 L. J. Ex. 427, n.; M. Dig. 75 .... 148, 149, 238
——— *v.* Vaucher (1851), 21 L. J. Ex. 305 (at p. 308); 6 Ex. 859 .... 55, 68, 151
Nickels *v.* Haslam (1844), 13 L. J. C. P. 146; 8 Scott, N. R. 97; 7 M. & G. 378; 8 Jur. 474 59
——— *v.* Ross (1849), 8 C. B. 679 (at p. 710) 20
Nobel's Explosive Co. *v.* Jones, Scott & Co. (1878), 17 Ch. D. 721 .... 161, 162
Normand's Patent, In re (1870), 6 Moo. P. C. C. N. S. 477 .. 135
Norton's Patent, In re (1863), 1 Moo. P. C. C. N. S. 339; 9 Jur. N. S. 419; 11 W. R. 720; 1 N. R. 557 .... 133, 136
Norton *v.* Brooks (1861), 7 H. & N. 499; 8 Jur. N. S. 155; 10 W. R. 111 117
Nunn *v.* D'Albuquerque (1865), 34 Beav. 595 180

O.

Oldham *v.* Langmead (before 1789), Cit. 3 T. R. 439, 441 114
Oxford and Cambridge Universities *v.* Richardson (1802), 6 Ves. 689 .... 161, 168
Oxley *v.* Holden (1860), 30 L. J. C. P. 68; 8 C. B. N. S. 666; 8 W. R. 626; 2 L. T. Rep. N. S. 464 .... 45, 47, 163

P.

Palmer *v.* Cooper (1853), 9 Ex. 231; L. R. 23 Ex. 82; 2 C. L. R. 430 .... 195, 203, 207
——— *v.* Wagstaff (1853), 8 Ex. 840; 17 Jur. 781; 22 L. J. Ex. 295; 1 W. R. 438; 1 C. L. R. 448 196
Parkes *v.* Stevens (1869), L. R. 8 Eq. 358 (at p. 367); 38 L. J. Ch. 627; 17 W. R. 846; L. R. 3 Ch. 36 .... 31, 66, 86, 152, 237
Patent Bottle Envelope Co. *v.* Seymer (1858), 5 C. B. N. S. 164; 5 Jur. N. S. 174; 28 L. J. C. P. 22 .... 32, 149
——— Type Founding Co. *v.* Richards (1859), 2 L. T. R. N. S. 359 195
——— *v.* Walter Lloyd (1860), 8 W. R. 353; Johns. 727.. 218
Patterson's Patent, In re (1849), 6 Moo. P. C. C. 469; 13 Jur. 593 134

Patterson *v.* Gas Light & Coke Co. (1876), L. R. 2 Ch. D.
  827 (at p. 832); 45 L. J. Ch. 843; 35 L. T.
  Rep. N. S. 11 15
———————— (1877), L. R. 3 App. Ca. 239 (at p. 243); 47
  L. J. Ch. 402; 38 L. T. Rep. N. S. 303;
  26 W. R. 482 ....14, 22, 44
———— *v.* Holland (1845), Hindmarch, 293 224
Penn *v.* Bibby (1866), L. R. 1 Eq. 538 (at p. 548)........... 206
—— *v.* Jack (1866), L. R. 2 Ch. App. Ca. 127; 36 L. J. Ch.
  455; 15 W. R. 208; 15 L. T. Rep. N. S. 399.. 31,
  61, 62
———————— (1866), 3 L. J. Eq. 308 ....169, 240
———————— (1866), L. R. 2 Eq. 314 (at p. 317); 14 L. T. R.
  N. S. 495; 14 W. R. 760 ....230, 231
———————— (1867), L. R. 5 Eq. 81 (at p. 86) 177, 178
—— *v.* Fernie (1866), L. R. 3 Eq. 308 240
Perkins's Patent, In re (1845), 2 Web. P. C. 6 (at p. 18) 126
Perry *v.* Mitchell (1840), 1 Web. P. C. 269 197
———————— (1854), 9 Ex. 494; 2 C. L. R. 1052; 23 L. J.
  Ex. 217 226
—— *v.* Skinner (1837), Hindmarsh, Patents, p. 207; 2 M. & W.
  471; M. & H. 122; 1 Jur. 433; 1 Web. P. C. 250; 6 L. J.
  Ex. 124 ....97, 98
Piggott *v.* Anglo-American Telegraph Co. (1868), 19 L. T. R.
  N. S. 46 217
Pinkus' Patent, In re (1847), 12 Jur. 234 ....133, 134
Pitman's Patent, In re (1871), 8 Moo. P. C. C. N. S. 293 (at
  p. 297); L. R. 4 P. C. 84 136
Plimpton *v.* Malcomson (1876), L. R. 3 Ch. D. 53 (at p. 557);
  45 L. J. Ch. 505; 34 L. T. Rep. N. S. 340;
  L. R. 20 Eq. 37 .... 51, 74, 80, 176, 191, 228
———————— (1876), 20 Sols. Jour. 1876, p. 860........ 207
———— *v.* Spiller (1877), L. R. 6 Ch. D. 412 ....,44, 47, 68, 170
Poole's Patent, In re (1867), 4 Moo. P. C. C. N. S. 452; L. R.
  1 C. P. 514; 36 L. J. P. C. 76 ....130, 135
Pow *v.* Taunton (1845), 9 Jur. 1056 28
Price's Patent Candle Co. *v.* Bauwen's Patent Candle Co. (1858),
  4 K. & J. 727 ....176, 180
Printing and Numerical Registering Co. *v.* Sampson (1875),
  44 L. J. Ch. 705; L. R. 19 Eq. 462; 32 L. T. Rep. N. S. 354.. 118

R.

R. *v.* Arkwright (1785), 1 Web. P. C. 64 (at p. 72); Dav. P. C.
  61; Printed Cases, fol. Lon. 1785; 1 Carp. P. C. 53..35, 49, 66, 72
R. *v.* Cutler (1847), 3 C. & K. 215; Macrory, 124; 14 Q. B.
  372 n. 28
R. *v.* Else (1785), 1 Web. P. C. 76; Bull, N. P. 76; Dav. P. C.
  144 55
R. *v.* Lister (1826), Web. P. L. 80 155
R. *v.* Mill (1850), 20 L. J. C. P. 16 (at p. 24); 10 C. B. 379;
  15 Jur. 59; 1 L. M. & P. 695; 14 Beav. 315 ....95, 96

	PAGE
R. v. Wheeler (1819), 2 B. & Ald. 345; 1 Carp. P. C. 394..10, 26,	105
Ralston v. Smith (1865), 11 H. L. C. 223; 20 C. B. N. S.28; 13 L. T. Rep. N. S. 1; 35 L. J. C. P. 49 31,	96
Renard v. Lewinstein (1864), 3 W. R. 665; 10 L. T. Rep. N. S.94	211
——————— (1864), 10 L. T. N. S. 177	169
——————— (1865), 2 Hem. & M. 528; 5 N. R. 301; 11 L. T. Rep. N. S. 766; 13 W. R. 382 143,	188
Roberts' Patent, In re (1839), 1 Web. P. C. 573 (at p. 575) ..	130
Roden v. London Small Arms Co. (1876), 46 L. J. Q. B. 213 ..	120
Rolls v. Isaacs (1878), L. R. 19 Ch. D. 268; W. N. 1878 (p. 37)	109
Rushton v. Crawley (1870), L. R. 10 Eq. 522 32,	85
Russell v. Cowley (1834), 1 Web. P. C. 459 (at p. 463); 2 Coop. C. C. 59 ....25, 156, 169,	217
—— v. Crichton (1837), 15 Dec. of Ct. of Sess. 1270; 1 Web. P. C. 667, n..	217
—— v. Ledsam (1843), 11 M. & W. 647..........204, 208,	209
——————— (1845), 14 M. & W. 574 (at p. 580); 14 L. J. Ex. 353.............................	155

S.

Samuda's Patent, In re (1846), Cit. Hind on Pat. 534........	99
Saxby v. Gloucester Waggon Co. (1880), L. R. 7 Q. B. D. 305; W. N. 1880 (at p. 28) 33,	222
Saxby's Patent, In re (1870), L. R. 3 P. C. 292; 7 Moo. P. C. C. N. S. 82; 19 W. R. 513	127
Scott and Young, Ex parte (1871), L. R. 6 Ch. D. 264; L. R. 6 Ch. 274; 19 W. R. 425	16
Seed v. Higgins (1860), 8 H. L. C. 550; 30 L. J. Q. B. 314; 6 Jur. N. S. 1264; 3 L. T. Rep. N. S. 101 ....85, 227, 234,	238
Sellers v. Dickenson (1850), 5 Ex. 312 (at p. 324); 20 L. J. Ex. 417 149,	238
Sharp's Patent, In re (1840), 1 Web. P. C. 641 (at p. 645); 10 L. J. Ch. 86; 3 Beav. 245	92
Shaw v. Beck (1853), 8 Ex. 392	230
Sheehan v. Great Eastern Rail. Co. (1880), L. R. 16 Ch. D. 59 142,	188
Simister's Patent, In re (1842), 1 Web. P. C. 721 (at p. 724); 4 Moo. P. C. C. 164	133
Simpson v. Holliday (1866), L. R. 1 H. L. 315; 35 L. J. Ch. 811................................27,	85
——————— (1865), 13 W. R. 577 (at p. 578); 12 L. T. Rep. N. S. 99; 21 Newton, Lond. Jour. N. S. 111; 5 N. R. 340 ....70, 74,	85
——————— (1864), 20 Newton's Lond. Jour. N. S. 105 (at p. 108) 83, 156,	234
Singer Sewing Machine Co. v. Wilson (1865), 5 N. R. 505; 12 L. T. Rep. N. S. 140; 13 W. R. 560	219
Smith's Patent, In re (1855), Macr. P. C. 232 97,	101
Smith v. Buckingham (1870), 18 W. R. 314; 21 L. T. R. N. S. 819	118

	PAGE
Smith v. Davidson (1857), 19 C. S. 691	40
—— v. Dickenson (1804), 3 B. & P. 630	107
—— v. London & North Western Rail. Co. (1853), 2 E. & B. 69 (at p. 76); 17 Jur. 1071	149, 150
—— v. London & South Western Rail. Co. (1854), Kay, 408; 23 L. J. Ch. 562; 23 L. T. R. 10; 2 Eq. Rep. 428; 2 W. R. 310; 23 L. T. R. 10	176
—— v. Scott (1859), 6 C. B. N. S. 771; 28 L. J. C. P. 325; 5 Jur. N. S. 1356	117
—— v. Upton (1843), 6 M. & G. 257	224
Soame's Patent, In re (1843), 1 Web. P. C. 560, 729 (at p. 733)	21, 124, 126
Spencer v. Jack (1864), 11 L. T. R. N. S. 242	237
Spicer v. Todd (1839), 1 D. P. C. 306	143
Spilsbury v. Clough (1842), 2 Q. B. 466; 2 G. & D. 17; 6 Jur. 579; 1 Web. P. C. 255; 11 L. J. Q. B. 109	93
Stead v. Anderson (1846), 2 Web. P. C. 147 (at p. 149)	39
—————— (1847), 4 C. B. 806; 2 Web. P. C. 151; 16 L. J. C. P. 250	146, 148, 155, 226
—— v. Williams (1843), 2 Web. P. C. 126 (at p. 136)	39, 47
—————— (1844), 2 Web. P. C. 137 (at p. 142); 7 M. & G. 318; 8 Scott, N. R. 449; 8 Jur. 930; 13 L. J. C. P. 218	41, 58
Steiner v. Heald (1851), 20 L. J. Ex. 410; 6 Ex. 607; 17 Jur. 875	29
Stevens v. Keating (1847), 2 Web. P. C. 176 (at p. 181); 2 Phill. 333 (at p. 335)	156, 191, 238
—————— (1850), 1 Mac. & G. 659	146
Stocker v. Rodgers (1843), 1 Car. & Kir. 99	241
Stocking v. Llewellyn (1842), 3 L. T. R. 33	192
Stoner v. Todd (1876), L. R. 4 Ch. D. 58; 46 L. J. Ch. 32; 35 L. T. Rep. N. S. 661; 25 W. R. 138	42, 62
Sturtz v. De la Rue (1828), 5 Russ. 322 (at p. 329); 1 Web. P. C. 83	58, 73, 192
Sugg v. Silber (1876), L. R. Q. B. D. 362	221
—————— (1877), L. R. 2 Q. B. D. 495	205
Swinborne v. Nelson (1853), 16 Beav. 416; 22 L. J. Ch. 331	213
Sykes v. Howarth (1879), L. R. 12 Ch. D. 826; 48 L. J. Ch. 769; 41 L. T. R. N. S. 79; 28 W. R. 215	157, 163, 165, 196, 205, 232

T.

Talbot v. La Roche (1854), 15 C. B. 310; 2 C. L. Rep. 836; M. Dig. 210	197
Tangye v. Stott (1865), 14 W. R. 386	176, 187
Taylor v. Hare (1805), 1 Web. P. C. 292, 293; 1 B. & P. N. R. 260	114, 119
Templeton v. Macfarlane (1848), 1 H. L. C. 595	48
Tennant's case (1802), 1 Web. P. C. 125; Dav. P. C. 429; 1 Carp. P. C. 177	9, 40
Terrell, In re (1883), L. R. 22 Ch. D. 473	244
Tetley v. Easton (1852), Mac. P. C. 48, 76	72, 82
—————— (1857), 2 C. B. N. S. 706; 26 L. J. C. P.	85

	PAGE
Thomas v. Foxwell (1858), 5 Jur. N. S. 37 (at p. 39)	151
——— v. Hunt (1864), 17 C. B. N. S. 183	120
——— v. Welch (1866), L. R. 1 C. P. 182 (at p. 192); 12 Jur. N. S. 316; 35 L. J. C. P. 200	62
Thorn v. Worthing Skating Rink Company (1876), L. R. 6 Ch. D. 417	155
Tielens v. Hooper (1850), 5 Ex. 830	120
Tolhausen's Patent, In re (1866), 14 W. R. 557	100
Townsend v. Haworth (1875), L. R. 12 Ch. D. 831, n.; Higgins' Dig. Pt. II. p. 60 (not fully reported anywhere)	158, 163, 165
Travell v. Carteret (35 Car. 2), 3 Lev. 135	104
Trotman's Patent, In re (1866), L. R. 1 P. C. 118; 3 Moo. P. C. C. N. S. 291	131, 132
Trotman v. Wood (1864), 16 C. B. N. S. 479	117
Turner v. Hancock (1881), 20 Ch. D. 303	244
——— v. Winter (1787), 1 Web. P. C. 77 (at p. 80); 1 T. R. 602; Dart, P. C. 145	49, 66, 229

U.

United Telephone Co. &c. v. Harrison, Cox, Walker & Co. (1882), L. R. 21 Ch. D. 720	44, 45, 156
Unwin v. Heath (1855), 25 L. J. C. P. 8	68, 69, 155

V.

Vavaseur v. Krupp (1878), L. R. 9 Ch. D. 357; 39 L. T. R. N. S. 437	176
Vincent's Patent, In re (1867), L. R. 2 Ch. 341; 15 W. R. 524	100

W.

Wallington v. Dale (1852), 7 Ex. 888; 23 L. J. Ex. 49	66, 237
Walton v. Bateman (1842), 1 Web. P. C. 613 (at p. 615)	37, 145, 155, 237
——— v. Lavater (1860), 3 L. T. Rep. N. S. 272; 8 C. B. N. S. 162; 29 L. J. C. P. 275; 6 Jur. N. S. 1251	117, 141, 147, 149, 164, 188
——— v. Potter (1841), 1 Web. P. C. 585 (at p. 592)	13, 25, 145, 155, 238
Warwick v. Hooper (1850), 3 M. & G. 60	120
Wegmann v. Corcoran (1879), L. R. 13 Ch. D. 65 (at p. 77); 39 L. T. Rep. N. S. 563; 27 W. R. 357	68, 79, 80
Westrupp & Gibbons' Patent, In re, Ex parte Wells (1836), 1 Web. P. C. 554	138
White v. Fenn (1867), 15 W. R. 348; 15 L. T. Rep. N. S. 505	152
Whitton v. Jennings (1860), 1 D. R. & S. 110	192

	PAGE
Wield's Patent, In re (1871), L. R. 4 P. C. 89; 8 Moo. P. C. C. N. S. 300	132, 138
Williams v. Williams (1819), 3 Mer. 157	107
Winan's Patent, In re (1872), 8 Moo. P. C. C. N. S. 306; L. R. 4 P. C. 93	135
Wirth's Patent, In re (1879), L. R. 12 Ch. D. 303; 28 W. R. 329	6
Wood v. Zimmer (1815), 1 Web. P. C. 44, 82; Holt, N. P. 58; Kay, P. C. 290	47, 80
Woodcroft's Patent, In re (1841), 1 Web. P. C. 740; 3 Moo. P. C. C. 171	133
Wren v. Weild (1868), 4 Q. B. 213	198
Wright v. Hitchcock (1870), L. R. 5 Ex. 37; 39 L. J. Ex. 97	59, 152, 165, 226

Y.

Young v. Fernie (1864), 12 W. R. 901 (at p. 903); 4 Giff. 577; 10 Jur. N. S. 926; 10 L. T. Rep. N. S. 861; 9 Prac. Mech. Jour. 2nd Series, 102; 4 N. R. 218 .... 25, 44, 228

ERRATA.

Page 83, line 4, *for* "malâ fide," *read* "mala fides."
,, ad fin., *for* "bonâ fide," *read* "bona fides."

The Law and Practice

RELATING TO

LETTERS PATENT FOR INVENTIONS

INTRODUCTION.

LETTERS patent for inventions are granted by the crown by virtue of its common law prerogative. By the creation of monopolies to first and true inventors in the right of using their inventions, a species of property is created in favour of inventors, as a reward for the benefits which they have conferred on humanity, by the exercise of their thought, knowledge and industry. It is to the interests of the community that persons should be induced to devote their time, energies and resources in furtherance of the development of arts and manufactures, and this was recognized in England from the earliest periods which can pretend to be described as civilized.

It was to the advantage of the whole community that inventors should be rewarded, and no measure of reward can be conceived more just and equitable, and bearing a closer relation to the benefit conferred by the particular inventor than to grant him the sole right of making, using and vending his invention for a limited period of time. In the corrupt ages of the Stuarts, it is not to be wondered at, that the prerogative of the crown to grant monopoly rights to first and true inventors, should have been made a lever for assuming a prerogative to grant monopoly rights in trade generally.

In the reign of James the First, to such an extent had this abuse been carried, that it was deemed advisable by the legislature that the rights of the crown in respect of letters patent should be declared by legislative enactment—this was the origin of the Statute of Monopolies.

It has been supposed that the prerogative of the crown to grant letters patent for inventions was created by this statute, but the most cursory perusal of its enactments and of the authorities which preceded it, shows clearly that, so far from the statute giving to the crown any right which it did not possess before it was passed, it has as its intention the limiting the right of the crown, and the declaring that, which had always been the common law upon the subject. In the first section of this Act, for instance, we find it recited "that all grants of monopolies and of the benefit of any penal laws, or of power to dispense with the law, or to compound for the forfeiture, are contrary to your Majesty's laws, which your Majesty's declaration is truly consonant and agreeable to the ancient and fundamental laws of this your realm. . . . That all monopolies, and all commissions, grants, licenses, charters and letters patent heretofore made or granted or hereafter to be made or granted . . . are altogether contrary to the laws of this realm, and so are and shall be utterly void and of none effect, and in no-wise to be put in use or execution."

Section 6 saved the granting of letters patent to inventors in the following words:—

"Provided also, and be it declared and enacted, that any declaration before mentioned shall not extend to any letters patent and grants of privilege for the term of fourteen years or under, hereafter to be made of the sole working or making of any manner of new manufactures within this realm, to the true and first inventor and inventors of such manufactures, which others at the time of making of such letters patents and grants shall not use, so as also they be not contrary to the law, nor mischievous to the state by raising of prices of commodities at home, or hurt of trade, or generally inconvenient; the said fourteen years to be accounted from the date of the first letters patents or grant of such privilege hereafter to be made, but that the same shall be of such force as they should be if this Act had never been made and of none other."

It will thus be seen that the Statute of Monopolies creates no statutory right, but merely saves the common law right of the crown; and by sect. 116 of the Patents Designs and Trade Marks Act, 1883, it is enacted, "Nothing in this Act shall take away, abridge or prejudicially affect the prerogative of the crown in relation to the granting of any letters patent, or to the withholding of the grant thereof." By sect. 46 of the same Act the word "invention" is defined as meaning "any manner of new manufacture the subject of letters patent and grant of privilege within sect. 6 of the Statute of Monopolies . . . . and includes an alleged invention."

So it is that in the present day, notwithstanding the various statutes which have been passed in relation to letters patent for inventions, these monopolies are still granted upon the mere motion of the sovereign, in the exercise of her royal prerogative, and that all that has been done, has been declaratory of the limits within which that prerogative should be exercised, and of the method of procedure to be adopted in obtaining letters patent for inventions.

For the purpose of supporting the validity of the letters patent it is necessary that the patentee should conform to certain requisites, and these requisites are indicated in the 6th section of the Statute of Monopolies. In the first place, he must be the true and first inventor of a new manufacture; the new manufacture must not be contrary to law, nor must it be mischievous to the State, by raising the prices of commodities at home; it must not be hurtful to trade, nor generally inconvenient. The

Act of 1883 has adopted this definition of an invention, and anything that does not conform with all these requisites is not entitled to be called an invention. The host of important decided cases as to the construction of the 6th section of the Statute of Monopolies, and the enormous expense, and labour and learning, which has been devoted to obtaining these decisions, no doubt induced the legislature to adopt a definition which had in some respects obtained a correct judicial meaning; but it is doubtful whether it was wise to re-enact it in a form which had, we may say, centuries ago, already become to some extent obsolete.

The protection of trade by means of Guilds, and of all those various protective schemes which were elaborated in the middle ages, have been found to be fallacious. Industries in this country are no longer protected by the artificial process of law, and therefore it is difficult to understand the correct meaning which would be given to the words in the 6th section of the Statute of Monopolies, which refer to an invention having a tendency to **raising the prices of commodities at home,** or to **hamper trade,** or to be **generally inconvenient,** terms exceedingly vague in themselves, and which the Courts have not had occasion to consider for a very great number of years.

These matters, and the construction which is to be placed upon the word "invention," will have to be dealt with hereafter, when we consider the cases which have been decided upon the matter.

CHAPTER I.

THE PATENTEE.

By sect. 46 of the Act of 1883, the word **patentee** is construed as meaning "the person for the time being entitled to the benefit of the patent;" consequently it may mean the original grantee, his executors and administrators, or the assignee of the original grantee. By sect. 4 of the same Act it is enacted:—

(1) "Any person, whether a British subject or not, may make an application for a patent."

It will be observed, that there is no limitation whatever preventing a person under incapacity, either by reason of infancy or otherwise, from obtaining a patent.

(2) "Two or more persons may make a joint application for a patent, and a patent may be granted to them jointly."

By sect. 5, (1) "An application for a patent must be made in the form set forth in the Schedule to this Act, or in such other form as may be from time to time prescribed; and must be left at, or sent by post to, the Patent Office, in the prescribed manner."

(2) "**An application** must contain a **declaration** to the effect that the applicant is in possession of an invention whereof he, or, in the case of a joint application, *one or more of the applicants* claims or claim to be the true and first inventor or inventors, and for which he or they desire or desires to obtain a patent, and must be accompanied by either a provisional or complete specification."

Before this Act it was competent for an **alien** to obtain

a patent; Lord Cairns, in the matter of *In re Wirth's Patent*(a), went even further than this: "I am quite clear that letters patent may be granted to a foreigner who is resident abroad for an invention communicated to him by another resident also abroad."

There does not appear to have ever been a question as to whether an **infant** or a **married woman** might, under the old law, have become a grantee of letters patent. The new law, however, is perfectly clear, and sweeps away any doubt that might have been entertained on the subject.

By sect. 99 of the Patent Act of 1883, it is found that due provision is made for enabling infants and persons under incapacity to take the requisite steps for obtaining letters patent. The Act of 1883, however, appears to abolish by implication one large class of grantees, viz. those persons who claimed to have letters patent granted to them for communications from abroad. It will be observed that sect. 6 of the Statute of Monopolies deals with new manufactures *within this realm*, and the construction which has been placed upon that statute has been, that the consideration for the grant of the patent could be equally supported by the process of inventing a new manufacture, as by the process of importing from abroad a manufacture which up to the time of such importation had been unknown within this realm.

In the case of *Darcy* v. *Allin* (b), it was held, "Where any man by his own charge and industry, or by his own wit and invention, doth bring any new trade into the realm, or any engine tending to the furtherance of a trade that never was used before, and that for the good of the realm, that in such cases the king may grant to him a monopoly patent for some reasonable time until the subjects may learn the same in con-

---

(a) L. R., 12 Ch. D. 303. (b) 1 Web. P. C. 6.

sideration of the good that he doth bring by his invention to the commonwealth, otherwise not."

So in *The Clothworkers of Ipswich case* (c), it was laid down that "the bringing of a new invention into the kingdom equally with the discovery of anything was sufficient to support the king's grant." It is true that these cases were prior to the Statute of Monopolies, but the Statute of Monopolies merely affirmed the common law, hence these cases are applicable. *Edgebury* v. *Stephens* (d) was decided after the statute; there it was held that "a grant of a monopoly may be to the first inventor, and if the invention be new in England, a patent may be granted though the thing was practised beyond the sea before; for the statute speaks of a new manufacture *within this realm,* so that if it be new here it is within the statute, for the Act intended to encourage new devices useful to the kingdom, and whether learned by travel or by study it is the same thing" (d).

The practice of granting letters patent to the **first importers** of manufactures new within this realm, has been uniformly sustained by our Courts of Law. It would appear, however, that the Act of 1883 is intended to abolish this class of patentee, for it will be seen, that after declaring that any person alien or otherwise may apply for a patent, it says that the application *must* contain a declaration to the effect that the applicant claims to be *the first and true inventor.* A form of this declaration is given in the first Schedule to the Act, and there is no provision whatever made for a declaration that the applicant is the first and true *importer.*

We have seen that the word "invention" is construed by the language of the 6th section of the Statute of Monopolies, that language has been held in *Edgebury* v. *Stephens* (d) and the succeeding authorities, to include an importer of an invention; but inasmuch as the Act

(c) Godbolt's R. 253.   (d) 1 Web. P. C. 35.

provides no machinery whereby an importer might apply for a patent, it may perhaps be taken as the intention of the legislature that henceforth that class of patentee shall be abolished, and that the patent should only be granted to the first and true inventor of the invention.

In *Milligan* v. *Marsh* (e) it was held by Vice-Chancellor Page-Wood that a person taking out a patent and making a declaration that he is a first inventor when in truth he is only an importer of a communicated invention, makes a false suggestion and the patent is void.

Only one of the applicants need make the declaration, so that a capitalist may join an inventor and obtain a valid joint patent.

Sect. 34 of the Act of 1883 makes provision for the granting of letters patent to the legal representative of a deceased inventor, provided application be made within six months from the decease of the inventor, the application must contain a declaration by the legal representative that he believes such person to be the true and first inventor of the invention.

We have now to deal with the construction of the words " first and true inventor."

The reason that the common law has created a prerogative of the crown to grant letters patent to first and true inventors, is that the public benefit by the consideration which the inventor gives in return for the monopoly privilege which is granted to him. That consideration may be divided into three parts.

In the first place, the patentee must be the actual inventor, that is, the consideration must move from him.

Secondly. He must have invented a new and useful invention.

Thirdly. He must publish his invention.

(e) 2 Jur., N. S. 1083.

CHAPTER II.

THE CONSIDERATION—BEING THE ACTUAL INVENTOR.

An actual inventor is a person who, either by accident or design, produces or discovers an art or manufacture. The process of invention may be divided into two parts. The operation of the mind, and the carrying out of the results of that operation by the hands. It is true that when an invention is the result of pure accident, the physical production may precede the operation of the mind in perceiving its applicability, still, as a general rule, it will be observed that the operation of the mind must precede the physical production. The operation of the mind must in all cases be that of the mind of the inventor. The carrying out of the results of the operation of the mind may be done by the hands of the inventor, or by those of anyone else whom he may employ for that purpose.

In *Tennant's case* (a), a material portion of the invention claimed was found to have been suggested by a chemist at Glasgow. Lord Ellenborough held, that the patent was bad because the plaintiff was not the inventor. It will be observed in this case, that although it is possible that the plaintiff was the first person to use the particular method for making a bleaching liquor, still, inasmuch as that method of producing this bleaching liquor was thought out by some one else and communicated to the plaintiff, he was held not to be an inventor. In considering this question we must not confuse the idea of **first manufacturer** with that of first inventor.

"A." may have invented something, it may have pleased him to try a few experiments with his invention, and then to abandon it without publication. "B." may

(a) 1 Web. P. C. 125.

subsequently have invented the same thing altogether independently of "A." If "B." applies for letters patent he is at law the first inventor; but should it be shown that the process of invention was not carried on in "B.'s" mind at all, but that "A." communicated his ideas to "B.," although with the full intention of abandoning them, "B." will not be the first inventor. Take, for instance, the case of *Dollond's Patent* (b), this was an improvement in the manufacture of object glasses for telescopes. Dr. H. had made and used identically similar object glasses for his own purposes, but he had in no way published his invention. Dollond, without any communication from Dr. H., had re-invented these object glasses; held that Dollond's patent was good.

In *R.* v. *Wheeler* (c), Abbott, C. J., delivering the judgment of the court, said: "If the patentee has not invented the matter or thing of which he represents himself to be inventor, the consideration of the royal grant fails." In *Barber* v. *Walduck* (d), it was proved that the **invention** was made by a **workman** in the workshop of the patentee, that he communicated it to his master: the patent was opposed on the ground that the patentee was not the inventor.

In *Bloxham* v. *Elsee* (e), the patentee had worked out the principle of his invention in his own mind, but he intrusted the mechanical details to Mr. D., an engineer. Mr. D. had suggested several parts of the machine to the patentee. An objection was taken that the patentee was not the inventor: the objection was overruled. It will be seen in this case, that the patentee's mind conceived the invention, and that Mr. D. was only, so to speak, the **intellectual hands** employed by the patentee to carry out that which he had previously conceived in his mind. The summing up of Mr. Baron

(b) 1 Web. P. C. 43.
(c) 2 B. & Ald. 345.
(d) 1 Carp. P. C. 438.
(e) 1 Web. P. C. 132, n.

Alderson, in the case of *Minter* v. *Wells*(*f*), is instructive upon this point:—" The patentee," said the learned judge, " claims under the patent, stating it in his petition to the crown, that he is the true inventor of the machine in question, and if it could be shown that he was not the true inventor, but that some one else had invented it, the crown is deceived in that suggestion, which was the foundation on which it granted the patent, and then the law is, that the patent obtained under such circumstances would be void, and no action could be maintained against the party for the infringement of the patent, ... If Sutton suggested the principle to Minter, then he, Sutton, would be the inventor; if, on the other hand, Minter suggested the principle to Sutton, and Sutton was assisting him, then Minter would be the first and true inventor, and Sutton would be a machine, so to speak, which Minter uses for the purpose of enabling him to carry his original conception into effect."

In *Lewis* v. *Marling* (*g*), Mr. Justice Bailey said : " If I discover a certain thing for myself, it is no objection to my claim to a patent that another also has made the discovery, provided I first introduce it into public use." The suggestion in that case having been that the patentee had acquired his invention by seeing a model of a similar machine which had been brought from America; it was disproved that he had seen the model, and consequently he was held to be the first and true inventor.

In *Cornish* v. *Keene* (*h*) Chief Justice Tindal said : " Sometimes it is a material question to determine whether the party who got the patent was the real and original inventor or not, because these patents are granted as a reward, not only for the benefit that is conferred upon the public by the discovery, but also the

(*f*) 1 Web. P. C. 127.   (*h*) 1 Web. P. C. 507.
(*g*) 10 B. & C. 22.

ingenuity of the first inventor; and although it is proved that it is a new discovery so far as the world is concerned, yet if anybody is able to show that although that was new with the party who got the patent, he was not the man whose ingenuity first discovered it, that he borrowed it from A. or B., or had taken it from a book that was printed in England, and which was open to all the world—then, although the public had the benefit of it it would be an important question whether he was the first and original inventor of it." There is no doubt that under the circumstances stated by the Chief Justice, the patentee would not be the original inventor.

Inasmuch as we have seen that the Act of 1883 probably abolishes *first importers*, and recognizes the right of all persons, whether British subjects or not, and whether resident in England or not, to become patentees, a serious question will arise for the consideration of the Courts as to whether the validity of a patent, and the claim to be a true and first inventor, must be supported upon an investigation of what has been published and become public property not only in England, but in any other part of the civilized world; and for the purpose of calling himself a first and true inventor, it will not only be, not sufficient for an inventor to say that he has not obtained the invention from a book printed or published in England, or from a communication made to him in England. But that he has not obtained the invention from a book published or printed in any part of the world, or from a communication made to him in any part of the world. In future the first and true inventor must in reality be an inventor, and the invention must be the result of the operation of his own mind.

It is probable that this change in the rights of first importers was not contemplated by the legislature, and that the omission of the words " within this realm," in the 5th section of the Act of 1883, was accidental. If it be accidental it is doubtful whether the Courts will venture so far as to correct such an omission by judicial decision; and the change in the law thus brought about will require a great deal of thought, and a great many decisions before its effect can be fully appreciated.

We do not propose to deal at length with the cases that succeed *Cornish* v. *Keene*. The principle laid down in cases we have cited has been invariably followed. In *Gibson* v. *Brand* (*i*), Chief Justice Tindal said: "A man may publish to the world that which is perfectly new in all its use, and has not before been enjoyed, and yet he may not be the first and true inventor, he may have borrowed it from some other person, or book. The legislature never intended that a person, who had taken his knowledge from the art of another, from the labours and assiduity or ingenuity of another, should be the man who was to receive the benefit of another's skill." The same judge, in *Walton* v. *Potter* (*k*), said: "If the subject-matter of the patent has been published in a dictionary, for example, and, if a man merely adopts it, the merit is so small that his patent for it would be worth nothing."

It is evident that cases may arise where the operation of one man's mind may have assisted the operation of another's mind. In this case it will be a question for the jury which was, so to speak, the dominant mind and which the servient mind, the dominant mind will be entitled to the patent. In *Allen* v. *Rawson* (*l*), Chief Justice Tindal said: "I think it is too much that a suggestion of a workman employed in the course of experiments of something calculated more easily to carry into effect the conceptions of the inventor should render the whole patent void."

In dealing with this branch of the subject, and show-

i) 1 Web. P. C. 628. (*l*) 1 C. B. 574.
(*k*) 1 Web. P. C. 592.

ing that one of the essential portions of the consideration for the grant of letters patent is the **labour of the mind** of the inventor, we may cite the case of *Patterson* v. *Gas Light and Coke Company* (m). In that case certain referees had been appointed under the City of London Gas Act to inquire into the subject of the purification of gas. The plaintiff was one of those referees. The referees drew up a report on the 31st January, 1872. The report contained a description of the subject-matter of the plaintiff's patent. Subsequently to the making of the report, but before its delivery to the Board of Trade the plaintiff, who had really discovered the invention, obtained provisional protection. The action was brought against the Gas Light and Coke Company for infringing his patent. The company alleged that the invention was not new, and also denied the title of the plaintiff to take out a patent in respect of it, on the ground presumably, that he had no consideration to offer to the public in return for the grant of letters patent, he having already disposed to the public of his knowledge upon the subject for other considerations. In the judgment of the House of Lords, Lord Blackburn said : " It seems to me clear that the duty of the referees under the Act was to ascertain how far the gas could be practically purified by each company. If they found that gas containing not more than a certain limited amount of impurity could be practically produced by any means, they were to prescribe the maximum amount accordingly, and they were by obvious implication, though it is not expressly enacted, to make public how this degree of purity could practically be obtained. It was not material to them to inquire whether these were means previously known, which the companies had failed to make use of from parsimony, negligence or ignorance, or whether there was some new idea which

---

(m) L. R., 3 App. C. at p. 243.

had been developed during the course of their inquiries, which made these old means practicably valuable when before they were not. They were not at all required to distinguish new from old. In all these respects the report was quite different from a specification. But, as soon as they became aware that the gas could be practicably brought to this degree of purity, their duty was to fix the maximum accordingly, and to make known to the public the means by which this could practicably be done. The report of the 31st January, 1872, is drawn up as it ought to have been. It shows that, by some means there explained, purity to a great extent could practicably be obtained, it makes no attempt to show how much of this was previously known though neglected, and it nowhere states that any part of what was now disclosed was invented by one of their own body." In the Court of Appeal Lord Justice James had said (*n*): "Although it is not necessary for the determination of this suit to pronounce any final decision on this point, we deem it right to say we think it at the least very questionable whether it can be competent for a member of final commission or committee to take out a patent for the subject-matter of their official investigation, . . . it is to be borne in mind that the report then made belonged absolutely to the State. Every fact and figure in it had been obtained at the public expense, every hour of every referee and of the secretary employed in the production of it was public time . . . the consideration for every patent is the communication of useful information to the public. What consideration is there when the information was already the property of the State."

These judgments, although going to a point which was not absolutely necessary for the decision of the case (for the case was decided upon the ground of want of novelty in the invention), tend to show that it was in the minds

(*n*) L. R., 2 Ch. D. at p. 832.

of the judges that the mental labour of making the discovery being an essential element for the consideration of the grant, if that mental labour had already been paid for by the State, it failed as a consideration to support the patent.

By sect. 35 of the Act of 1883, "A patent granted to a true and first inventor shall not be invalidated by an application in fraud of him, or by provisional protection obtained thereon, or by any use or publication of the invention subsequent to that fraudulent application during the period of provisional protection." This clause is only a re-enactment of that which had been decided to be the law previous to the Act. In *Ex parte Scott and Young* (*o*), the servant had filed a provisional specification of an invention, after which the master filed a specification for a similar invention, and subsequently filed a complete specification, and obtained letters patent. It was held that, under the circumstances, the Great Seal might be affixed to the letters patent of the servant's invention, and that the patent might bear the date of his provisional specification.

In the case of *Ex parte Bates and Redgate* (*p*), it was held, that leaving a provisional specification, and obtaining a provisional protection, does not prevent a second applicant from leaving a specification of a similar invention, and obtaining valid letters patent for the invention before six months have elapsed from the time when the first provisional specification was left, and in such a case letters patent will not be granted to the first applicant for any part of his invention, which is covered by the letters patent already obtained by the second applicant, but in this case there was no suggestion of fraud on the part of the second applicant. This decision has, however, been doubted in *Re Deering's Patent* (*q*),

(*o*) L. R., 6 Ch. D. 264.   (*q*) 13 Ch. D. 393.
(*p*) L. R., 4 Ch. 577.

by Lord Cairns, who said: "I may, however, state my objections to that decision" (*Bates and Redgate*), "which I never could thoroughly understand; it has always seemed to me that if Parliament held out to inventors the advantage they could get from provisional protection, the inventor should have the enjoyment of that advantage for the six months granted to him. Parliament intended the six months to be for the completion of the invention, and for perfecting the specification, and never said that the applicant should be deprived of or lose that privilege for want of any due diligence on his part."

The difficult questions, however, which arise in these cases, seem to be set at rest by the 14th section of the Act of 1883: "Where the application for a patent in respect of an invention has been accepted, the invention may, during the period between the date of the application and the date of sealing such patent, be used and published without prejudice to the patent to be granted for the same. And such protection from the consequences of use and publication is in this Act referred to as provisional protection."

The general question of concurrent applicants, where there is no fraud, that is, where each applicant is in a position to offer the consideration of mental labour, will be considered in the next Chapter. It is only material here so far as concurrent application is brought about by reason of one man fraudulently appropriating the invention of another.

We have intimated that in all probability it will be held that the Act of 1883 has disqualified a true and first importer from becoming a patentee; but the provisions of the Act are not so clear as to warrant our omitting to give some account of the law which has hitherto been in force, and the more so since it is evident that on the 1st January, 1884 (the date when the Act of 1883 comes into force), there will be in existence large numbers of patents granted to first importers, which will still have many years to run and which in all probability will at some time or other be the subject matter of litigation.

The right of the Crown to grant letters patent to true and first importers of inventions appears to have been a common law right. We find that so far back as 1567 a patent had been granted to one Hastings (*r*) for the making of frisadoes in consideration of his having imported the skill of manufacturing them from abroad. So in Mathey's case, "It was granted unto him the sole making of knives with bone hafts and plates of lattice, because, as the patent suggested, he brought the first use thereof from beyond the seas." This was in the reign of Elizabeth. In the clothworkers of Ipswich case we have this (*s*) said, "The king granted unto B. that none besides himself should make ordnances for battery in the time of war: such grant was adjudged void. But if a man hath brought in a new invention and a new trade in the kingdom in peril of his life and consumption of his estate or stock, &c., or if a man hath made a new discovery of anything, in such cases the king, of his grace and favor in recompense of his costs and travail, may grant by charter unto him that he only shall use such a trade or trafique for a certain time; because at first the people of the kingdom are ignorant, and have not the knowledge or skill to use it. But when that patent is expired the king cannot make a new grant thereof." This was in 1615.

Then came the Statute of Monopolies, and we have seen that the 6th section of that Act carefully excepted "the sole working or making of any manner of new manufactures **within this realm**, to the true and first inventor or inventors of such manufactures, which others

---

(*r*) 1 Web. P. C. 6.   (*s*) 1 Web. P. C. 6; 1 Godb. 252, 254.

at the time of making such letters patents and grants shall not use."

Afterwards came the decisions of *Darcy* v. *Allin* (*t*), and *Edgebury* v. *Stevens* (*u*), where it is said, "for the statute speaks of new manufactures **within this realm**, so that if it be new here it is within the statute, for the Act intended to encourage new devices useful to the kingdom, and whether learned by travel or by study it is the same thing." See the remarks of Eyre, C. J., in *Boulton* v. *Bull* (*x*).

In the early days of manufacturing enterprise, when true inventors were so exceedingly rare as scarcely ever to be heard of, the word inventor had not acquired the meaning which it has at present, and seems to have been used to designate a **first introducer** rather than a first inventor. In the early reports shortly succeeding the Statute of Monopolies we do not find the judges in any difficulty in dealing with the words "true and first inventor," showing that the word **inventor** had not the precise meaning which it has since acquired.

In *Marsden* v. *Saville Street Co.* (*y*) in the Court of Appeal, Jessel, M. R., said, speaking of imported inventions, "It has been argued that before the Statute of James such patents were valid and were allowed by the judges, and that the statute merely restricts the duration of the patent and does not destroy the right as it previously existed. Even supposing that were so, the statute defines who are considered to be worthy recipients of the grant of such a monopoly, as it was then called, and the definition so given has been followed ever since. It is difficult to say *à priori* on what principle a person who did not invent anything, but who merely imported from abroad into this realm the invention of another, was treated by the judges as being the first and true inventor.

(*t*) 1 Web. P. C. 6. (*x*) 2 H. Blac. 491.
(*u*) 1 Web. P. C. 35. (*y*) L. R., 3 Ex. D. 203.

I have never been able to discover the principle; and although I have often made enquiry of others, and of some who are more familiar with the patent law than even I am, although I cannot pretend not to possess a considerable familiarity with it, I could never get a satisfactory answer. The only answer was, "It has been so decided and you are bound by the decisions." But it is an anomaly as far as I know, not depending on any principle whatever. It has never been declared by any judge or authority that there is such a principle, and, not being able to find one, all I can say is that I must look on it as a sort of anomalous decision which has acquired by time and recognition the force of law."

A patent granted to a British subject, in his own name, for an invention communicated to him by a foreigner, the subject of a state in amity with this country, is not void, although such patent be in truth taken out and held by the grantee in trust for such foreigner (z).

Sect. 23 of the Act of 1883, provides for the registration of owners of patents. Sect. 85 prohibits the registration of any trust. This does not abolish trusts, but merely prohibits the registration of trusts.

The importer of an invention need not be a meritorious importer, but may only be a mere agent, *Beard* v. *Egerton* (a).

The importer need not have acquired the information from a foreigner abroad, but may have done so from a British subject abroad (b).

But a communication made **in England** by one British subject to another, of an invention, does not make the person, to whom the communication is made, the first and true inventor within the meaning of the statute

---

(z) *Beard* v. *Egerton*, 3 C. B. 97. (b) *Nickels* v. *Ross*, 8 C. B. at p. 710, per Earl, C. J.

(a) *Supra*, at p. 129.

21 Jac. 1, c. 3, so as to enable him to take out letters patent for the invention (c).

When a patent is taken out as for an original invention the subject of the patent being, in fact, a communication from abroad, the patent is void. *Milligan* v. *Marsh* (d).

This latter case very much strengthens our previously expressed opinion, that the Act of 1883 abolishes patents for imported inventions, since if the directions of the Act be followed, it is impossible to take out a patent for such an invention without making a false suggestion within the meaning of *Milligan* v. *Marsh*.

"The merit of an importer is less than of an inventor. . . . . and it is an argument against the patent, that it was imported and not invented. I do not say it takes away the merit, but it makes it much smaller." Per Lord Brougham in *re Soame's Patent* (e).

We have now shown what is meant when it is said that the consideration for a patent must move from the patentee personally.

(c) *Marsden* v. *Saville Street Co.*, C. A.; L. R., 3 Ex. D. 203.

(d) 2 Jur. N. S. 1083.

(e) 1 Web. P. C. 733.

CHAPTER III.

THE CONSIDERATION (*continued*)—A NEW AND USEFUL INVENTION.

THE second branch of the consideration is that the inventor must have invented **a new and useful invention**. It is evident that a person may have invented a manufacture which, although new to him, may not be new so far as the world is concerned. He may have had all the work and labour of discovering for himself a process which, although not generally known, yet the previous knowledge of which may amount to prior user. In such a case, inasmuch as the public are considered at law to be in full possession of the invention, it is evident that the applicant for letters patent has no consideration to offer in return for the grant. The 6th section of the Statute of Monopolies defines a new invention as "any manner of new manufacture which others at the time of making such letters patent shall not use."

We have seen that the Act of 1883 has adopted this definition of an invention. We have now to consider the legal meaning which has been placed upon the words "New Manufactures."

A new manufacture does not mean, as it is erroneously sometimes supposed, only **a new article** of manufacture, but it also means **a new process** or method of manufacturing something new or old; it does not mean a new principle of manufacturing, but it means a new application of principles. No man can claim an invention in **a principle** (*a*), for that would be to invent the

---

(*a* Boulton v. Bull, 2 H. Bl. 479; Hornblower v. Boulton, 8 T. R. 101; Jupe v. Pratt, 1 Web. P. C. 146; Neilson v. Harford, 1 Web. P. C. 342; The Housechill Co. v. Neilson, 1 Web. P. C. 673; Crossley v. Potter, Mac. P. C. 240; Patterson v. The Gas Light Co., L. R., 3 App. Cas. 246.

laws of nature, which have always existed. Man merely discovers the principle, and if, when he discovers a principle he can discover a method of utilizing the principle so as to make it applicable to the production of a new manufacture, he can obtain a patent for the method. In *Hornblower* v. *Boulton* (b), decided in 1799, the patent was granted for a method for lessening the consumption of steam and fuel in fire engines, by applying certain principles of combustion. It was held that the invention could be made the subject of a patent. The language of the learned judges does not seem very clearly to expound the doctrine upon which that judgment was based; but Mr. Justice Grose said, "I am inclined to think that the patent cannot be granted for the mere principle; but I think that, although in words the privilege granted is to exercise the method of making or doing anything, yet if that thing to be made or done be a manufacture, and the mode of making that manufacture is described, it thus becomes in effect (by whatever name it may be called) not a patent for the mere principle, but for the manufacture of the thing so made, and not merely for the principle upon which it is made." In *Boulton* v. *Bull* (c) the Lord Chief Justice Eyre said: "When the effect produced is some new substance or composition of things, it should seem that the privilege of sole working or making ought to be for such new substance or composition, without regard to the mechanism or process by which it has been produced, which, though perhaps also new, will be only useful as producing the new substance. When the effect produced is no substance or composition of things, the patent can only be for the mechanism, if new mechanism is used, or for the process, if it be a new method of operating with or without old mechanism, by which the effect is produced." Mr. Justice

(b) 8 T. Rep. 95.   (c) 2 H. Bl. 463.

Heath speaking said, "What then falls within the scope of the proviso? such manufactures as are reducible to two classes: the first class includes machinery, the second, substances, such as medicines formed by chemical and other processes, where the vendible substance is the thing produced, and that which operates preserves no permanent form; in the first class the machine, and in the second the substance produced, is the subject for the patent. I approve of the term 'manufacture' in the statute, because it precludes all nice refinements; it gives us to understand the reason of the proviso—that it was introduced for the benefit of trade." With reference to this judgment, we may point out that a new chemical substance is not a new manufacture, as the words "new manufacture" are understood in modern times, but that in the case of manufacturing a new chemical substance, the process of making that substance is the subject of the patent, and not the substance when made.

Upon perusing the cases which we propose to quote, it will be seen that the more modern view of the construction of the words "new manufacture" has been the result of a great deal of development. At first the judges seemed to be inclined to limit the subject-matter of letters patent to new articles produced; but as the arts and manufactures of the country progressed and increased, it was seen that by far the most important inventions were inventions in the **process** of making old and well-known articles of commerce, and so it became evident that should the construction of the words "new manufactures" be entirely limited to the production of new articles, to the exclusion of the process of manufacturing old articles by cheaper, better and more improved methods, the inducement which the common law intended to give to inventors would be curtailed to the narrowest possible limits.

Hull v. *Jarvis* (*d*) was an action for the infringement of a patent for the improvement of the manufacture of lace by the use of the flame of gas for the purpose of singeing the fluffy ends of the surface of lace manufactured from cotton. For the defendants it was contended that the process was not new. Fire and flame had been applied for similar purposes before the plaintiff's invention. The mere doing that with the flame of gas could not be the subject matter of a patent. The patent, which was clearly only for a process, was supported. In *Jones* v. *Pearce* (*e*)—the patentee had used the principle of suspension to the manufacture of wheels; the patent was supported because, although the principle could not be patented, the method of applying that principle to the manufacture of wheels was properly the subject of a patent. In *Russell* v. *Cowley* (*f*) the patent which was for an improved process of manufacturing iron tubes was supported. Lord Lyndhurst, in giving judgment, said: "It is an invention to manufacture tubes for gas and other purposes by welding them without the use of any mandril or internal support, by which certain advantages are produced."

In *Walton* v. *Potter* (*g*), Chief Justice Tindal said: "Now there can be no doubt whatever, that although one man has obtained a patent for a given object, there are many modes open for a man of ingenuity to obtain a patent for the same object; there may be many roads leading to one place, and if a man has, by dint of his own genius and discovery after a patent has been obtained been able to give to the public without reference to the former one, or borrowing from the former one, a

(*d*) 1 Web. P. C. 100. See also *Booth* v. *Kennard*, 1 Hurl. & N. 527; *Higgs* v. *Godwin*, 27 L. J., Q. B. 421; *Hills* v. *London Gas Light Co.*, 29 L. J., Ex. 409;

Young v. *Fernie*, 12 W. R. 903; *Newall* v. *Elliott*, 13 W. R. 11.
(*e*) 1 Web. P. C. 122.
(*f*) 1 Web. P. C. 459.
(*g*) 1 Web. P. C. at p. 590.

new and superior mode of arriving at the same end, there can be no objection to his taking out a patent for that purpose." In this case, the learned judge by the word "object" must have meant the method of producing an article.

The same judge in *Gibson* v. *Brand* (h), said: "The patent is taken out 'for a new or improved process for the manufacture of silk, and silk in combination with certain other fibrous substances,' taken out therefore strictly for a process . . . . . undoubtedly there is a very strong reason to suppose if the specification is carefully and properly prepared, so as to point out with great distinctness and minuteness what the process is, that such a patent may be good in law. Such certainly was the opinion of Chief Justice Eyre, in *Boulton* v. *Watt* (i), and such also appears to have been the opinion (carefully guarding against any abuse of that doctrine) of Lord Tenterden in the case of *The King* v. *Wheeler* (k), who says that, 'the subject-matter of letters patent, *i.e.* the word "manufacture," as used in the Statute of James, is generally understood to denote either a thing made, which is useful for its own sake, and vendible, or to mean an engine or instrument, or some part of an engine or instrument to be employed either in the making of some previously-known article, or in some other useful purpose . . . . . or it may perhaps extend also to a new process to be carried out by known implements or elements acting upon known substances, and ultimately producing some other known substance, but producing it in a cheaper or more expeditious manner or to a better or more useful account.'"

Since the date of these earlier decisions the law seems to have been considered as settled upon the subject. In *Bewley* v. *Hancock* (l), Lord Cranworth said: "A

(h) 1 Web. P. C. 633.
(i) 2 H. Bl. 468.
k 2 B. & A. 350.
l) 6 De G., M. & G. 402.

discovery that the mixture of two or more simple substances in certain definite proportions will form a compound substance valuable for medical or other qualities, would afford a good ground for a patent. A discovery of some machinery, whereby such a mixture might be more quickly and effectually accomplished, might be the foundation of another patent." In *Simpson* v. *Holiday* (*m*), the specification said, " I mix aniline with dry arsenic acid and allow the mixture to stand for some time, or I accelerate the operation by heating it to, or nearly to, its boiling point until it assumes a rich purple colour." The patentee claimed " the manufacture or preparation of red or purple dyes by heating aniline dyes with arsenic acid as hereinbefore described." Lord Chelmsford, in giving judgment, said : " There is nothing on the face of the specification to show that the invention described is not, in every part of it, the subject of a patent." It is obvious that there may be many different processes of accomplishing the same object; if some of the processes are old, and that which is claimed is merely a new method, the subject of the invention will be confined to that method (*n*).

Hereafter, in considering the specification, we shall have to discuss the limitations within which the patent for a new process will be held valid, and the cases which have been decided upon the point.

Any **addition to or subtraction from any known machine** or process causing the old machine or process to accomplish an object in a more speedy, perfect or economical manner, is evidently the subject of a patent. In *Hornblower* v. *Boulton* (*o*) Mr. Justice Grose said: "A doubt is entertained whether there can be a patent for the addition of an old manufacture, this doubt rests altogether upon *Bircot's case* (*p*), if that were to be considered as law at

(*m*) L. R., 1 H. L. 315. (*o*) 8 T. Rep. 104.
(*n*) *Bovill* v. *Pimm*, 11 Exch. 739. (*p*) 3 Inst. 184.

this date (1799) it would set aside many patents for many ingenious inventions . . . . . if indeed a patent could not be granted for the addition it would be depriving the public of one of the best benefits of the statute of James." In *Lister* v. *Leather* (*q*), Lord Campbell said: "The assertion that all patents for improvements of existing patents must be void, is obviously untenable." In *Fox* v. *Dellestable* (*r*), V. C. Malins said: "No doubt a man may make an **invention** which is partly covered by an **existing patent**, but he cannot use it without the license of the patentee. He may wait for the expiration of the patent and take out one himself. If his invention be novel, that patent will be valid."

An application of an old machine or an **old material for a new purpose**, may be the subject of a patent; for instance, *Muntz* v. *Foster* (*s*) was an action for an infringement of a patent for the manufacture of metal plates to be used for sheathing the bottoms of ships. The improvement consisted of using an alloy of zinc and copper in certain proportions for the manufacture of the plates, and for this purpose copper alone had hitherto been used. The alloy of zinc and copper was to produce an old and well-known material, still the application of that old material to sheathing of ships had not before been discovered, and upon its being shown that such an application was a great improvement on the old method of sheathing with copper, it was held that the patent could be sustained.

The mere application of a **known instrument or machine to a new purpose** will not support a patent unless the means or method of the application is also new (*t*).

In *Reg.* v. *Cutler* (*u*) Lord Denman said: "With

q 8 E. & B. at p. 1017.
(*r* 15 W. R. at p. 195.
s 2 Web. P. C. 103.
t *Poe* v. *Taunton*, 9 Jur. 1056.
u 3 C. & K. 215.

regard to the third and fourth claims, in which the defendant claims the application of tubes in the construction of tubular flues, it appears to me that he has no right to take out a patent for the mere application of particular things to any particular purpose. If he had made a new combination, that would have been a new discovery, and a proper subject for a patent . . . I think that the application of an article to produce any particular result, the party having no claim either to the mode of producing the article, or to the mode of applying it for attaining that result, forms no ground for a patent." Lord Denman's distinction between the mere application of an old instrument to a new purpose and a new combination, appears to have been followed, and to be a correct exposition of the law.

In the case of *Steiner* v. *Heald* (*x*), in the Exchequer Chamber, the head-note is inexplicable and erroneous. If the case itself is read, it will be found to be in accordance with the other decided cases on this subject: In the ordinary process of dyeing, by means of madder, the colouring matter was obtained from fresh madder by the application of hot-water; the refuse, after boiling, was called spent madder. It had long been known to dyers, that a portion of the colouring remained in the spent madder, but it was not known how to extract it, as it remained in combination with the plant; recently it was discovered that by means of acid and hot-water the pure colouring matter of madder, called garancine, could be obtained from fresh madder, and that this process extracted the colouring matter of the plant. The plaintiff obtained a patent for the new manufacture of garancine, by applying the same process of acid and hot-water to the spent madder; since his invention the spent madder, which was previously worthless, became valuable.

(*x*) 20 L. J. Exch. 410.

At the trial Chief Baron Pollock directed the jury to find a verdict for the defendant, upon the ground apparently that there was no subject for a patent; in reversing this decision Mr. Justice Pearson said: "Now spent madder might be a very different thing from fresh madder in its properties, or it might be in effect the same thing as fresh madder in its properties, chemical and otherwise, with the difference only that part of its colouring matter had been already extracted. Again, the properties, chemical and otherwise, might or might not have been known to chemists and other scientific persons, so that they could find out whether fresh madder and spent madder were different or substantially the same things. The points appear to us to be questions of fact, and materially to affect the validity or invalidity of a patent." It will appear, therefore, that the Court were of opinion that it was a question of fact whether spent madder and fresh madder were the same thing in their chemical properties; if they were, no patent; if they were not, the validity of the patent would be sustained, but the fact must be decided by the jury.

In *Bush* v. *Fox* (*y*) Chief Baron Pollock graphically illustrated the point we are now discussing, he said: "I think if one man invents a new mode of looking at the moon, somebody else cannot take out a new patent for looking at the sun. If a man were to take out a patent for a telescope to be used to make observations on land, I do not think anyone could say, 'I will take out another patent for another telescope to be used for taking observations on the sea.'" That case was ultimately confirmed in the House of Lords ( ). In *Brook* v. *Aston*, Baron Martin said (*a*): "The application of a well-known tool to work previously untried materials, or to produce new forms, is not a subject of a patent."

y Macrorie's P. C. 164.　　　*a)* 8 E. & B. 185.
(*z* 5 H. L. C. 707.

It is evident to anyone considering these cases, that the border line is exceedingly fine. In *Penn* v. *Bibby* (b) Lord Chelmsford, L. C., recognized the difficulty of stating any definition which should be applicable to any case. He said: " It is very difficult to extract any principle from the various decisions on this subject which can be applied with certainty to every case, nor indeed is it easy to reconcile them to each other." He then proceeds to dissent from the definition given by Lord Campbell in *Brook* v. *Aston*, doubting the accuracy of the report, and proceeds to say: " Lord Chief Justice Cockburn approaches much nearer to the enunciation of a principle, or at least of a rule for judging in these cases, in *Harwood* v. *G. N. R.* (c), where he says, " although authorities established the proposition that the same means, apparatus, or mechanical contrivance cannot be applied to the same purpose, or to purposes so nearly cognate and similar as that the application of it in one case naturally leads to the application of it when required in some other, still the question in every case is one of degree, whether the amount of affinity or similarity which exists between the two purposes is such that they are substantially the same, and that determines whether the invention is so sufficiently meritorious as to be deserving of a patent.'" The case of *Harwood* v. *G. N. R.*, quoted above by the Lord Chancellor, was carried to the House of Lords, where Lord Chelmsford, then Lord Chancellor, said: " The question is, whether there can be any invention of the plaintiff in having taken that thing, which was a fish for the bridge, and having applied it as a fish for the railway, upon that I think the law is well and rightly settled . . . . . . viz., that you cannot have a patent for a well-known mechanical appliance, merely because

(b) L. R. 2 Ch. 127.
(c) 29 L. J., Q. B. 193; also *Ralston* v. *Smith*, 11 H. L. Cas.
223; *Jordan* v. *Moore*, L. R., 1 C. P. 624; *Parkes* v. *Stevens*, L. R., 8 Eq. 367; L. R., 5 Ch. 36.

it is applied in a manner or to a purpose which is analogous to the manner or purpose in or by which it has hitherto been notoriously used (*d*)." It may be noticed that where the **object** of a patent is **old**, and the **means** to effect it only are **new**, the Court construes the invention strictly, as it looks jealously at the claims of inventors seeking to limit the right of the public to a well-known object (*e*).

A new combination is an invention consisting of the discovery that two or more known processes, materials, or implements when used together will become applicable to a new purpose, or will effect an old purpose in a better, cheaper or more expeditious manner than it had before been done.

In *Huddard* v. *Grimshaw* (*f*), Lord Ellenborough said: " I suppose it will not now be disputed that a new combination of old materials, so as to produce a new effect, may be the subject of a patent." There may be a valid patent for new combination of materials previously in use for the same purpose (*g*).

In *Foxwell* v. *Bostock* (*h*), Lord Westbury said : " If a combination of machinery for effecting certain results has previously existed and is well known, and an improvement is afterwards discovered, consisting, for example, of the introduction of some new parts, or an altered arrangement in some particulars of the existing constituent parts of the machine, an improved arrangement or improved combination may be patented."

Bovill's patent consisted of a combination of a blast, with an exhaust of air to millstones, for the purpose of preventing the heat generated in grinding corn and

d 11 H. L. Cas. 654.

e *Curtis* v. *Platt*, 3 Ch. D. 135, n.; *Rushton* v. *Crawley*, L. R. 10 Eq. 522; *The Patent Bottle Envelope Co.* v. *Seymer*, 5 C. B., N. S. 164; *Horton* v. *Mabon*, 12 C. B.,
N. S. 437; *Ormson* v. *Clarke*, 14 C. B., N. S. 475.

f Daw. P. C. 267.

g Per Lord Eldon, *Hill* v. *Thompson*, 1 Web. P. C. 237.

(*h* 12 W. R. 725.

saving the dust generated. It was proved that a blast and an exhaust had been used separately. But that the **combination was a substantial improvement.** The patent was held good (*i*).

In *Crane* v. *Price* (*k*), the patentee, in his specification, after specifically disclaiming the use of the hot blast or the use of anthracite coal, proceeded: " What I do claim as my invention is, the application of anthracite or stone coal or culm *combined* with the using of hot air blast in the smelting and manufacture of iron from ironstone, mine or ore as above described." The patent was held valid for the combination. This decision was afterwards questioned by Lord Justice James in *Murray* v. *Clayton* (*l*), but not on the ground that a combination could not form the subject of a patent. In *Murray* v. *Clayton*, the decision was followed and a patent of this description was upheld.

A patent was granted in 1870 for railway signalling apparatus; in 1871 another patent was granted for other improvements in railway signalling apparatus; in 1874 the plaintiffs obtained a patent for a combination which, in effect, was constituted of the improvements in the 1870 and 1871 patents; any person of ordinary knowledge of the subject would, by placing the two inventions of 1870 and 1871 side by side, be able to effect the desired combination without making any further experiment or gaining any further information. Field, J., held the 1874 patent void (*m*).

In *Cannington* v. *Nuttall* (*n*), it was held that the patent could be sustained, although **each principle or process in it was previously well known,** provided that the mode

---

(*i*) *Bovill* v. *Keyworth*, 7 E. & B. 725; *Brunton* v. *Hawkes*, 4 B. & Ald. 550; *Lewis* v. *Davis*, 1 Web. P. C. 488; *Carpenter* v. *Smith*, 1 Web. P. C. 538; *Allen* v. *Rawson*, 1 C. B. 551; *Lister* v. *Leather*, 27 L. J. Q. B. 295; *Dangerfield* v. *Jones*, 13 L. T. R., N. S. 142.

(*k*) 1 Web. P. C. 393.

(*l*) L. R., 7 Ch. 584.

(*m*) *Saxby* v. *Gloucester Wagon Co.*, L. R., 7 Q. B. D. 305.

(*n*) L. R., 5 H. L. 205.

of combining these processes was new and produced a beneficial result, and provided also that the specification claimed not the old processes or any other, but only the new combination. This case is very instructive, as clearly demonstrating what is meant by a " new combination."

Having now considered the interpretation which has been placed by the Courts upon the word " manufacture," we next examine what has been held to be a **" new manufacture,"** that is to say, to what extent prior user is an answer to an action for the infringement of a patent. It is evident, that, if the alleged new manufacture can be shown to have been in the possession of the public before the application for the grant of letters patent, that there is no consideration for the grant. The patentee offers to the public, in return for the monopoly privilege, his information and knowledge respecting a new manufacture; if the public is already possessed of the information or knowledge the supposed inventor has nothing to give. We shall see hereafter, when we discuss the practice of the Courts in actions for the infringement of patents, that the **burden of proof** lies on the alleged infringer when he sets up a defence of **prior user**, *i. e.* of want of novelty in the alleged manufacture at the date of the patent; and it is as well to keep this in mind in reading the cases which have been decided as to what amounts to prior user.

We have seen that the Statute of Monopolies is a mere declaration of that which was the law before it was passed; it was always held by the Courts that the principle of a patent grant was not an arbitrary advantage granted by the Crown to one subject in detriment to the rest, but that it was an advantage granted by the Crown to persons who introduced a new manufacture, and that it was granted upon principle, not for the benefit of the patentee but for the benefit of the public: it being considered to the benefit of the public that reasonable encouragement should be given to inventors to induce them to devote their time, energies and resources to the improvement of the arts and manufactures of the realm.

In the case of *Hasting's Patent* (r), decided in 1567, the patent was in consideration of the patentee having brought into the country the making of frisadoes as they were made in Haarlem, in Amsterdam, being not used in England. The infringers defended the patentees' bill in the Exchequer Chamber, on the ground that they had made baies very like to Mr. Hasting's frisadoes, prior to the date of Mr. Hasting's patent; they were therefore not restrained from making baies like his frisadoes. The monopoly patent granted to "one Humphrey, of the Tower, 'for the sole and only use of a sieve or instrument for melting of lead, supposing it was his own invention, and therefore prohibited all others to use the same for a time;' and because others used the like instrument in Derbyshire, contrary to the intent of his patent, therefore he did sue them in the Exchequer Chamber by English bill, in which Court the question was whether it was newly invented by him, whereby he might have the sole privilege, or else used before at Mendip, in West country, which if it were there before used then the Court were of opinion that he should not have the sole use thereof (s)."

The general question in disputed patents is whether the invention was known and in use before the patent? In *Rex* v. *Arkwright*(t), decided in 1785, Mr. Justice Buller gave a definition of a novelty which now would be considered too wide. "Thus the case stands as to the several component parts of this machine, and if

(r) 1 Web. P. C. 6.
(s) 1 Web. P. C. 7; *Darcy* v. *Allin*, 1 Web. P. C. 6; *Mitchell* v. *Reynolds*, 19 Mod. R. 130;

Liardet v. *Johnson*, 1 Web. P. C. 52 and 53.
(t) 1 Web. P. C. 64.

upon them you are satisfied that none of them were inventions unknown at the time this patent was granted, or that they were not invented by the defendant upon either of these points, the prosecutor is entitled to your verdict."

When we speak of an invention being new, we mean that it must be new so far as the public are concerned, that is, so far as the means of information of the public goes. If a man had invented a machine and made it and used it **secretly**, so that no one but himself had access to it, and the general public had no means of information upon it, there is no doubt that a subsequent inventor, re-inventing, so to speak, the same machine, and disclosing his knowledge to the public in his specification, would be entitled to a valid patent. A machine made by the person who kept it secret would not amount to such a public knowledge as would anticipate the invention of the patentee, but if the first-made machine had been used in such a manner that other persons had been enabled to acquire the knowledge of its use and application, there would be a prior user to void the subsequent patent. Lord Chief Justice Tindal said, in *Cornish* v. *Keene* (*u*): "If it was known at all to the world publicly, or practised openly so that any other person might have the means of acquiring a knowledge of it as well as the inventor, then the patent would be void." In *Carpenter* v. *Smith* (*x*), Lord Abinger, C. B., analyzed the meaning of the words "**public use.**" "Public use does not mean a use or exercise by the public, but a use or exercise in a public manner." Taking that as a definition of the meaning of the words "public use," it will be apparent that the question of prior user is one of fact, and one which will have to be considered by

---

u 1 Web. P. C. 508.

x 1 Web. P. C. 534. See also *Lewis* v. *Marling*, 10 B. & C. 26; *Minter* v. *Mower*, 1 Web. P. C. 139; *Morgan* v. *Seaward*, 2 M. & W. 544; *Betts* v. *Menzies*, 1 E. & E. 1008; *Harwood* v. *G. N. R.*, 29 L. J., Q. B. 193.

a **jury** or a judge sitting as a jury upon the facts of each particular case.

The decided cases only offer illustrations of that which has been held to be public use or prior user in the different cases which have come before the Courts. In *Walton* v. *Bateman* (*y*), Cresswell, J., said, referring to the words in the statute, " which others at the time of making such letters patent and grants did not use," said: " Now that has been held to mean a user, not by way of experiment, but a public user, in distinguishing which the knowledge of the parties as to the article in use will be material for your consideration. . . . . . Whether it is a *manufacture* within the meaning of this Act I apprehend to be a question of law." The learned judge then proceeds to sum up to the jury upon the question of fact as to prior user. " First, was any article made before, answering the purposes or having the properties of that which the plaintiff has made and claimed as in the patent . . . . . then even supposing that article did embody the principles of the plaintiff's, so as to present to persons using it the properties, qualities and advantages in principle of that article which the plaintiff makes, the question for you will be whether that user is not to be considered rather in the nature of an **experiment** than of any public use of the article, so as to deprive the plaintiff of the fruit of his discovery in respect of this manufacture." The learned judge then proceeds to quote the words of Tindal, C. J., in *Cornish* v. *Keene* (*z*): " ' The question raised for the jury was this, whether various instances brought forward by the defendants amounted to proof, that before or at the time of taking out the patent the manufacture was in public use in England, or whether it fell short of that point and proved only that experiments had been made in various quarters and had been after-

(*y*) 1 Web. P. C. 615 to 619.   (*z*) 1 Web. P. C. 519.

wards abandoned.'" It is very difficult to reconcile the meaning of Mr. Justice Cresswell when he says, that " the question of prior user is one for the jury," with his remarks in the latter part of the judgment. "The third issue is much wider. The defendants say that the alleged invention was not, nor is, a new manufacture within the meaning of the statute concerning monopolies. Now that is put to him as a question of law . . . and I am confirmed now, on further consideration, in the opinion I previously expressed, that there is sufficient of a new manufacture in this case to justify and maintain the patent that has been granted. I think that there is a new principle developed, carried out and embodied in the mode of using that principle." The learned judge must have had present in his mind that the point of law was as to whether the manufacture was a manufacture in the meaning of the statute or not, for the **novelty** of the manufacture is certainly **a question of fact.**

As further illustrating the distinction between " public use " and " secret use," we may quote the words of Mr. Justice Williams in *Hancock* v. *Somervell*, which is quoted in " Newton's London Journal," Vol. XXXIX. p. 158. " The defendants say that the invention had been substantially published and was in use, not in secret use, but in public use in England before the date of the patent, and if that is so, it would entitle the defendants no doubt to a verdict upon this novelty issue. Upon that part of the case the view that it seems to me ought to be taken by you is this, you will first consider whether the material was before the public; it is not necessary that it should be used by the public if it is in public use, not in secret use. . . . I should here say that I do not think it necessary the use should be actually for sale; if it were in public use it need not be sold; it would be sufficient, for instance, if it were in use, handed about the country for the purpose of attracting customers. If you should think that the material being so in use, it was so palpable that you could make it when you got the material, that substantially the disclosure of the material was a disclosure of the means of making it, that would be a public use."

In *Stead* v. *Anderson* (z), Baron Parke placed some considerable limitation of the meaning of the words "public use" in saying, "if the mode of forming and laying blocks at Sir W. Worsley's had been precisely similar to the plaintiff's, that would have been sufficient user to destroy the plaintiff's patent, though put in practice in a spot to which the public had not free access."

It is difficult to draw the line precisely between public and secret use: we do not suppose that for the purpose of showing that some use was secret use, it would be necessary to show an intention of secrecy, but in all cases it will be a matter of fact whether the use was so private and so secret as to make it practically impossible that the public should become acquainted with the manufacture.

Mr. Justice Erle, in *Heath* v. *Smith* (a), cast a doubt even upon whether **secret use** would not amount to anticipation. He said, "If one party only had used the process and had brought out the article for profit and kept the method entirely secret, I am not prepared to say that then the patent would have been valid." But this seems to be in direct contradiction to the decision in *Dolland's Case* (b). In that case the objection to Dolland's Patent was, that he was not the inventor of the method of making new object glasses, but that Dr. Hall had made the same discovery before him; but it was held, that inasmuch as Dr. Hall had confined it to his closet, and the public were not acquainted with it, Dolland was to be considered the inventor (c).

(z) 2 Web. P. C. 149. See also *Stead* v. *Williams*, 2 Web. P. C. 136.

(a) 3 E. & B. 256.

(b) 1 Web. P. C. 43.

(c) See also the remarks of Buller, J., in *Boulton* v. *Bull*, 2 H. Bl. 463 to 470, and Mr. Justice Dallas in *Hill* v. *Thompson*, 1 Web. P. C. 244.

In *Betts* v. *Neilson* (*d*) it is said, "There may be public use of a patented article, **without actual sale** of the goods manufactured."

There are some conflicting cases on the subject of **secret use.** It does not appear to be open to much doubt that purely secret use, without publication, even if accompanied with the sale of the article manufactured, provided the article itself, by its appearance or other qualities, does not disclose the invention, ought not to invalidate the letters patent granted to a subsequent inventor, since he is in the position to and does give to the public the full consideration required by the Statute of Monopolies and the common law, for the patent grant which he applies for. On the other hand, if the secret use has been by himself, and he only applies for letters patent when he has any fear of his invention being discovered, then, probably, the previous secret use of the inventor would be held to invalidate his patent; but that must be on the ground of want of *bona fides* on the part of the inventor, and not on the ground of prior user, and want of *bona fides* has always been held to invalidate letters patent (*e*). This question is discussed hereafter (p. 47).

In *Smith* v. *Davidson*, a Scotch case (*f*), the Lord President said, "In order to invalidate letters patent on the ground of previous use it is necessary not only that the use shall have been prior to the date of letters patent, but that it should be a public and not a secret use." The remarks of Lord Bramwell, in *Hills* v. *London Gaslight Co.* (*g*), on this subject were as follows: "If a person has invented anything which is the subject of a patent, and has kept it to himself or communicated it privately to one or two, in fact has not made it

d L. R., 3 Ch. 129.
(*e*, See *Tennant's case*, 1 Web. P. C. 125.
f 19 C. S. 691.
g) 5 H. & N. 336.

public knowledge, if anyone else discovers that invention it is new, that is to say, new in the sense that the first invention has not been published."

There is another description of anticipation which is capable of invalidating a patent besides that of public use, and that is **prior publication**. Prior publication means the printing, writing or publishing of some document to which the public have access, containing such a description of the invention as will enable a practical man to carry it out from the description given. Vague hints or descriptions of experiments, incomplete, or imperfect, are not sufficient to invalidate a subsequent patent. It is not necessary that that which is described in the book or publication should have been carried out in practice, it equally anticipates the patent (*h*). The question will always be one of fact, depending on the circumstances of each particular case, and the point which should be left to the consideration of the jury is, whether upon the whole evidence there has been such a publication as to make the description part of the public stock of information (*i*).

It is necessary that the description in the publication which is relied upon as evidence of prior publication, should be such as will when carried out produce the patented article; otherwise, however similar the description may be, if it will not produce the alleged invention it will not amount to anticipation (*j*).

Vice-Chancellor Wood, in *Betts* v. *Menzies* (*k*), said, "I think that if a man sits down and takes out a patent from his own conjectures without ever having tried the experiments set forth in it, that will not invalidate a subsequent patent taken out and practically

---

(*h*) See *The Househill Company* v. *Neilson* in the House of Lords, 1 Web. P. C. 718, n.

(*i*) *Stead* v. *Williams*, 2 Web.

P. C. 142.

(*j*) *Muntz* v. *Foster*, 2 Web. P. C. 94.

(*k*) 3 Jur. N. S. 358.

worked, especially when it turns out that the method prescribed by the earlier patent is practically useless." This remark of the learned Vice-Chancellor indicates how difficult a thing it is to lay down a general rule which shall bind every case, indeed no such general rule has ever been framed. It is evident that if a man were to describe an invention in a book or in a specification, and describe it so minutely and accurately that any practical person could from the description produce the invented matter, it would be immaterial whether the writer had tried experiments or had ascertained whether his invention would work in practice or not. If it should afterwards turn out to work in practice, and work as described, without any further inventive power and without any further invention being necessary, the description in the book or specification would be sufficient to invalidate any subsequent patent for the same invention.

In *Betts* v. *Menzies* (*ante*) the Vice-Chancellor had before him a case where the method described in the earlier publication was practically useless. In that event there is no doubt that the description would not invalidate a subsequent patent, because further invention would be necessary to bring the matter to a successful issue.

When *Betts* v. *Menzies* (*l*) came before the House of Lords, Lord Westbury said: "To defeat a new patent, it must be clear that the antecedent specification disclosed a practical mode of producing the result which was the object and effect of the subsequent discovery; a barren general description therefore, though containing some **suggestive information** or involving some **speculative theory**, could not be treated as avoiding for want of novelty a subsequent specification or invention, unless it was ascertained that the antecedent publication involved

(*l*, 10 H. L. C. 117. See also *Stoner* v. *Todd*, L. R., 4 Ch. D. 58.

the same amount of **useful information**." In the same case the opinion of the judges having been taken by the House of Lords as to whether the Court could pronounce Betts' patent to be void simply on the comparison of two specifications without evidence to prove identity of invention, and also without evidence that Dobbs' specification disclosed a practical mode of producing the result, or some part of the result described in Betts' patent; Mr. Justice Blackburn, subsequently Lord Blackburn, gave it as his opinion, "that **to avoid a patent on the ground of want of novelty**, it is necessary to show that part of what the patentee claimed as a new invention was at the date of the patent already a publicly-known invention; this may be shown by proving that the invention was already disclosed in a publication accessible to the public . . . . . . it is not necessary to show that the invention thus made publicly known had already been put in actual use . . . . . . as soon as it has been ascertained that the description in the book makes known an invention, that is to say, that it adds to the public stock of knowledge what would without any further discovery enable a person to produce a result in the nature of a new manufacture. . . . . . . If Dobbs had made it part of the public knowledge how to produce a new material as a practical result, and Betts had afterwards claimed to have a patent for, amongst other things, producing that result, he would have claimed that which was not new, and if Dobbs had not made it part of the public knowledge how to produce the result, then Betts would not have claimed anything already known. The Court cannot tell without evidence whether what Dobbs disclosed would produce a result, and, therefore, as it seems to me, cannot pronounce the first patent void without evidence. I therefore answer your lordships' question in the negative" (*m*).

(*m*) See also *Betts* v. *Neilson* 429; *Neilson* v. *Betts*, L. R., 5 H. and *Betts* v. *de Vitre*, L. R., 3 Ch. L. 1.

The cases which have been decided have generally been upon the subject of antecedent publication by means of a **specification**, but it is evident that the publication of **a book** or **newspaper**, or in any other form which gives the public a means of information, is equally potent as an anticipation of a subsequent patent (*n*). *Hills* v. *London Gas Light Company* (*o*) illustrates very clearly the principle laid down by Lord Westbury in *Betts* v. *Menzies*. The plaintiff obtained a patent for the employment of hydrated oxide of iron in purifying coal gas. A specification was put in evidence as published some ten years prior to the plaintiff's patent by one Croll, in which he said that coal gas could be purified by using the oxide of manganese, the oxide of zinc, or the oxide of iron. Now there are two descriptions of oxide of iron, hydrated and anhydrous. Anhydrous oxides of iron will not purify coal gas. It was held, therefore, that inasmuch as further experiments were required to discover that the action of hydrated oxide of iron was different from that of anhydrous oxide of iron in the purification of coal gas, that the antecedent specification did not anticipate the plaintiff's specification.

In *Hills* v. *Evans*(*p*) Lord Westbury said: "The antecedent statement must, in order to invalidate the subsequent patent, be such that a person of ordinary knowledge of the subject would at once perceive and understand and be able practically to apply the discovery without the necessity of making further experiments."

It is not necessary that the book containing the description of the invention should be sold so as to constitute an anticipation. Mere exhibition in a book-

---

n *Young* v. *Fernie*, 12 W. R. 901; *Plimpton* v. *Spiller*, L. R., 6 Ch. D. 412; also *Patterson* v. *Gas Light and Coke Co.*, L. R., 3 App. Cas. 239, *United Telephone Co.* v.

Harrison, Cox, Walker & Co., L. R., 21 Ch. D. 720.

o 29 L. J., Ex. 409.

p 31 L. J., Ch. 463.

seller's window for sale is sufficient publication, or sending it to a bookseller's in this country to be published. "There is no difference between a foreign inventor and an English one if, when the inventor is a foreigner, he publishes the book in a foreign language and sends it over to the booksellers in this country for the purpose of being sold" (*q*). Prior publication in a foreign journal and in a foreign language will invalidate an English patent if it can be shown that a single copy was deposited in England in a public place, and was open to public inspection (*r*).

An inventor may invalidate his own invention by previous publication in a specification. For instance, if an inventor applies for letters patent and files a specification, and after the publication of the specification abandons it and begins again applying for letters patent for the same invention, the previous publication of the specification will invalidate a subsequent patent. Prior to the Act of 1883, it would have been otherwise if he made his application for a second patent prior to the expiration of the period of provisional protection for the first invention, and therefore before the first specification had been published, provided that he had not in the meantime published his own invention (*s*).

The secret manufacture and sale by the inventor himself of a subsequently-patented article prior to the date of the patent, would of itself constitute an anticipation of the invention. This branch of the subject is surrounded with considerable difficulty, for bearing in mind that the consideration which the inventor gives for the patent is the information which he is in a position to give to the world, it is difficult to under-

---

(*q*) Per M. R. in *Lang* v. *Gisborne*, 31 Bevan, 135.

(*r*) *United Telephone Co.* v. *Harrison, Cox, Walker & Co.*, L. R., 21 Ch. D. 720.

(*s*) *Oxley* v. *Holden*, 30 L. J., C. P. 68.

stand upon what principle, if he keeps that information to himself and manufactures an article which of itself does not disclose his invention, he should not have a patent; since he is always in a position to give the information to the public, and to give a valid consideration for the grant. Unless indeed we regard the grant of letters patent, as not only the result of a contract between two parties, the state and the inventor, but also as somewhat after the nature of a reward for invention, which is only given for merit. There is, as we have pointed out before, no merit in publishing an invention which you find it difficult to keep any longer secret. Of course it would be otherwise where the article itself, by its appearance or by its properties, discloses the invention; the Courts, in their decisions, seem to have recognized the difficulty of this question. Baron Parke, in *Morgan* v. *Seaward* (*l*), said: " For if the inventor could sell his invention, keeping the secret to himself, and, when it was likely to be discovered by another, take out a patent, he might have practically a monopoly for a very much longer period than fourteen years." It does not seem to have been expressly decided that if an article sold did not disclose the invention, the use of the invention, if kept secret, would invalidate a subsequent patent by the inventor. Baron Parke seems to have thought that it would; on the other hand, if the original inventor manufactured articles, but kept the invention secret so that no one else could practise it, and someone else were to re-invent the same matter subsequently, can it be said that the secret use of the invention by the first inventor would invalidate the patent of the second inventor? and if not the patent of the second inventor, why, upon principle, should one person from whom the consideration would move personally be in a worse position than another? It may be said, perhaps, that the

(*l*) 2 M. & W. 544.

common law contemplated *bona fides* on the part of the inventor, and a *bonâ fide* discovery of the invention to the public within a reasonable time, and that the working of the invention in secret and subsequent application for the patent was strong evidence of *mala fides*, and consequently would avoid the patent on the ground of a constructive fraud upon the public (*u*).

Mere **experiments** with a view to discovery have been frequently held not to invalidate a subsequent patent; few inventions could be made without trial, and there are some things of such magnitude that the trials cannot practically be conducted in private: hence it has been held that the mere making of experiments, with a view to invention, does not invalidate a patent (*x*).

Not only must the invention be new, but **the whole of the invention** which is claimed in the specification **must be new** (*y*); and if any material part of it can be shown to have been anticipated, there would be a valid objection to the patent, and an action for infringement, even of the parts that are new, would not be maintainable.

We shall show hereafter that the claiming of too much in a specification, that is to say, the claiming of things which are not new, is not incurable, but that it operates in such a way as to prevent the inventor from

(*u*) As to publication by sale see *Wood* v. *Zimmer*, 1 Web. P. C. 44; *Losh* v. *Hague*, 1 Web. P. C. 205; *Gibson* v. *Brand*, 1 Web. P. C. 628; *Carpenter* v. *Smith*, 1 Web. P. C. 536; *Mullins* v. *Hart*, 5 Car. & K. 297; *Heath* v. *Smith*, 2 Web. P. C. 268; *Honiball* v. *Bloomer*, 2 Web. P. C. 200; *Oxley* v. *Holden*, 8 C. B. N. S. 666.

(*x*) *Newall* v. *Elliott*, 4 C. B., N. S. 269; *Hills* v. *London Gas Light Company*, 29 L. J. Ex. 409. See also *Jones* v. *Pearce*, 1 Web. P. C. 122; *Bramah* v. *Hardcastle*, Holroyd, 81; *Cornish* v. *Keene*, 1 Web. P. C. 508; *Galloway* v. *Bleaden*, 1 Web. P. C. 525; *Stead* v. *Williams*, 2 Web. P. C. 135; *Houschill Company* v. *Neilson*, 1 Web. P. C. 673.

(*y*) *Plimpton* v. *Spiller*, L. R. 6 Ch. D. 412, & per Jessel, M. R. in *Frearson* v. *Loe*, L. R. 9 Ch. D. 58.

successfully maintaining an action against an infringer until he has taken the proper steps to obtain a disclaimer of the tainted portion, so to speak, of his specification. In *Bramah* v. *Hardcastle* (z) Kenyon, J., said : "Unlearned men look at the specification, and suppose everything new that is there ; if the whole be not new, it is hanging terrors over them." In *Hill* v. *Thompson* (a), per Dallas, J., " If any part of the alleged discovery, being a material part, fail (the discovery in its entirety forming one entire consideration), the patent is altogether void." In *Brunton* v. *Hawkes* (b) Abbott, C. J., said : " I feel myself compelled to say that I think so much of the plaintiff's invention, as respects the anchor, is not new, and that the whole patent is therefore void." A process incidental to the manufacture, which is not one of the substantial elements of the claim, will not invalidate a patent (c).

A description of two processes, one of which is old, and the other new, a claim of the combination of the two would be valid for the combination ; but if the claim is not for the combination, but for the two processes, then the patent is void (d).

When a part of a described invention is old, the question will always arise as to whether the claim is for the several parts as described, or for the combination. We shall treat this subject at length when we deal with the specification.

We now come to the consideration of the question of **utility**, for not only must the invention be new, but it must be new and useful. The 6th section of the Statute of Monopolies does not refer to the necessity of utility in the invention, but saving, as it does, the common law

z 1 Carp. P. C. 168.
(a) 1 Web. P. C. 249.
b 4 B. & Ald. 541.
(c) Munt. v. Foster, 2 Web. P.
C. 112.
d *Templeton* v. *Macfarlane*, 1 H. L. C. 595 ; *McCormick* v. *Gray*, 5 H. & N. 25.

prerogative of the Crown in respect of inventions, it refers us back to what had previously been held to be the necessary elements of an invention. In *Darcy* v. *Allin* (e), decided in 1602, it was held, the invention must tend to the furtherance of trade, and be for the good of the realm, and that the monopoly was granted in consideration of the good that the inventor doth bring by his invention to the commonwealth, otherwise not. Consequently an essential element of a valid grant is, that it should be for something which is for the good of the realm, that is, it must be useful (*f*).

In *Boulton* v. *Bull* (*g*), Rooke, J., said: "The public have a right to receive a meritorious consideration in return for the protection granted." In the same case, Buller, J., said: "The invention professes to lessen the consumption of steam, and to make the patent good the method must be capable of lessening the consumption to such an extent as to make the invention useful." And in the case of *The King* v. *Arkwright* (*h*), the same judge, in leaving the matters to the jury, said: "There is another question, whether the stripe in it makes a material alteration, for if it appears, as some of the witnesses say, to do as well without the stripes, and to answer the same purpose if you suppose the stripes never to have been used before, that is not such an invention as will support the patent."

It will always be a question for the consideration of the **jury**, whether the invention is useful, that is, whether that which is new is a sufficient advance or improvement upon what was already known by the public as to add to a material extent to the public stock of knowledge. It does not mean that there must necessarily be a great deal

---

(*e*) Noy. R. 182.
(*f*) *Edgebury* v. *Stephens*, 1 Web. P. C. 35; *R.* v. *Arkwright*, 1 Web. P. C. 72; *Turner* v. *Winter*, 1 Web. P. C. 80.
(*g*) 2 H. Bl. 478.
(*h*) 1 Web. P. C. 72.

of invention, or an extensive operation, to support the patent, but that the invention when carried out in some way materially improves the process of manufacture, either by cheapening the article produced, or by improving its quality, or by improving the method of producing, or the uses to which it can be put.

Each of the cases which have been decided upon the question of utility deal, and necessarily must deal, with an independent state of facts, and consequently, no case can be said to be an authority for another case; but they go to show the general principle that "utility" means a **substantial improvement, and not** necessarily **an extensive process**; for instance, a man might invent a large and complicated machine for the manufacture of boots, which, when completed, would do nothing which was not done before, and would not make them any quicker or any cheaper than they were made before. Such a machine would not form the subject of a patent. On the other hand, a man might discover a new needle for stitching boots, which would economise half-an-hour in the manufacture of each boot; such a needle would be the subject of a patent, although the whole improvement might consist of a bend.

In *Crane* v. *Price*, Tindal, C. J., said: "If the invention be new and useful to the public, it is not material whether it be the result of long experiments and profound research, or whether by some sudden or lucky thought, or mere accident of discovery" (*i*).

We have seen that the invention must be *new* in every part. It is not, however, necessary that it should be *useful* in every part. Provided always, that useless parts have not been added to the specification for the purpose of deception, or of misleading the public as to what the real nature of the invention is, and how it is

---

i Crane v. *Price*, 1 Web. P. C. at p. 111.

to be performed (*k*). The invention further need not be useful for every purpose to which it can be applied, provided it be useful for some purpose to which it can be applied (*l*).

In *Frearson* v. *Loe* (*m*), Sir George Jessel said: "It is not because a patentee has attempted to claim as an advantage something else to which he is not entitled that the improvement he has made is to be held not worthy of a patent. I am not to say that because even half the advantages said to arise from his invention may not be new he is not to be protected in respect of the other half." It will be observed that in this case the Master of the Rolls does not refer to the novelty of the invention claimed, but to the novelty of the advantages. A large number of patents which are applied for are intituled "improvements in the manufacture of ———," and sometimes it has been considered that when that which is claimed is really no substantial improvement at all, the patent is bad for a false suggestion" (*n*).

It is always a question for the jury whether the invention be useful or not (*o*).

In *Plimpton* v. *Malcolmson* (*p*), Sir George Jessel said: "The cases cited may be rather used as illustrations of what will amount to sufficient evidence than as deciding anything in principle beyond this, that it must be sufficiently known." This would apply to the utility issue as well as that of novelty. In such matters cases merely offer illustrations, and cannot be said to lay down any rigid principles of law.

(*k*) *Lewis* v. *Marling*, 1 Web. P. C. 496.
(*l*) *Haworth* v. *Hardcastle*, 1 Web. P. C. 483.
(*m*) L. R., 9 Ch. D. 64.
(*n*) In the case of *Losh* v. *Hague*, 1 Web. P. C. 202.
(*o*) *Hill* v. *Thompson*, 1 Web. P. C. 237; *Bloxham* v. *Elsee*, 1 C. & P. 565; *Cornish* v. *Keene*, 1 Web. P. C. 506.
(*p*) L. R., 3 Ch. D. 557.

CHAPTER IV.

THE CONSIDERATION (*continued*)—THE SPECIFICATION.

THE third condition which supports a consideration for a valid patent, is that the patentee must publish his invention, that is to say, that in the specification which he files, and which forms the basis of the description of the subject-matter of his patent, he must give such an account of his invention, of the way of working it, and of what he particularly claims, as to enable an ordinary skilled person to carry out the invention without further assistance or discovery. By the 5th section of the Act of 1883, it is provided:—

"(1) The application for a patent must be made in the form set forth in the first schedule of this Act, or in such other form as may be from time to time prescribed, and must be left at or sent by post to the Patent Office in the prescribed manner.

"(2) An application must contain a declaration to the effect that the applicant is in possession of an invention whereof he, or in the case of a joint application, one or more of the applicants claims or claim, to be the true and first inventor or inventors, and for which he or they desires or desire, to obtain a patent; and must be accompanied by either a provisional or complete specification.

"(3) A provisional specification must describe the nature of the invention, and be accompanied by drawings if required.

"(4) A complete specification, whether left on application or subsequently, must particularly describe and ascertain the nature of the invention, and in what manner it is to be performed, and must be accompanied by drawings if required.

"(5) A specification, whether provisional or complete, must commence with the title, and in the case of a complete specification must end with a distinct statement of the invention claimed."

Sect. 6 of the same Act vests in an examiner the duty of reporting to the comptroller whether the nature of the invention has been fairly described, and the application, specification, and drawings (if any) have been prepared in the prescribed manner, and the title sufficiently indicates the subject-matter of the invention.

Sect. 7 provides for the report of the examiner, and for an appeal from the decision of the comptroller should he refuse the application, to the law officer, who may affirm, reverse or vary the decision of the comptroller. By sect. 8 (1), "If the applicant does not leave a complete specification with his application, he may leave it at any subsequent time within nine months from the date of application." (2) "Unless the complete specification is left within that time, the application shall be deemed to be abandoned." By sect. 9, "Where a complete specification is left after a provisional specification, the comptroller shall refer both specifications to an examiner, for the purpose of ascertaining whether the complete specification has been prepared in the prescribed manner, and whether the invention particularly described in the complete specification is substantially the same as that which is described in the provisional specification." Sub-sect. 2 provides for the refusal of the complete specification by the comptroller upon an adverse report of the examiner; and sub-sect. 3 gives the machinery for appealing to the law officer; by sect. 10, "On the acceptance of a complete specification, the comptroller shall advertise the acceptance, and the application and specification or specifications with the drawings (if any), and shall be open to public inspection." By sect. 18, sub-sect. 1, "An applicant or patentee may from time to time, by request in writing left at the Patent Office, seek leave to amend his specification, including drawings forming part thereof, by way of disclaimer, correction or explanation, stating the nature of such amendment, and his reasons for the same." Sub-sects. 2, 3, 4, 5, 6, 7, 8 and 9, deal with the practice to be observed upon amendment, to which we shall refer hereafter; and sub-sect. 10 enacts that "the foregoing provisions of this section do not apply when and so long as any action for infringement or other legal proceeding in relation to a patent is pending."

Such are the provisions of the new Act in respect of the requirements of the specification. It leaves the law respecting the necessary disclosures to be made in the specification very much as it was before; and the changes which are made are more changes of practice than anything else.

The specification is the means which is provided by the state, whereby a patentee publishes his invention, that is, dedicates it to the public. We have observed that two descriptions of specifications are provided for, one called "provisional," and the other "complete;" the applicant for letters patent may, if he so pleases, in the first instance, file a complete specification, or he may file a specification which, for want of a better word, has been described as provisional; subsequently, and within the prescribed time, filing a complete specification, which particularly describes and ascertains his invention. It is only necessary, however, that the provisional specification should describe the nature of the invention; and although it is not absolutely necessary that full details should be given as to the method of working the invention, care should be taken to ascertain to what extent and in what direction the invention goes.

There are three things, in the specification, which must **agree** with each other—the title, the provisional specification, and the complete specification.

The Title.

The title of the specification must disclose the object of the invention (*a*).

The title is a part of the specification, and should be read into it so that it may limit the patentee's claim, which otherwise would be too large (*b*).

In the case of *Rex* v. *Else* (*c*), the title of the patent was held to contain the claim, there being no other claim.

It has frequently been held that the **title must not go too far;** for instance, a man who had invented a new street lamp, and described his invention in the title as being "a method or methods of more completely lighting cities, towns and villages," was held to have vitiated his patent by going too far in his title. His claim should have been for a new or improved street lamp (*d*). So care must be taken that an improvement in buttons, for instance, is not described as an improvement in the manufacture of buttons; if the improvement is in the article, it must be so stated, and if in the process, likewise. In *Campion* v. *Benyon* (*e*), the title was a new and improved method of making and manufacturing double canvas and sail cloth with hemp and flax, without any starch whatever; the title, therefore, described an invention, the novelty and utility of which

---

(*a*) *Househill Co.* v. *Neilson,* 1 Web. P. C. 678.
(*b*) *Newton* v. *Vaucher,* 21 L. J., Ex. 308.
(*c*) 1 Web. P. C. 76.
(*d*) *Cochrane* v. *Smethurst,* Davy's P. C. 354.
(*e*) 6 B. Mo. 71.

was to omit the use of starch, but upon reading the specification we find that the real invention was an improved mode of twisting the threads to be applied to the making of unstarched cloth, the patent was held bad. In the case of *Bloxam* v. *Elsee* (*f*), the title for the invention was for a machine for making paper in single sheets without seam or joining from 1 to 12 feet and upwards wide, and from 1 to 45 feet and upwards in length. It was found that to vary the width of the paper it was necessary to have a different machine, and that consequently the title did not **correspond with the invention**, and the title was held bad. In *Felton* v. *Greaves* (*g*), the title was "a machine for an expeditious and correct mode of giving a fine edge to knives, razors, scissors and other cutting instruments." The machine would not sharpen scissors:—Held bad. These cases seem to have been decided upon the ground that an incorrect or too extensive title is evidence of fraud upon the Crown. For instance, in *Brunton* v. *Hawkes* (*h*), Best, J., said, "that the patent was taken out for more than the patentee was entitled to, that, in my opinion, avoids the patent *in toto*, for the king is deceived." In *Cook* v. *Pearce* (*i*), however, Tindal, C. J., in the Exchequer Chamber, said: "This was an action on the case against the defendant for the infringement of a patent taken out by the plaintiff for improvements in carriages. The 6th plea, after setting out the specification, averred that 'although the said alleged invention in the declaration of letters patent respectively mentioned is therein styled and described as improvements in carriages, yet the said invention in truth, and in fact, is not an invention of improvements of carriages generally, but certain alleged improvements in the fixing and adapting of German shutters in those carriages only in which German

f 6 B. & C. 169.
g 3 C. & P. 611.
h 4 B. & Ald. 552.
i 8 Q. B. 1051.

shutters are used, and that German shutters cannot be used in divers and very many carriages, to wit, coaches, &c.,' and so the defendants say that the title of the said invention is too large and general, and by reason thereof the said letters patent are void and of no force. . . . . It has been observed that the decision (in the Court below) does not proceed upon the ground that the title of this patent must be held of necessity to claim more than the invention as explained by the specification, as if the title had been 'an invention and improvement of *all* carriages,' and the specification had limited the invention to the improvement of one or more species of carriages only, or if the title had been for the invention of two things, and the specification had shown it to be an invention of one only out of the two; in such cases it may be readily admitted that the patent would be void, in the first, because there was no specification enrolled agreeing with the title, and in the second, upon the principle laid down by Mr. Justice Bayley, in his judgment in *Brunton* v. *Hawkes:* 'that the entire discovery of all the things for which the patent was taken out may be held to be the consideration upon the patent which was granted by the Crown;' but such an objection would not apply to the case now before us, for the words 'improvements in carriages' do not necessarily imply in all carriages, but in their ordinary use may well be held to be satisfied by an invention for improvements in some carriages only, but the ground of the decision is as before stated confined to the vagueness and generality of the title, and to that only. Now the mere vagueness of the title appears to us to be an objection that may well be taken on the part of the Crown before it grants the patent, but to afford no ground to avoid the patent after it has been granted. If such title did not agree with the specification when enrolled, or if there had been any fraud practised on the Crown in obtaining the payment with such title, the patent in those cases might undoubtedly be held void. . . . . . . We think it would be unsafe to lay down the rule in terms so large as it appears to have been adopted by the Court below, for that it would endanger the validity of very many patents which had hitherto been free from exception, if every patent must be held to be void simply on the ground that its title was conceived in such terms as to be capable of comprising some other invention besides that contained in the specification in the absence at the same time of any proof of an intention to commit any fraud upon the Crown, or of deceiving or misleading the public "(*k*). It will be seen, therefore, that although **variance** between the title and the specification is held to vitiate the patent as in *Felton* v. *Greaves*, that mere excess and generality in the title will not vitiate the patent in the absence of any evidence of fraud upon the Crown (*l*).

In *Neilson* v. *Harford* (*m*), Abinger, C. B., said, "If the specification is **consistent** with the title, that would be sufficient;" and Baron Parke said, "The title of the patent is for the improved application of air, though that is ambiguous. It is sufficiently explained by the specification, and is not at variance with it."

It is evident that the question of **variance** between the title and the specification is one upon which the decided cases can have no bearing. All that can be gleaned from previous decisions of the Courts is that variance is a fatal blemish; but in the immense variety of inventions it is evident that the same variance will never occur in any two cases, and it will be a question for the Court in each

k This decision was followed in *Crossley* v. *Potter* by Pollock, C. B. See Macr. P. C. 242.

l *Sturtz* v. *De la Rue*, 5 Russ.

322; *Morgan* v. *Seaward*, 1 Web. P. C. 196; *Stead* v. *Williams*, 2 Web. P. C. 137.

m 1 Web. P. C. 331.

individual case that comes before it to decide whether, in that case, the specification and the title vary or differ from each other; and although the decided authorities will be of assistance to the Court in showing to what extent variance has been held in prior cases to vitiate the patent, it is evident that no prior decision will be absolutely binding (*n*).

THE PROVISIONAL SPECIFICATION.

It was found that application for letters patent, being made merely upon the title of an invention, caused a great deal of inconvenience and uncertainty, therefore by the Patent Law Amendment Act, 1852, the provisional specification was created. Prior to the passing of that Act applicants for letters patent, when they made their application, merely deposited the title of their invention. By sect. 6 of that Act a provisional specification was required, which should give some more definite information as to the nature of the invention for which protection was sought than could be possibly given in a mere title.

It is very difficult to clearly define the distinction between that which is absolutely necessary in the provisional specification and that which is absolutely necessary in a complete specification.

Sect. 8 of the Act of 1852, to which we have referred, says that "the law officer must be satisfied that the provisional specification describes the nature of the invention," and we have seen that the exact words of that section are retained in sub-sect. 3 of sect. 5 of the Act of 1883; and probably the legislature had in view the desirability of retaining the effect of the numerous valuable decisions of the Courts of law upon the construction

(*n*) *Bainbridge* v. *Wigley*, Higgins' Digest, 155; *Hill* v. *Thompson*, 1 Web. P. C. 239; *Nickels* v. *Haslam*, 13 L. J., C. P. 146; *Croll* v. *Edge*, 9 C. B. 479; *Wright* v. *Hitchcock*, L. R. 5 Ex. 37.

which should be placed upon what is a sufficient description of the nature of an invention. It will be observed that the complete specification to which we shall refer at greater length hereafter must not only describe the nature of the invention, but must also *ascertain* the nature of the invention and in what manner it is to be performed; but both a provisional specification and a complete specification must commence with a title, and the complete specification must conclude with a distinct statement of the invention claimed.

The cases which we have quoted, and which were decided prior to the year 1852, as to the fatal nature of a variation between the title and the specification, will apply equally to the consideration of a variance between a provisional and a complete specification. It is evident, however, that the object of the legislature in creating a provisional specification, and founding upon it a period of provisional protection, was to enable the inventor in that interval to improve and perfect his invention, and to clearly ascertain what was new, and what was old, in that which he proposed to patent. That being so, it is obvious that it could not have been the intention of the legislature that, when framing a complete specification the inventor should be bound to follow implicitly every detail which he had given in his provisional specification, or that he should be prevented from adding to or subtracting from his invention: for, in that case, the object of the legislature would be defeated.

In *Newall* v. *Elliott* (m) Pollock, C. B., said: "The object of the statute which requires a provisional specification is nothing more than a legislative recognition of the custom which called upon every patentee, when he applies for a patent, to give some notion of what his invention is; that has been followed by Act of Parliament, requiring it to be done; but the object in both

m) 10 Jur., N. S. 955.

cases is to ascertain the identity of the invention, and make it certain that the patentee shall ultimately obtain his patent for that invention which he presented to the Attorney-General in the first instance .... I have no doubt that the object of the Act of Parliament was not to ascertain the **entirety** of the invention, but the **identity** of the invention, so as to enable the Attorney-General, and, in fact, to enable a jury ultimately to determine whether the invention fully specified was the same invention as that which was presented to the notice of the Attorney-General by the provisional specification." Mr. Baron Channell in the same case, at p. 960, describes a provisional specification as a "short note or minute of that which was ultimately disclosed in the full specification." It will be observed that in the cases to which we drew attention upon the subject of variance between title and specification, the point always was as to whether the title and the specification varied in the description of the **nature** of the invention; and the same principle holds good when considering the variation between the provisional and complete specification, the question always is, Do they differ in their description of the nature of the invention? In *Newall* v. *Elliott* (n) Mr. Justice Byles said: "The office of the provisional specification is only to describe generally and fairly the nature of the invention, and not to enter into all the minute details as to the manner in which the invention is to be carried out" (o).

Lord Chelmsford, in *Penn* v. *Bibby* (p), said: "The relation which the provisional specification bears to the complete specification is much the same as that which before the Patent Law Amendment Act a title bore to the specification ..... the only objection then which is open upon the complete specification, is whether

(n) 4 C. B., N. S. 269.   R. 723.
(o) *Foxwell* v. *Bostock*, 12 W.   (p) L. R., 2 Ch. Ap. C. 127.

it is sufficient in itself, and whether it agrees with the provisional specification. Now, by agreement is not meant a perfect correspondence, but merely that there shall be nothing in the complete specification at variance with the provisional." The learned Lord Chancellor then proceeds to quote *Newall's case*, to which we have referred, and proceeds: "Nor is it at all necessary that the specification should extend to everything comprehended in the provisional specification. Perhaps a better illustration of this proposition could not be given than that which was offered in the course of the argument. If the patentee were to introduce into his complete specification everything which was warranted by the terms of the provisional specification, and afterwards found that a part of that which he had claimed would invalidate his patent for want of novelty, or for any other reason, he might afterwards cure the objection by a disclaimer. Now if he would be allowed to disclaim in such a case, which is a matter of indulgence, he must have a right to waive his claim to any portion of the grant which the allowance of the provisional specification had entitled him to demand. It is clear, therefore, that unless a complete specification in this case claims something *different* from the provisional specification, the objection to the patent under consideration cannot prevail."

In the absence of fraud, any part, whether in the description or the claim of the provisional specification, may be omitted in the complete specification without the necessity of any disclaimer (r). In *Stoner* v. *Todd* (s), Jessel, M. R., said: "I must consider first the nature of a provisional specification, and the effect of a provisional specification on a final specification of

r *Thomas* v. *Welch*, L. R., 1 C. P. 192. See also the remarks of Lord Chelmsford in *Penn* v. *Bibby*, quoted above.

s L. R., 4 Ch. D. 58.

the same invention. A provisional specification was never intended to be more than a mode of protecting an inventor; until the time of filing a final specification, it was not intended to contain a complete description of the thing so as to enable any workman of ordinary skill to make it, but only to disclose the invention, fairly no doubt, but in its rough state, until the inventor could perfect its details, the provisional specification as such is not and cannot be known to the public. It is never published unless with the final specification, when they become parts of the same document."

In the case of *Bailey* v. *Roberton* (*t*), decided in the House of Lords, the provisional specification stated the object of the invention to be the preserving of animal substances in the fresh state, and the patentees claimed the use of a solution composed of a certain quantity of gelatine mixed with bisulphite of lime, but in the complete specification they claimed as solution No. 1 a solution composed of bisulphite of lime alone, and gave no direction how this solution was to be used. Bisulphite of lime had been used by a prior patentee. In the action for infringement against the defendants who had used bisulphite of lime pure and simple, it was held that the complete specification, if large enough to cover the employment of bisulphite of lime for the preservation of animal substances as practised by the defenders, would claim an invention larger than and different from that disclosed in the provisional specification. It will be observed that in this case the invention, which was described in the provisional specification, was the coating of animal substances with a film of a mixture of gelatine and bisulphite of lime; the complete specification claimed the dipping of the animal substance into a solution of bisulphite of lime in water; it is apparent, therefore, to anyone acquainted with the

(*t*) L. R., 3 Ap. C. 1055.

action of antiseptic substances upon animal decomposition, that the operation of a film of gelatine with bisulphite of lime is entirely different from the operation of a solution of bisulphite of lime; it is a totally different idea, and therefore a different invention; the complete specification, therefore, was not an extension, curtailment or modification of the provisional specification, but was a description of a totally different invention, and so it was held bad for variance.

Thus we see that the provisional specification is a mere extension of the title; but since variance between the title and the specification vitiated the patent before the inauguration of the provisional specification, variance between the provisional and complete specification also vitiates a patent; but it is quite open to a patentee to extend, improve or curtail the claim which he has made in his provisional specification when he comes to file his complete specification.

THE COMPLETE SPECIFICATION.

We now come to the more important subject of the requirements of a complete specification. The complete specification is, as we have seen, one of the essential considerations which the patentee gives for the grant which is made to him. **It is the disclosure of his invention**, and of the mode of performing it. It contains the information which he is bound to give to the public. That information must be *bonâ fide*, full, complete, and unambiguous; it must disclose the invention, the nature of it, the intention of it, the way of performing it, and an exact statement of what is claimed by the patentee.

These conditions are imposed by the common law; they were maintained intact by the Statute of Monopolies, by the Patent Law Amendment Act, 1852, and are now specifically re-enacted in the Act of 1883.

The specification must be **sufficient**—that is, it must

give a sufficient description of the invention to enable a person skilled in the art to which it refers to perform the invention from the description which it gives. It must be *bonâ fide*—there must be no reserve on the part of the inventor. He must disclose what he knows; he must conceal nothing, and thus he must give to the public the full benefit of his invention. In *Harmar* v. *Playne*(*u*), Lord Ellenborough said:—" The object of requiring the specification to be enrolled seemed to be to enable persons of reasonable intelligence and skill in the subject-matter to tell from an inspection of the specification itself what the invention was for which the patent was granted, and how it was to be executed." In *Morgan* v. *Seaward* (*x*), Mr. Baron Alderson said:—" The patentee ought to state in his specification the precise way of doing it (referring to the invention); if it cannot completely be done by following the specification, then a person will not infringe the patent by doing it. If this were an infringement it would be an infringement to do that perfectly, which, according to the specification, requires something else to be done to make it perfect. If that be correct, you would prevent a man from having a perfect engine. He says, practically speaking, the difference in the length of the rods would not be very material, the difference being small. But the whole question is small, therefore it ought to have been specified, and if it could not be ascertained fully it should have been so stated." We quote this decision at length, because the exposition of the law which it contains is still absolutely correct. The subsequent cases to which we purpose to draw attention have implicitly followed the judgment of Mr. Baron Alderson (*y*).

The specification is a portion of the patent (*z*).

(*u*) Dav. P. C. 316.
(*x*) 1 Web. P. C. at p. 182.
(*y*) *Neilson* v. *Thompson*, 1 Web. R. 278.
(*z*) *Hornblower* v. *Boulton*, 8 T. R. 95; *Crossley* v. *Beverley*, 9 B. & C. 62.

T. F

In the case of *The King* v. *Arkwright* (*a*), Mr. Justice Buller said, "The public have a right to a fair, full, and true description of the invention in the specification."

It is incumbent on a patentee to give a specification of his invention in the fairest and most unequivocal terms of which the subject is capable (*b*). In the same case, Mr. Justice Buller said:—"Many cases upon patents have arisen within our memory, most of which have been decided against the patentees upon the ground of their not having made a full and fair discovery of their inventions. Whenever it appears that the patentee has made a fair disclosure I have always had a strong bias in his favour, because in that case he is entitled to the protection which the law gives him." In *Newbery* v. *James* (*c*), Lord Eldon said:—"In order to support a patent, the specification should be so clear as to enable all the world to use the invention as soon as the term for which it was granted was at an end."

We have next to consider the bearing of the different decisions upon the question of what amounts to **sufficiency** in a specification. It is always a question of fact whether the specification is sufficient or not, taking care to distinguish between sufficiency of description and an attempt to cover too much—it is for the jury to say whether from the description given the invention could be carried out. It is for the Court to determine whether the inventor has claimed that which is not new among that which is new (*d*). The question of the sufficiency of the specification is a question for the jury (*e*).

---

a Dav. P. C. 61.
b Per Mr. Justice Ashurst, in *Turner* v. *Winter*, Dav. P. C. 151.
c 2 Mer. 151.
d *Hill* v. *Thompson*, 3 Mer.

626.
e *Bickford* v. *Skewes*, 1 Q. B. 938; *Wallington* v. *Dale*, 7 Exch. 888; *Parkes* v. *Stephens*, L. R., 8 Eq. 358.

The **intelligibility** of the specification is a question for the jury (*f*). The **construction** of the specification is in the same manner as the construction of all documents—a question of law. The duty of the judge at Nisi Prius is to **tell the jury** the specification says so-and-so, placing a meaning upon the different words used and the different sentences used in the specification. It is then for the jury to say it is intelligible or it is not, it is sufficient or it is not sufficient, but the Court will determine in all cases whether or not the patent is defective by reason of the patentee having endeavoured to describe or to claim too much (*g*).

We will deal with these different heads in their natural order, first, as to **construction**, next as to intelligibility, and then as to sufficiency. The object of the Courts is not to defeat patents. In *Hullett* v. *Hague* (*h*), Lord Tenterden said :—" I cannot forbear saying that I think a great deal too much critical acumen has been applied to the construction of patents, as if the object was to defeat, and not to sustain, them." The patentee is to be presumed not to claim things which he must have known to be in use (*i*).

The leaning of the Courts is invariably in favour of the patentee, and specifications will **not** be **construed astutely** so as to overthrow a patent. Sir George Jessel, in the case of *Hinks* v. *The Safety Lighting Co.* (*j*), said: " I am anxious, as I believe every judge is who knows anything of patent law, to support honest *bonâ fide* inventors who have actually invented something novel and useful, and to prevent their patents being overturned on mere technical objections or on mere cavillings

(*f*) *Neilson* v. *Harford*, 1 Web. P. C. 295.

(*g*) *Hill* v. *Thompson*, 3 Mer. 626; *Beard* v. *Egerton*, 19 L. J., C. P. 38.

(*h*) 2 B. & Ad. 377.

(*i*) *Haworth* v. *Hardcastle*, 1 Web. P. C. 484.

(*j*) L. R., 4 Ch. D. 612.

with the language of their specifications, so as to deprive the inventor of the benefit of his invention; that is sometimes called a benevolent mode of construction, perhaps that is not the best term to use, but it may be described as construing the language of the specification fairly, with a judicial anxiety to support a really useful invention, if it can be supported by a reasonable construction of a patent; beyond that the benevolent mode of construction does not go." And the same judge, in *Plimpton* v. *Spiller*(*k*), adopted the remark that "the judge is not to be astute to find flaws in small matters in a specification with a view to overthrow it."

Lord Chelmsford, in *Harrison* v. *Anderston Foundry Co.*(*l*), said, "the language should be construed according to its ordinary meaning, the understanding of technical words being, of course, confined to those who are conversant with the subject-matter of the invention, and if the specification is thus sufficiently intelligible it performs all that is required of it." In *Clark* v. *Adie*(*m*) it was held that the words used in the specification must be construed like the words in any other instrument, in their natural sense, according to the general purpose of the instrument in which they are found.

The title of a specification and the specification itself is one document, and an ambiguity in the specification must be construed by the light which is thrown upon it by the title (*n*). In the case of *Unwin* v. *Heath* (*o*), in the course of an opinion given by the judges to the House of Lords, Mr. Justice Crompton said, "I think it will be a narrow and a dangerous construction to limit the

l L. R., 6 Ch. D. 122.
l L. R., 1 Ap. C. 581.
m L. R. 2 Ap. C. 423; *Dudgeon* v. *Thompson*, L. R., 3 App. Ca. 34; *Wegmann* v. *Corcoran*.

L. R., 13 Ch. D. 77.
n *Newton* v. *Vaucher*, 6 Exch. 864.
o 25 L. J., C. P. 8.

invention claimed in express words by the mode and process of working which the plaintiff sets forth as a means of carrying his invention into effect."

The claims in specifications frequently claim the invention in a general manner with the words added "as herein described." It has been held that the meaning of the words "as herein described" is not limited where the invention is for a mode of construction or manufacture, and not for a particular method of carrying out the principle which is described in the specification. In *Betts* v. *Menzies* (*p*) Mr. Justice Blackburn, giving his opinion to the House of Lords, said, "I agree with what was said by Mr. Justice Crompton in the Court below that, if a general claim for the use of an invention were cut down and limited to the use of the invention in the particular way pointed out by reason of the words ' as herein described,' it will be a narrow rule of construction, generally working to the detriment of patentees, and, what weighs more with me, generally giving an effect to specifications different from what the persons drawing them intended or those reading them understand."

In the case of *Unwin* v. *Heath* (*supra*), Mr. Justice Williams said, "but if the invention described and claimed by the patentee in this case is not the particular process specified, but the employment of carburet of manganese in the process of the conversion of iron into steel, and if the description of the process in the specification, instead of being a description of the invention, is only one mode of carrying the invention into effect, an entirely different doctrine becomes applicable to the question, viz., that *if the patent is taken out for the application of a principle coupled with the mode of carrying the principle into effect the patentee is entitled to protection from all other modes of doing so, whether known or not known at the time of the specification."*

(*p*) 10 H. L. C. 140.

There are numerous authorities which bear out the general rule of construction which has been laid down, viz., that a specification of an invention must be construed by the same rules and upon the same principles that are applied to other written documents, and if, on the one hand, minute cavilling at the words of a specification is not to be allowed as against a patentee, so, on the other hand, the interpretation must not be strained in favour of a patentee. Lord Westbury, in *Simpson* v. *Holliday* (*p*), said :—" It was contended before me, and the Vice-Chancellor is reported to have said, that it has been settled by authority that the most liberal construction is to be given to the patent that will sustain it. . . . . I am not aware of any such authority."

A patent may be, as we have seen, for the application of a newly-discovered principle of manufacture or, for that of an old principle to a new object or, for a new method of carrying out an old principle applied to an old object. It frequently becomes a matter of construction upon the specification as to which of these branches of invention the specification is intended to apply, and there have been several cases upon the subject. It is evident that inasmuch as the patent will be valid provided a fair description of a new invention in either branch is given, that, in construing the specification of a patent a decided case upon some other specification will be of very little value. We do not propose, therefore, to discuss at length the constructions which have been placed upon specifications in particular cases. The words " improvements . . . . in the manner hereinafter mentioned," followed by a claim concluding with the words " as above described," have been held to limit the claim to the particular machine described in the specification or to the particular method

p 13 W. R. 578.

of carrying out the process and not to include the principle of the process or any other method than that described of carrying it out (*q*).

We have seen, and we shall see more fully at length hereafter, that it is incumbent on a patentee in drawing the specification to distinguish that which is new in his invention from that which is old. In the case of *Holmes* v. *London and North Western Railway* (*r*), A. obtained a patent for an improved turning-table for railway purposes, and in his specification gave a description of the machinery, of which no part was new except certain suspending rods; the combination, however, was both new and useful. In the specification the patentee claimed as his invention "An improved turning-table hereinbefore described, such my invention being, to the best of my knowledge and belief, entirely new." It was held, that no construction of the claim could be put upon it as including a combination of the various parts which were old, but that it must be construed as meaning that the patentee claimed the several parts of the invention as being new, and the combination being the only part which was new, the patent was held void. In the case of *Hills* v. *London Gaslight Company* (*s*), it was held, that where the meaning of a document depends upon its terms and not on matters of fact, dehors the document, the question will be for the judge, even although the terms are technical or scientific; and where an ambiguity is raised by evidence, dehors the document, which is plain upon the face of it, the ambiguity being as to a term which imports one thing in a scientific sense, and another in a commercial sense. Query, whether it is for the judge or the jury. We should venture to say, that it would undoubtedly be for the jury. The question not being one at all as to the construction of the document,

(*q*) *Barker* v. *Grace*, 1 Ex. 339.
(*r*) 22 L. J., C. P. 57.
(*s*) 27 L. J., Exch. 60.

but being as a matter of fact, did the writer of the specification use the scientific term or the commercial term? A specification is to be construed with reference to the state of knowledge at the time it is published (*t*).

When drawings are attached to a specification, although the drawings may be used in construing the specification as explanatory of the text, they will not be allowed to be used in limiting the claim in a manner not provided for by the specification (*u*).

When two documents such as specifications are before the Court for comparison, the Court must interpret the meaning of the words, but the jury must say if they are identical (*x*). It is evident that, inasmuch as technical expressions are used in different trades and businesses, and that it is impossible for one person to be acquainted with every trade and every business, and every technical expression used in such trade and business, it is not necessary that the specification should be **intelligible** to any one, it is sufficient that it should be intelligible to a person reasonably skilled in the trade to which it particularly refers, and it must be intelligible to them without the necessity of their making new inventions of their own or additions to the specification or experiments (*y*).

In *Arkwright* v. *Nightingale* (*z*), Lord Loughborough, in charging the jury, said: "The clearness of the specification must be according to the subject-matter of it; it is addressed to the persons in the profession having skill in the subject, not to men of ignorance, and if it is under-

---

t *Heath* v. *Unwin*, 22 L. J., C. P. 7.

u *Hinks* v. *Safety Lighting Co.*, L. R., 4 Ch. D. 607. See also *Clark* v. *Adie*, L. R., 2 Ap. Cas. 315.

x *Betts* v. *Menzies*, 10 H. L. C. 117; *Muntz* v. *Foster*, 2 Web.

P. C. 105; *Tetley* v. *Easton*, Mac. P. C. 68. But see *Bush* v. *Fox*, 5 H. L. C. 707; *Booth* v. *Kennard*, 2 H. & N. 84. Also *Hills* v. *Evans*, 31 L. J., Ch. 457.

y *Reg.* v. *Arkwright*, 1 Web. P. C. 66.

z 1 Web. P. C. 61.

stood by those whose business leads them to be conversant in such subjects, it is intelligible." And in *Hornblower* v. *Boulton* (*a*), to which we have previously referred, Mr. Justice Grose said : " If the specification be such as to enable artists to adopt the invention and to make the manufacture, it is sufficient."

In *Harmar* v. *Playne* (*b*), Lord Ellenborough graphically puts it: " No sort of specification would probably enable a ploughman utterly ignorant of the art to make a watch." But it is necessary that the specification should be in such terms as to enable persons of ordinary ability to understand it, and it will not be sufficient to show that one individual of extraordinary ability or of very exceptional technical knowledge is enabled to understand the specification (*c*). In *Neilson* v. *Harford* (*d*), Baron Parke puts it to the jury : " You are not to ask yourselves the question whether persons of great skill, a first-rate engineer, or a second-class engineer, as described by Mr. Farey, whether they would do it, because generally these persons are men of great science and philosophical knowledge, and they would, upon a mere hint in the specification, probably invent a machine which would answer the purpose extremely well; but that is not the description of persons to whom this specification is supposed to be addressed: it is supposed to be addressed to a practical workman, who brings the ordinary degree of knowledge, and the ordinary degree of capacity, to the subject."

In the process of the invention it is necessary to use some old or well-known apparatus; it is not necessary in the specification to describe the apparatus, save in such terms as it is generally known by in the particular business to which it belongs (*e*).

(*a*) 8 T. Rep. 104.
(*b*) Dav. P. C. 318.
(*c*) *Sturz* v. *De la Rue*, 5 Russ. 327.
(*d*) 1 Web. P. C. 314.
(*e*) *Crossley* v. *Beverley*, 3 C. & P. 513; *Househill Co.* v. *Neilson*, 1 Web. P. C. 676.

In *Heath v. Unwin* (*f*), Mr. Baron Alderson said: "Every specification is to be read as if by persons acquainted with the general facts of the mechanical or chemical sciences involved in such invention; thus, if a particular mechanical process is specified, and there are for some parts of it, as specified, other well-known **mechanical equivalents**, the specification in those parts is in truth the specification of the well-known equivalent also, to those to whose general knowledge we refer: viz., mechanics and readers of specifications; and so it is with chemical equivalents also in a specification which is to be read by chemists. But it may be that there are equivalents, mechanical and chemical, existing, but previously unknown to ordinary skilful mechanics and chemists. These are not included in the specification but must be expressly stated there."

An error in a specification which may be said, in a sense, to be a technical error, will not vitiate a specification, although it be an error in description, provided it be such an error that an ordinary skilled workman would at once observe and be in a position to correct; provided it is not such an error as would require experiments to show that it was an error (*g*).

In *Plimpton v. Malcolmson* (*h*), Sir George Jessel said: "It is plain that the specification of a patent is not addressed to people who are ignorant of the subject-matter. It is addressed to people who know something about it; but there are various kinds of people who know something about it, if it is a mechanical invention, as this is; you have, first of all, scientific mechanicians of the first class, eminent engineers; then you have scientific mechanicians of the second class, managers of great manufactures, great employers of labour, persons who have studied

---

f, 2 Web. P. C. 245.
g See *Simpson v. Holliday*,
per Lord Westbury, 13 W. R. 578.
h) L. R., 3 Ch. D. 568.

mechanics, but not to the extent of the first class, and scientific engineers, but still to a great extent for the purpose of conducting the manufacture of complicated and unusual machines, and who therefore must have made the subject a matter of considerable study; and in this class I should include foremen, being men of superior intelligence, who, like their masters, would be capable of invention, and, like the scientific engineers, would be able to find out what was meant even with slight hints and still more from imperfect description, and would be able to supplement so as to succeed even from a defective description, and, even more than that, would be able to correct an erroneous description—that is what I would say to be the two first classes, which I will call the scientific classes; the other class consists of the ordinary workman, using that amount of skill and intelligence which is fairly to be expected from him, not a careless man, but a careful man, though not possessed of that great scientific knowledge or power of invention which would enable him by himself unaided to supplement a defective description or correct an erroneous description. Now, as I understand it, to be a good specification it must be intelligible to the **third** class I have mentioned, and that is the result of the law." This judgment very precisely lays down the law upon the subject of intelligibility generally.

The next question, as to what is a **sufficient** specification, is by far the most important branch of the subject.

We have seen that the consideration for the grant of letters patent is, that the inventor shall particularly describe and ascertain the nature of his invention, and in what manner it is to be performed; consequently for a specification to be sufficient it must particularly ascertain—(1) What the invention itself is; (2) How the invention is to be carried out. Under the first head the inventor must describe exactly and accurately what he has invented, and if in the course of the description of his invention it should be necessary for him to describe something which is old but which he wishes to use in the process of his invention, he must be careful to say, "This is old and I do not claim it as a part of my invention." There are two reasons why the inventor should be called upon to particularly state what he has invented; one is, that the public may be placed in a position to use the invention so soon as the period of protection has elapsed; and the other is, that the public may be protected by being carefully informed what it is that during the period of protection they are not to use. In *Macfarlane* v. *Price* (*g*), Lord Ellenborough said: "The patentee in his specification ought to inform the person who consults it what is new and what is old; he should say, 'my improvement consists in this ....' A person ought to be warned by the specification against the use of the particular invention, but it would exceed the wit of man to discover from what he is warned in a case like this." And the same judge, in *Harmar* v. *Playne* (*h*), maintained the same opinion.

The **degree of sufficiency** which is required by the law is very aptly and accurately put by Eyre, C. J., in *Boulton* v. *Bull* (*i*): "Suppose a newly-invented chemical process, and the specification should direct that some particular chemical substance should be poured upon gold in a state of fusion, it would be necessary that, in order to carry out this operation, the gold should be put into a crucible, and should be melted in that crucible, but it would be hardly necessary to state in the specification the manner in which, or the utensils with which, the operation of putting gold in a state of fusion was to be performed. These are mere incidents, which every man acquainted with the subject is familiar." In taking this distinction as a guide, however, we must be

g 1 Web. P. C. 74.
h Dav. P. C. 311.
i, 2 H. Bl. 498.

careful to remember that could it be shown that the chemical process would only be successful when the gold was melted in a particular kind of crucible, or at a particular temperature, that then, unless the description was given of the temperature and of the crucible, the specification would be insufficient.

It will be evident that, in any action for infringement, the statement of claim must relate to an infringement of something which is described and claimed in the specification, and consequently the invention, which must be proved, must be one of something which is found described in the specification. If that which is alleged to be an infringement is not described in the specification, then there can be no infringement of the patent. If anything cannot be completely done by following the specification then a person will not infringe the patent by doing it (*j*). The disclosure in the specification of the nature of the invention must be *bonâ fide*, but it need not go farther than the knowledge of the inventor at the time extends (*k*). If a patentee **suppresses** anything, or if he **misleads,** or if he does **not communicate** all he knows, his specification is bad. So if he says that there are many modes of doing a thing, when, in fact, only one will do, this will also avoid the patent (*l*). The object of the patent is to benefit the world, and not to obstruct a subsequent invention; consequently, if the specification is worded in such a manner as to grasp at more than the patentee has actually invented, and to endeavour to cover, so to speak, wholesale problematic inventions, the patent will be void (*m*).

There is a head-note to the case of *Betts* v. *Neilson* (*n*) which is apt to mislead, the head-note is this : " Whether

(*j*) *Morgan* v. *Seaward*, 1 Web. P. C. 182.

(*k*) *Lewis* v. *Marling*, 1 Web. P. C. 496.

(*l*) Per Mr. Justice Bailey, in

Lewis v. *Marling*, 1 Web. P. C. 496.

(*m*) *Crossley* v. *Potter*, Mac. P. C. 245.

(*n*) L. R., 3 Ch. Ap. 429.

a specification contains a sufficient description can only be ascertained by experiments, and in making an experiment knowledge and means may be employed which have been acquired since the date of the patent." It is evident that this head-note is incorrect, and if the case be read it will be found that the judgment of Lord Chelmsford was, not that the specification of the plaintiff could be held sufficient or insufficient upon experiments tried on the specification itself, with the assistance of subsequently-acquired knowledge, but that the specification, which was alleged to anticipate the plaintiff's patent, might be read for the purpose of determining whether there was anticipation or not, or whether there had been prior publication or not in the light of knowledge acquired by the general public since the date of the specification. This would be undoubtedly correct, because the question always is, in dealing with matters of prior publication, Was the supposed invention of the plaintiff's, at the time when he obtained his patent, already part of the public stock of knowledge or not? The public stock of knowledge consisted of the specification, which is put forth as anticipating the patent, together with all knowledge on the subject which can be proved to have been published or used prior to the date of the plaintiff's patent, and so in reading a specification with a view to ascertaining whether it anticipates a subsequent patent you must read into that specification all subsequently-acquired knowledge of the subject prior to the date of the patent; but in discussing the sufficiency of the specification which is actually in dispute, you cannot make use of information which has been acquired since the publication, for otherwise it would be held that the patent, which was void at first for insufficiency of specification, might become valid at some subsequent date by further discovery, which is obviously absurd.

The question of the sufficiency of a specification is one which must be dealt with on each particular case as it arises; a single word added to a specification may make that which was insufficient sufficient, and that which would be a sufficient description of one invention would be found to be an insufficient description of another, consequently there can be no absolutely fixed rules of construction in dealing with specifications.

In *Wegmann* v. *Corcoran* (o) it was held that the specification of a patent was bad if one of the materials to be used was described by a generic comprising a variety of species, the majority of which would be unsuitable. The specification of a patent is bad if a skilled mechanic would not, without performing a series of experiments, be able to construct the machine from the description.

The specification (*p*) of a machine for crushing meal, described the rollers as "to have a surface consisting of material containing so much silica as not to colour the meal or flour. I prefer to make them of iron, coated with china, and finally turned with diamond tools;" and the claim was, *inter alia*, for the use of material "of the hardness required." It appeared that the rollers must be made of very hard china, such as had scarcely been made in Europe during this century, and specially tough, and must be fixed in a peculiar manner to an iron core or spindle, which carried them; and, according to the evidence, a miller or a skilled mechanic would not, without making a series of experiments, discover of what china the rollers must be made, or how they must be fixed to the spindle. Held by the Court of Appeal, confirming the judgment of Mr. Justice Fry, that the specification was insufficient and the patent invalid. Mr. Justice Fry had said: "Though the grantee of a patent for an invention communicated to him by a foreign resi-

(o) L. R., 13 Ch. 65.   (*p*) *Wegmann* v. *Corcoran*, supra.

dent abroad is only bound to tell the public what he himself knows, yet if the original inventor has not told him enough to enable him so to describe the invention as that it could be constructed by the aid only of the specification, the patent will be invalid. As we have seen, it is doubtful whether this does not only affect those patents which were obtained before the Act of 1883, known as " communications from abroad."

It will be seen that the last-mentioned case is distinguishable from the case of *Plimpton* v. *Malcolmson* (*p*). In *Weymann* v. *Corcoran* the question was whether the patentee, having disclosed a useful invention, was bound to disclose something more, which he himself did not know, but which was within the knowledge of the person communicating from abroad; in that case it was properly held that he was not so bound, but it is obvious that he was bound to describe an invention in his specification which of itself was useful, and that he was bound to tell all that he himself knew.

We have seen that *bona fides* in the description of the invention is one of the essential elements of the consideration for the grant. The patentee must say not only that which is sufficient to carry out the invention, but he must say all he knows, and he must give every improvement which is within his knowledge at the time and which assists the process or manufacture. *Wood* v. *Zimmer* (*q*), decided so far back as 1815, gives a very clear idea of the law upon this branch of the subject. In this action to try the validity of Zinck's patent " for a method of making verdigris," it appeared that the method described in the specification was sufficient to make verdigris, but that Zinck had been accustomed, clandestinely, to put aquafortis into the boiler, whereby the metallic copper was dissolved more rapidly, but the verdigris produced was neither better nor cheaper

(*p*) L. R., 3 Ch. D. 531.   (*q*) 1 Web. P. C. 82.

than that made according to the specification. Gibbs, C. J., said: "It is said that the method described makes verdigris, and that the specification is therefore sufficient—the law is not so. A man who applies for a patent, and possesses a mode of carrying out that invention in the most beneficial manner, must disclose the means of producing it in equal perfection and with as little expense and labour as it costs the inventor himself. The price that he pays for his patent is, that he will enable the public, at the expiration of his privilege, to make it in the same way and with the same advantages. If anything that gives an advantageous operation to the thing invented be concealed, the specification is void. Now, though the specification should enable a person to make verdigris substantially as good without the aquafortis as with it, still, inasmuch as it would be made with more labour by the omission of aquafortis, it is **prejudicial concealment** and a breach of the terms which the patentee makes with the public."

In this case it must have been proved that the patentee, at the time when he obtained his letters patent and filed his specification, knew of the benefit to be derived by the use of aquafortis. It is evident that if he did not know it at the time, but discovered it subsequently during the currency of the patent, that then it would form an improvement upon his invention, and not one which he could possibly have disclosed at the time he filed his specification, and therefore there would be no *mala fides* on his part in not describing it.

The remarks of Gibbs, C. J., in *Bovill* v. *Moore* (*q*) go to the same extent; and in *Crossley* v. *Beverley* (*r*), Bailey, J., said: "It is the duty of the inventor if, between the period of taking out the patent and enrolling the specification, he makes discoveries which will enable him better to effect the thing for which the patent was obtained,

(*q*) Dav. P. C. 400.   (*r*) 1 Web. P. C. 117.

not only that he is at liberty to introduce them into his patent, but that it is his bounden duty so to do, and it is not sufficient for him to communicate to the public the knowledge which he had at the time he obtained the patent, but he ought to communicate to the public the knowledge he had obtained before the specification." In *Morgan* v. *Seaward* (*s*), Alderson, B., said: "If the patentee is acquainted with any particular mode by which his invention may be most conveniently carried into effect he ought to state it in his specification: that was laid down in a case before Lord Mansfield; there the question arose on a patent for steel trusses. It appeared that the patentee in some parts of his process used tallow to facilitate the invention for which he had obtained a patent, and in his specification he made no mention of the use of tallow. The Court held the specification to be bad, because they said: 'You ought not to put people to find out that tallow is useful in carrying into effect the invention of steel trusses. You ought to tell the public so if that is the best mode of doing it, for you are bound to make a *bonâ fide*, full, and candid disclosure.'" The case referred to by the learned judge was the case of *Liardet* v. *Johnson* (*t*).

In *Tetley* v. *Easton* (*u*), Pollock, C. B., said: "A man has no right to patent a principle and then give to the public the humblest instrument that can be made from his principle, and reserve to himself all the better part of it;" and in *Heath* v. *Unwin* (*v*), Coleridge, C. J., said: "If the inventor of an alleged discovery, knowing two equivalent agents for effecting the end, could, by the disclosure of one, preclude the public from the benefit of the other, he might, for his own profit, force upon the public an expensive and difficult process, keeping back the simple

s) 1 Web. P. C. 174.
t) 1 Web. P. C. 53; and Bull. N. P. 76.
u) Mac. P. C. 76.
v) 2 Web. P. C. 243.

and cheap one, it would be directly contrary to the good faith required from a patentee in his communication to the public."

Upon the same ground of *malâ fide* it has been held, in a large number of cases, that if the patentee in his specification gives details which are not necessary to the invention, which of themselves do not constitute an invention, and which are merely put in for the purpose of misleading the public as to either what is the nature of the invention or how it is to be carried into effect, then the patent will be void. Bailey, C. J., in *Lewis* v. *Marling* (w), said: " If the party knew that it was unnecessary the patent would be bad, on the ground that this was deception; but if he thought it was proper, and only by a subsequent discovery finds out it is not necessary, I think that it forms no ground of objection."

If the **extraneous matter** is put into the specification, *bonâ fide* thinking that it was necessary, the patent will not be held to be void; if it was put in *malâ fide*, with the intention of deceiving or knowing it was extraneous and useless, the patent would be void. If the extraneous matter is in itself misleading, and would prevent a skilled workman from successfully carrying out the invention, whether it is put in *malâ fide* or *bonâ fide*, the patent will be void. It will be seen that in the latter case the specification is insufficient, and in the former two cases the question is one simply of *bonâ fide* on the part of the inventor (x).

We now come to that portion of the specification which is described as " **the claim.**" By sect. 5, sub-sect. 5, of the Act of 1883, it is provided that " a specification,

(w) 1 Web. P. C. 496.
(x) *Simpson* v. *Holliday*, 20 Newton's London Journal, N. S. 108. *Crompton* v. *Ibbertson*, 1 Web. P. C. 83; *Bickford* v. *Skewes*, 1 Web. P. C. 218; *Neilson* v. *Harford*, 8 M. & W. 806.

whether provisional or complete, must commence with the title, and in the case of a complete specification must end with a distinct statement of the invention claimed." This is, perhaps, emphasizing, in a more distinct manner than had been provided before the passing of this Act, the necessity of the inventor making a distinct and unambiguous claim. He **must not claim too much**, and yet he **must claim sufficient** to show a useful manufacture, and he must distinguish in his claim what it is that is new in the process which he has described and what is old. So far as this goes, there is no doubt that the old law provided for similar declarations on the part of the inventor.

In *Bovill* v. *Moore* (y), Gibbs, C. J., said: "If the plaintiff has in this specification asserted to himself a larger extent of invention than belongs to him, if he states himself to have invented that which was well known before, then the specification will be bad, because that will affect to give him, through the means of this patent, a larger privilege than could be legally given to him." In the case of *Gibson* v. *Brand* (z), Tindall, C. J., said: "Looking at the specification in the case, it appears to me that this patent cannot be supported at law, because the plaintiffs have in the course of it claimed more than they are entitled to."

The Court must be taken to distinguish between **describing too much and claiming too much**. In the course of a well-drawn specification it is frequently necessary to describe something which is old, and if, provided the claim says that the old parts do not constitute a portion of the invention, the description of the old parts in the specification will not invalidate the patent. But if two methods of doing a thing are

---

y Dav. P. C. 404.   z 1 Web. P. C. 631.

described, one of which will answer and the other will not, it will be interpreted, unless one of them is specifically disclaimed, that both parts are claimed as being new and useful, and one of them not being useful the patent will be invalidated, because it is said there is a false suggestion in the specification (a). In *Rushton* v. *Crawley* (b), Malins, V.-C., said: "The public must be told in very distinct language in every specification what are the articles they may use and what they may not use. Therefore, if a man makes a discovery, and instead of limiting himself in his specification to that which properly is a discovery (if it be one), makes his specification too extensive, and claims more than he is entitled to claim, that is calculated to embarrass the public; that is, I apprehend, a fatal objection to the patent."

In reading specifications, one frequently comes across a claim in these words: "I claim as my invention the appliances and combinations hereinbefore described." This claim is perfectly good (c), provided there is nothing described in the patent which is old. If there be anything old, the claim should proceed: "I do not claim so-and-so, and so-and-so, as part of my invention."

Under the new Act, it will be seen that for the validity of the patent to be supported, the specification *must* contain a claim; under the old law, if no claim was inserted the patentee was taken to claim everything that was described in the specification (d), it not being absolutely necessary that there should be a claim in the specification at all, provided nothing was described in the specification which could be shown to have been antici-

---

(a) *Simpson* v. *Holliday*, 13 W. R. 578; L. R., 1 H. L. 315, per Lord Westbury.

(b) L. R., 10 Eq. 527.

(c) *Seed* v. *Higgins*, 8 H. L. C. 550.

(d) *Tetley* v. *Easton*, 2 C. B., N. S. 706.

pated (*e*). For instance, if the invention be for an **improvement upon an old process** very great care should be taken that the improvement alone is made the subject of the claim; so if it be for a **combination of old well-known parts**, care must be taken that it be clearly shown that the patentee claims the combination, and not the parts. James, V.-C., in *Parkes* v. *Stephens* (*f*), said: " It is obvious that a patentee does not comply as he ought to do with the condition of his grant if the improvement is only to be found, like a piece of gold, mixed up with a great quantity of alloy. And if a person desiring to find out what was claimed as new would have to get rid of a large portion of the specification, by eliminating from it all that was old and commonplace, all that was the subject of other patents, or of other improvements, bringing to the subject not only the knowledge of an ordinary skilled artizan, but of a patent lawyer or agent."

In *Harrison* v. *The Anderston Foundry Co.* (*g*), it was finally held by the House of Lords that if the combination and application of old machinery be new and beneficial the invention of this combination may be protected by a patent. The specification commenced: " The invention consists of a new or improved simple and most efficient mode of and arrangement of mechanism for connecting the set or sets of compound or multiple shuttle boxes of looms for weaving stripe, check or other ornamental or figured fabrics requiring two, three or more shuttle boxes in each set." The specification then described in detail and by reference to drawings the arrangement of mechanism in question, and then continued: " What we believe to be novel and original, and therefore claim as the invention secured to us by letters patent, is – (1) The construction and arrangement of the

e, *Lister* v. *Leather*, 8 E. & B. 1004.
f, L. R., 8 Eq. 365.
g, L. R., 1 App. C. 578.

parts and portion of the mechanism, and (2) a shuttle-box moving and holding mechanism as herein distinguished generally for actuating the shuttle-boxes of power-looms, all substantially in the new or improved manner herein described and shown in the drawings or any mere modification thereof." A great number of the parts of the machine were admittedly old, and one of the questions in this case was, whether the first claim above set forth was a sufficient claim to a combination. Lord Cairns, in giving judgment, said : "It is as I read it a claim for a combination, that is to say, a combination of all the movements going to make up the whole mechanism described; it must, for the present at least, be assumed that this combination, as a combination, is novel, that it is, to use the words of the Lord President, a new combination of old parts to produce a new result or to produce a known result in a more useful and beneficial way; it is not doubted that a combination such as this is may be the subject of a patent, what, then, are the objections to the first claim viewed as a claim for the combination; the first is an objection said to be founded upon the case of *Foxwell* v. *Bostock* (*h*), decided by the late Lord Westbury. It is said to be determined in that case that where there is a patent for a combination there must be a discovery or explanation of the novelty, and the specification must show what is the novelty and what the merit of the invention. I cannot think that, as applied to a patent for a combination, this is or was meant to be the effect of the decision in *Foxwell* v. *Bostock*. If there is a patent for a combination the combination itself is *ex necessitate* the novelty, and the combination is also the merit, if it be a merit, which remains to be proved by evidence."

In the same case Lord Hatherley said: "The judges extended, as it appears to me with great respect, the

(*h*) 4 De G., J. & S. 298.

doctrine of *Foxwell* v. *Bostock* in their application of it in this case; it was there held, and that I think was all that was held, that it is not competent to a man to take a well-known existing machine, and, having made some small improvement, to place that before the public and say, 'I have made a better machine, there is this sewing machine invented by so-and-so, I have improved upon that. That is mine! it is a much better machine than his;' that will not do; you must state clearly and distinctly what it is in which you say you have made an improvement. To use an illustration which was adopted, I think, by James, L. J., in another case, 'I think it will not do if you invented the gridiron pendulum to say, I have invented a better clock than anybody else, not telling the public what you have done to make it better than any other clock which is known.'"

In *Clark* v. *Adie* (*i*), Lord Hatherley said, speaking of *Foxwell* v. *Bostock:* "You must in some way or other inform those whom you are dealing with, by which I mean the general public, whom you wish to exclude for a certain limited number of years from using your invention, you must inform them in some mode or other whether you have sub-divided, if I may so term it, your machine into these separate parts and claim for each the merit of novelty, or whether you are simply making a combination of things *per se* old but which have never been used before in combination, and which make up, as you say, your machine, for which you claim protection, as a novel and useful machine."

These two judgments of the House of Lords show the extent to which the law went prior to the Act of 1883. We have seen that since the Act of 1883 the claim is an absolute essential, and the words of the statute are, "A distinct statement of the invention claimed." To what extent the words "a distinct state-

i L. R., 2 App. C. 328.

ment" will be construed it is at present difficult to say; but it will undoubtedly be advisable for inventors to be more careful that their claims are more accurately defined, it being very probable that the law as it at present stands will be held to be much more stringent in its requirements than it was before the Act of 1883.

CHAPTER V.

AMENDMENT OF SPECIFICATIONS.

THE Patents, &c. Act, 1883, provides for the amendment of specifications in two ways, **compulsorily** and **voluntarily**. We have seen that sect. 6 directs that the comptroller shall refer the specification to an examiner. Sect. 7 provides that (1). " If the examiner reports that the nature of the invention is not fairly described, or that the application, specification, or drawings have not been prepared in the prescribed manner, or that the title does not sufficiently indicate the subject-matter of the invention, the comptroller may require that the application, specification, or drawings be amended before he proceeds with the application." Sub-sects. 2, 3, 4, provide for an appeal to the law officer; and sub-sects. 5 and 6 give directions as to what should be done when there are two applications for substantially the same invention.

Sect. 9, sub-sect. 1, requires that the examiner shall report to the comptroller as to " whether the complete specification has been prepared in the prescribed manner, and whether the invention particularly described in the complete specification is substantially the same as that which is described in the provisional specification." If the examiner reports that these conditions have not been complied with, the comptroller *may* refuse to accept the complete specification until it has been amended to his satisfaction, subject to appeal to the law officer.

Sub-sect. 3: The law officer shall, if required, hear the applicant and the comptroller, and may make an order determining whether, and subject to what conditions, if any, the complete specification shall be accepted. By sub-sect. 4 the application is rendered void, except in the case of an appeal, unless a complete specification is "*accepted*" within twelve months from the date of application. Sect. 94 provides: "Where any discretionary power is by this Act given to the comptroller, he shall not exercise that power adversely to the applicant for a patent, or for amendment of a specification . . . . without (if so required within the prescribed time by the applicant) giving the applicant the opportunity of being heard personally or by his agent."

These provisions of the law are entirely novel. It will be particularly observed that **compulsory amendment** is strictly **limited to matters of form.** The comptroller has no power to order an amendment on the ground that too much is claimed, or that there is want of novelty, or that the invention is not subject matter for a patent. It is very difficult to predicate what judicial decisions will be given to the words "that the nature of the invention is not fairly described." Is the examiner to be in the position of an expert witness, and to decide whether or not the description is sufficient to enable a skilled artizan to carry the invention into effect within the meaning of Jessel, M. R., in *Plimpton* v. *Malcolmson* (a)? or is he merely to see that the language is correct, and that, without going technically into the matter, the specification *appears* to fairly describe the invention? If the former is his province, it is difficult to see how it is to be carried into effect, since there is no machinery in the Act for the receiving of skilled evidence, such as would be necessary for the purpose of arriving at a satisfactory conclusion upon such a point. The applicant or his agent are alone to be heard. It is true that by sect. 38, when the applicant *appeals* he may call witnesses before the law officer, but surely the statute does

(a) L. R., 3 Ch. D. 568.

not contemplate that questions should be gone into which, it is evident, can only be decided on appeal, and even then not satisfactorily without the procedure and care of a regular formal trial.

Under such circumstances, it may fairly be presumed that the meaning of the section is, that the examiner shall report whether the specification, on the face of it, appears to fairly describe the invention.

In construing sect. 9, it will probably be held that a minute and scientific inspection of the specification is not within the contemplation of the statute.

Sect. 18 provides for the **amendment** of the specification by the applicant or patentee. There are several reported cases showing that at common law mere clerical errors in a specification might formerly be amended by the Master of the Rolls and the Lord Chancellor upon petition, but these amendments were strictly limited to verbal or clerical errors arising from mistake or inadvertence (*h*). We have seen that a patent for a very meritorious invention may be utterly vitiated by the patentee claiming something which is not new; so, also, a patent might be rendered void by reason of innocent misdescription or misrepresentation.

The **common law power** of amendment being found **insufficient** for the purposes of justice in such cases, the Act 5 & 6 Will. 4, c. 83, was passed, enabling "*any person who as grantee, assignee, or otherwise, hath obtained, or shall hereafter obtain, letters patent*, &c.," with the leave of the law officer, might **disclaim** any part of the "title of the invention or of the specification, stating the reason for such disclaimer"; or might, with such leave as aforesaid, "enter a **memorandum of** any **alteration** in such title or specification (not being such disclaimer or such alteration as shall extend the exclusive right granted by the said letters patent), &c., &c." The

h) In re Sharp's Patent, 1 Web. P. C. 645.

case of *Spilsbury* v. *Clough* (c) having very much limited the meaning of the words of the statute, printed above in italics, the Act 7 & 8 Vict. c. 69, was passed, giving power to the original **patentee, or his assignees,** or both jointly, in the event of any interest in the patent remaining in the original patentee, to file a disclaimer or memorandum of alteration.

It will be observed that prior to the Act of 1883 any **disclaimer or amendment** made by the patentee was entirely **at his own peril,** and that in any subsequent action involving the validity of the patent objection might be taken to the disclaimer or amendment on the ground that it really extended the patent beyond its original limits.

The provisions of sect. 18 of the Act of 1883 are as follows:—

"(1) An applicant or a patentee may from time to time, by request in writing left at the Patent Office, seek leave to amend his specification, including drawings forming part thereof, by way of disclaimer, correction, or explanation, stating the nature of such amendment and his reasons for the same.

"(2) The request, and the nature of such proposed amendment shall be advertised in the prescribed manner, and at any time within one month from its first advertisement any person may give notice at the Patent Office of opposition to the amendment.

"(3) Where such notice is given the comptroller shall give notice of the opposition to the person making the request, and shall hear and decide the case subject to an appeal to the law officer.

"(4) The law officer shall, if required, hear the person making the request and the person so giving notice, and being in the opinion of the law officer entitled to be heard in opposition to the request, and shall determine

(c) 2 Q. B. 466.

whether and subject to what conditions, if any, the amendment ought to be allowed.

"(5) When no notice of opposition is given, or the person so giving notice does not appear, the comptroller shall determine whether, and subject to what conditions, if any, the amendment ought to be allowed.

"(6) When leave to amend is refused by the comptroller, the person making the request may appeal from his decision to the law officer.

"(7) The law officer shall, if required, hear the person making the request and the comptroller, and may make an order determining whether and subject to what conditions, if any, the amendment ought to be allowed.

"(8) No amendment shall be allowed that would make the specification as amended, claim an invention substantially larger than or substantially different from the invention claimed by the specification as it stood before amendment.

"(9) Leave to amend shall be conclusive as to the right of the party to make the amendment allowed, except in case of fraud, and the amendment shall in all Courts and for all purposes be deemed to form part of the specification.

"(10) The foregoing provisions of this section do not apply when and so long as any action for infringement or other legal proceeding in relation to a patent is pending."

Sect. 19. " In an action for infringement of a patent, and in a proceeding for revocation of a patent, the Court or a judge may at any time order that the patentee shall, subject to such terms as to costs or otherwise as the Court or a judge may impose, be at liberty to apply at the Patent Office for leave to amend his specification by way of disclaimer, and may direct that in the meantime the trial or hearing of the action shall be postponed."

Sect. 20. " Where an amendment, by way of disclaimer, correction or explanation, has been allowed under this Act no damages shall be given in any action in respect of the use of the invention before the disclaimer, correction or explanation, unless the patentee establishes to the satisfaction of the Court that his original claim was framed in good faith and with reasonable skill and knowledge."

Sect. 46 defines the word patentee, referred to in sect. 18, sub-sect. (1), as meaning "The person for the time being entitled to the benefit of a patent."

It will be observed that the **amendments** under the new Act are **to be by disclaimer, correction or explanation,** provided the amendment does not cause the specification to claim an invention **substantially larger or different** The Act of Will. IV., after using the words "disclaimer" and "alteration," provided that no extension should take place in the "**exclusive right**" granted by the letters patent.

It was always a question of great difficulty whether or not a disclaimer or alteration extended the "exclusive right" of the patentee. For instance, if in his original specification, after describing several improvements in a process of manufacture, he proceeded to claim them all, and it should turn out that one of his improvements was old, the whole patent was bad and the patentee had no exclusive right at all; if he then disclaimed the objectionable portion, his patent became good as to all the rest. There was clearly, therefore, an extension of the exclusive right, notwithstanding that this was the very case the statute was passed to meet. Mr. Justice Maule's view of the Act of Will. IV., was:—" Whereas there were previously many small and trifling objections by which, if they were sustained against any one of many important inventions, the whole was avoided. In such cases amendments may now be made by means of a disclaimer" (*d*).

(*d*) *R. v. Mill*, 20 L. J., C. P. at page 21.

Romilly, M. R., in the same case (*d*), at the Rolls, said, "It is proper they (patentees) should be allowed to correct errors in their patents by removing from the specification parts which are not material or substantial, or which they have since discovered not to be new inventions; but this power ought to be exercised with great care and discretion." There is a case reported in Macrory's Patent Cases at page 116, where Sir Richard Bethell, when Solicitor General, allowed a patentee to enter a disclaimer, the effect of which was to enable him to claim for a combination, the original clause being for the several parts of the described invention. When afterwards he became Lord Westbury he described the words of this statute as vague and indefinite, and said, "Possibly they mean that the patent must not, by the operation of the disclaimer, be made to include or comprehend something which was not originally contained in the patent. The invention claimed may be reduced or diminished, but it must not be extended or enlarged (*e*)."

The case of *Ralston* v. *Smith* (*f*) shows the difficulty which the Courts had in reconciling a disclaimer which might make a patent valid which was void *ab initio*, with the prohibition against extending the exclusive right. The judgment of Lord Chelmsford, as reported, is remarkable for its cautious vagueness, and the care which seems to have been exercised not to lay down anything approaching to a general principle. Under the new Act it is not the exclusive right which must not be extended, but the invention must not be substantially larger or different. It is presumed that the law officers will not find so much difficulty in dealing with these words as with the words of the old statute. Moreover, **an amendment once made cannot afterwards be objected to** on any ground whatever, excepting that of **fraud**.

d, 14 Beavan, 315.
e Foxwell v. Bostock, 4 De G., J. & S. 306.
f 11 H. L. C. 223.

The amendment becomes part and parcel of the original specification in all courts and for all purposes.

Under the Statute of Will. IV. no disclaimer or amendment could be given in evidence in any action or suit (save and except in any proceedings by *scire facias*) pending at the time the disclaimer or amendment was enrolled. The object of this was obvious. It would have been unjust that a defendant should be held guilty of infringing a patent when at the time the action was brought against him the patent was void. The saving clause relating to *scire facias* was always exercised subject to just provision as to costs, and was inserted with a view to prevent a patent being repealed on account of some trifling error which might have been cured by disclaimer or alteration. The entry of a disclaimer under the old Act did not make a void patent valid *ab initio*, " so as to make any person a wrongdoer by relation," and in *Perry* v. *Skinner* (*g*) it was held, that the words " from thenceforth " must be read into the specification. Proceedings by *scire facias* are abolished by sect. 26 of the new Act, and a petition to the Court is substituted, the grounds for the petition being the same as heretofore in *scire facias*. Although we have seen that sub-s. 10 of sect. 18 prohibits any amendment *under that section* pending legal proceedings (including proceedings by way of revocation), sect. 19 provides machinery for saving a patent in the event of the Court or judge being of opinion that **a disclaimer** should be allowed upon such terms as may appear just (*h*). It will be observed that the Court or judge have no power to permit amendment by " correction or explanation " under this section.

In *Dudgeon* v. *Thompson* (*i*), an interdict granted prior

(*g*) Hindmarch, p. 207; 2 M. & W. 471.

(*h*) As to what are just terms, see *In re Smith's Patent*, Macr.

P. C. 232; and *In re Medlock's Patent*, Newton, London Journal, New Series, vol. 22, p. 69.

(*i*) L. R., 3 App. Cases, 34.

to the amendment was refused to be enforced after the amendment, on the ground that the amendment materially altered the patent, and that it was quite possible that there was no infringement of the patent as altered. In *Kynoch v. National Arms Company, Limited* (*k*), it was held that the law officer could not order an applicant for leave to disclaim to pay costs. Sect. 38 of the Act of 1883 cures this defect, giving the law officer full discretion as to costs, with provision that his order may be made a rule of Court.

Sect. 20 speaks for itself; may be it is intended to overrule *Perry v. Skinner* (*l*), quoted above. Under the Act of Will. IV., when a patentee sought to disclaim it was necessary that he should give his reasons for the proposed disclaimer, but he was not compelled to state reasons for a proposed alteration. Under the present statute he must give his reasons for any amendment, whatever the form of the amendment may be. The reasons will, of course, vary with each case. Either that the patentee has discovered that parts of the invention claimed are not new, or are useless, or are not sufficiently described, or that they will not work. It will be observed that the **reasons** are not required to be advertised. The subject of opposition to the amendment proposed will be dealt with in the next chapter. It may be observed that there is nothing in the Act of 1883 to withdraw from the Master of the Rolls the common law power of amending clerical errors in specifications. See *In re Johnson's patent* (*m*).

k 37 L. J., Rep. N. S. 31.   *m*) L. R., 5 Ch. D. 503.
l, 2 M. & W. 471.

CHAPTER VI.

OPPOSITION.

SECTION 10 of the Act of 1883 provides that upon acceptance of the complete specification, but before sealing the patent, the comptroller shall advertise the acceptance, and that then the application and specifications, with the drawings, if any, shall be open to public inspection.

Section 11 is as follows:—(1) "Any person may at any time within two months from the date of the advertisement of the acceptance of a complete specification, give notice to the Patent Office of opposition to the grant of the patent on the ground of the applicant having obtained the invention from him, or from a person of whom he is the legal representative, or on the ground that the invention has been patented in this country on an application of prior date, or on the ground of an examiner having reported to the comptroller that the specification appears to him to comprise the same invention as is comprised in a specification bearing the same or a similar title and accompanying a previous application, **but on no other ground.**"

Prior to the passing of this Act any ground was available for the purpose of opposition which would have been available for the purpose of destroying the validity of the patent. Prior user was a frequent ground of opposition (*In re Samuda* (a)), so also was an alleged dedication to the public by the inventor himself (*In re Adamson's Patent* (b)), but it was always considered necessary that the ground of the opposition should be proved beyond the shadow of a doubt (*In re Tolhausen's*

(a) Hindmarch, at page 534.   (b) 6 De G., M. & G. 420.

Patent (c), and also *In re Vincent's Patent* (d)). If there was any doubt the patent ought to be sealed, so as to give the inventor the benefit of an exhaustive trial. These two latter cases indicate the course the law officer should take, where the ground of opposition is an allegation that the applicant has obtained the invention from the opposing party. Such a question might very frequently raise questions of fact of great delicacy, and the question of the credibility of witnesses. Such questions should be left for trial in open court, more particularly as it will be observed that any such opposing party has an ample and unfettered remedy by petition to revoke the patent under sect. 26. The other two grounds of opposition are such as can readily be proved or disproved, hence the power of the law officer can be exercised with less prejudice to the interests of justice. It will make no difference in the exercise of the discretion of the law officer upon the report of the comptroller, if the specification appears to him to comprise the same invention as is comprised in a previous application, that the validity, of the first patent is in dispute (e).

The second sub-section provides:—"Where such notice is given, the comptroller shall give notice of the opposition to the applicant, and shall, on the expiration of those two months, after hearing the applicant and the person so giving notice, if desirous of being heard, decide on the case, but subject to appeal to the law officer.

(3) "The law officer shall, if required, hear the applicant and any person so giving notice, and being, in the opinion of the law officer, entitled to be heard in opposition to the grant, and shall determine whether the grant ought or ought not to be made.

(4) "The law officer may, if he thinks fit, obtain the assistance of an expert, who shall be paid such remune-

c 11 W. R. 551.
d L. R., 2 Ch. 341.

e *In re Manceaux's Patent*, L. R., 2 Ch. 272.

ration as the law officer with the consent of the treasury shall appoint."

Sect. 38 of the Act gives power to the law officers to examine witnesses on oath, to make rules from time to time regulating references and appeals, together with the practice and procedure before them, and in any such proceedings they may make such orders as to costs as they may deem just, such orders to be enforceable as rules of Court.

In the absence of opposition, or in the event of any opposition being decided in favour of the patentee, the patent will be sealed. (Sect. 12.)

Provisions are made in sect. 18 for opposition to the amendment of any specification—opposition to an amendment may be made upon any ground—the only restriction being that the opposition must, in the opinion of the law officer, be by a person entitled to be heard. Any person who would be injuriously affected by a void patent becoming valid is a person entitled to be heard (*f*).

(*f*) See the conditions imposed in *Re Medlock's Patent*, reported in Newton's London Journal, New Series, vol. 22, p. 69, and also in *Re Smith's Patent*, Macr. P. C. 232, in which cases it appears that great care was taken to protect the vested interests of persons who had acquired rights by reason of the imperfect condition of the original specification.

CHAPTER VII.

THE GRANT.

Prior to the Act of 1883 letters patent were issued under **the great seal of England**, and, consequently, by the Lord Chancellor, as keeper of the great seal. The process of sealing a patent was surrounded with all the formalities and expense which surrounds an important Act of State. Letters patent derived their authority from the fact that the great seal was attached to them, for "all the king's subjects are bound to take notice of the king's great seal" (a). Sect. 84 of the Act provides: "There shall be **a seal for the Patent Office**, and impressions thereof shall be judicially noticed and admitted in evidence;" and sect. 12: (1) "If there is no opposition, or, in case of opposition, if the determination is in favour of the grant of a patent, the comptroller shall cause a patent to be sealed with the seal of the Patent Office. (2) A patent so sealed shall have the same effect as if it were sealed with the great seal of the United Kingdom." Form D. in the first schedule to the Act gives the form in which in future letters patent are to be issued.

Letters patent consist of six material parts:—

    1st. The address.
    2nd. The recitals.
    3rd. The grant.
    4th. The prohibition.
    5th. The conditions.
    6th. The construction of the grant.

a *East India Co* v. *Sandys*, Skin. 225.

THE ADDRESS.

The address is a public address from the sovereign to "all to whom these presents shall come." Mr. Hindmarch gives the reason for this as being, that it contains bargains made between the public and patentee (*b*).

THE RECITALS.

The recitals are four in number. **The first** recites the patentee's name and address, that he has made a declaration that he is in possession of an invention and is followed by the title of the invention. That he has declared that he is the true and first inventor of the invention, and that the same is not in use by any other person to the best of his knowledge and belief.

It will be remembered that previously to the Act of 1883, there were two forms in use; one when the inventor was the first and true inventor, and the other for a communicated invention; the latter running, "that in consequence of a communication from a foreigner residing abroad, he is in possession of an invention, &c." We have seen that communications from abroad have, in all probability, been abolished by the Act of 1883, and that if he would avoid making a false suggestion, and so destroy his patent, the inventor must himself become the patentee (*c*)

This recital contains the "**suggestions**" which have been made to the sovereign prior to the patent being granted and the representations upon which it has been granted. If either of these suggestions or representations be untrue the patent is void. We cannot do better to illustrate the exact meaning of a **false suggestion** than to quote the language of Parke, B., in *Morgan* v. *Seaward* (*d*). In that case the false suggestion complained of was in the title of the specification, which it was alleged

(*b*) Page 40. (*d*) 2 M. & W. 544.
(*c*) Ante, pp. 7 & 21.

did not disclose the true nature of the invention. "This brings me to the question," said the learned judge, "whether this patent, which suggests that certain inventions are improvements, is avoided if there be one which is not so; and upon the authorities we feel obliged to hold that the patent is void upon the ground of fraud on the Crown, without entering into the question whether the utility of each and every part of the invention is essential to a patent, where such utility is not suggested in the patent itself as the ground of the grant. That a false suggestion of the grantee avoids an ordinary grant of lands or tenements from the Crown is a maxim of the common law, and such a grant is void, not against the Crown merely, but in a suit against a third person (e). It is on the same principle that a patent for two or more inventions, when one is not new, is void altogether, as in *Hill* v. *Thompson* (f); *Brunton* v. *Hawkes* (g); for, although the statute invalidates a patent for want of novelty, and, consequently, by force of the statute the patent would be void, so far as related to that which was old, yet the principle on which the patent has been held to be void altogether is, that the consideration for the grant is the novelty of all, and the consideration failing, or in other words the Crown being deceived in its grant, the patent is void, and no action maintainable upon it. We cannot help seeing on the face of this patent, as set out in the record, that an *improvement* in steam-engines is suggested by the patentee, and is part of the consideration for the grant, and we must reluctantly hold that the patent is void for the falsity of that suggestion. In the case of *Lewis* v. *Marling* (h), this view of the case, that the patent was void for a false suggestion, does not appear by the report

e *Travell* v. *Carteret*, 3 Lev. 135; *Alcock* v. *Cooke*, 5 Bing. 340.
f 8 Taun. 375.
g 1 B. & Ald. 541.
h 10 B. & C. 22.

to have been pressed on the attention of the Court or been considered by it. The decision went upon the ground that the brush was not an essential part of the machine, and that want of utility did not vitiate the patent, and besides, the improvement by the introduction of the brush is not recited in the patent itself, as one of the subjects of it which may make a difference." It will be observed here that the learned judge draws a careful difference between an insufficient description in the specification and a false suggestion. In the cases cited below letters patent were held void for false suggestion (*i*). And the following cases are illustrations of the distinction drawn by Mr. Baron Parke:—*Lewis* v. *Murling* (supra) and *Haworth* v. *Hardcastle* (*k*). Also *Bainbridge* v. *Wigley* (*l*); *Hill* v. *Thompson* (*m*).

The **second recital** deals with the prayer of the application for the grant.

The **third recital** recites that a complete specification has been filed, particularly describing the nature of the invention. Here, again, a **false suggestion** will avoid the patent, so that if the complete specification is imperfect, the patent will be void upon two grounds, the one being the failure of consideration, and the other the false suggestion; and a false suggestion is equally fatal whether it is wilfully false or otherwise.

The **fourth recital** gives the common law motive for the grant, which is the encouragement of inventions for the public good. There will be something analogous to a false suggestion if the subject matter of the patent be immoral or illegal, and hence the patent will at common law be void. By sect. 86 of the Act the comptroller may refuse to grant a patent for an invention of which the use would, in his opinion, be contrary to law or

---

(*i*) *Jessop's Case,* 2 H. Bl. 489;
R. v. *Wheeler,* 2 B. & Ald. 345;
Felton v. *Greaves,* 3 C. & P. 61.

(*k*) 1 Bing. N. C. 189.
(*l*) 1 Carp. P. C. 270.
(*m*) 1 Web. P. C. 239.

morality. A serious oversight in the Act appears to be that there is no appeal from the comptroller when he exercises the power given by this section.

THE GRANT.

"Know ye, therefore, that we of our especial grace, certain knowledge, and mere motion do by these presents, for us, &c., give and grant unto the said patentee our especial licence, full power, sole privilege, and authority, that the said patentee by himself, his agents, or licensees, and no others, may at all times hereafter during the term of years herein mentioned, make, use, exercise and vend the said invention .... in such manner as to him or them may seem meet, and that the said patentee shall have and enjoy the whole profit and advantage from time to time accruing by reason of the said invention, during the term of fourteen years from the date hereunder written of these presents."

This language is intended to preserve intact the **royal prerogative** to grant or withhold a patent—which right was by the common law absolute and undoubted. We have seen that this prerogative is carefully preserved by sect. 116 of the Act.

It is the granting portion of the letters patent which creates the property in the invention. We have seen that this species of property is purely artificial in its nature; it is the most equitable and natural method which the state can devise for the reward and encouragement of inventors; it is merely a right yielding nothing until the invention is made practically useful to humanity. **A trade mark** is also an exclusive right, but it **differs from a patent**, insomuch that it has not merit and the benefit of mankind as its consideration. A trade mark is only a right to guarantee the genuine origin of an article. Anyone else may make the article, but they are only prevented from stamping it with the same mark. A patent prevents the public from making the article or using the invention. There is no property which partakes of the nature of an exclusive right save that of a patent, copyright, or trade mark. There is no exclusive right in **a secret**. A man may only use a secret to his own profit so long as no one is in a position, by reason of knowing the secret, to use it. But the original possessor of a secret cannot, by any process of law, prevent a person from acquiring the knowledge of his secret, or, having acquired it, from making such use of it by publication or otherwise, as he may think proper (*p*). In *Newbery* v. *James* (*q*), although an agreement had been made to preserve a secret, the Court refused to grant an injunction on the ground that there was no means of enforcing it. Lord Eldon, L. C., said in *Williams* v. *Williams* (*r*), " So far as the injunction goes to restrain the defendant from communicating the secret upon general principles, I do not think that the Court ought to struggle to protect this sort of secrets in medicine. The Court is bound indeed to protect them in cases of patents to the full extent of what was intended by the grant of the patent, because the patentee is a purchaser from the public, and bound to communicate his secret to the public."

If the **plaintiff's secret**, however, be one which he **intends to patent,** and the defendant has acquired the information during the progress of experiments, or from the confidence of the plaintiff, he will not be allowed to make such use of the knowledge so acquired as to subsequently invalidate the plaintiff's patent, or to take out a patent for the invention himself, and if he do he will be liable in damages to the plaintiff (*s*). It will be observed that the word "patentee" is used in the grant; the old

(*p*) *Canham* v. *Jones*, 2 Ves. & B. 218.
(*q*) 2 Mer. 446.
(*r*) 3 Mer. 157.
(*s*) *Smith* v. *Dickenson*, 3 B. & P. 630.

form was, "to the said John Smith, his executors, administrators or assigns;" a "patentee" is, under the 46th section, construed as being "the person for the time being entitled to the benefit of a patent;" we shall see presently that this includes assignees, executors and administrators, together with receivers and trustees in bankruptcy, but the subject of the devolution of patent rights is too extensive and important to be dealt with under this head.

THE PROHIBITION.

The prohibition in the patent commands "all our subjects, that they do not at any time during the continuance of the said term of fourteen years either directly or indirectly make use or put in practice the said invention, or any part of the same, nor in anywise imitate the same, nor make or cause to be made any addition thereto or subtraction therefrom, whereby to pretend themselves the inventors thereof, without the consent, licence or agreement of the said patentee in writing under his hand and seal, on pain of incurring such penalties as may be justly inflicted on such offenders for their contempt of this our royal command, and of being answerable to the patentee according to law for his damages thereby occasioned."

It is very difficult to understand the form of letters patent which is appended to the Act of 1883. It is presumed that the Act was intended to amend, simplify and codify the law of patents. The form above quoted is an imitation of forms previously in use. It is not easy to understand what the "penalties" referred to in the prohibition are, and how are they to be put in force or recovered? The Act certainly does not mention penalties as a form of punishment for infringers.

THE CONDITIONS.

We find in the " conditions " that the grant is to be avoided " if it should appear to us, &c., or six or more of our Privy Council, that this our grant is contrary to law or prejudicial or inconvenient to our subjects generally, or that the said invention is not a new invention as to the public use and exercise thereof within our United Kingdom of Great Britain and Ireland and Isle of Man, or that the patentee is not the first and true inventor thereof within this realm as aforesaid." This proviso raises some questions of importance. The only proceedings mentioned in the Act for the repeal of letters patent are proceedings in the High Court of Justice. What is the proceeding before " six of our Privy Council " ? It can scarcely be believed that reference is here made in a new codifying Act to the old prerogative claim of power to revoke, which has not been put in practice for two hundred and fifty years. If it be intended to have such a system of avoiding patents, surely it would be well to provide for it in a more certain manner than merely to mention it as one of the conditions in the patent itself. In the next place we find here, for the first time, an intimation that **" novelty "** means novelty within the kingdom; in the recitals of the patent it is recited as being novelty universally, and throughout the Act itself we find that " novelty " is not limited to novelty within the kingdom. Again, we find here for the first time the inventor described as " the first and true inventor **within this realm."** In the Act and in the recitals of the patent he is described as the " first and true inventor." We have shown that the omission of the words " within this realm " makes an immense difference not only in the class of persons who may be grantees of letters patent, but also in the nature of the evidence of " prior user " which may be given in an action either for infringement or revocation. The ambiguity of the form of letters patent which is given, and the by no means clear provisions of the Act upon these matters, will in all probability result in a plentiful crop of litigation (*t*).

The next proviso is one for the determination of the patent in the event of the prescribed **fees not being paid**, and the last provides for the supply of the patented article for the use of the public service on reasonable terms. This proviso in no way binds the Crown if the patented article should be required for the public service to purchase it from the patentee upon reasonable terms and conditions. (*In re Daine's Patent*)(*u*).

Prior to the Act of 1883 letters patent did not operate as against the Crown. The Crown might make use of the invention without in any way recognising any rights of the inventor or patentee (*x*). But should the Crown have employed a contractor, as distinguished from a servant, to manufacture the patented article, the usual proceedings for infringement might be brought against the contractor, since he is the person using the patent, and not the Crown. There being two methods of infringing: first, making and vending; and secondly, using. The contractor infringes by doing the first, and it makes no difference that the Crown also infringes by using the invention (*y*).

This case was subsequently affirmed in the House of Lords. Lord Hatherley said, "The Crown has no right to authorize others who are not their officers, servants, or agents, to use a patented invention without a license from the patentee;" and Lord Selborne added, "I agree with the Court of Queen's Bench that this decision (*Feather* v. *R.*) is not to be extended by any reasoning from the convenience of the Crown, or of the public service, or from any idea that it practically comes to the same thing, whether the Crown manufactures itself or gives orders to other manufacturers."

The right of the Crown to use a patented invention for the public service without being under any obligation to remunerate the inventor has been abolished by sect. 27 of the Act of 1883.

(1) "A patent shall have to all intents the like effects as against her Majesty the Queen, her heirs and successors, as it has against a subject.

(2) "But the officers or authorities administering any department of the service of the Crown may, by themselves, their agents, contractors (z), or others, at any time after the application, use the invention for the services of the Crown on terms to be before or after the use thereof agreed on, with the approval of the Treasury, between those officers or authorities and the patentee, or, in default of such agreement, on such terms as may be settled by the Treasury after hearing all parties interested."

Sect. 44 deals with the acquisition by the Secretary of State for War of any inventions dealing with instruments or munitions of war, and with the non-publication of specifications describing such inventions, and generally with the preservation for the public benefit of the secret of them.

THE CONSTRUCTION.

"And lastly, we do by these presents for us, our heirs and successors, grant unto the said patentee that these our letters patent shall be construed in the most beneficial sense for the advantage of the said patentee." These words are inserted in the patent for the purpose of preventing the common rule of construction of grants of the Crown when founded upon a petition being read most strongly against the grantee. This favourable construction will not, however, in any way save the validity of the patent if it can be shown to have been granted upon a false suggestion.

(z) *Dixon* v. *London Small Arms Co.*, supra.

CHAPTER VIII.

THE DEVOLUTION OF A PATENT.

WE have seen that a "**patentee**" is "the person for the time being entitled to the benefit of a patent." This includes the first inventor and any person or persons in whom the patent may have become vested by operation of law or by assignment.

The property of a patent passes, **by operation of law,** when the patentee dies or becomes **a bankrupt.** Upon the **death of** a patentee his interest in the property passes to his executors or administrators as the case may be in the like manner to the rest of his personal estate. Any step which in the Act is required to be taken by the patentee, may be taken by the executor or administrator, and sect. 34 of the Act provides that—"(1) If a person, possessed of an invention, dies without making application for a patent for the invention, application may be made by, and a patent for the invention granted to, his legal representative." This undoubtedly, seeing the terms of the grant itself, will mean his legal **personal representative.** Some letters patent of the Crown (not for inventions) have a limitation to heirs or heirs male, such, for instance, as patents of nobility. The Act proceeds—"(2) Every such application must be made within six months of the decease of such person, and must contain a declaration by the legal representative that he believes such person to be the true and first inventor of the invention."

If the patentee becomes bankrupt the property in the patent will pass to his receiver, trustee or assignee in bankruptcy (a). It is doubtful whether the doctrine of apparent possession can be said to affect a patent right. The Lord Chancellor, in 1812, seems to have thought that it did (b). This, however, can hardly be quoted as an authority. The persons in whom the patent vests, by reason of bankruptcy, are placed in all respects in the position of the original patentee, and may sue in respect of infringements (c).

The second method of devolution is **by assignment,** *inter vivos.* This may be done either by absolute assignment of the whole of the patent, or by absolute assignment of the patent right for a limited area, or by assignment by way of mortgage, or by the grantees of licenses.

The right of the original inventor to assign the exclusive right which has been granted to him is recognised in the patent itself, which is granted to the said A. B., his executors, administrators or assigns. Without these words of limitation the property in the patent right would be merely personal, attaching to the person of the first inventor and becoming extinguished by his death.

The patent itself being a deed the **assignment must be** also **by deed** (d). So, also, **licenses should be under seal,** the prohibition in the grant itself being "without the consent, license or agreement of the said patentee in writing under his hand and seal."

A license granted by a patentee, but not under seal, is, however, not void in the sense that the licensee, having used the patent, is not bound to pay the royalties contracted for. In *Chanter* v. *Dewhurst* (e), it was held that the defendants having obtained the license they had

---

(a) *Hine* v. *Stevenson,* 3 B. & P. 565, also *Bloxam* v. *Elsee,* 9 D. & R. 215; *M'Alpine* v. *Mangnall,* 15 L. J., C. P. 298.

(b) See *Ex parte Granger;* Godson on Patents, 2nd ed. p. 225.

(c) *Bloxam* v. *Elsee, supra.*

(d) Co. Lit. 9 b, 172 a.

(e) 12 M. & W. 823.

bargained for, and kept it, were bound to pay for it; and secondly, that the license was not void as not being under seal. Baron Alderson said: "The defendants, in making the machine in question, are merely acting as agents for the patentee .... in my opinion a license, for this purpose, need not be under seal."

Although the words of the grant are "under his hand and seal," the document is not a deed since it need not be delivered as a deed, nor need it be stamped as such (*f*).

By sect. 36 of the Act, "a patentee may **assign** his patent **for any place** in or part of the United Kingdom or Isle of Man, as effectually as if the patent were originally granted to extend to that place or part only." Having assigned a patent, the original patentee cannot manufacture the patented article, and when an action is brought against him by his assignee he cannot set up that the patent was not valid; **he is estopped by his deed** (*g*). But where the plaintiff, **fraudulently asserting** that he had a **right to a patent**, induced the defendant to come to terms with him for a license to use that patent, the defendant, in an action upon that agreement, is not estopped from alleging the want of title in the plaintiff as a defence (*h*). But it would be otherwise in the absence of fraud and where both parties are innocent, in that case the assignee or licensee would not be allowed to set up as a defence the bad title of the assignor or licensor (*i*).

In *Bowman* v. *Taylor and others* (*k*), the plaintiff sued the defendants for the non-payment of certain royalties due from the defendants to the plaintiff under a license under seal for the use of the plaintiff's patent. The defendants defended on the grounds (1) that the invention was not a

---

f *Chanter* v. *Johnson*, 14 M. & W. 111.

g *Oldham* v. *Langmead*, cit. in *Hayne* v. *Maltby*, 3 T. R. 319.

h *Hayne* v. *Maltby*, 3 T. R. 438.

i See *Taylor* v. *Hare*, 1 Web. P. C. 292, 293.

k 2 A. & E. 278.

new invention, (2) that the plaintiff was not the first and true inventor, (3) that the specification was not sufficient—pleas which in effect endeavoured to put in issue the validity of the plaintiff's title. Upon demurrer, Taunton, J., said, "The law of estoppel is not so unjust or absurd as it has been too much the custom to represent. The principle is, that where a man has entered into a solemn engagement by deed under his hand and seal as to certain facts, he shall not be permitted to deny any matter which he has so asserted. The question here is, whether there is a matter so asserted by the defendant under his hand and seal that he shall not be permitted to deny it in pleading. It is said that the allegation in the deed is made **by way of recital,** but I do not see that a statement such as this is the less positive because it is introduced by a 'whereas.' Then the defendant has pleaded that the supposed invention in the declaration and letters patent mentioned was not nor is a new invention. These words 'was not nor is a new invention' must be understood in the same sense as the words 'had invented' in the recital of the deed set out in the declaration, and must refer to the time of granting the patent, and if the invention could not then be termed a new invention, it could not, I think, have been truly said in the deed, that the plaintiff 'had invented' the improvements in the sense in which the deed uses the words. Then the plea directly negatives the deed, and comes within the rule that a party shall not deny what he has asserted by his solemn instrument under hand and seal." The learned judge then proceeds to distinguish *Hayne* v. *Maltby* (*l*), but for some reason does not refer to the element of **fraud** in that case, which certainly would take it out of the operation of the doctrine of estoppel.

Where, however, the **license is not under seal** there

will be **no estoppel**, and the defendant may show the invalidity of the plaintiff's patent by way of showing failure of consideration (*l*).

Bosseman v. *Wright* (*m*) was decided on the ground of partial as against total failure of consideration, and has no reference to the doctrine of estoppel, although it seems sometimes to have been thought that it had.

In *Clark* v. *Adie* (*n*), James, L. J., said, "A licensee cannot under any pretence whatever bring his licensor into litigation as to the novelty of any part of the patent." This case was afterwards affirmed in the House of Lords (*o*). But it appears that if the license has been determined prior to the expiration of the term of the patent the ex-licensees may contest the validity of the patent, notwithstanding the covenants or recitals in the license (*p*). In giving judgment, Lord Cottenham said, "That is exactly coming to the point which I put, whether, at law, the party was estopped from disputing the patentee's right, after having once dealt with him as the proprietor of that right. And it appears from the authority of that case (*Hayne* v. *Maltby* (*q*)), and from the other cases, that from the time of the last payment (*i.e.* expiration of license), if the manufacturer can successfully resist the patent right of the party claiming the rent, that he may do so in answer to an action for the rent for the use of the patent during that year." The language is not clearly reported, but this appears to mean—to an action for the use and occupation, so to speak, of the patent after the expiration of the license.

The following cases have been decided uniformly, and show that parties to a deed of assignment or license are estopped from denying the validity of the patent, and

l *Chanter* v. *Leese*, 1 Web. P. C. 295.
m 6 W. R. 719.
n L. R., 3 Ch. D. 111.
(*o*) L. R., 2 App. Cas. 123.
p *Nelson* v. *Fothergill*, 1 Web. P. C. 287.
(*q*) 3 T. R. 138.

that there is no implied **warranty** on the part of the assignor or licensor. *Cutler* v. *Bower* (*q*), *Smith* v. *Scott* (*r*), *Walton* v. *Lavater* (*s*), *Norton* v. *Brooks* (*t*), *Crossley* v. *Dixon* (*u*).

Where the license is by parol and has been acted upon, and so long as the licensee has thought fit to claim the benefit of it, he is estopped from denying the validity of the patent, but no term being fixed for the duration of the verbal license he may determine it at any time (*x*). As to estoppel by judgment, see *Goucher* v. *Clayton*.

When the defendant has assigned his patent to the plaintiff, he cannot afterwards deny the validity of his own patent—*Walton* v. *Lavater*, *supra*. A licensee cannot take advantage of a judgment obtained by third parties against the patentee declaring the patent bad (*y*). But a licensee, in an action by the patentee, may claim to place the most **favourable construction** on the specifications, which will support the validity of the patent, if another construction would make it bad (*z*).

An assignment of patent rights in a **partnership** dissolution deed will estop the retiring partner from subsequently setting up the invalidity of the patent by way of defence to an action brought by his late partners (*a*). But where the plaintiff and defendant had been partners, and had worked as such the defendant's patent, there being no deed between the plaintiff and defendant which inferred the validity of the patent, held that plaintiff was not estopped from denying the validity of the patent (*b*). And where partners are joined as defendants

---

(*q*) 11 Q. B. 973.
(*r*) 6 C. B., N. S. 771, and 28 L. J., C. P. 325.
(*s*) 3 L. T. R., N. S. 272.
(*t*) 7 H. & N. 499.
(*u*) 10 H. L. Cas. 293, and 11 Jur., N. S. 107.
(*x*) *Crossley* v. *Dixon*, 32 L. J. Ch. 617.

(*y*) *The Grover and Baker Sewing Machine Co.* v. *Millard*, 8 Jur., N. S. 714.
(*z*) *Trotman* v. *Wood*, 16 C. B., N. S. 479.
(*a*) *Chambers* v. *Crichley*, 33 Beav. 274.
(*b*) *Axmann* v. *Lund*, 22 W. R. 789.

in an action for infringement, and one is assignor of the patent, the other is not debarred from setting up the pleas of invalidity (*c*).

Fraudulent agreements for the assignment of patents, such, for instance, as bubble patents, will be set aside (*d*). But in the absence of fraud the agreement will be enforced, and it is no defence to the action that the plaintiff has not invented the alleged invention (*e*).

Executors may assign a patent prior to registration of the probate (*f*).

Specific performance of an agreement to assign letters patent may be decreed (*g*). Even though the agreement be to assign patents for future inventions (*h*).

Licenses differ from assignments, in that the patentee granting a license does not part with his whole interest, but grants merely a right to use the patent for the whole term or any portion of the whole term. The license may be exclusive or otherwise.

Sect. 22 of the Act of 1883 provides for the granting of **compulsory licenses.**

"If on the petition of any person interested it is proved to the Board of Trade that by reason of the default of a patentee to grant licenses on reasonable terms—

"(a) The patent is not being worked in the United Kingdom; or

"(b) The reasonable requirements of the public with respect to the invention cannot be supplied; or

"(c) Any person is prevented from working or using to the best advantage an invention of which he is possessed, the Board may order the patentee to grant

c *Heugh* v. *Chamberlain,* 25 W. R. 742.

(*d* *Lovell* v. *Hicks,* 2 Y. & C. 46.

e *Smith* v. *Buckingham,* 18 W. R. 314.

f) *Ellwood* v. *Christy,* 10 Jur., N. S. 1079.

g) *Lewin* v. *Brown,* 14 W. R. 640.

(*h* *Printing and Numerical Registering Co.* v. *Sampson,* 44 L. J., Ch. 705.

licenses on such terms as to the amount of royalties, security for payment or otherwise, as the Board, having regard to the nature of the invention and the circumstances of the case, may deem just, and any such order may be enforced by mandamus."

These provisions are entirely novel; "(a) and (b)" are capable of being reasonably construed, as to "(c)" it is difficult to understand how the Board of Trade will come to a decision as to whether " a person is prevented from working or using, to the best advantage, an invention of which he is possessed." The "invention" must be protected by letters patent (see the construction given in sect. 46).

The proceedings under sect. 22 will be regulated by rules to be made by the Board of Trade in pursuance of the power given by sect. 101, sub-sect. 1 (g), and sub-sects. 3, 4 and 5.

Money paid by a licensee for royalties cannot be recovered when it is ascertained that the patent was void *ab initio* (i). And if the licensees have kept the license and used it, the licensor can recover from them the agreed royalties, although the patent may have been void and the license not under seal (j). But if the consideration for the money paid is that an application for a patent should be made and a license to use the patent granted, no application being made for the patent there is a total failure of consideration, and the price paid may be recovered (k). But otherwise, if the licensor knew from the first that the patent was void (l), **a license is not assignable** (m). A license to a man and his assigns means a license with power to licensee to sub-license

---

(i) *Taylor* v. *Hare*, 1 B. & P. Rep., N. S. 70.
(N. R.) 260.
(j) *Chanter* v. *Dewhurst*, 12 M. & W. 823.
(k) *Knowles* v. *Bovill*, 22 L. T.

(l) *Chanter* v. *Leese*, 4 M. & W. 295.
(m) Per Maule, J., in *Bowen* v. *Hodges*, 22 L. J., C. P. 198.

(*ideal*). A licensee may covenant not to manufacture without applying the patented invention; such a covenant is not in restraint of trade (*n*). **A license may be created by parol**, but if no time is fixed for its duration it may be determined at will, and after the determination there will be no estoppel to the ex-licensee to dispute the validity of the patent (*o*). A patentee having granted a license cannot prevent anyone **vending the articles** which have been made in pursuance of the license (*p*). And an inventor selling the patented article abroad cannot restrain its importation and sale in this country. Although an assignee of the patent in this country might restrain the importation of an article made by the original inventor or his assignee abroad (*q*). **A latent ambiguity** in a license by deed may be explained by parol evidence in the same manner as other deeds (*r*). A licensor may in the license deed stipulate for a forfeiture in the event of royalties not being paid (*s*), but such forfeiture may be waived (*t*). The licensor may also agree that he will take all necessary steps to support the validity of the patent (*u*).

Sect. 23 of the Act provides:—"(1) There shall be kept at the Patent Office a book called the Register of Patents, wherein shall be entered the names and addresses of grantees of patents, notifications of assignments and of transmissions of patents, of licenses under patents and of amendments, extensions and revocations of patents, and such other matters affecting the validity or proprietorship of patents as may from time to time be pre-

n *Jones* v. *Lees*, 1 H. & N. 189.

o *Crossley* v. *Dixon*, L. J., 32 Ch. 617, H. L.

p *Thomas* v. *Hunt*, 17 C. B., N. S. 183.

q *Betts* v. *Willmott*, L. R., 6 Ch. 239.

r *Roden* v. *The London Small Arms Co.*, 46 L. J., Q. B. 213.

s *Tielens* v. *Hooper*, 5 Ex. 830.

t *Warwick* v. *Hooper*, 3 M. & G. 60.

u *Henderson* v. *Mostyn Copper Co.*, L. R., 3 C. P. 202.

scribed; (2) the register of patents shall be *primâ facie* evidence of any matters by this Act directed or authorized to be inserted therein; (3) copies of deeds, licenses and any other documents affecting the proprietorship in any letters patent or in any license thereunder, must be supplied to the comptroller in the prescribed manner for filing in the Patent Office.

By sect. 85, "**There shall not be entered in any register** kept under this Act, or be receivable by the comptroller, any notice of any **trust**, expressed, implied, or constructive." Sect. 87 provides for the entry in the register, at the request of the person becoming entitled, of any assignment or transmission of interest. The person registered shall have power to deal with such interest as he has registered, absolutely: "Provided that any equities in respect of such patent, &c., may be enforced in like manner, as in respect of any other personal property." Sect. 88 deals with the inspection of registers, and the obtaining of certified copies. By sect. 89 sealed copies are to be received in evidence.

Sect. 90 empowers the Court (High Court of Justice) to order the alteration of the registers, upon the application of persons aggrieved, and upon sufficient cause shown. The comptroller may himself correct errors in registers which are merely of a clerical nature, sect. 91.

Sect. 35 of the **Act of 1852**, after providing for the registration of proprietors, assignments, &c., of patents, proceeded: "Provided always, that, until such entries shall have been made, the grantee or grantees of letters patent shall be deemed and taken to be the sole and exclusive proprietor or proprietors of such letters patent, and of all licenses and privileges thereby given or granted."

It will be observed that the Act of 1883, quoted above, **materially differs from this enactment.** Hence *Chollett*

v. *Hoffman* (x), and *Hassall* v. *Wright* (y), will not now apply.

Prior to the Act of 1883, the High Court of Justice exercised jurisdiction to alter and amend the register of patents (z).

The register should be amended whenever a fraudulent entry has been made. A patentee assigned half a patent to A., and afterwards he assigned the whole to B. by deed, reciting that he had already granted a license to work and use to A. B.'s assignment was first registered:—Held, that B. had **constructive notice** of A.'s rights, and an entry was ordered to be made in the register that the license referred to in B.'s assignment was the deed of assignment to A., subsequently entered (a).

(x) 7 Ell. & B. 686.
(y) 40 L. J., Ch. 145.
(z) In re *Morgan's Patent*, 21 W. R. 215.

(a) In re *Morey's Patent*, 25 Beav. 581, and Higgins' Digest, 339.

CHAPTER IX.

EXTENSION OF TERM OF PATENT.

SECT. 25 of the Act of 1883 provides:

"(1) A patentee may, after advertising in manner directed by any rules made under this section his intention to do so, present a **petition to her Majesty in Council**, praying that his patent may be extended for a further time; but such petition must be presented at least six months before the time limited for the expiration of the patent.

"(2) Any person may **enter a caveat**, addressed to the Registrar of the Council at the Council Office, against the extension.

"(3) If her Majesty shall be pleased to refer any such petition to the Judicial Committee of the Privy Council, the said Committee shall proceed to consider the same, and the petitioner and any person who has entered a caveat shall be entitled to be heard by himself or by council on the petition.

"(4) The Judicial Committee shall, in considering their decision, have regard to the nature and merits of the invention in relation to the public, to the profits made by the patentee as such, and to all the circumstances of the case.

"(5) If the Judicial Committee report that the patentee has been inadequately remunerated by his patent, it shall be lawful for her Majesty in Council to extend the term of the patent for a further term, not exceeding seven, or, in exceptional cases, fourteen years; or to order the grant of a new patent for the term therein mentioned, and containing any restrictions, conditions, and provisions that the Judicial Committee may think fit.

"(6) It shall be lawful for her Majesty in Council to make from time to time rules of procedure and practice for regulating proceedings on such petitions, and subject thereto such proceedings shall be regulated according to the existing procedure and practice in patent matters of the Judicial Committee.

"(7) The costs of all parties of and incident to such proceedings shall be in the discretion of the Judicial Committee; and the orders of the Committee respecting costs shall be enforceable as if they were orders of a division of the High Court of Justice."

These provisions have made **no substantial alteration in the law.** Prior to the Act 5 & 6 Will. IV. c. 83, there was no power in the Crown to extend the duration of letters patent, and should an inventor have desired to apply for an extension of the term of his grant, he could only do so by applying for and obtaining a **special Act of Parliament** in his favour. The Act of Will. IV., and the amending Act of 2 & 3 Vict. c. 67, introduced the method of petitioning and obtaining an extension to the Privy Council.

It had been found that the procedure to obtain an Act upon each occasion, when an extension was sought, was too costly and cumbrous, hence the modern course of procedure was devised.

This being shortly the history of jurisdiction of the Privy Council, at first an impression gained ground that the Privy Council were to put themselves in the position of Parliament, and not in that of a court of law, in considering the claims of applicants who appeared before them; that they were to weigh the claims of the **public interest** very heavily in the balance as against the inventor. In *Re Soame's Patent* (*y*) Lord Brougham

(*y*) 1 Web. P. C. 733.

said: "If this case were to be disposed of upon the ground which in arguing such cases have sometimes been assumed to be the fit one, that there must not only be merit and benefit to the public, and (which is essential) a want of sufficient remuneration in the course of using the patent; but that, moreover, the case is to be tried here as on a bill in parliament introduced to prolong the patent; then, I apprehend, there can really be no doubt whatever that in this case no bill would ever have passed through the two houses of parliament."

The true construction is, however, not so severe as that, although still sufficiently severe. In re *Morgan's Patent* (z) Lord Brougham said: "It is by no means their (the Privy Council) course to put themselves precisely in the situation of the Legislature, and never to grant an extension where an Act of Parliament would not have been obtained. At the same time there are some limits to this. They are to look to a certain degree at the position in which they are placed, and to consider that they here represent the Legislature, and that they are invested with somewhat similar powers of discretion to those exercised formerly by the whole three branches of parliament."

Such is **the spirit in which the Privy Council will approach the subject** of an extension, not benevolently to the applicant, but still with not so stern a regard to the interests of the public as parliament would entertain.

In considering their decision the Privy Council will consider:—

1. The nature and merits of the invention in relation to the public.
2. The adequacy or inadequacy of the profits made by the inventor as such.
3. The circumstances of the case.

In re Erard's Patent (a) Lord Lyndhurst said, "In cases

(z) 1 Web. P. C. 739.   (a) 1 Web. P. C. 559.

of this kind we expect a very strong **case of hardship** to be made out as well as a strong case upon the **utility of the invention**;" and the same privy councillor in *Soame's case* (b) said, " We consider the invention as very meritorious, the result of a great deal of labour, care, and science, and that it is extremely useful in its effects. We are satisfied by reasonable evidence that the party has sustained very **considerable loss**, and under these circumstances we think that the period ought to be extended."

It will be observed that the three considerations for the Privy Council laid down by the Act of 1883 are almost identical to the grounds of extension as given by Lord Brougham in *Re Derosne's Patent* (c): " The parties must show in the first place some invention, in the next place a benefit to the public, and in the third place that they have not had adequate remuneration."

It is immaterial whether or not the application is opposed. The Privy Council will require every necessary ground for extension to be **strictly proved** before they advise an extension (d), and this even though the Crown through the attorney-general consents (e).

" The merit of an **importer** is less than of an inventor. We are sitting judicially, and it is an argument against the patent that it is imported and not invented. I do not say it takes away the merit, but it makes it much smaller (f)."

Extension of the term will be granted to **assignees**, as they have, so to speak, purchased the merit of the original inventor, but the argument against importers will apply with equal force against assignees (g).

Merit here means the consideration which has been

---

b 1 Web. P. C. 560.
c 2 Web. P. C. 1.
d *In re Perkins' Patent*, 2 Web. P. C. 18.
e *In re Cardwell's Patent*, 10 Moo. P. C. C. 490.
f Per Lord Brougham *In re Soame's Patent*, 1 Web. P. C. 733.
g See *In re Napier's Patent*, 13 Moo. P. C. C. 543.

given to the state for the patent; it does not mean the merit of the inventor, but the **merit of the consideration** which he has given. An inventor may have diligently worked for years in a most deserving manner and yet have produced an improvement of the most trifling nature—the merit of the person in this case will not be considered. On the other hand, the invention, although a great one, may have been handed to him from abroad without thought or trouble on his part. This is what Lord Brougham contemplates when he says that the merit of an importer is less than that of an inventor. Again, the invention may have been a very simple one, produced by an inventor with a moment of thought, and yet of great importance to the world. This latter case would be one of merit—simplicity of an invention being an element of its value (*h*).

The Privy Council will not inquire into the **novelty or utility** of a patent, except in so far as such novelty or utility may form elements in the consideration of the merit of the invention (*i*).

Non-user of the patent creates a strong presumption against the merit of an invention, which presumption can only be rebutted by the strongest evidence (*k*). But the same objection being raised *In re Hughes' Patent* (*l*), the application was granted after strong and unanswered evidence of merit though the patent had not been used in England during the whole term (*m*).

In *re Betts' Patent* (*n*) Lord Chelmsford said, " Dobbs' specification may have given the petitioner the idea of the possibility of uniting the two metals of tin and lead,

---

(*h*) *In re Muntz' Patent*, 2 Web. P. C. 119.

(*i*) *In re Saxby's Patent*, L. R., 3 P. C. 292.

(*k*) See *In re Allan's Patent*, L. R., 1 P. C. 507, where an application was rejected on that ground.

(*l*) L. R., 4 App. Cas. 174.

(*m*) See also *In re M'Dougal's Patent*, L. R., 2 P. C. 1, and *In re Herbert's Patent*, L. R., 1 P. C. 399.

(*n*) 1 Moo. P. C. C., N. S. 49.

and may thus have deprived him of the merit of originality. But in Dobbs' hands the discovery was barren; the petitioner, however, who followed out his suggestion, and after repeated experiments gave it a practical application, is the **real benefactor to the public**, and is entitled to claim that description of **merit** which constitutes one of the grounds for extending the term of a patent" (*o*).

Merit is a vague term. Different persons have different ideas as to wherein it consists. Each case that comes before the Privy Council must of necessity, therefore, be decided upon the facts of that particular case. It is otherwise with the other necessary condition for an extension, viz., the inadequacy of the remuneration of the inventor. Here figures can be dealt with, and a nearer approach to uniformity of decision obtained. It is possible, therefore, to gather from the various decisions a reasonably accurate set of rules for the guidance of the applicant for an extension on the ground of the inadequacy of the remuneration.

The **sufficiency of the remuneration** will be estimated with a view to the **importance of the invention** and the **benefit the public** have derived from it. That which would be ample remuneration for one patent would be considered inadequate for another. Refining sugar by filtering it through animal charcoal was an invention of great value and importance. The patent was extended for six years on the ground that although there had been a considerable profit, it bore no relation to the great merit of the invention (*p*). So *In re Newton's Patent* (*q*) the Privy Council granted an extension on the ground that there had not been sufficient remuneration considering the value of the invention.

An English patent may be renewed though a foreign one has been taken out and allowed to expire (*r*).

o) Also see *In re Hills' Patent*, 1 Moo. P. C. C., N. S. 265.

p) *In re Derosne's Patent*, 2 Web. P. C. 1.

q) 11 Moo. P. C. C. 156.

r) *In re Adair's Patent*, L. R., 6 App. Cas. 176.

If the patentee is a manufacturer of the patented article, the privy council will not endeavour to distinguish accurately **his profits** as a patentee from his profits **as a manufacturer,** but will consider the gross amount of profits (*s*). In this case Lord Brougham said, "We cannot weigh in golden scales the proportions between manufacturers' profits and patentees, but we must take it in the gross, and apply our minds as men of the world, men of business—neither unfairly towards the inventor, nor extravagantly and romantically towards him in his favour—neither against him pressing, nor in his favour straining. We must ascertain whether he has, in the eyes of men of ordinary but enlightened understandings, judging fairly between him and the public, had a sufficient remuneration."

The ground of this view of the case appears to be that the possession of the patent has placed the manufacturer in an advantageous position in obtaining orders (*t*).

In the accounts which the patentee must file upon an application for an extension, when he is a manufacturer of the patented article he should, so far as possible, distinguish profits as a manufacturer from profits as a patentee (*u*); and in cases where it can be shown that the reasoning in *Johnson's case* (*supra*) does not apply, he will be allowed to deduct his profits as a manufacturer before an estimate is taken of his profits as a patentee (*w*).

But where he ascribed two-thirds of the profits to the manufacturer, and only one-third to the patent, it was held to be unreasonable (*x*).

It will be observed that the cases quoted above appear to conflict with the principles laid down by Lord

---

(*s*) *In re Muntz' Patent,* 2 Web. P. C. 120.

(*t*) *In re Johnson's Patent,* 8 Moo. P. C. C., N. S. 291.

(*u*) *In re Betts' Patent,* 1 Moo. P. C. C., N. S. 49.

(*w*) Ib.

(*x*) *In re Hills' Patent,* 1 Moo. P. C. C., N. S. 258.

Brougham in *Muntz' case* (y). These words cannot be read as meaning that no regard whatever will be paid to the fact, that a great portion of the patentees' plant, expenditure, or time, is devoted to the business of an ordinary manufacture, from which some profits would be derived, even if no patent were in existence, but that no attempt will be made to go into minute details of figures. The profits will be treated in gross, and then their lordships will apply their general knowledge, as men of the world, in coming to a conclusion as to how much the patentee has received from the profits of his invention.

In estimating profits, a deduction will be allowed for the **expenses of experiments** in bringing the invention to perfection (z). And also in respect of the **costs of litigation** necessary to maintain the validity of the patent, and to restrain infringers (a). But not where actions have been compromised, improvidently, and costs abandoned without sufficient reason (b). The **expenses of taking out the patent** will be allowed as a deduction (c). So also will the **expenses incurred in bringing the invention in general public use** (d). And a deduction will be allowed in respect of the **personal expenses of the patentee**, and by way of salary for the exclusive devotion of his time in bringing the patent into practical operation and public notice (e). A patentee residing in America, for the purpose of getting the patented article into general use in England, employed **an agent**, and allowed him half profits. This half was allowed to be deducted (f).

But, on the other hand, the patentee must add to his

(y) 2 Web. P. C. 120.

(z) *In re Bates' Patent*, 1 Web. P. C. 739, and *In re Kay's Patent*, 1 Web. P. C. 572.

(a) *In re Galloway's Patent*, 1 Web. P. C. 729.

(b) *In re Hills' Patent*, 1 Moo. P. C. C., N. S. 258.

(c) *In re Roberts' Patent*, 1 Web. P. C. 575.

(d) *In re Galloway's Patent*, supra.

(e) *In re Carr's Patent*, L. R., 1 P. C. 539.

(f) *In re Poole's Patent*, 4 Moo. P. C. C., N. S. 452.

profits the profits arising out of the manufacture of the patented article, even though intended for exportation(*g*). So also he must add the **profits** which have been made **by** his **licensees** (*h*). And in *Re Johnson's* patent, Lord Justice James said : " Their lordships are of opinion, that where the question to be considered is, whether an invention has been sufficiently remunerated or not, in taking into consideration the remuneration received, they must have regard to the remuneration which the invention has brought in to the patentee or the person who claims the right of the patentee, *whether it be in one country or another.*"

We have seen by sub-section 6 of the section of the Act of 1883 now under consideration, the rules of the privy council, which have been heretofore in force, are to continue until amended or altered.

Rule 9 is as follows :—" A party applying for an extension of a patent . . . . must lodge at the council office six printed copies of the specification, and also four copies of the **balance sheet of expenditure and receipts** relating to the patent in question, which accounts are to be proved on oath before the lords of the committee at the hearing." This must be done within one week of the hearing, rule 10.

The judicial committee will not enter into the accounts in a case for extension unless they have been filed in accordance with this rule (*i*).

But in exceptional cases, the filing of perfect accounts may be excused (*j*). Where the estate of a deceased patentee was of little value, and no accounts had ever been kept, the petitioner, the administratrix and widow of

---

(*g*) *In re Hardy's Patent*, 6 Moo. P. C. C. 441.

(*h*) *In re Trotman's Patent*, L. R. 1 P. C. 118 ; 3 Moo. P. C. C., N. S. 291.

(*i*) *In re Johnson's* and *Atkinson's Patent*, L. R., 5 P. C. 87.

(*j*) *In re Lowe's Patent*, 10 Jur. 363.

the patentee was examined to prove an allegation in the petition, to the effect that not only had there been no profits, but a considerable loss (*k*).

The **account** of profit and loss ought to be **clear and precise** (*l*). The application will be refused if the petitioner's accounts are unsatisfactory (*m*). The accounts furnished by the petitioner not containing sufficiently full and accurate information in respect of the patent, or the remuneration received by him, the judicial committee declined to recommend a prolongation of the term (*n*). In one case, the accounts being *primâ facie* unsatisfactory, the judicial committee directed the question of accounts to be taken before considering the merits of the invention (*o*). And where the accounts were *primâ facie* satisfactory, the petitioners were allowed to prove the merits of the invention before going into the accounts (*p*). The books of the petitioner in respect to profits arising from his patent having been lost during his bankruptcy, the account of profit and loss was taken upon his own evidence (*q*). This was an exception to the general rule, which is, that evidence will not be received from the petitioner.

Where a patentee, whether English or foreign, has obtained **foreign patents, they should be stated** in a petition for prolongation, and the fullest information afforded as to the profits thereof. A patentee should preserve the clearest evidence of everything which has been paid or received on account of the patent. Whether or not his remuneration has been adequate, his furnishing a satisfactory account is a condition precedent to his obtaining an extension of his term (*r*).

The third head of subjects to be inquired into, upon an application for prolongation, consist of the various grounds of objections to an extension which have been allowed hitherto by the committee, and which are included in the general term used in sub-sect. 4, viz., "**All the circumstances of the case.**"

That the invention has not been brought into **public use** is a good ground of objection(*s*). So is **negligence** on the part of the patentee **in restraining infringement**(*t*). That the **invention was practically useless** as originally described in the specification, but was subsequently made practicable by subsequent improvements, introduced from abroad, is also a good ground for objection (*u*). But, otherwise, where the invention was useful and meritorious, in its original form, subsequent improvements form no ground in support of objection (*x*). When the non-profitable use of the patent has been caused by the fault of the patentee himself, objection will be allowed (*y*). So also where a patentee has **delayed, intentionally**, putting his invention into practice, unless he can show that shortness of funds, or other reasons, placed it out of his power to avoid the delay (*z*).

We have seen that the novelty or utility of a patent will not be inquired into, except so far as they bear upon the merit of the invention. Nor will the validity of the patent be inquired into, excepting in cases where it is **obvious the patent is invalid.** In *Re Hills'*

(*r*) *In re Adair's Patent*, L. R., 6 App. Cas. 176.

(*s*) *In re Pucker's Patent*, 12 Jur. 234.

(*t*) *In re Simister's Patent*, 1 Web. P. C. 724; also *In re Pucker's Patent*, supra.

(*u*) *In re Woodcroft's Patent,* 1 Web. P. C. 740.

(*x*) *In re Galloway's Patent*, 1 Web. P. C. 727.

(*y*) *In re Patterson's Patent*, 6 Moo. P. C. C. 469.

(*z*) *In re Norton's Patent*, 1 Moo. P. C. C., N. S. 339.

Patent (*a*). Sir J. T. Coleridge said: "Their lordships have not in these cases been in the habit of trying the validity of patents. They will not, of course, recommend the extension of a patent which is manifestly bad; but, on the other hand, they will not generally enter into questions of doubtful validity. They lay aside, therefore, the questions of **want of novelty** and **want of utility**, so far as they affect the validity of the patent. Indeed the learned counsel for the opponents disclaimed, and very properly, any intention of impeaching its validity directly; but they contended that, both with respect to the novelty and the utility of the invention, the degree of merit to be attributed to the petitioner ought to be taken into account; and in their lordship's judgment they are right in that contention. Unless the patent be very clearly invalid, so that it would be altogether nugatory to prolong that patent, the court usually has been rather inclined to assume that the patent may be a good patent, and so leave the question to any legal consideration that may arise in a contest between the parties who are interested in it" (*b*).

An illustration of what is meant by the patent being **clearly bad** is given in *Re M'Innes' Patent* (*c*). The patent was for a metallic soap to be used for the purpose of preserving metals from rust. The specification was very widely worded. Sir W. Earle said, "Their lordships taking into consideration with reference to the public interest that the individual substance for the application of which the patent is sought to be prolonged is not specially defined, every kind of metallic soap being within the limits of the specification, are of opinion that many questions affecting the patent might be raised if any metallic soap was used by the public in ignorance of

---

a 1 Moo. P. C. C., N. S. 262.
b Per Lord Langdale, M. R., *In re Pucker's Patent*, 12 Jur. 231.
c 5 Moo. P. C. C., N. S. at p. 78.

the specification being as wide as it is. On the whole, therefore, their lordships are of opinion that they ought not to recommend her Majesty under such circumstances to grant a prolongation."

In consequence of sect. 25 of the Patent Law Amendment Act, 1852, and of sect. 7 of 16 & 17 Vict. c. 115, which provided that letters patent obtained in the United Kingdom for patented foreign inventions should not continue in force after the expiration of the foreign patent, and that any prolongation of letters patent should be made subject to that condition. **An inquiry into foreign patents** and their duration was always an essential element of the proceedings before the privy council (*d*).

These Acts are, however, specifically repealed, and by sect. 45, sub-sects. 2 and 3, of the Act of 1883 it is provided, "Every patent granted **before** the commencement of this Act, or on an application there pending, shall remain unaffected by the provisions of this Act relating to patents binding the Crown, and to compulsory licenses. In all other respects (including the amount and time of payment of fees) this Act shall extend to all patents granted before the commencement of this Act, or on applications then pending, in substitution for such enactments as would have applied thereto if this Act had not been passed."

Thus it will be seen that after the commencement of the Act any prolongation of letters patent will be made regardless of foreign patents or their duration.

Prior to the Act of 1883 it had been held, in a series of cases, that **executors and administrators** of a grantee of

(*d*) *In re Bodmer's Patent*, 8 Moo. P. C. C. 282; *In re Aubé's Patent*, 9 Moo. P. C. C. 43; *In re Newton's Patent*, 15 Moo. P. C. C. 176; *In re Betts' Patent*, 1 Moo. P. C. C., N. S. 49; *In re Poole's Patent*, 4 Moo. P. C. C., N. S. 452; *In re Normand's Patent*, 6 Moo. P. C. C., N. S. 477; *In re Winan's Patent*, 8 Moo. P. C. C., N. S. 306; *In re Johnson's Patent*, 8 Moo. P. C. C., N. S. 287; *In re Blake's Patent*, L. R., 4 P. C. 535.

letters patent might petition for an extension (e). So might the assignee of a patent, even though a public company (f). So might the executor of an assignee (g).

The Act of 1883 gives a **patentee** the right to petition, and, bearing in mind that the **definition of the word patentee** is by sect. 46, "Any person for the time being entitled to the benefit of a patent," it will be observed that the greatest latitude is given as to persons who may petition. The committee will still regard different classes of petitioners in different lights.

In *Re Norton's Patent*, quoted above, Sir John Romilly, then Master of the Rolls, said, "Under the late statute, 7 & 8 Vict. c. 69, s. 4, a person is not excluded from applying for an extension of a patent upon the ground of his being the assignee of the patent; but it must always be borne in mind that the assignee of a patent does not, unless under peculiar circumstances, apply on the same favourable footing that the original inventor does. The ground that the merits of the inventor ought to be properly rewarded, in dealing with an invention which has proved useful and beneficial to the public, does not exist in the case of an assignee, unless the assignee be a person who has assisted the patentee with funds to enable him to perfect and bring out his invention, and has thus enabled him to bring it into use."

And in *Re Pitman's Patent* (h) Sir J. W. Colvile said: "There are no doubt cases in which their lordships have granted applications by the assignees of the patentee for extension of the term, and have also considered, in some respects, the expenses incurred by the assignee in bringing the patent into notice, and for the merit as it may be said of the assignee in patronizing the patentee, and in pushing the patent into notice; but the general

---

e *In re Heath's Patent*, 8 Moo. P. C. C. 217.

f *In re Norton's Patent*.

g *In re Bodmer's Patent*, 1 Moo. P. C. C., N. S. 239.

h 8 Moo. P. C. C., N. S. 297.

rule which their lordships entertain in applications on the part of assignees is, as was stated by Lord Brougham in *Re Morgan's Patent* (i), that by so doing 'they are, though not directly, yet mediately and consequentially, as it were, giving a benefit to the inventor, because, if the assignee is not remunerated at all, it might be said that the chance of the patentee of making an advantageous conveyance to the assignee would be materially diminished, and consequently his interest damnified. For this reason consideration has been given to the claims of the assignee who has an interest in the patent.'"

There is no case showing that an extension has ever been granted to licensees; but it may be suggested that at any rate *exclusive* licensees are "persons for the time being entitled to the benefit of a patent," although, of course, very exceptional circumstances indeed would have to be shown to warrant an extension to them.

It is difficult to estimate the effect of sect. 36 of the Act of 1883 upon this branch of the subject. Sect. 36 provides that: "A patentee may assign his patent for any place in or part of the United Kingdom or Isle of Man, as effectually as if the patent were originally granted to extend to that place or part only."

Will the privy council, on the application of an assignee for a portion of the kingdom, extend the patent for that portion, or must all parties to the patent join in the petition?

It is evident that whilst one district assignee of an electric light patent, for example, may have been amply remunerated, another may not have been remunerated at all, owing to the action of local authorities or other matters entirely beyond the assignee's control. How could the committee in justice refuse the latter an extension? On the other hand, how could they grant it to the other?

(i) 1 Web. P. C. 737.

Then again, if a patent may be extended for one district and not for another we shall have the enormous practical difficulties and public inconveniences of an article being patented in one county and free in another, a state of affairs which, we venture to say, would be intolerable to the public.

Any person may enter a **caveat against the extension**, and may be heard at the bar in support of their opposition; and where unreasonable opposition is offered, they will be ordered to pay the petitioner's costs (*k*). But where the opposition is well founded and successful, costs will be allowed to the opposing party (*l*). If the petition be **abandoned, costs will be given to opposers**, and they need not give the petitioner notice of their intended application for the same (*m*). Where the petitioner had fairly and honestly stated his case, both the things against and the things for him in his petition, and the inquiry had been prolonged by the opposition, the costs of the opposition refused, although the petition had been dismissed on the ground of sufficient remuneration.

Where two or more parties have opposed the petition separately and successfully, the committee will sometimes order a **fixed sum** to be paid by the petitioner to the opponents, to be apportioned between them in lieu of saddling him with several separate sets of **taxed costs** (*n*). We thus see that, whilst on the one hand an unwarranted application for an extension may be very costly, unreasonable opposition may be equally so.

An extension of a patent having once been granted, the privy council have no jurisdiction to entertain a

k In re Downton's Patent, 1 Web. P. C. 567.

(*l) In re Westrupp and Gibbins' Patent*, 1 Web. P. C. 554.

m In re Bridson's Patent, 7 Moo. P. C. C. 499. See, however, *In re Milner's Patent*, 9 Moo. P.

C. C. 39.

n In re Jones' Patent, 9 Moo. P. C. C. 11. Also *In re Hills' Patent*, 1 Moo. P. C. C., N. S. 258, and *In re Wield's Patent*, 8 Moo. P. C. C., N. S. 300.

petition for a **further prolongation,** their power being exhausted; and this objection may be taken by an opposing party, even though omitted from the objections filed by them (*o*).

The rules of practice to be observed upon application for extensions of letters patent will be found hereafter.

(*o*) *In re Goucher's Patent,* 2 Moo. P. C. C., N. S. 532.

CHAPTER X.

CONFIRMATION.

The Statute 5 & 6 Will. IV. c. 83, provided a remedy for cases of hardship, such as, where an invention had been invented or used and subsequently abandoned before the date of the patent in a manner unknown to the patentee at the time of his application. There would be a sufficient prior user to invalidate the patent, and yet there would be great merit probably in the patentee, and a great benefit to the public. The patentee might petition the privy council to confirm the patent, that is, to declare it valid, notwithstanding such prior user. The proceedings on such a petition were similar to those upon a petition for extension.

The Act of 1883 repeals the statute 5 & 6 Will. IV. c. 83, and with it all proceedings for confirmation; and this method of clothing an invalid patent with validity is abolished. A perusal of sect. 45, sub-sect. 2 & 3, shows that this applies to patents existing at the commencement of the Act, as well as to those to be hereafter applied for and granted.

It is not strictly the purpose of a law work to criticise the enactments of the legislature, saving in their construction and application from an administrative point of view, otherwise a great deal might be said as to the evidence of abolishing that which was intended for and operated merely as a relief under very hard and exceptional circumstances.

CHAPTER XI.

REMEDIES OF THE PATENTEE AND OF THE PUBLIC—ACTION FOR INFRINGEMENT.

An action for infringement is the remedy which the patentee has, and the means which is given to him for enforcing his patent privileges.

The courts are bound to take notice of the patent, and are bound to give legal effect to it, provided it cannot be shown to have been granted contrary to law.

PARTIES TO THE ACTION.

The Act of 1883 gives no directions as to what persons may be **plaintiffs or defendants** in an action for infringement, and therefore leaves the question of the parties to the action as it was before the passing of the Act.

The **original grantee**, it is obvious, so long as he has not parted with the whole of his interest in the patent, may be a plaintiff. And so may the **assignees** of a patent (a), even though he has acquired the right by assignment of two separate moieties, and the party sued is the original grantee (b).

The **assignee of a portion** of a patent may sue for an infringement of that part. Erle, C. J., in giving judgment in *Dunnicliff* v. *Mallett* (c), said: "The question is whether an assignment of part of a patent is valid. I incline to think that it is. It is every day's practice for the sake of economy to include in one patent several things which are in their nature perfectly distinct and

---

(a) *Electric Telegraph Co.* v. *Brett*, 10 C. B. 838.

(b) *Walton* v. *Lavater*, 8 C. B., N. S. 162.

(c) 7 C. B., N. S. 209.

severable. . . . . Being therefore inclined to think that a patent severable in its nature may be severed by the assignment of a part, I see no reason for holding that the assignee of a separate part which is the subject of infringement may not maintain an action." The plaintiff in such an action would not be allowed to sever his part from the rest of the patent, and he would be liable to be defeated if it could be shown that the patent in any of its parts was void. But, on the other hand, he would have to show that his part alone would have been sufficient to support a patent, *i.e.*, that it contains a new and useful invention. Sect. 33, however, of the Act of 1883, provides, " Every patent . . . . . shall be granted for one invention only, but may contain more than one claim; but it shall not be competent for any person in an action or other proceeding to take any objection to a patent on the ground that it comprises more than one invention."

By sect. 36, " A patentee may assign his patent for any place in or part of the United Kingdom, or Isle of Man, as effectually as if the patent were originally granted to extend to that place or part only." The **assignee for a district** will be in a position to bring an action for infringement, but it is obvious that the infringement must be within his district, otherwise he will be unable to prove damage.

One of several joint owners of a patent may bring an action in his own name to restrain infringement, or for damages, without joining his other co-owners (*d*), and he may sue alone for an account of profits, and for payment to the plaintiff of such part of such profits as the plaintiff should be entitled to.

Abinger, C. B., in *Derosne* v. *Fairie* (*e*), said that "a mere **licensee** could maintain no action against anyone else for the infringement of a patent." He might, how-

(*d* Sheehan v. Great Eastern Rail. Co., L. R., 16 Ch. D. 59;   *Dent* v. *Turpin*, 2 J. & H. 139. (*e* 1 Web. P. C. 155.

ever, **use the name of the grantor** of the license for the purpose provided he were an **exclusive licensee** (*f*).

A mere licensee would have no exclusive right to use the invention; he is only a person who is permitted to use it. The grantor of such a license might grant a dozen other such licenses without prejudicing the rights of the license; but an exclusive licensee has a right of property in the monopoly, and stands very much in the same position as an assignee for a district. The term exclusive, as applied to a licensee, meaning exclusive within an area.

When the exclusive licensee finds it necessary to protect his rights by bringing an action in the name of the licensor he is liable to give the licensor security for the costs (*g*) which, in the event of defeat, the licensor would have to pay. The right, however, to assign for particular districts will make this branch of the subject unimportant, since exclusive licenses were only a scheme for the purpose of, in effect, assigning for districts.

The **assignees or trustees** in bankruptcy of a patentee may maintain action for infringement in their own name (*h*), and so may the **executors or administrators** of a patentee.

As defendants, a person physically using a patented invention is liable, such as a **contractor** (*i*). When a person in the position of **a servant** uses a patented invention, the master, in law, is the person who physically uses the invention as well as the servant, and the master may be sued. If a servant uses an invention in the course of his employment the master is liable, even though the master has told the servant to avoid infringing

---

(*f*) *Renard* v. *Levinstein,* 2 Hem. & M. 528.

(*g*) *Evans* v. *Rees,* 2 Q. B. 334; *Spicer* v. *Todd,* 1 D. P. C. 306.

(*h*) *Bloxam* v. *Elsee,* 6 B. & C. 169.

(*i*) *Denley* v. *Blore,* 38 Lond. Jour. 224.

the patent (*k*). The **directors of a company** whose servants infringe an invention are personally liable (*l*).

An architect specifying the use of a patented invention is not liable (*m*).

Aliens infringing a patent in this country by vending or otherwise are liable if they come within the jurisdiction of the courts (*n*). A person ordering goods to be made in England which are an infringement of a patent, although intended for exportation to him abroad, infringes the patent. "He that causes or procures to be made may be well said to have made himself." Per Tindal, C. J. (*o*).

(*k*) *Betts* v. *De Vitre*, L. R., 3 Ch. App. Cas. 441.
(*l*) Ibid.
(*m*) *Denley* v. *Blore*, 38 Lond. Jour. 224.
(*n*) *Caldwell* v. *Vanvlissengen*, 9 Hare, 415.
(*o*) *Gibson* v. *Brand*, 11 L. J., C. P. 186.

CHAPTER XII.

THE CAUSE OF ACTION—INFRINGEMENT.

The infringement of a patent is the doing that which the patent prohibits from being done (*a*). The words of the Royal Command are as follows: "We do by these presents for us, our heirs and successors, strictly command all our subjects whatsoever within our United Kingdom of Great Britain and Ireland and the Isle of Man, that they do not at any time during the continuance of the said term of fourteen years, either directly or indirectly make use of or put in practice the said invention, or any part of the same, nor in anywise imitate the same, nor make or cause to be made any addition thereto or subtraction therefrom, whereby to pretend themselves the inventors thereof, without the consent, license or agreement of the said patentee in writing under his hand and seal, on pain, &c."

The **question of infringement** or no infringement is one of fact, and therefore **is for the jury** (*b*). But this refers to the mere infringement alone within the meaning of Tindal, C. J., in *Muntz* v. *Foster* (*c*), when he told the jury that "for the purpose of inquiring whether the defendants have infringed the patent or not, we are to assume that it is a good patent, that no objection arises either to the nature of the grant or the specification which has been enrolled by the plaintiff."

If the patent is invalid there can be no infringement in the sense that a patent which has no legal existence

---

(*a*) *Walton* v. *Bateman*, 1 Web. P. C. 616.   P. C. 586; *De la Rue* v. *Dickenson*, 7 E. & B. 738.
(*b*) *Walton* v. *Potter*, 1 Web.   (*c*) 2 Web. P. C. 99.

T.   L

cannot be infringed. But assuming that it has a legal existence, the question is for the jury. This explains the apparently contradictory decision in *Curtis* v. *Platt* (d) in the House of Lords. The question of infringement was there taken as involving the validity of the patent.

It is equally an infringement whether the defendant acted in **ignorance** of the plaintiff's patent or not. In *Heath* v. *Unwin* (e) Parke, B., delivering the judgment of the Court, said: "There was therefore no intention to imitate the patentee's invention, and we do not think the defendant can be considered to be guilty of any indirect infringement if he did not intend to imitate at all." This judgment certainly gives an erroneous impression of the law, and Shadwell, V. C., when the same case came before him (*f*), said: "The party complaining of the act is not the less prejudiced by it because it was committed unintentionally; and my opinion is that, if a party has done an act that is injurious to the rights of another (though without any intention of doing him an injury) he is answerable for the consequences." In *Stevens* v. *Keating* (g) the Lord Chancellor disapproved of the case in the Court of Exchequer; "and I must decline to act upon the principle which it lays down."

Subsequently, when *Heath* v. *Unwin* came before the House of Lords, the opinion of the judges being taken, Parke, B. (*h*), acknowledged the error into which the Court had fallen, and approved of *Stevens* v. *Keating*.

In *Stead* v. *Anderson* (*i*) Wilde, C. J., graphically puts it: "The question of infringement depends not on what the defendant intends, but on what he does."

So it is immaterial **whether the defendant was aware** that the thing was patented or not, since in law every person in the realm is taken to have notice of a patent

---

d 35 L. J., Ch. 852.
e 11 L. J., Ex. at p. 156.
f 15 Sim. 553.
g 1 Mac. & G. 659.
h 25 L. J., C. P. at p. 19.
i 2 Web. P. C. 156.

in the same way that he is taken to be aware of the law (*k*).

And the converse is also sound—if a person intending to infringe a patent does not in fact do so, he will not be taken to have infringed (*l*).

In *M'Cormick* v. *Gray* (*m*) the specification, after describing several parts of reaping machines, including some cutting blades of peculiar construction, claimed: " The construction of reaping machines according to the improvements before described—that is to say, the constructing and placing of holding fingers, cutting blades, and gathering reels, respectively, as before described, and the embodiment of those parts as so constructed and placed, all or any of them in machines for reaping purposes, whether such machines are constructed in other respects as before described, or however else the same may in other respects be constructed."

The defendant made and sold cutting blades similar to those described by the plaintiff's patent, which were *capable of being used* in the plaintiff's reaping machine. Bramwell, B., in giving judgment, said :—" A man could not make the blade of a knife without infringing this person's patent, because you may intend to put it into a machine, or you may not. I think it is a very clear case, and I am satisfied there is no difference between making a thing with one intent and making it with another, because I always understood, that if a man may do a thing, he may do it with whatever intent he pleases." It will be observed, that in this case, to make the knives was no infringement, and there was no evidence of the defendant having applied them to reaping machines (*n*).

(*k*) *Walton* v. *Lavater*, 29 L. J., C. P. 275; *Curtis* v. *Platt*, 11 L. T. R., N. S. 245.

(*l*) *Newall* v. *Elliott*, 10 Jur., N. S. 954.

(*m*) 31 L. J., Ex. 42.

(*n*) See, however, *Bancroft* v. *Warden*, Romilly's Notes of Cases, 103.

Thus we see that infringement, as taken apart from the question of validity, is a matter of fact, and that intention is not material to the conclusion.

To prove infringement, it must be shown that there is a **substantial resemblance** (*o*). The infringement must be of a part for which the patent was granted, and not merely of a part described in the specification (*p*).

A patented article sold by a patentee carries with it the right of being used and sold anywhere (*q*).

It is impossible to surmise how the Courts will deal with sect. 36 of the Act of 1883, which enables a patentee to assign his patent for any place or part of the kingdom as effectually as if the patent were originally granted to extend to that place or part only.

Supposing a patentee to assign a patent for making brushes for London to A, and for Liverpool to B. Will the purchaser of brushes from A in London be infringing the rights of B by using the brushes in Liverpool, and will he be liable to an action? If he is not liable to be sued, of what use is the right of assignment for a part only, since the assignee, for one place, could make the brushes in that place, and sell them universally to the detriment of assignees for other places.

The amount of prior user which will be sufficient to invalidate a patent, differs considerably from the amount **of user** which will be held to infringe a patent: " these are different questions, depending on wholly different considerations, the one upon the extent of previous knowledge, the other upon the effect of the grant" (*r*). We have seen that by sect. 33 of the Act of 1883, a patent may still contain more than one claim, and in such a case,

---

o *Stead* v. *Anderson*, 2 Web. P. C. 155.

p *Croll* v. *Edge*, M. Dig. 191.

q *Betts* v. *Willmott*, L. R., 6 Ch. App. Cas. 239.

r) Per Turner, V. C., in *Caldwell* v. *Vanvlissengen*, 9 Hare, 428; *Newton* v. *Grand Junction Rail. Co.*, 5 Ex. 331.

provided every claim which is made is valid, a patent may be infringed by infringing any one claim. In *Gillett* v. *Wilby* (s) Coltman, J., said:—" If they are all new (the parts claimed), and the defendant has infringed any one of them, it will be sufficient to support the action, and it is not necessary that he should have infringed them all." In *Newton* v. *The Grand Junction Rail. Co.* (t), Pollock, C. B., said:—"But in considering the question of infringement, all that is to be looked at is, whether the defendant has pirated a part of that to which the patent applies; and if he has used that part for the purposes for which the patentee adapted his invention, and for which he has taken out his patent, and the jury are of opinion that the difference is merely colourable, it is an infringement," and in *Sellers* v. *Dickenson* (u), the same judge said:— " There may be an **infringement by using so much of a combination as is material** . . . . if a portion of a patent for a new arrangement of machinery is in itself new and useful, and another person, for the purpose of producing the same effect, uses that portion of the arrangement, and substitutes for the other matters combined with it another mechanical equivalent, that would be an infringement of the patent."

"Where a patent is for a combination of two, three, or more old inventions, a user of any of them would not be an infringement of the patent; but where there is an invention consisting of several parts, the imitation or pirating of any part of the invention is an infringement of the patent " (v).

Speaking of this case in *Clark* v. *Adie* (w), James, L. J., said: " Upon the authority of *Smith* v. *L. & N. W.*

(s) 9 Carr. & P. 336.
(t) 5 Ex. 334.
(u) 5 Ex. 324.
(v) Per Campbell, C. J., in *Smith* v. *L. & N. W. Rail. Co.*,
2 E. & B. 76; *The Patent Bottle Envelope Co.* v. *Seymer*, 5 C. B., N. S. 172.
(w) L. R., 10 Ch. App. Cas. 674.

Railway Co., it has been strongly contended before us that whenever there is a patent for a combination, that patent gives protection, not indeed to every distinct thing that enters into the combination, but to every combination, arrangement and aggregate of two or more of those distinct things, even although such subordinate combination is not expressly or impliedly claimed in the specification. This, in our opinion, is so startling a violation of every principle of patent law, that we doubt whether we could follow any authority, short of the House of Lords, in applying such a doctrine. If a patent for a combination of several parts is in reality a patent, and gives really a monopoly for every combination of any two or more of those parts, then it follows, from the very first principle of patent law, that if any conceivable combination of any two or more parts was old, the patent would be bad. On the other hand, if the patentees say, 'No, we do not claim to protect every combination of those parts, but only those subordinate combinations, or parts of the combination, which are new and useful,' then such a claim would be entirely inconsistent with the leading case of *Foxwell* v. *Bostock* (*x*), which, we may be permitted to say, is as good sense as it is sound and intelligible law . . . . . I will state what we conceive to be the real principle which underlies the case of *Lister* v. *Leather* (*y*), and which reconciles it with the other cases, and with general principles, and common sense. A patent for a new combination or arrangement is to be entitled to the same protection, and on the same principles, as every other patent. In fact every, or almost every patent, is a patent for a new combination. The patent is for the entire combination, but there is, or may be, an essence or **substance of the invention** underlying the mere accident of form, and that invention, like every other invention, may be pirated by a theft in a disguised

x) 12 W. R. 723.   *y*) 8 E. & B. 1004.

or mutilated form, and it will be in every case a question of fact, whether the alleged piracy is the same in substance and effect, or is a substantially new or different combination."

Where, however, the **application** by the defendant of a portion of the invention of the plaintiff is **for a different object**, and with a view of carrying out a principle totally newly discovered by the defendant, and which was unknown to the plaintiff, there is no infringement, although at first sight there appears to be some similarity of process (*z*).

We have seen that sect. 5, sub-sect. 5, provides that a complete specification must conclude with a distinct statement of the invention claimed ; so that, if the invention be a combination, it must be so stated ; if for parts, they must be claimed. It is apprehended that there will in future be no **infringement** if the defendant cannot be shown to have infringed, directly or indirectly, **a part or parts of the claim.** In *Lister* v. *Leather* (*a*) it was held that a valid patent for an entire combination, or for a process, gives protection to every part that is new and material, for the purpose of effecting that particular combination or process, without any express claim of particular parts, and notwithstanding that parts of the combination are old. In future, if any parts are desired to be protected, as well as the combination or process, the claim will have to be so drawn as to include those parts.

The jury will always have to consider whether the infringing machine process or combination is a **substantial imitation** (*b*). No fine lines can be drawn as to what amounts to a substantial imitation. In *Clarke* v. *Adie* (*c*), in the House of Lords, Lord Blackburn said, "I incline to

---

(*z*) *Newton* v. *Vaucher*, 6 Ex. 859. See also *Morewood* v. *Tupper*, 3 C. L. Rep. 718.

(*a*) 8 E. & B. 1004.

(*b*) *Thomas* v. *Foxwell*, 5 Jur. N. S. 39.

(*c*) L. R., 2 App. Cas. 335.

agree with what was said in the Exchequer Chamber in the case of *Lister* v. *Leather* (d), that you cannot decide in the abstract whether the using of two parts, A and B, of a combination of A, B, and C is or is not using part of that invention, nor can you decide in the abstract the other question, which was somewhat discussed in the case of the sewing machine (*Foxwell* v. *Bostock*) (e), whether or no the specification shows that A or B is sufficiently claimed as a part of the invention or not. I do not think that either of those questions can be decided in the abstract. I would wish, like the Exchequer Chamber in *Lister* v. *Leather*, before deciding it, to have before me the nature of the machine, in order that I may see what A, B, and C are, and what is their relation to each other."

In *Parkes* v. *Stevens* (f), James, V.-C., said, "The authority of that case (*Lister* v. *Leather*) has been pressed upon me as if it really established this, which would be a most startling proposition, that a patent for a combination or arrangement would be a distinct patent for everything that was new and material and that went to make up the combination .... the judgment if read well will be found to give no warrant whatever for such, I must call it, baseless notion. The law is summed up thus. The cases establish that a valid patent for an entire combination for a process gives protection to each part thereof that is new and material *for that process*, which is really nothing more than stating in other words that you not only have no right to steal the whole, but you have no right to steal any part of a man's invention; and the question in every case is a question of fact—is it really and **substantially a part of the invention**" (g). This judgment was affirmed on appeal (h).

(d 8 E. & B. 1004.
e 12 W. R. 723.
f L. R., 8 Eq. 358.
g See also *Wright* v. *Hitch-*

cock, L. R., 5 Ex. 37; on the other side *White* v. *Fenn*, 15 W. R. 348.
(h, 5 Ch. Ap. Cas. 36.

If a man in the course of producing an improved combination substantially uses a combination which already forms the subject of a patent he thereby infringes the patent, notwithstanding that the combination he is making has a different end in view than that which has been patented (*i*).

But, on the other hand, where a patent is for a combination a person who takes a new and material part of the combination, but **not for a similar or analogous purpose** to that to which it was applied in the patent, does not infringe the patent (*k*).

If the invention be for a combination or process whereby an already well-known object is produced, it will be no infringement to make **another combination, even of the same materials** (provided they be also old and well-known), for the purpose of attaining the same object, for the patent is for the *means* of attaining the object, and if other means are employed there is no infringement. The patent is also for the *method* of combining the old and well-known materials, and if **another method** is adopted there is no infringement (*l*).

When the defendant has set himself to work to **evade the plaintiff's patent** by fraudulently making a colourable imitation, or substituting a mechanical or chemical equivalent, the cases show that the Courts will look strictly at what he has done, and will take care that he does not overstep the line which he is endeavouring to keep within.

The question of fraudulent evasion is, as we have shown, one of fact. "A slight departure from the specification, for the purpose of evasion only, would, of course, be a fraud upon the patent; and therefore the question will be, whether the mode of working by the

---

(*i*) Per Lord Westbury in *Cannington* v. *Nuttall*, L. R., 5 H. L. at p. 230.

(*k*) *Lister* v. *Eastwood*, 9 L. T. R., N. S. 766.

(*l*) *Curtis* v. *Platt*, in the House of Lords, 35 L. J., Ch. 852.

defendant has, or has not, been essentially or substantially different (*m*).

In *Dudgeon* v. *Thompson* (*n*) Lord Cairns makes strong objection to the use of the term **colourable imitation**, in connection with the infringement of patents, and proceeds:—"If there is a patented invention, and if you, the defendant, are found to have taken that invention, it will not save you from the punishment or from the restraint of the Court, that you have, at the same time that you have taken the invention, dressed it up colourably, added something to it; taken, it may be, something away from it, so that the whole of it may be said, as is said in this injunction, Here is a machine, which is either the plaintiff's machine, or differs from it only colourably. But underlying all that there must be a taking of the invention of the plaintiff. There used to be a theory in this country, that persons might infringe upon the equity of a statute, if it could not be shown that they had infringed the words of the statute; it was said that they had infringed the equity of the statute, and I know there is by some confusion of ideas, a notion sometimes entertained that there may be something like an infringement of the equity of a patent. My lords, I cannot think that there is any sound principle of that kind in our law; that which is protected is that which is specified, and that which is held to be an infringement must be an infringement of that which is specified. But I agree it will not be the less an infringement because it has been coloured or disguised by additions or subtractions, which additions or subtractions may exist, and yet the thing protected by the specification be taken notwithstanding."

Summing up the cases, therefore, we come to this. Strictly speaking, there is no such thing as a colourable imitation: either the defendant has infringed the thing

m Per Dallas, J., in *Hill* v. Thompson, 1 Web. P. C. 242.   (*n*) L. R., 3 App. Cas. at p. 43.

specified or he has not. At the same time there is an essence or substance to every invention underlying the mere accident of form or words. If the defendant has imitated and adopted the **essence of the invention** he will not be allowed to escape because he has not adopted the form or words in which the essence of the invention is clothed (n).

There is a description of imitation which is produced by the substitution of **chemical or mechanical equivalents**. To the unscientific eye there is a total dissimilarity between the infringing machine or process and the original; but, none the less, it is a mere imitation—it is a robbery of the ideas and intentions of the first inventor, but a robbery conducted in a scientific manner.

We have seen that a patent cannot be granted for the discovery of a mere principle (o), but that, if the principle when discovered is at the same time applied, a valid grant may be made for the application of the principle. The essence of the patent is the fact of applying the newly-discovered principle to a particular end. Now a mechanical or chemical **equivalent is another method** of producing the same result, a method which a skilled mechanic or chemist, having once seen the original invention, could at once suggest and apply without the necessity of any inventive power whatever. Equivalents

(n) *Thorn* v. *The Worthing Skating Rink Co.*, L. R., 6 Ch. D. 417; *Flower* v. *Lloyd*, W. N. 1877, p. 132; *Barrett* v. *Vernon*, 45 L. T. R. (N. S.) 755; *Bailey* v. *Roberton*, L. R., 3 App. Cas. 1055. And the older cases, *Bovill* v. *Moore*, Dav. P. C. 405; *Forsyth* v. *Riviere*, 1 Web. P. C. 97; *R.* v. *Lister*, Web. P. L. 80; *Minter* v. *Wells*, 1 Web. P. C. 130; *Morgan* v. *Seaward*, per Alderson, B., 1 Web. P. C. 171; *Walton* v. *Potter*, 1 Web. P. C. 586; *Neilson* v. *Harford*, 1 Web. P. C. 310; *Walton* v. *Bateman*, per Cresswell, J., 1 Web. P. C. 616; *Muntz* v. *Foster*, per Tindal, C. J., 2 Web. P. C. 101; *Russell* v. *Ledsam*, 14 M. & W. 580; *Gamble* v. *Kurtz*, 3 C. B. 425; *Stead* v. *Anderson*, 2 Web. P. C. 156; *Unwin* v. *Heath*, 25 L. J., C. P. 9; *Curtis* v. *Platt*, 35 L. J., Ch. 852; *Murray* v. *Clayton*, L. R., 7 Ch. App. Ca. 585.

(o) Ante, p. 22.

may be substituted for parts as well as for the whole invention, so that it may happen that a patent is taken out which consists of three parts. An equivalent may be substituted for each part, so that in effect the whole invention may be changed and yet there may be a most flagrant infringement.

Take, for instance, the case of *Stevens* v. *Keating* (*p*). Here the patent was for the manufacture of cement. The cement was made from gypsum (sulphate of lime) by admixing it with pearlash (carbonate of potash) and sulphuric acid. Chemically, the effect was this: Sulphate of potash was produced; this, combined with the sulphate of lime, produced a double salt, which, when submitted to a high temperature and subsequently ground to a fine powder, constituted the cement. The principle of this discovery was that sulphate of lime combined with salts of potash or soda, and when so combined, produced a substance which set very hard. The defendant substituted for the pearlash and sulphuric acid a chemical equivalent, borate of soda (borax), and heated that with gypsum, producing in the same manner a double salt, and with the same resulting property of setting. This was properly held to be an infringement.

In *Russell* v. *Cowley* (*q*) the invention claimed was that of bringing to a welding heat a long piece of iron of the proper quality; after having turned up its edges and drawing it through a hole of the proper size of the intended tube, so as to compress together the edges and give it a complete circular form. The defendants turned up the skelp, and, after heating it in the furnace, passed it through two rollers with grooves:—Held, that the two rollers with grooves were a mere mechanical equivalent for the hole through which the iron was passed under the patent (*r*).

(*p*) 2 Web. P. C. 181.
(*q*) 1 Web. P. C. 463.
(*r*) See also *Jupe* v. *Pratt*, 1 Web. P. C. 146; *Heath* v. *Unwin*, per Parke, B., 2 Web. P. C. 227; *The Electric Telegraph Co.* v. *Brett*,

There are three ways in which a patent may be infringed:—

1. By making the patented article or working the process.
2. By using.
3. By selling.

BY MAKING.

A person may infringe a patent by making the article himself, or by his agent, or by his servants. The agent and servants, it is true, will be considered as equally infringing the patent, and actions may be brought against them individually, but that in no way absolves the person who employs them for that purpose. In *Sykes* v. *Howarth* (s) a patent consisted of the application of cards or strips of leather covered with wire or rollers at "wide distances." A person who contracted to clothe rollers and supplied to a "nailer" cards of such width that when applied to the rollers they must of necessity leave wide spaces, and who himself paid the nailer, was held to have infringed the patent, though he alleged that his business was that of a card-maker only and did not include the nailer's work. In giving judgment, Fry, J., said: "I have come to the conclusion that the nailer must be deemed to have been the agent, for the purpose of nailing on, of the defendant . . . . there is a contract to clothe in the manner prescribed by the particulars given to the defendant, and that contract was carried into effect by a person paid by the defendant— the defendant himself receiving the total amount for which he contracted. The consequence is that in my judgment all the defences fail."

10 C.B. 838; *Hancock* v. *Moulton*, Johnson's Patentees Annual, 3rd ed. 208; *Bateman* v. *Gray*, Mac. P. C. 102; *Simpson* v. *Holliday*, 20 Newton's Lond. Journ. (N. S.) 111; *United Telephone Co.* v. *Harrison, Cox, Walker & Co.*, L. R., 21 Ch. D. 896.

(s) L. R., 12 Ch. D. 826.

We have seen that **it is an infringement to colourably imitate an invention.** It is no infringement to make, use, or vend the elements which afterwards enter into the combination. In *Townsend* v. *Haworth* (t), Jessel, M. R., said, " The chief of these chemical substances are substances which are perfectly well known, and most of them are common substances; they are all old chemical compounds, and there is no claim in the patent at all except for the peculiar use of these chemical compounds for the purpose of preserving the cloth from mildew. No judge has ever said that the vendor of an ordinary ingredient does a wrong if the purchaser coming to him says, ' I want your compound because I want to preserve my cloth from mildew. I wish to try the question with the patentee.' No one would doubt that that sale would be perfectly legal. You cannot make out the proposition that any person selling any article, either organic or inorganic, either produced by nature or produced by art, which could in any way be used in the making of a patented article can be sued as an infringer, because he knows that the purchaser intends to make use of it for that purpose."

The working and making must be by way of using the invention, as distinguished from **experimenting** with it, so as to operate as an infringement. In *Higgs* v. *Godwin* (u) the patent was for obtaining a commercially saleable manure by treating sewage with slaked lime. The defendant used the process by way of experiment to purify water—held no infringement. In *Frearson* v. *Loe* (v), Jessel, M. R., adverting to this branch of the subject, said, " The other point raised was a curious one and by no means free from difficulty, and what occurred with regard to that was this: that the defendant at

t) L. R., 12 Ch. D. 831, note.
u E. R. & E. 529. See also *Jones* v. *Pearce*, 1 Web. P. C. 122,
and *Muntz* v. *Foster*, 2 Web. P. C. 93 and 96.
v, L. R., 9 Ch. D. 48.

various times made screw blanks, as he said, not in all more than 2 lbs., by various contrivances, by which no doubt screw blanks were made; according to the plaintiff's patent of 1870, as well as that of 1875, they seem to have been an infringement of both. He said he did this merely by way of experiment, and no doubt if a man makes things merely by way of *bonâ fide* experiment, and not with the intention of selling and making use of the thing so made for the purpose of which a patent has been granted, but with the view of improving upon the invention, the subject of the patent, or with a view of seeing whether an improvement can be made or not, that is not an invasion of the exclusive rights granted by the patent. Patent rights were never granted to prevent persons of ingenuity exercising their talents in a fair way. But if there be neither using nor vending of the invention for profit, the mere making for the purpose of experiment and not for a fraudulent purpose ought not to be considered within the meaning of the prohibition, and if it were, it is certainly not the subject for an injunction."

It will be remembered that prior to the Act of 1883 letters patent did not operate as against the Crown; questions sometimes arose as to whether persons acting in the **service of the Crown** might manufacture a patented article or use a patented process.

When the persons using the invention were servants of the Crown, and acting in pursuance of their duty as servants, they were protected; but if they were contractors contracting with the Crown they were not protected, but stood in exactly the same position as other subjects (*x*).

Sect. 27 of the Act of 1883 provides that a patent should bind the Crown, but that the Crown may use the inven-

---

(*x*) *Dixon* v. *The London Small Arms Co.*, L. R., 10 Q. B. 130, and L. R., 1 App. Cas. 632, reversing decision of Court of Appeal, L. R., 1 Q. B. D. 384; also *Feather* v. *R.*, 6 B. & S. 257.

tion " by agents or *contractors* " on terms to be before or after the use agreed upon.

BY USING.

It frequently occurs that very fine questions arise as to what constitutes **using** a patented invention. The general rule may be thus stated: That if the defendant has put the invention to the purpose for which it was intended he has used it in this country. In the case of *Nielson* v. *Betts* (y), in the House of Lords, the facts were as follows: Betts, the plaintiff in the suit, was the patentee of an invention for the manufacture of capsules for the purpose of covering bottles of liquid (wine, beer, or otherwise), and protecting them from the action of the atmosphere. Betts' patent did not extend to Scotland. Nielson and his co-appellants, defendants in the suit, were persons who bottled beer in Glasgow for the Indian market. They bottled the beer and covered it with capsules, which were made in Germany in pursuance of Betts' specification. The beer was shipped by the appellants in vessels which called at Liverpool to complete their cargoes; on some occasions the beer was transshipped in England, but no cases of beer were opened, nor was any of the beer sold in this country. Held, by the House of Lords, that, inasmuch as the object of Betts' invention was to make a capsule that would preserve the beer, whilst the beer was in England it was being preserved by the use of Betts' invention, and consequently that there was an infringement of the patent. Lord Chelmsford, in giving judgment in the Court below, said: " It is the employment of the machine or article for the purpose for which it was designed which constitutes its active use, and whether the capsules were intended for ornament or for protection of the contents of the bottles upon which they were placed, the whole time they were in England they may be correctly said to

(y L. R., 5 H. L. 1.

be in active use for the very objects for which they were placed upon the bottles by the vendors. If the beer, after being purchased in Glasgow, had been sent to England, and had been afterwards sold here, there can be no doubt, I suppose, that this would have been an infringement, because it would have been a profitable user of the invention, and I cannot see how it can cease to be a user because England is not the final destination of the beer."

The case of *Nobel's Explosive Co.* v. *Jones, Scott & Co.*, is instructive upon the question of user. The subject of the plaintiff's patent, dynamite, is a mechanical compound of nitro-glycerine and infusorial earth. The compounding of nitro-glycerine in this manner is done for and effects the purpose of rendering it less liable to explosion from concussion. The object of the patent was, therefore, to enable nitro-glycerine to be kept and handled with safety. Held, by Bacon, V.-C., that the mere storage of dynamite made abroad, and only landed in this country for the purpose of transhipment, amounted to an infringement of the plaintiff's patent. This decision was reversed in the Court of Appeal, but upon another point, to be mentioned presently, and without in any manner impugning the correctness of the Vice-Chancellor's decision on this question (*y*).

In the case of *Caldwell* v. *Vanvlissengen* (*z*), it was held by Turner, V.-C., that **foreign ships coming into British ports,** fitted with screw propellers, which were made in pursuance of the specification of an English patent, thereby infringed the patent. If the injunction which was granted be carefully read, it will be found to amount to a restraint from propelling the vessels with the propellers, not from having the ships merely fitted with them. Legally speaking, the user of propellers differs from that of capsules or dynamite in this important respect, that the

(*y*) L. R., 17 Ch. D. 721. See also *The Universities of Oxford and*

Cambridge v. *Richardson*, 6 Ves. 689.

(*z*) L. J. R., 21 Ch. 97.

one is in use only when in motion; the others are at use, the one when merely affixed to the bottles, and the other when merely in possession. Subject to the applicability of the arguments adduced in the case of dynamite, **mere possession**, unaccompanied with user, does not constitute an infringement of Letters Patent.

In the case of *Adair* v. *Young* (z), certain pumps, which were an infringement of the plaintiff's patent, were fitted on board a British ship. There was no evidence of their having been used. Held, by the Court of Appeal, that there had been no infringement, but as there was evidence of an intention to use the pumps, an injunction would be granted against the use of the pumps.

Sect. 43 of the Act of 1883 provides:—"(1) A patent shall not prevent the use of an invention for the **purposes of the navigation of a foreign vessel** within the jurisdiction of any of Her Majesty's Courts in the United Kingdom or Isle of Man, or the use of an invention in a foreign vessel within that jurisdiction, provided it is not used therein for or in connection with the manufacture or preparation of anything intended to be sold in or exported from the United Kingdom or Isle of Man. (2) But this section shall not extend to vessels of any foreign state of which the laws authorize subjects of such foreign state, having patents or like privileges, for the exclusive use or exercise of inventions within its territories, to prevent or interfere with the use of such inventions in British vessels while in the ports of such foreign state, or in the waters within the jurisdiction of its Courts, where such inventions are not so used for the manufacture or preparation of anything intended to be sold in or exported from the territories of such foreign state."

A patent is not infringed by being used on board an English vessel abroad (a).

In the case of *Nobel's Explosive Co.* v. *Jones & Scott* (b), mentioned above, the Court of Appeal reversed the decision of Vice-Chancellor Bacon, on the grounds that the defendants had not infringed the plaintiff's patent, they having merely acted as Custom House agents for the transhipment of the dynamite, and their functions being confined to obtaining papers necessary for such transhipment, and that they never had any ownership in or exercised any control over the dynamite.

This decision shows that the Courts will not recognize that a person infringes a patent by **aiding and abetting**, so to speak, another to do so. There must be some actual infringement on the part of the defendant (c).

SELLING.

A person infringes letters patent who sells the patented article within this realm. It is a putting in practice of the invention within the terms of the grant.

The **purchase** of the patented article is not of itself an infringement of the patent, nor is the **mere possession**, since these do not come within the prohibition in the grant, which is against making use of, or putting in practice, the said invention (d).

This is always with exceptions such as in the case of dynamite, where the mere possession involves *ex necessitate* the use; and the **importation** of the patented article will not of itself amount to an infringement.

The possession of the patented article, combined with **exposure for sale**, if no sale is in fact effected, is no infringement (e).

But the making of the patented article, as we have seen, is an infringement, whether a sale was effected, or attempted or not (f).

(c) See also *Townsend* v. *Haworth*, L. R., 12 Ch. D. 831; *Sykes* v. *Howarth*, 12 Ch. D. 826.

(d) See *Minter* v. *Williams*, 1 Web. P. C. 135.

(e) *Ibid.*

(f) *Muntz* v. *Foster*, 2 Web. P. C. 101; *Oxley* v. *Holden*, 8 C. B. (N. S.) 666.

Where the patent is for a process the manufacture of an article by the process abroad and sale in this country is an infringement. In *Elmslie* v. *Boursier* (g) Sir W. M. James, V.-C., said: "It is said that tinfoil can be made by the plaintiff's process at less cost than by the old method; and it is conceded that nobody in England can use the plaintiff's process of making cast tinfoil as distinguished from rolled tinfoil without a license from the plaintiff. If that cannot be done in England it would be a very strange thing if a person in England could send an order to some one in France, get the same thing manufactured there in exactly the same way, and bring it here so as to compete with the person to whom the Crown has granted 'the whole profit, benefit, commodity, and advantage' arising from the patent. It would be a short mode of destroying 'every profit, benefit, commodity, and advantage' which a patentee could have from such a thing, if all that the man had to do was to get the thing made abroad, import it into this country, and then sell it here in competition with the English patentee."

In *Walton* v. *Lavater* (h) Erle, C. J., said: "But it appears to me that the main purpose of the patent is to give the profit to the patentee, and that the main mode of defeating that purpose would be by selling the patented article; and it seems to me that without proof of the making of the article by the infringer, evidence that he sold the patented article for profit would be good evidence upon which a jury might find that he had infringed the patent. With respect to the defendant not being liable, because the articles were imported from abroad, I should say that, even if it was a simple case of importation, without any proof of knowledge of the article being patented or of the infringement, it would

g L. R., 9 Eq. at p 222.   *h* 29 L. J., C. P. 275.

be sufficient evidence of infringement that the defendant had imported and *sold*" (*i*).

Selling known chemical substances with knowledge of and a view to their being used for the purpose of infringing a patent is no offence, provided the vendor takes no actual personal part in the infringement (*k*).

A patentee selling the patented article sells with it the right of free disposition as to that article, and if he sells the article in France, the purchaser may import and sell it in England. Lord Hatherly in *Betts* v. *Willmott*(*l*), said: "Inasmuch as he has the right of vending the goods in France, or Belgium, or England, or in any other quarter of the globe, he transfers with the goods necessarily the license to use them wherever the purchaser pleases. When a man has purchased an article he expects to have the control of it, and there must be some clear and explicit agreement to the contrary to justify the vendor in saying that he has not given the purchaser his license to sell the article, or to use it wherever he pleases *as against himself.*"

But when the patentee has assigned his patent in France and kept it to himself in England, the French assignee may not, nor may a purchaser from him import and vend or use the goods made in France in England (*m*). In this case the sale of the article can only imply such license as the vendor himself has, and the vendor has no right to sell in England.

Conversely, if the patentee had assigned his patent rights in England he could not manufacture in France and sell in England, and the sale of an article in France

---

(*i*) See also *Wright* v. *Hitchcock*, 39 L. J., Ex. 97.

(*k*) *Townsend* v. *Haworth*, Higgins' Digest of Patent Cases, Pt. 2, p. 60; *Sykes* v. *Howarth*, L. R., 12 Ch. D. 826.

(*l*) L. R., 6 Ch. App. Cas. at p. 245.

(*m*) See the rule laid down in *Caldwell* v. *Vanvlissengen*, 9 Hare, 415.

would carry with it no implied right to import into or sell in England. But if the rights under the patent are vested in one and the same person for both France and England, or if there are no monopoly rights in France but only in England, the patentee could make and sell in France and restrain the purchaser from selling or using the article in England, unless indeed there was a special agreement for that purpose; and then such agreement could not be held to attach to the article so as to prevent any person in whose hands it might come from importing it (*n*).

(*n*) *Betts* v. *Willmott*, 6 Ch. App. Cas. 239.

CHAPTER XIII.

THE REMEDY—INJUNCTION.

The remedy sought or granted in an action for infringement may consist of an injunction, together with an account of sales and profits, or damages.

The judicature acts and the rules which have been made for the governing of the practice of the courts have introduced great changes in the method of procedure. The old practice of moving for an injunction by a suit in the Court of Chancery, and of trying the validity of the patent at common law, has disappeared; and in its place the patentee seeking to enforce his rights commences but **one action in which he claims, and if entitled to, obtains every remedy** which was formerly granted to him by the dual process.

Every patentee proceeding against an infringer must prove the validity of his patent and his title to an injunction; that being so, and the right to the injunction hanging so completely upon the question of validity, it is obvious that the new procedure and the new power of both divisions of the High Court of Justice to grant complete and sufficient remedies and to try every question is of great advantage to persons in possession of patent rights.

There are two forms of injunction, the interlocutory injunction and the perpetual injunction.

The interlocutory injunction stands very much upon the same footing, and will be granted for similar reasons and upon the same conditions that an injunction was formerly awarded by the Court of Chancery when an action was directed to be tried at common law.

The perpetual injunction is granted after trial, and binds the parties against whom it is granted during the continuation of the term of the patent.

An interlocutory injunction will be granted whenever there has been such **working, user and enjoyment** of the patent rights as will satisfy the Court that there are strong *primâ facie* reasons for acting on the supposition that the patent is valid.

Lord Eldon, in the case of the *Universities of Oxford and Cambridge* v. *Richardson* (*o*), said: " It is then said in cases of this sort the universal rule is that if the title is not clear at law the Court will not grant or sustain an injunction until it is made clear at law. With all deference to Lord Mansfield, I cannot accede to that proposition so unqualified. There are many instances in my own memory in which this Court has granted or continued an injunction to the hearing under such circumstances. In the case of patent rights, if the party gets his patent and puts his invention in execution and has proceeded to a sale, that may be called possession under it; however doubtful it may be whether the patent can be sustained, this Court has lately said **possession under a colour of title** is ground enough to enjoin, and to continue the injunction, till it shall be proved at law that it is only colour and not real title."

And in *Gardner* v. *Broadbent* (*p*) Sir J. Stuart, V.-C., said: "I wish it to be understood that the law of the Court is that laid down by Lord Eldon in the *Universities of Oxford and Cambridge* v. *Richardson*."

There having been a trial as to the validity of the patent, which has terminated in favour of the patentee, will be considered by the Court sufficient reason for granting an interlocutory injunction.

Where the patentee has worked and enjoyed the patent for many years without dispute, an interlocutory

---

o, 6 Ves. 689.   (*p*) 2 Jur., N. S. 1041.

injunction will be granted. In *Dudgeon* v. *Thompson* (*q*) Jessel, M. R., said: "The Court can grant an injunction before the hearing where the patent is an old one and the patentee has been in long and undisturbed enjoyment of it, or where its validity has been established elsewhere, and the Court sees no reason to doubt the propriety of the result, or where the conduct of the defendant is such as to enable the Court to say that, as against the defendant himself, there is no reason to doubt the validity of the patent."

So in *Betts* v. *Menzies* (*r*), Wood, V.-C., said, "The law of this Court is, that where the patentee has had long enjoyment, then he shall have an injunction to protect his rights until trial, even although his rights under his patent be doubtful." On the other hand, we find Lord Westbury laying it down in *Hills* v. *Evans* (*s*), "It is the habit and the rule of the Court not to grant that injunction (to restrain infringement), at all events at the hearing, and **not to make it perpetual unless the legal validity** of the patent has been **conclusively established.**"

Sometimes an application for an interim injunction is advisable where there has not been long user of the patent, or a decision in favour of the patentee. In such cases the plaintiff must be prepared to give *primâ facie* satisfactory evidence of the validity of his patent (*t*).

These decisions certainly appear contradictory, but perhaps this principle may be gleaned from them—that the Court will consider the **balance of convenience** in each particular case. If it should appear that irremediable injury will be sustained by the defendant if an

(*q*) *Russell* v. *Cowley*, 2 Coop. C. C. 59 (n.); but see *Crosskill* v. *Evory*, 10 L. T. R. 459.

(*r*) 3 Jur., N. S. at p. 358. See also *Davenport* v. *Goldberg*, 2 H. & M. 282; *Penn* v. *Bibby*, 3 L. J., Eq. 308; *Muntz* v. *Foster*, 2 Web.

P. C. 95.

(*s*) 4 De G., F. & J. at p. 289.

(*t*) *Gardner* v. *Broadhurst*, 2 Jur., N. S. 1041; *Davenport* v. *Jepson*, 1 N. R. 73; *Renard* v. *Levinstein*, 10 L. T., N. S. 177.

injunction goes which may afterwards appear unfounded, the Court will require a very strong case to be made out by the plaintiff before granting such an injunction (*u*), and the converse would equally appear.

In *Bickford* v. *Skewes* (*v*), Shadwell, V.-C., said, " I have nothing to do with any other case than the case before me."

The Court will not infrequently **grant or refuse** the **injunction** until the hearing **upon terms** ; the terms on the plaintiff being that he shall be answerable in damages, or on the defendant that he shall keep an account of the material manufactured, or of the articles sold, in pursuance of the patent process. And in considering which course should be adopted the Court will be influenced chiefly by the balance of convenience and the probability of injury to either side (*w*).

In *Plimpton* v. *Spiller*, James, L. J., said, " The Court, not forming an opinion very strongly either one way or the other whether there is an infringement or not, but considering it as a fairly open question to be determined at the hearing, and not to be prejudiced by any observations in the first instance, reserves the question of infringement as one which will have to be tried at the hearing and which it will then have to consider. There will always be, no doubt, the greatest possible difficulty in determining what is the best mode of keeping things *in statu quo*—for that is really what the Court has to do, to keep things *in statu quo*—until the final decision of the question; and then, of course, the Court says, 'We will not stop a going trade. We will not adopt a course which will result in a very great difficulty in giving compensation on the one side or on the other. We have to deal with it as a practical question, in the best way we can.' I think, on

---

(*u*) *Neilson* v. *Forman*, 2 Coop. 61 n.).

(*v*) 1 Web. P. C. 213.

(*w*) *Neilson* v. *Thompson*, 1 Web. P. C. 278 ; *Bridson* v. *M'Alpine*, 8 Beav. 229 ; L. R., 4 Ch. D. 289.

the whole, that the Master of the Rolls has made the right order, viz., by granting the injunction and putting the plaintiff upon an undertaking to abide by such order (if any) as to damages as the Court may think fit to make if he should ultimately turn out to be in the wrong, and that it would not be right in this case merely to put the defendant upon the terms of keeping an account which, I conceive, might be a very clumsy and inefficient mode of recompensing the plaintiff if he should turn out ultimately to be in the right." In the same case the present Master of the Rolls, Sir W. B. Brett, said, "There will be a hardship on the one side or on the other, and the question is on which side does the balance appear to lie? Now, if the trade of a defendant be an old and an established trade, I should say that the hardship upon him would be too great if any injunction were granted. But where, as here, the trade of the defendant is a new trade, and he is the seller of goods to a vast number of people, it seems to me to be less inconvenient and less likely to produce irreparable damage to stop him from selling, than it would be to allow him to sell and merely keep an account, thus forcing the plaintiff to commence a multitude of actions against the purchasers."

Injunctions are now granted pursuant to the Judicature Act, 1873, sect. 25, sub-sect. 8 :—"A mandamus or an injunction may be granted, or a receiver appointed, by an interlocutory order of the Court in all cases in which it shall appear to the Court to be just or convenient that such order should be made; and any such order may be made, either unconditionally or upon such terms and conditions as the Court shall think just; and if an injunction is asked either before, or at, or after the hearing of any cause or matter, to prevent any threatened or apprehended waste or trespass, such injunction may be granted, if the Court shall think fit, whether the person against whom such injunction is sought is or is not in possession under any claim of title or otherwise, or (if out of possession) does or does not claim a right to do the act sought to be restrained under any colour of title; and whether the estates claimed by both, or either of the parties, are legal or equitable."

It will be observed that this section confers upon the Court very wide limits within which, in its discretion, it may grant injunctions. It sweeps away a great deal of the technical rules which had been from time to time laid down by the Court of Chancery for the granting of injunctions, and it practically substitutes for them the opinion of the judge trying each particular action as to the balance of convenience upon a consideration of the facts of the case.

The basis of an injunction is the threat actual or implied on the part of the defendant, that he is about to do an act which is in violation of the plaintiff's rights; so that not only must it be clear that the plaintiff has rights, but also that the defendant has done something which induces the Court to believe that he is about to infringe those rights.

The fact that he has been guilty of an infringement of the patent rights will, under circumstances, be evidence that he intends to continue his infringement, but whether he has actually infringed the patent or not, it will be sufficient if he has **threatened to infringe it**. Actual infringement is merely evidence upon which the Court implies an intention to continue in the same course.

In *Frearson* v. *Loe* (*r*), Jessel, M. R., said:—" I am not aware of any suit or action in the Court of Chancery which has been successful on the part of a patentee, without infringement having been proved; but, in my opinion, on principle there is no reason why a patentee should not succeed in obtaining an injunction without proving actual infringement. I think for this reason:

r L. R., 9 Ch. D. at p. 65.

where the defendant alleges an intention to infringe, and claims the right to infringe, the mischief done by the threatened infringement of the patentee is very great, and I see no reason why a patentee should not be entitled to the same protection as every other person is entitled to claim from the Court from threatened injury, where that threatened injury will be very serious. No part of the jurisdiction of the old Court of Chancery was considered more valuable than that exercise of jurisdiction which prevented material injury being inflicted, and no subject was more frequently the cause of bills for injunction than the class of cases which were brought to restrain threatened injury, as distinguished from injury which was already accomplished. It seems to me, when you consider the nature of a patent right, that where there is a deliberate intention expressed, and about to be carried into execution, to infringe certain letters patent under the claim of a right to use the invention patented, the plaintiff is entitled to come to this Court to restrain that threatened injury. Of course it must be plain that what is threatened to be done is an infringement."

The actual infringement of the patent is taken by the Court to imply an intention to continue the infringement, notwithstanding any promises not to do so, and an injunction will be granted. Vice-Chancellor Shadwell, in *Losh* v. *Hague* (y), said:—" If a threat had been used, and the defendant **revokes the threat**, that I can understand as making the plaintiff satisfied; but if once the thing complained of has been done, I apprehend this Court interferes, notwithstanding any promise the defendant may make not to do the same thing again."

If the fact of actual infringement is relied upon, and not a mere threat, it will be necessary to show very clearly that what has been done amounts to an infringement. In *Hancock* v. *Moulton* (z), it was held that the

(y) 1 Web. P. C. 200.   (z) M. Dig. 506.

evidence must be so perfect, that if it were a motion to commit for the breach of an injunction, the Court would commit upon it. If the evidence of infringement is conflicting, either by reason that it is denied that the acts complained of were done, or that such acts as were done did not amount to an infringement of the patent, the Court should not grant an interim injunction before the hearing of the action (*a*).

If the evidence relied upon for the injunction is the sale by the defendant of the patented article, and not the manufacture, the plaintiff must show that such patented article was not made by himself or his licensees (*c*).

In the case of *Adair* v. *Young* (*b*), the defendant was the captain of a ship which was fitted with certain pumps which were an infringement of the plaintiff's patent. No act of using the pumps was proved; but it was shown that the ship was not supplied with other pumps. It was held that the possession of the pumps under such circumstances, although not of itself amounting to an infringement, was evidence upon which the Court would act that the defendant intended to use the pumps, should occasion require. And the Court, Brett and Cotton, L. JJ., James, L. J., dissenting, granted an injunction.

Lord Justice James, in giving his reasons for dissenting, said: "I think that an injunction ought not to be granted against a man unless he has done something which he ought not to have done, or permitted something which he ought to have prevented. Now, a master who comes on board ought not to be answerable on the ground that, when he takes the command, there is on board a pump which infringes the patent. He does

a) *The Electric Telegraph Co.* v. *Nott,* 2 Coop. 41.
b L. R., 12 Ch. D. 13.
c Betts v. *Willmott,* L. R., 6 Ch. App. Cas. 239.

not, owing to his qualified possession, become at once an infringer. He had no power to take a pump out of the ship; he had nothing to do with putting it there, and he was not wrong in allowing it to remain there, for he could not lawfully remove it. An injunction, therefore, can only be granted on the principle of *quia timet*, and in applying that principle I think that it would be a right exercise of the discretion of the Court not to grant an injunction against a master who has done nothing wrong when there is no difficulty in finding and suing the owner of the ship."

The Court, however, seem to have been of opinion that the ground upon which an injunction should be granted is not whether the defendant has done anything wrong or not, but whether there was evidence of an intention to use the patented invention. The Court held that the circumstances of the case showed an intention in the captain to use the invention.

No injunction will be granted where the patentee has **not proceeded with reasonable speed** to prosecute infringers (*d*). But in cases where there are several infringers he is not justified in commencing a vast multitude of actions and applying for injunctions in each (*e*). His proper course is to " select that which he thought the best in order to try the question fairly, and proceed in that case to obtain his interlocutory injunction. He might write at the same time to all the others who were *in simili casu*, and say to them: 'Are you willing to take this as a notice to you that the present case is to determine yours? Otherwise I shall proceed against you by way of interlocutory injunction; and if you will not object on the ground of delay, I do not mean to file bills against all of you at once. Am I to understand that you make no objection of that kind? If you do not object I

(*d*) *Losh* v. *Hague*, 1 Web. P. C. 201; *Bacon* v. *Jones*, 4 My. & Cr. 438; *Bridson* v. *Benecke*, 12 Beav. 1.

(*e*) *Foxwell* v. *Webster*, 3 N. R. 103, at p. 180.

shall file a bill against only one of you.' I do not think any court could complain of a patentee for taking the course I am suggesting" (*f*).

Where machines have been manufactured or articles made in infringement of patent rights, an injunction will be granted to prevent their use or sale even after the patent has expired (*g*).

The injunction falls with the **expiration of the patent** (*h*).

After trial and judgment, and upon application for a perpetual injunction, when the nature of the infringing matter will permit of it, an order will be made that the articles (machinery or otherwise) **be delivered up to the plaintiff or destroyed** (*i*). This was done in *Plimpton* v. *Malcolmson* (supra), the reference to this cause is M.R., 28th Jan., 1876, B. 381. An inquiry will, when necessary, be directed as to the articles manufactured which are in the defendant's possession, and that they be destroyed, *Betts* v. *De Vitre*, V.-C. W., 1865, A. 119. The defendant will also be ordered to make discovery upon oath of the articles or machinery which he may have in his possession, and which infringe the plaintiff's patent, so that they may be delivered up and destroyed; this was done in *Tangye* v. *Scott*, V.-C. W., 12th Feb., 1866, B. 461. **The right of property in the articles** which infringe the patent remain in the infringer, although the Court may order the articles to be destroyed (*j*).

These mandatory orders are never made except after trial, and when the plaintiff has fully established to the

f Per Sir W. Page-Wood, V.-C., *Bovill* v. *Crate*, L. R., 1 Eq. at p. 391. See also *Hancock* v. *Moulton*, M. Dig. 206; *Smith* v. *The London and South Western Rail. Co.*, Kay, 408.

g *Crossley* v. *Beverley*, 1 Web. P. C. 119; *Crossley* v. *The Derby Gas Light Co.*, 4 L. J., Ch. 25. See also *Price's Patent Candle Co.* v. *Bauwen's Patent Candle Co.*, 4 K. and J. 727.

h *Daw* v. *Eley*, L. R., 3 Eq. 496.

i *Frearson* v. *Loe*, L. R., 9 Ch. D. at p. 67.

j *Vavasseur* v. *Krupp*, L. R., 9 Ch. D. 351.

satisfaction of the Court the validity of his patent and the fact of the defendant's infringement.

DAMAGES.

In addition to an injunction, the defendant may be entitled, when there has been actual infringement as distinguished from an intention to infringe, to either damages or an account of sales and profits.

He is **not entitled to both damages and an account,** but he must elect which he will take (*k*). An account of sales and profits amounts to a condonation of the infringement (*l*).

The **measure of damage** is the loss which the plaintiff has actually sustained, irrespective of the costs of the action. The question of damages is not synonymous with an account of profits, the basis of calculation being entirely different. In calculating damages, the Court will not take into account any **manufacturer's profit** which the plaintiff might have made (*m*). But it is submitted that consideration should be had where the patentee is the manufacturer, and has granted no licenses, to the damage which he has sustained by reason of the **commercial competition** to which he has been subjected.

In estimating damages, the Court will inquire into the **extent of infringement** and the amount of goods manufactured by the defendant, care being taken to distinguish this inquiry from that as to sales and profits. In the one case the quantity of business is inquired into, in the other the amount of profit. It is evident that the smaller the price at which the articles have been sold, the greater the damage to the patentee by reason of the market depre-

---

(*k*) *De Vitre* v. *Betts,* L. R., 6 H. L. 319; *Neilson* v. *Betts,* L. R., 5 H. L. 1; *Needham* v. *Oxley,* 11 W. R. 852.

(*l*) Per Lord Westbury, *Neilson* v. *Betts, supra.*

(*m*) *Penn* v. *Jack,* L. R., 5 Eq. at p. 86.

T.　　　　　　　　　　　　　　　N

ciation of the profits to be made by his invention by reason of the competition.

In *Betts* v. *De Vibre* (n), Sir W. Page-Wood, V.-C., said: "I confess it appears to me that if the damages are to be assessed, it would be proper to take the identical course that was taken in *Hills* v. *Evans*, for this reason, that damages of this description, namely, damages for the infringement of a patent where there has been no license granted at any time for the use of that patent, can only be ascertained on those very vague and guess-like data which, it appears, juries have been obliged to act upon in ascertaining what the actual loss has been that has occurred to a patentee by the user by some wrongdoer of his patent right. The difficulty one sees must be very great where there are no licenses existing. Where there are licenses existing, the difficulty would be next to nothing, because you would simply ascertain the amount sold, and fix the wrongdoer with that amount."

In *Penn* v. *Jack*, licenses had been granted, and the same Vice-Chancellor fixed the amount of damage at the amount which would have been received had the defendant been working under a license.

Where licenses have been granted, no account will be taken of profits which have been lost by reason of competition (*o*).

Where bills to restrain the infringement of a patent have been filed against both the person who manufactures, and the person who uses the article, and issues of fact have been found for the plaintiff, it is the right of the plaintiff to have, not only an account against the manufacturer, but also damages against the person using the article, wherever it be found (*p*).

In aid of the inquiry as to damages, directed by the

(*n*) 34 L. J., Ch. at p. 290.   (*p*) Head note to *Penn* v. *Bibby*,
(*o*) *Penn* v. *Jack*, L. R., 5 Eq.   L. R., 3 Eq. 308.
at p. 85.

judgment for a perpetual injunction, **the defendant must give full discovery,** and will be required to set out the names and addresses of the persons to whom machines, made in infringement of the patent, have been sold; but not the names of the agents concerned in the transaction (*q*).

ACCOUNT OF SALES AND PROFITS.

In cases where it is deemed to the advantage of the plaintiff, he may elect, in lieu of damages, to take an account of sales and profits; that is, to condone the infringement upon the footing that the defendant has been acting as the plaintiff's agent in selling or using the invention.

The plaintiff will not, however, be allowed to claim an account **if he has tacitly permitted the defendant to infringe his patent,** relying upon an ultimate account of profits. In *Crossley* v. *The Derby Gas Light Co.* (*r*), Lord Brougham said: "It is a principle of equity, that a party who claims a right should not lie by, and by his silence or acquiescence induce another to go on spending his money and incurring risk, and afterwards, if profit has been made, come and claim a share in that profit without having ever been exposed to share in the losses which might have been sustained. Upon this the defendants rely; but it was to be considered, on the other hand, whether the plaintiff did not explain the delay which has taken place, and whether the conduct of the defendants has not been such as to lull the plaintiff's suspicions to sleep."

Prior to the Judicature Acts it was held a rule in Courts of Equity, that in consequence of the terms of

(*q*) *Murray* v. *Clayton*, 15 Eq. 115.   (*r*) 1 Web. P. C. 120.

21 & 22 Vict. c. 27, no relief could be awarded for damages or an account, unless an injunction could be granted at the same time. All other relief being merely incidental to the injunction (r). Thus, where a **patent had expired** after bill filed, but before an injunction could be granted, the Court declined to consider the question of damages (s). But now, in pursuance of sect. 24, subsect. 6, of the Judicature Act, 1873, a Court of Equity may give full relief; and so, wherever a court of law would, prior to the passing of the Act, have granted damages or an account, similar orders will be made by either branch of the High Court of Justice, irrespective of the question of injunction.

Where it appears at the trial that **the defendant has made no profit,** although the plaintiff may be entitled to damages, he will not be entitled to an account (t).

Where the defendant has acted in ignorance of the patent, and before action has offered to submit to an account and to pay to plaintiff the amount of profits, the Court should exercise its discretion in disallowing costs (u), although it may grant the injunction. In such a case the plaintiff will proceed to an account at his peril, running the risk of nothing being found due.

The practice of the Courts as to injunctions, damages, and accounts, will be dealt with hereafter under the head of "Practice."

r *Price's Patent Candle Co. v. Bauwen's Patent Candle Co.,* 1 K. & J. 727.

s *Betts v. Gallais,* L. R., 10 Eq. 392.

(t) *Bacon v. Spottiswood,* 1 Beav. 387.

(u) *Nunn v. D'Albuquerque,* 34 Beav. 595.

CHAPTER XIV.

REVOCATION.

WE have seen that the patentee has his remedy in an action for infringement. The public has also a remedy by petition for revocation.

Sect. 26 of the Act of 1883 provides:—

" (1) The proceeding by **scire facias** to repeal a patent is hereby **abolished.**

" (2) **Revocation** of a patent may be obtained on petition to the Court.

" (3) Every ground on which a patent might, at the commencement of this Act, be repealed by scire facias shall be available by way of defence to an action for infringement, and shall also be a ground of revocation.

" (4) A petition for revocation of a patent may be presented by:—

> " (a) The Attorney-General in England or Ireland, or the Lord Advocate in Scotland.
>
> " (b) Any person authorized by the Attorney-General in England or Ireland, or the Lord Advocate in Scotland.
>
> " (c) Any person alleging that the patent was obtained in fraud of his rights, or of the rights of any person under or through whom he claims.
>
> " (d) Any person alleging that he, or any person under or through whom he claims, was the true inventor of any invention included in the claim of the patentee.

"(e) Any person alleging that he, or any person under or through whom he claims an interest in any trade, business, or manufacture, had publicly manufactured, used, or sold within this realm before the date of the patent anything claimed by the patentee as his invention.

"(5) The plaintiff must deliver with his petition particulars of the objections on which he means to rely, and no evidence shall, except by leave of the Court or a judge, be admitted in proof of any objection of which particulars are not so delivered.

"(6) Particulars delivered may be from time to time amended by leave of the Court or a judge.

"(7) The defendant shall be entitled to bring in and give evidence in support of the patent, and if the plaintiff gives evidence impeaching the validity of the patent the defendant shall be entitled to reply.

"(8) Where a patent has been revoked on the ground of fraud the comptroller may, on the application of the true inventor, made in accordance with the provisions of this Act, grant to him a patent in lieu of and bearing the same date as the date of revocation of the patent so revoked, but the patent so granted shall cease on the expiration of the term for which the revoked patent was granted."

Practically speaking, scire facias had fallen into desuetude before the passing of this Act; other methods of disputing the validity of patents were found, or thought to be, more to the advantage of persons opposing them. It is presumed, however, that the new procedure will find more favour, being simpler, more speedy, and more similar to the ordinary action for infringement than the old action of scire facias.

The grounds upon which a patent may be revoked are similar to those upon which it might have been cancelled by scire facias (*x*). These are in the Fourth Institute said to be: "*Firstly*, when the king by his letters patent doth grant by several letters patent one and the self-same thing to several persons, the former patentee shall have a scire facias to repeal the second patent; *secondly*, when the king granteth anything that is grantable upon a false suggestion, the king by his prerogative jure regio may have a scire facias to repeal his own grant. When the king doth grant anything which by law he cannot grant, he jure regio (for the advancement of justice and right) may have a scire facias to repeal his own letters patents."

And it was held in *Sir Oliver Butler's case* (y), that "where a patent is granted to the prejudice of the subject, the king, of right, is to permit him on his petition to use his name for the repeal of it in a scire facias at the king's suit, and to hinder multiplicity of actions upon the case."

Thus it will be seen that formerly any person might, on behalf of the public, proceed by scire facias to repeal a patent, although security for costs was required. Sub-sect. 4 of sect. 26 has very considerably narrowed and limited this general right.

Practically speaking, any ground which may be set up as a defence to an action for infringement may be employed as a ground for revocation—such as that the person to whom the letters patent were granted was not the first and true inventor, or that the invention was not new or useful, or that it was not true that the invention had not been practised before, or that the said invention did not come within the meaning of the words " a new manufacture," or that the specification was insufficient and did not disclose the nature of the invention.

The petition is to be presented to the High Court of Justice in England or in Ireland. By sect. 109 it is provided: (1) "Proceedings in Scotland for revocation of a patent shall be in the form of an action of *reduction* at the instance of the Lord Advocate, or at the instance of a

(y) Vent. 344.

party having interest with his concurrence, which concurrence may be given on just cause shown only." And in respect to Ireland we find that, by sect. 110, "All parties shall, notwithstanding anything in this Act, have in Ireland their remedies under or in respect of a patent as if the same had been granted to extend to Ireland only."

The general result of these sections seems to be that the proceeding for revocation may be taken in any part of the United Kingdom, and that the question may be dealt with by the Courts of either portion independently; so that it will be possible for letters patent to have been cancelled so far as England is concerned, and yet to continue in force for Scotland and Ireland, and vice versâ.

It will be observed that in sect. 26, sub-sect. 4 (d), " Any person *alleging* that he, &c. . . . . may petition," and by sub-sect. (3), any ground which might be available for scire facias may form the ground for revocation. It is not quite clear whether this section requires the petitioner *to prove* that he was the real inventor, or that the patent was obtained in fraud of his rights, provided he shows some ground upon which the patent should be repealed. It will be observed that there is no provision that the petition should be supported by an affidavit verifying the same. It may be that a petitioner might bring himself within this section by alleging in the petition that he was the inventor or had used the patent prior to the date of the patent, and might then abandon this branch of his case and proceed to prove any one of the other grounds which sub-sect. 3 enables him to rely upon.

We have dealt with the several grounds of revocation in previous chapters, under the title of infringement, and it will be unnecessary to do more here than to refer the reader to them. In a subsequent chapter will be found the practice to be observed in the course of proceedings for revocation.

CHAPTER XV.

INTERNATIONAL AND COLONIAL ARRANGEMENTS.

SECTS. 103 and 104 of the Patents Act, 1883, gives power to the Crown to enter into arrangements with foreign and colonial governments with respect to the mutual protection of patent rights. And, in respect to any foreign State which has entered into such arrangements, any person who has applied for protection for any invention in any such State shall be entitled to a patent for his invention in priority to other applicants, and such patent shall have the same date as the date of the protection obtained in such foreign State, provided that the application for letters patent in this country is made within seven months from the date of the application for protection in such foreign State.

Then follows a provision that a patent granted under such circumstances shall not entitle the patentee to bring actions in respect of infringements which may have happened prior to the date of the acceptance of his final specification.

It will be dangerous for persons to adopt foreign discoveries or inventions before the expiration of the seven months from the date of the foreign application: for, in the event of a patent being applied for under this section, the whole of the capital invested in the adoption of such invention may be found to have been lost. Regard particularly being had to the fact that by sub-sect. 2 any use of the invention in this country within the seven months by any number of persons will in no way invalidate the patent rights subsequently obtained; and that the persons who have used the invention will not have obtained any vested rights to continue the use of the invention.

The application for a patent under this section must be made in the same manner as ordinary applications. The section only applies with respect to such foreign States with respect to which her Majesty shall from time to time, by Order in Council, declare them to be applicable, and so long only in the case of each State as the Order in Council shall continue in force with respect to that State.

Where it is made to appear to her Majesty that the legislature of any British possession has made satisfactory provision for the protection of inventions patented in this country, her Majesty may, by Order in Council, apply the provisions of the last preceding section, with such variations or additions, if any, as to her Majesty in Council may seem fit, to such British possession.

Orders in Council in pursuance of this section shall have the like effect as if the provisions they contain had been incorporated in the Act.

Practice.

CHAPTER I.

ACTION FOR INFRINGEMENT.

An action for infringement is commenced **by writ** issued out of the High Court of Justice.

The writ may be endorsed merely **for damages** for infringement(a), or **for an account** of sales and profits(a), and it may be endorsed for an injunction claiming that the defendant may be restrained from continuing to infringe the patent (a), and for a mandatory order that the defendant may be ordered to deliver up to the plaintiff the articles made in infringement of the patent which are in his custody or power, or in the custody or power of his servants or agents, so that they may be broken up or destroyed (b). The plaintiff may not claim both an account of sales and profits and damages for infringement; the two claims being inconsistent, since, if an account is taken, the infringement is condoned (c).

(a) Form, p. 251.
(b) Form, p. 251. See *Tangye* v. *Stott*, 14 W. R. 386; *Betts* v. *De Vitre*, 34 L. J., Ch. 289.
(c) Per Lord Westbury in *Neilson* v. *Betts*, L. R., 5 H. L. 1. See also *De Vitre* v. *Betts*, L. R., 6 H. L. 321; *Needham* v. *Orley*, 11 W. R. 852. But see *Hills* v. *Evans*, 4 De G. F. & J. 288.

CHAPTER II.

PARTIES.

The parties to the writ may be—**as plaintiffs**, any person for the time being entitled to the benefit of the patent. **An ordinary licensee** cannot be plaintiff, as he is merely licensed to use, and not entitled to any monopoly; but an **exclusive licensee** may sue, using the name of the grantor of the licence in the action (*a*). **An assignee** may sue in his own name, even though he has acquired the right by assignment of two separate moieties, and the party sued is the original grantee (*b*). An assignee of a portion of a patent may be plaintiff (*c*); so, also, it is submitted, may an assignee for a place or part of the United Kingdom, under sect. 36 of the Act of 1883. **Assignees or trustees under a bankruptcy petition** may sue (*d*), and an assignee may maintain an action, although the assignment has not been registered (*e*). One of several joint owners may recover (*f*), **and one of several co-owners** of a patent has a right to sue alone for the recovery of profits due for the use of a patent; and an objection by a defendant that other persons should have been joined as plaintiffs should be made promptly under Rules of Court 1875, Ord. XVI. rules 13 and 14, and may not be postponed till the hearing, where no impediment exists to raising the objection at once (*g*).

(*a* *Renard* v. *Levinstein*, 2 H. & M. 628.

b *Walton* v. *Lavater*, 8 C. B., N. S. 162; *Electric Telegraph Co.* v. *Brett*, 10 C. B. 838.

c *Dunnicliff* v. *Mallett*, 7 C. B., N. S. 209.

d *Bloxam* v. *Elsee*, 6 B. & C. 169.

e *Hassall* v. *Wright*, L. R., 10 Eq. 509.

f *Davenport* v. *Richards*, 3 L. T. R., N. S. 503.

g *Shehan* v. *Great Eastern Rail. Co.*, L. R., 16 Ch. D. 59.

A mere agent to introduce, sell, and grant licences for the use of a foreign patent in this country is not entitled to take proceedings to restrain infringement (*h*).

As defendants, all persons physically infringing, or threatening to infringe, the patent may be joined. An **architect,** specifying the use of a patent, should not be joined, but the **contractor** doing the work may (*i*). The **directors of a company** may be sued in their personal capacity for an infringement by the servants of the company (*k*). Where the principals are out of the jurisdiction, the court will restrain the manager or workmen (*l*).

(*h*) *Adams* v. *North British Rail. Co.*, 29 L. T. R., N. S. 367.

(*i*) *Denley* v. *Blore*, 38 Lond. Jour. 224.

(*k*) *Betts* v. *De Vitre*, L. R., 3 Ch. 441.

(*l*) See *Betts* v. *Neilson*, 6 N. R. 221.

CHAPTER III.

INTERLOCUTORY INJUNCTION.

An interlocutory injunction may be granted **ex parte**, after the issue of the writ, and before service. An ex parte injunction will only be granted when it can be shown that great injury will accrue to the plaintiff by delay, and when he can clearly establish his title and the fact of infringement (*a*). Interlocutory injunctions are always upon terms as to damages (*b*).

Notice of motion having been given, an interlocutory injunction will be granted after appearance, or with leave, upon notice of motion to be served with the writ.

By sect. 25 of the Judicature Act, 1873, sub-sect. 8: " A mandamus or an injunction may be granted, or a receiver appointed by an interlocutory order of the Court, in all cases in which it shall appear to the Court to be just or convenient that such order should be made; and any such order may be made either unconditionally or upon such terms and conditions as the Court shall think just; and if an injunction is asked either before, or at, or after the hearing of any cause or matter to prevent any threatened or apprehended waste or trespass, such injunction may be granted if the Court shall think fit, whether the person against whom such injunction is sought is or is not in possession under any claim of title or otherwise, or (if out of possession) does or does not claim a right to do the act sought to be restrained under

---

(*a*) *Gardner* v. *Broadbent*, 2 Jur., N. S. 1011.

(*b*) *Graham* v. *Campbell*, L. R., 7 Ch. D. 190.

any colour of title; and whether the estates claimed by both or either of the parties are legal or equitable."

Ord. L. rule 6, directs that: "An application for an order under sect. 25, sub-sect. 8, or under rules 2 or 3 of this order, may be made to the Court or a judge by any party. If the application be by the plaintiff for an order under the said sub-sect 8, it may be made either ex parte or with notice . . . . ."

A master of the Queen's Bench Division has no power to grant an injunction. Order LIV. Rule 12.

An interlocutory injunction will only be granted when there is a fair **primâ facie case of validity.** This may be made out by long undisturbed enjoyment, or by the question having been previously tried in a court of law (c), or where the defendant has admitted the validity of the patent (d), or is so placed in his relationship to the patentee as to be estopped from denying its validity (e).

The injunction may be **refused upon terms** that the defendant keep an account *pendente lite* (f). But it is open to the plaintiff to show that if he succeeds the defendant's position is such that he will be unable to pay the damages or the amount of the account (g).

The evidence to be used upon an application for an interlocutory injunction is upon affidavit.

The affidavit should clearly point out in what the alleged infringement consists (h). If the plaintiff is the

(c) *Dudgeon* v. *Thompson*, 22 W. R. 464; *Plimpton* v. *Malcolmson*, L. R. 20 Eq. 37; *Collard* v. *Allison*, 4 My. & Cr. 433; *Stephens* v. *Keating*, 2 Ph. 335; *Bridson* v. *McAlpine*, 8 Beav. 229; *Bridson* v. *Benecke*, 12 Beav. 1, and cases quoted *supra*, under the head "Injunction."

(d) *Dircks* v. *Mellor*, 26 Lond. Jour. 268.

(e) *Clarke* v. *Fergusson*, 1 Giff. 184.

(f) *Jones* v. *Pearce*, 2 Coop. 58; *Mitchell* v. *Barker*, 39 Lond. Jour. 531; *Muntz* v. *Grenfell*, 2 Coop. 61 (n.).

(g) *Newall* v. *Wilson*, 2 De G., M. & G. 282.

(h) *Hill* v. *Thompson*, 3 Mer. 624; *Betts* v. *Willmott*, L. R., 6 Ch. 239.

first inventor, he must distinctly swear to the fact, as also to the novelty and utility of the invention, and to the due filing of a sufficient specification (*i*). If the plaintiff is an assignee he must swear to the best of his belief (*k*). The affidavits in either case must state the facts as at the time of swearing, and it is not sufficient to swear that the invention was believed to be new when the patent was granted (*l*). An injunction granted prior to statement of claim will be dissolved if the statement of claim when delivered does not agree with the affidavits upon which the injunction was granted (*m*).

Forms of injunction upon undertaking as to damages (*n*), and of order refusing injunction upon terms (*o*), will be found in the Appendix.

(*i*) *Hill* v. *Thompson*, 3 Mer. 624; *Sturtz* v. *De La Rue* (per Lord Lyndhurst), 5 Russ. 329; *Whitton* v. *Jennings*, 1 Dr. & S. 110.

(*k*) *Gardner* v. *Broadbent*, 2 Jur., N. S. 1011.

(*l*) *Hill* v. *Thompson*, 3 Mer. 624.

(*m*) *Stocking* v. *Llewellyn*, 3 L. T. Rep. 33.

(*n*) Form 5.

(*o*) Form 6.

CHAPTER IV.

STATEMENT OF CLAIM.

The Rules of Court of 1883 have rendered the form of pleadings of less importance than hitherto. Ord. XIX. rule 26, provides: "No technical objection shall be raised to any pleading on the ground of any alleged want of form;" but by rule 27 the power of the Court to strike out pleadings on the grounds that they are unnecessary, scandalous, or embarrassing, is preserved.

Ord. XIX. rule 4, requires all material facts to be pleaded, and prohibits the pleading of evidence. Rule 5 is as follows:—" The forms in Appendices (C., D., and E.), when applicable, and when they are not applicable forms of the like character, as near as may be, shall be used for all pleadings, and where such forms are applicable and sufficient, any longer forms shall be deemed prolix, and the costs occasioned by such prolixity shall be disallowed to or borne by the party so using the same, as the case may be."

The forms mentioned relate to pleadings in an action for the infringement of a patent, but there is no provision made for the case where infringement has only been threatened, nor for the case when a mandatory order or an account of sales and profits is required (*a*).

It will be observed that the statement of claim in patent cases, which is rendered obligatory by Ord. XIX. rule 5, contains no allegation as to the matters going to constitute the validity of the patent, nor does it give the date, time, or place of the infringement; but it refers to the particulars of breaches which are delivered "herewith."

(*a*) See Form, p. 258.

CHAPTER V.

PARTICULARS OF BREACHES.

Particulars of breaches were required to be delivered in every action for the infringement of a patent by sect. 41 of the Patent Law Amendment Act, 1852; and now by sect. 29 (1) of the Act of 1883, it is provided:—
"In an action for infringement of a patent the plaintiff must deliver with his statement of claim, or by order of the Court or a judge at any subsequent time, particulars of the breaches complained of; (4) at the hearing no evidence shall, except by leave of the Court or a judge, be admitted in proof of any alleged infringement, or objection of which particulars are not so delivered; (5) particulars delivered may be from time to time amended by leave of the Court or a judge."

Particulars of breaches are particulars of the times, places, occasions, and manner in which the plaintiff says the defendant has infringed his letters patent. The **defendant must have full, fair, and distinct notice of the case to be made against him** (*a*). In *Batty* v. *Kynock* (*b*), Sir James Bacon, V.-C., said: "All that is required and provided by the Patent Law Amendment Act, 1852, which has made no alteration in the practice to be observed in these cases, is that the defendants shall not be taken by surprise, and it is the duty of the judge to take care that by the particulars of breaches they shall have full and fair notice of the case that they will have to meet."

a) *Needham* v. *Oxley*, 1 H. & M. 248. *b* L. R., 19 Eq. at p. 231.

It had undoubtedly prior to the passing of the Patent Law Amendment Act, 1852, been the practice of the Courts to compel plaintiffs to give particulars of breaches, and the cases which were then decided as to the sufficiency of particulars are applicable now; for then, as now, the object was that the defendant should be warned with reasonable certainty of the case that was to be made against him.

Particulars stated that "A particular improvement had been used by A. B. (giving names and addresses) *and divers other people within this kingdom and elsewhere.*" The judges struck out the words "*and divers other people*" (c).

The words "carriage builders generally throughout Great Britain" does not sufficiently comply with the statute, nor do the words "used and applied by carriage builders generally;" and the words "in or near London, in or near Liverpool, &c., and in or near various other of the principal towns of Great Britain," are too general (d).

Vice-Chancellor Sir W. Page-Wood said in *Morgan* v. *Fuller* (d): "An allegation of general user does not of course admit of being met precisely . . . . . The real object is to secure to both parties a fair trial" (e).

"And the plaintiffs state these particular instances by way of example only, and not so as to preclude them from proving any of the infringements mentioned in the former particulars of breaches." This clause was ordered to be struck out of the amended particulars (f).

If the particulars delivered are too general the defendant should apply **for further and better particulars.**

(c) *Fisher* v. *Dewick*, 1 Web. P. C. 551 (n.)

(d) *Morgan* v. *Fuller*, L. R., 2 Eq. 297.

(e) See also *Jones* v. *Berger*, 1 Web. P. C. 544; *Holland* v.

Fox, 1 C. L. R. 440; *Palmer* v. *Cooper*, 9 Ex. 231.

(f) *The Patent Type Founding Co.* v. *Richards*, 2 L. T. R., N. S. 359.

If at the trial evidence is tendered which comes within the literal meaning of the particulars it will be admitted, notwithstanding that the particulars are too general, as **the defendant should have objected to the particulars,** and not wait until the trial to take his objection (*g*).

The plaintiff having delivered particulars of breaches specifying certain sales by the defendant of rollers, and in particular to Shaw and Smith, the defendant, in answer to interrogatories, admitted sales to Hirst. Fry, J., in giving judgment, said : " In this case I think I must admit the evidence tendered in respect of Hirst's case. It is said that in respect of those cases which are not mentioned by name in the particulars of breaches, the plaintiff cannot give evidence. It may be that the particulars were not sufficient, or tended to embarrass. But the defendant did not apply for amended particulars, according to the case of *Hall* v. *Bolland*. It appears to me I have to inquire what is the meaning of the particulars. I find the case of Hirst is within the literal meaning of the particulars. If I had found that the case of Hirst was likely to create surprise, or likely to introduce any point not raised by *Smith's* or *Shaw's* case, I should probably have given an opportunity to the defendant to bring fresh evidence. I have asked whether there is any witness not here whom the defendants would desire to bring in respect of Hirst's case, and have received no satisfactory answer on that point, and must assume there is no such witness (*h*)."

In *Flower* v. *Lloyd* (*i*), Field, J., said : " I cannot follow the cases which have been cited ; we have advanced in our ideas since they were decided (*k*). If the

---

g *Hall* v. *Bolland*, 25 L. J., Ex. 301.

h *Sykes* v. *Howarth*, L. R., 12 Eq. 826.

i Solicitors' Journal, 1876, p. 860.

k *Bentley* v. *Keighley*, 7 M. & G. 652 ; *Palmer* v. *Wagstaff*, 8 Ex. 840.

defendants know that their processes have been used by other persons in London and Birmingham, besides those specified, they must know the persons by whom they have been used, and must give more specific information. I do not say that they need give the name and address of every such person, but they must give fair information. If they can give no further information, the words in question are useless, and too indefinite, and must be struck out."

When the patent consists of two or more processes, or distinct and separable inventions, **particulars of breaches should distinguish which of the processes** it is alleged has been infringed, and should particularly indicate what parts of the defendant's machine or manufactured article is claimed to constitute an infringement; but when the process was one entire invention, the Court declined to compel the plaintiff to point out the particular parts of the specification which were alleged to be infringed. Jervis, C. J., said: "If the two processes described in the specification are wholly distinct from each other, and the defendant's process may be an infringement of the one and not of the other, he ought to have better particulars; but if the whole is substantially one process, he is not entitled to them . . . We must not make the particulars more complicated than the specification (*l*)."

Particulars of breaches, as we have seen, may also be ordered in actions which are not strictly actions for the infringement of patents; this is done under the ordinary jurisdiction of the Court (*m*). In an action charging that the defendant falsely and maliciously wrote and told persons who had bought certain machines of the plaintiff's that the machines were infringements of his, the defendant's patents, the defendant having pleaded not guilty,

(*l*) *Talbot* v. *La Roche*, 15 C. B. 310. See also *The Electric Telegraph Co.* v. *Nott*, 4 C. B. 462.

(*m*) *Perry* v. *Mitchell*, 1 Web. P. C. 269.

the Court ordered the defendant to deliver particulars, showing in what parts the plaintiff's machines were an infringement of the defendant's patents, and pointing out by reference to the page and line of the defendant's specifications, which part of the inventions therein described he alleged to have been infringed (*n*).

(*n*) *Wren and others* v. *Weild*, L. R., 4 Q. B. 213.

CHAPTER VI.

STATEMENT OF DEFENCE.

The statement of defence in patent actions is now, under the Rules of the Supreme Court, 1883, a very brief and concise document, giving no particulars or details whatever, and remitting the plaintiff to the particulars of objections, and the answers to the interrogatories for information as to the case which is to be made against him. Under Ord. XIX. rule 5, the form given in Appendix (D.) sect. VI. is rendered obligatory. That form merely gives headings of defence which is all that is to be allowed; for instance:—"(1) That the defendant did not infringe the patent; (2) The invention was not new; (3) The plaintiff was not the first and true inventor; (4) The invention was not useful; (5) The patent was not assigned to the plaintiff." And to these might be added:—That the title did not disclose the nature of the invention (*a*); that the title, the provisional specification, and the complete specification, or any two of them, did not substantially refer to the same invention (*b*); that the specification was not sufficient (*c*); that the claim in the specification was not sufficient to distinguish what was new from what was old (*d*); that the patent was obtained in fraud of the defendant, as, for instance, when a person employed to carry out or assist in experiments, applies for letters patent himself, or where the patentee has obtained the invention from the confidence of the defendant.

It will be observed that any one of these defences will

(*a*) Ante, pp. 55—59. (*c*) Ante, p. 64.
(*b*) Ante, pp. 55, 58. (*d*) Ante, pp. 83—85.

be sufficient to constitute a complete defence to the action; and that the greater portion of them are of a nature to require elaborate and costly evidence to prove or disprove them. Too much care cannot, therefore, be taken in preparing a statement of defence to avoid setting up defences which it is not expected will be satisfactorily proved at the trial, regard being had to the provisions of the Rules of 1883 as to costs; otherwise, even if the defendant succeeds in the action, he may be mulcted in heavy costs to the other side.

CHAPTER VII.

PARTICULARS OF OBJECTIONS.

SECT. 21, sub-sect. (2) of the Act of 1883, provides:— "The defendant must deliver with his statement of defence, or by order of the Court, or a judge at any subsequent time, particulars of any objections on which he relies in support thereof; (3) If the defendant disputes the validity of the patent, the particulars, delivered by him, must state on what grounds he disputes it; and if one of those grounds is want of novelty, must state the time and place of the previous publication or user alleged by him; (4) At the hearing, no evidence shall, except by leave of the Court, or a judge, be admitted in proof of any alleged infringement or objection, of which particulars are not so delivered; (5) Particulars delivered, may be from time to time amended, by leave of the Court, or a judge; (6) On taxation of costs, regard shall be had to the particulars delivered by the plaintiff and by the defendant; and they respectively shall not be allowed any costs in respect of any particulars delivered by them, unless the same is certified by the Court or a judge to have been proven, or to have been reasonable and proper, without regard to the general costs of the case."

This last sub-section will make it imperative upon the plaintiff or defendant, who has succeeded in an action, to obtain a certificate from the judge who has tried the case that each one of the particulars delivered by him has been proved or was reasonable and proper. It will be observed that the words of the section are "*shall not be allowed any costs;*" this leaves no discretion in the Court except as to certifying.

Ord. XIX. rule 6, of the Rules of the Supreme Court, 1883, provides: "In all cases in which the party pleading relies on any misrepresentation, fraud, breach of trust, wilful default, or undue influence, and in all other cases in which particulars may be necessary beyond such as are exemplified in the forms aforesaid, particulars (with dates and items if necessary) shall be stated in the pleading: provided that if the particulars be of debt, expenses, or damages, and exceed three folios, the fact must be so stated, and a reference to full particulars already delivered or to be delivered with the pleading."

It is not easy to reconcile the practice under this rule with the language of the 29th sect. of the Patent Act, or, indeed, with the form of defence given in the form to the rules quoted above. Ord. XIX. rule 6, provides that particulars shall be incorporated with the pleading; on the other hand, the form and the Patent Act seem to indicate a separate document. Hitherto the practice has been to deliver a separate document, and it is apprehended that when the balance of convenience is considered the Courts will hold that in respect of a patent action the practice has remained unchanged.

The particulars of objection may allege that the invention was not new at the date of the patent. We have on a previous occasion intimated that it is possible that sections of the Act of 1883 may be construed as admitting objections on the ground of want of novelty, on the ground of prior user, or publication in any portion of the world. Such a change would revolutionise the law of patents.

Prior user.—The objection on the ground of prior user **must state the time and place** when such user occurred; but it will be observed that **the persons by whom used** is not mentioned in sub-sect. (3). The Act, however, does not direct that such particulars shall not be required. The Patent Law Amendment Act, 1852, sect. 41, required that the place of prior user should be given, and was silent as to times or persons. Notwithstanding this, in *Palmer* v. *Cooper* (a), Baron Alderson went even further than to require the names of the persons who had used the invention, and the **present addresses** of such persons were ordered to be given, " As otherwise the plaintiff would not know where to go for his evidence." The object of particulars is, in the words of Tindal, C. J. (b), " Not, indeed, to limit the defence, but to limit the expense of the parties, and more particularly to prevent the patentee from being upset by some unexpected turn of the evidence. Under the fifth section (5 & 6 Will. 4, c. 83), therefore, it was intended that the defendant should give an honest statement of the objections on which he means to rely." In *Palmer* v. *Cooper* (a), Parke, B., said : " The defendant's particulars ought to give the plaintiff such information as will enable him to make the necessary inquiries at the place named."

It will be evident, therefore, that there are cases where to omit giving the names and addresses of the persons who are alleged to have anticipated the invention would be to supply the plaintiff with objections which would be practically useless.

There are cases where the names and addresses have been refused. In *Carpenter* v. *Smith* (c), the objections stated that the invention had been used by " the defendant and divers persons." It was refused to order the defendant

(a) 9 Ex. 231. See also *Bulnois* v. *Mackenzie*, 4 Bing. N. C. 432 ; *Galloway* v. *Bleaden*, 1 Web. P. C. 268 (n.)

(b) *Fisher* v. *Dewick*, 1 Web. P. C. 267.

(c) 1 Web. P. C. 268 (n.)

either to give the names and addresses of the "divers persons," or to have those words struck out.

It may be argued that the reason of such refusal was that a disclosure was required of the witnesses and case of the defendant. It is obvious that, although it is a recognized principle that one litigant shall not be permitted to inquire as to what witnesses the other is about to call at the trial, still that by far the more important principle is that neither party should be taken by surprise, and that the plaintiff should have a fair opportunity of critically examining every alleged anticipation which may be attempted to be established against him.

It does not of necessity follow that persons who have anticipated the invention should be the only and necessary witnesses of such anticipation. On the whole, therefore, it is submitted that names and addresses of such persons should be given in particulars of objections.

General words are inadmissible in particulars; for instance, expressions such as "and divers other people" (d), and "Inter alia at Sheffield, Birmingham, and London" (e). But in *Bentley* v. *Keighley* (f), Mr. Justice Maule, under special circumstances, allowed the words "and others" to be sufficient.

When the allegation of the defendant is that the patent is void by reason of a portion of the described invention being old, the particulars should clearly distinguish which part is alleged to be old, as well as the times and places of prior user (g).

Evidence will be admitted at the trial, provided the language of the particulars of objections is large enough to admit it; for instance, if the plaintiff has allowed such

---

d *Fisher* v. *Dewick*, 1 Web. P. C. 551 n; *Galloway* v. *Bleaden*, 1 Web. P. C. 268 n

(e) *Holland* v. *Fox*, 1 C. L. R. 440.

f 7 M. & G. 652. See also *Jones* v. *Berger*, 1 Web. P. C. 549.

(g) *Heath* v. *Unwin*, 10 M. & W. 684; *Russel* v. *Ledsam*, 11 M. & W. 647.

words as "and elsewhere" to stand until the trial, the defendant will be allowed to give evidence of prior user **anywhere** (*h*). The proper course for the plaintiff to take should the defendant deliver vague particulars is to issue a summons before a judge in chambers for further and better particulars, or, in the alternative, to have the objectionable words struck out (*i*).

In *Sugg* v. *Silber* (*k*), Mellish, L. J., said: "The authorities cited by Mr. Cave were cases where objections had been taken to the notices of objection at the time when they were delivered, and further and better particulars were asked for. In my opinion there is a very large difference between a case where a judge has been applied to and has ordered further particulars in order to state an objection more specifically, and a case where at the trial the plaintiff asserts that the defendant ought to be prevented from availing himself of an objection. It is perfectly obvious that, if Mr. Cave was right in saying that the two questions are the same, and that wherever the Court would order further particulars because the objection had not been particularly specified, it would also hold that the party was precluded from raising it at the trial. Nobody would be foolish enough to apply to a judge for further particulars."

Although the objections did not specifically point out that the invention consisted of several claims, yet the objection that the invention is not the subject-matter of a patent, is sufficient to open the objection that the whole, or some particular part of it, is not the subject-matter of a patent, and that consequently the patent is bad (*l*).

The defendant may, by leave of a Court or judge,

(*h*) *Hull* v. *Bolland*, 25 L. J., Ex. 304; *Sykes* v. *Howarth*, L. R., 12 Eq. 826.
(*i*) *Fisher* v. *Dewick*, 1 Web. P. C. 551 (n.); *Carpenter* v. *Walker*, 1 Web. P. C. 268 (n.); *Holland* v.
Fox, 1 C. L. R. 440.
(*k*) L. R., 2 Q. B. D. 495.
(*l*) See also *Hull* v. *Bolland*, 1 H. & N. 134; and *Neilson* v. *Harford*, 1 Web. P. C. 331.

from time to time, and upon such terms as under the circumstances of the case may be deemed equitable, amend the particulars which he has delivered; this is done by summons.

Page-Wood, V.-C., in *Penn* v. *Bibby* (m), permitted a defendant in his amended particulars, to preface his statement of the specific instances of alleged prior user, with the words " amongst other instances " in order to give him an opportunity to apply for leave to re-amend by inserting any further instances of prior user which he might discover.

The terms upon which amendment is permitted are, first, that the plaintiff should be at liberty, if he pleases, to discontinue the action, and to be in the same position as to costs, as if the proposed amended particulars had been delivered in the first instance (n), and, secondly, that the defendant should be put under such terms as to costs, as to the judge or Court seem just. The particulars of objections give notice to the plaintiff of the case which is to be made against him; thereupon he may discontinue or not, as he pleases, paying defendant's costs. The defendant should not be permitted to keep back his most salient objections, and so to entice the plaintiff to proceed and incur costs, and then to amend his particulars at the last moment.

Forms of order for further particulars will be found in the Appendix (o).

The defendant will not be allowed at the hearing of the action to introduce **evidence of prior user, not disclosed in the particulars of objection,** although such evidence may have only come to his knowledge since the delivery of the particulars of objection. His proper

(m) L. R., 1 Eq. 548.

n *Baird* v. *Moule's Patent Earth Closet Co.*, L. R., 17 Ch. D. 139 (n.); also *Aceling* v. *Maclaren*, same page; also *Edison Telephone Co.* v. *India Rubber Co.*, L. R., 17 Ch. D. 137.

(o) Pages 259, 261.

course is to obtain leave by summons or by serving short notice of motion **for leave to amend,** when an order will be made upon the terms mentioned above; and it is submitted with an added term to delay the trial should it appear just that the plaintiff should have time to investigate the new evidence (*p*).

Objections on the ground of **prior publication** stand very much upon the same footing as those on the ground of prior user.

If the prior publication is alleged to be in books or newspapers, the plaintiff is entitled to be told the name of the book or newspaper, and to give such details of the books or newspapers as will enable them to be found and identified by the plaintiff (*q*).

In *Plimpton* v. *Spiller* (*r*), the particulars were—"before the date of the alleged letters patent the alleged invention had been published in England in the 'Commissioners of Patents Journal,' of the 6th February, 1863, and in the 'Scientific American,' of the 24th January, 1863, and in drawings and sketches deposited in the Patent Office library, in July, 1865." Mr. Justice Field directed that the defendant should amend his particulars by stating the **date of the American patent,** and in whose name it had been granted. And also by giving the **pages of the publications** mentioned, but not the lines. And also by giving such written details as would enable the drawings mentioned to be identified, and to state whether the drawings were or were not contained in books, and what books. Notice of objections, on the ground that the grantee of the letters patent was not the first and true inventor, does not stand upon the

(*p*) *Daw* v. *Eley,* L. R., 1 Eq. 38.
(*q*) *Jones* v. *Berger,* 5 M. & G. 208; *Palmer* v. *Cooper,* 9 Ex. 231.
(*r*) 20 Solicitors' Journal, 1876, p. 860. See also *Flower* v. *Lloyd,* same reference.

same footing as objections on the ground of prior user or publication. Sect. 29, sub-sect. 3, does not require the defendant to state more than generally on what grounds he objects, and a statement that his objection is that the **plaintiff was not the true inventor**, that is, that the consideration did not move from him, will be sufficient, care being taken to distinguish this objection from that of prior user or publication.

When the objection is, that the grantee was not the true inventor, the Court will not require the defendant to say who was the true inventor (s). The fact upon which the objection is based, is the want of consideration, not the fact of some one having performed the invention before. The performance of the invention by some one else before the patent would not, of necessity, invalidate the patent. As, for instance, if it were done in secret; but if the invention was communicated to the grantee, the patent would be void for want of consideration. Now the foundation of the objection is, the fact of that communication, and the knowledge of this, and the time and place of it, might be within the patentee's knowledge only, and might not be extracted from him until in the witness box.

The objection that the specification is insufficient is enough without explaining in what way it is insufficient (t). A litigant could scarcely be required to argue his case on paper before he went into Court, and the sufficiency or insufficiency of a specification is to a great extent a matter of mere argument.

In *Jones* v. *Berger* (u), it was held that objections that the specification " did not sufficiently distinguish between what was old and what was new," and that the

---

s *Russell* v. *Ledsam*, 11 M. & W. 647. But see *Jones* v. *Berger*, 1 Web. P. C. 544.

t *Heath* v. *Unwin*, 10 M. & W. 687.

(u) 5 M. & G. 208.

inventor "did not disclose the most beneficial method with which he was then acquainted of practising his said invention," were sufficient.

We have seen that Ord. XIX. rule 6, requires **particulars in case of fraud** to be delivered with the statement of defence.

Fraud is a valid objection to a patent. The practice of the Court is to require accurate and detailed particulars of any fraudulent acts alleged. The species of "fraud, covin, or misrepresentation" should be given (x).

(x) *Russell* v. *Ledsam*, 11 M. & W. 647.

CHAPTER VIII.

INTERROGATORIES.

Ord. XXXI. rule 1, of the Rules of the Supreme Court, 1883, provides that either party to an action, with leave of the Court or a judge, may interrogate the other party.

Interrogatories must be relevant to the issue, and will not be allowed to be used for the purpose of cross-examination. Since it is not possible to say precisely what the issues between the parties are before the statement of defence is delivered, neither party, except under special circumstances, will be allowed to interrogate until that stage of the action has been reached (*a*).

Rule 26 provides that 5*l*. should be brought into Court by the party desiring to interrogate before he shall be at liberty to do so.

The general rules as to interrogatories in ordinary actions apply equally to actions for infringement.

The plaintiff may interrogate the defendant, and the defendant must **answer as to what infringement** he has been guilty of; and he must disclose, if asked, the names and addresses of all persons, whether in England or abroad, from whom he may have received money for the use of articles alleged to be made in infringement of the patent (*b*).

Where a defendant alleged that his process was secret, he was bound to answer whether he used the materials mentioned in the specification, and whether he used any additional materials, but not to disclose the proportions

---

(*a*) *Mercier* v. *Cotton*, L. R., 1 Q. B. D. 112.

(*b*) *Crossley* v. *Stewart*, 1 N. R. 426; *Howe* v. *McKernan*, 30 Beav. 516.

in which he used the specified materials, or what the additional materials were (c).

When there is nothing to show that the defendant has infringed the patent, and he has denied on oath having infringed the patent, the plaintiff will not be permitted to interrogate as to the articles made and sold by the defendant, there being nothing to show that the articles sold infringe the patent. If *Lea* v. *Saxby* (d) be read, this proposition will be seen to follow.

Crossly v. *Tomey* (e) was an action to restrain infringement. The defendant in interrogatories was required to state whether he was not making articles in all respects identical with those of the plaintiff, and to set forth in what respects they differed, and by what process they were made. It was held that the defendant, who alleged prior user by himself and others, had sufficiently answered by stating that, save so far as the articles manufactured by him before the date of the patent were similar to those of the plaintiff, the articles he now made differed from those made by the plaintiff, but he could not show in what they differed without ocular demonstration. It was also held in this case, that when the defendant alleged prior user by other persons, he was bound to set forth the names of some of those persons. In the argument of this case, it appears that some confusion existed as to the necessary requirements of particulars of objections and answers to interrogatories. It must be remembered that the answers to interrogatories are on oath, and it can never have been intended by the legislature, when the stringent requirements of particulars of objections were created, that the defendant should be bound to swear to these particulars; the penalty upon a defendant giving particulars, which at the trial he is not prepared to prove, is that he is mulcted in costs. But

(c) *Renard* v. *Levinstein*, 3 N. R. 665.
(d) 32 L. T. R., N. S. 731.
(e) L. R., 2 Ch. D. 533.

it was never intended that he should be prohibited from giving particulars, which, although based upon mere suspicion, he may hope to prove at the trial, perhaps out of the plaintiff's own mouth (*f*).

In *Bovill* v. *Smith* (*g*), the following interrogatory was disallowed, "Does not the defendant allege that the plaintiff's invention was publicly used within this realm before the date of the plaintiff's patent? Set forth particularly when, and in what place or places, and in what manner, does the defendant allege that the plaintiff's invention, or any or what part thereof, was publicly used within this realm before the date of the plaintiff's patent." Sir W. Page-Wood, V.-C., said that the plaintiff was not entitled to enquire generally into the way in which the defendant shaped his case in order to find out whether some of the persons alleged by him to have used the process before the date of the patent, were the persons against whom the plaintiff had succeeded in other suits, though he might have asked if the process was the same as that used by A. B., or any one person specifically named, who had been a defendant in some former suit.

A defendant who submits to answer must answer fully: he cannot, by denying the plaintiff's title, escape answering. Discovery of title deeds and of professional communications form an exception. The plaintiff and defendant had both patents for making gelatine; the plaintiff interrogated as to the article manufactured by the defendant, and as to the names and addresses of the customers, and as to prices and profits. The defendant denied all infringement. He said he had made his article according to his own, and not according to the plaintiff's, patent, and he declined to give an account of such article. Held, that notwithstanding his denial, he

---

f. See, however, *Finnegan* v. *James*, as to answers to interrogatories, L. R., 19 Eq. 72.

g L. R., 2 Eq. 459. See also *Daw* v. *Eley*, 2 H. & M. 725.

was bound to do so (*h*). It is doubtful whether this case would be followed now, for it is difficult to understand how the question could be relevant to the issue. It might be relevant after judgment, but before judgment the issue is, infringement or no infringement. The names of the customers could not bear upon this question.

After trial, and in pursuance of the terms of the judgment, if the plaintiff has been successful he is entitled to interrogate the defendant, or to require that the defendant "should make and file an affidavit stating what machines of the same construction as that supplied by him to A. or B., including such machines as are in his possession or power," see *Seton*, 4*th ed.*, *p.* 352. The answer or affidavit of the defendant must be complete. In *Murray* v. *Clayton* (*i*), a patentee of improvements in brick-cutting machines, who was a manufacturer of the machines by an agent at the agents' works and not a licensor, having obtained a perpetual injunction against the defendants, (who were also manufacturers of brick cutting machines), from infringement, the defendants were ordered to file an affidavit stating the number of machines made by them since the date of the patent, and the names and addresses of the persons to whom the same had been sold, and of the agents concerned in the transactions. Upon motion to vary the order, it was held, that the plaintiff was entitled to have discovery of the names and addresses of the purchasers, but not of the agents concerned, there being nothing to show that any agents had been employed.

In answering interrogatories filed by a defendant for the examination of the plaintiff, the general rule applies that he who is bound to answer must answer fully (*k*).

Interrogatories for the examination of a plaintiff are

(*h*) *Swinborne* v. *Nelson*, 16 Beav. 416.

(*i*) L. R., 15 Eq. 115.

(*k*) *Hoffman* v. *Posthill*, L. R., 4 Ch. App. Cas. 673.

on a different footing from those for the examination of a defendant in this respect, that a plaintiff is not entitled to discovery of the defendant's case, but a defendant may ask any questions tending to destroy the plaintiff's claim (*l*).

In determining whether a question is one of fact, and, therefore, to be answered, it makes no difference that it is asked with reference to a written document (*l*).

A defendant in a suit for infringement of a patent in order to prove that there was no novelty in the plaintiff's patent, interrogated the plaintiff as to the inventions described in the specifications of various patents, and asked him to show in what respects they differed from his. The plaintiff declined to answer these interrogatories on the ground that the questions were **not questions of fact, and that they related to the plaintiff's case**; the defendant excepted to the answer, and the exceptions were allowed (*l*).

A plaintiff in a patent suit was required by interrogatories to set out a correspondence between himself and a third party, and also to state the particulars of the infringement of his patent on which he relied. He refused to answer these questions on the ground that the defendant might obtain an order in chambers to inspect the correspondence; and that he had sufficiently set out the particulars of the infringement in his bill. These answers were held to be sufficient (*l*).

We have set out the effect of this case at length, because it is founded upon and exemplifies in many ways the principle upon which a defendant may examine a plaintiff. Lord Justice Giffard, in giving judgment, said, " As regards the case of *Daw* v. *Eley* (*m*), it must be always remembered that that was the case of a plaintiff exhibiting interrogatories to a defendant, and it

---

(*l*) *Hoffman* v. *Pothill*, L. R. 1 Ch. App. Cas. 673. (*m*) 2 H. & M. 725.

was there held that the plaintiff could not call on the defendant to set forth the particulars of his defence. But when you come to the case of a defendant asking questions of a plaintiff, it is a very different thing. It is the defendant's business to destroy the plaintiff's case, and there the defendant has a right to ask all questions which are fairly calculated to show that the patent is not a good patent, or that what he alleges to be an infringement is not an infringement." Lord Justice Selwyn had said, "Our decision in this case will leave it entirely within the power of the learned Vice-Chancellor to order that all the costs occasioned by the interrogatories, the answer, the exceptions, the hearing the exceptions before him, and the hearing of this appeal, shall be dealt with as he, in his discretion, shall think fit; and if it shall appear that the power which the Court, for the purpose of justice and discovery, gives to the parties to administer interrogatories to each other has been abused, I have no doubt the learned Vice-Chancellor will take care that justice shall be done, and will make the party who is to blame pay all the costs of the improper exercise of this power."

CHAPTER IX.

INSPECTION.

Sect. 30 of the Patents, &c. Act of 1883, provides : " In an action for infringement of a patent, the Court or a judge may, on the application of either party, make such order for an injunction, **inspection**, or account, and impose such terms and give such directions respecting the same and the proceedings thereon, as the Court or a judge may see fit."

The power to order an inspection was always assumed by the Courts; in *Bovill* v. *Moore* (a), Lord Eldon said: "There is no use in this Court directing an action to be brought, if it does not possess the power to have the action properly tried. The plaintiff has a patent for a machine used in making bobbin lace. The defendant is a manufacturer of that article; and, as the plaintiff alleges, he is making it with a machine constructed upon the principle of the machine protected by the plaintiff's patent. Now the manufactory of the defendant is carried on in secret. The machine which the defendant uses to make bobbin lace, and which the plaintiff alleges to be a piracy of his invention, is in the defendant's own possession, and no one can have access to it without his permission. The evidence of the piracy, at present, is the bobbin lace made by the defendant. The witnesses say that this lace must have been manufactured by the plaintiff's machine, or by a machine similar to it in principle. This is obviously in a great measure conjecture. No Court can be content with evidence of this description. There must be an order that plaintiff's

a 2 Coop. C. P. 56 (n.)

witnesses shall be permitted before the trial of the action to inspect the defendant's machine, and to see it work."

The object which the Court has in view in all cases where an inspection is permitted, is to ensure that **the true facts of the case shall be carefully sifted**; but at the same time the Court will take care that the process of the law is not abused, and that an action for infringement shall not be made a means and lever for the discovery of other person's secrets.

The Court requires before granting an order for inspection that a strong primâ facie case shall be made out of infringement (*b*). And when the interests of justice requires, the inspection will be granted to scientific witnesses, who will be required to keep any secrets which they may have discovered, and which do not affect the question of infringement (*c*). And in *Flower* v. *Lloyd* (*d*) the Court of Appeal strictly limited the inspection to scientific men, and excluded the plaintiff from being present.

In *Piggott* v. *The Anglo-American Telegraph Co.* (*e*), it was alleged that an inspection would disclose important secrets. Giffard, V.-C., in refusing an order to inspect, said: "Of late years greater readiness has been shown by the Equity Courts to allow inspection in patent cases than by the Courts of Common Law. But it has never been considered as a matter of right, nor have the Equity Courts considered themselves as precluded from exercising a proper discretion in applications of this description. The Court ought to be satisfied of two things: that there really is a case to be tried at the hearing of the cause, and that the inspection asked for is of

---

(*b*) *Morgan* v. *Seaward*, 1 Web. P. C. 169; *Russell* v. *Cowley*, 1 Web. P. C. 458; *Bovill* v. *Moore*, *supra*; *Keynaston* v. *East India Co.*, 3 Swan. 248; *East India Co.*
v. *Keynaston*, 3 Bl. Ap. Cas. 153.
(*c*) See *Russell* v. *Crichton*, 15 Dec. Ct. of Sess. 1270.
(*d*) W. N. 1876, 169, 230.
(*e*) 19 L. T. Rep., N. S. 46.

material importance to the plaintiff's case *as made out by his evidence.*"

In *Batley* v. *Kynock* (*f*), Sir James Bacon, V.-C., said: "Upon the single point which is raised before me, there can be no doubt that the plaintiff in such a suit as this is entitled to an inspection of the means which the defendants employ in the manufacture of the articles alleged to be violations of the plaintiff's patent, when such **inspection is essential for the purpose of enabling the plaintiff to prove his case**; upon the materials before me that is not made out. There is no allegation by the plaintiff that he cannot make out his case without inspection. But there is on the part of the defendants a plain allegation that inspection is not necessary for the purposes of the suit; upon that only I must decide this question. I would rather not go into the other matters which have been referred to. The description in the specification and the allegation in the bill—but as I read both the description in the specification and the allegation in the bill—I find that the charge made by the plaintiff is that the cartridges, the right of manufacturing which is vested in him exclusively, have been imitated and copied by the defendant, and if that fact can be made out the plaintiff's case can be clearly established. The mode of making that out is by examination of the cartridges, the means by which they have been made, whether by a machine or hammer or a screw cannot signify in the least if the cartridges of the defendant when made are made upon the principle of the patent claimed by the plaintiff."

The Court, in the case of *The Patent Type Founding Co.* v. *Walter* (*g*), assumed the jurisdiction to order the defendant to deliver to the plaintiff a **sample of the type made by him so that the plaintiff might have the same**

(*f*) L. R., 19 Eq. 91.   (*g*) 8 W. R. 353.

analysed, for the purpose of ascertaining whether the composition was similar to the plaintiff's patented composition.

In some cases where it is necessary, the Court will order the defendant and the plaintiff to give **mutual inspection,** and to show both the patented machine and the alleged infringement at work, and to permit either party to take away any of the work or samples of the work which has been done in their presence (*h*).

The application may be made on motion to the Court or by summons; it is usually made upon the application for an interim injunction, but it is immaterial at what stage of the proceedings the application is made. The evidence in support must be on affidavit, and a primâ facie case of infringement must be made out, and that the inspection is material to the plaintiff's case.

Order L. of the Rules of the Supreme Court, 1883, contains some provisions as to inspection which must be noticed.

Rule 3 provides for the inspection of property and the taking of samples, or for "any observations to be made or experiment to be tried which may be necessary or expedient for the purpose of obtaining full information or evidence." Rule 4: "It shall be lawful for any judge, by whom any cause or matter may be heard or tried with or without a jury, or before whom any cause or matter may be brought by way of appeal, to inspect any property *or thing* concerning which any question may arise therein."

This last mentioned rule was introduced by the Rules of 1883. Before, the parties must have consented to a view being had. In *Jackson* v. *The Duke of Newcastle* (*i*),

---

(*h*) *Davenport* v. *Jepson*, 1 N. R. 307. See also *The Singer Sewing Machine Co.* v. *Wilson*,

(*i*) 33 L. J., Ch. 698.
5 N. R. 505.

Lord Westbury said: "A judge is bound to pronounce his decision according to the evidence before him, but his inspection of the premises may bring him to a conclusion directly opposite to that which is established by the evidence."

CHAPTER X.

THE TRIAL.

The constitution of the Court which is to hear and determine patent actions is provided for by sect. 28, sub-sect. 1, of the Act of 1883. "In an action or proceeding for infringement or revocation of a patent, the Court may, if it thinks fit, and shall, on the request of either of the parties to the proceeding, call in the aid of an assessor, specially qualified, and hear and try the case wholly or partially, with his assistance; the action shall be tried without a jury, unless the Court shall otherwise direct."

This section is not very clear in its terms. Does it mean that in the event of an assessor being employed, that then the action shall be tried without a jury, or does it mean that all patent actions shall be tried without a jury, unless the Court otherwise directs?

Under the old statute, either party had an absolute right to have the questions of fact decided by a jury, and the Court had no power to deprive them of this right (*a*).

Under the 57th sect. of the Judicature Act, 1873, the Court had power, without the consent of the parties, "in any such cause or matter requiring any prolonged examination of documents or accounts, or *any scientific* or local *investigation* which cannot, in the opinion of the Court, or a judge, conveniently be made before a jury, or conducted by the Court through its other ordinary officers, the Court or a judge may at any time, on

---

(*a*) *Sugg* v. *Silber*, L. R., 1 Q. B. D. 362.

such terms as may be thought proper, order any question or issue of fact, or any question of account arising therein, to be tried either before an official referee, to be appointed as hereinafter provided, or before a special referee to be agreed on between the parties; and any such special referee so agreed on, shall have the same powers and duties, and proceed in the same manner as an official referee. All such trials before referees shall be conducted in such manner as may be prescribed by rules of court, and subject thereto in such manner as the Court or judge ordering the same shall direct."

In the case of *Saxby* v. *The Gloucester Wagon Co.* (*b*), Mr. Justice Hawkins was of opinion that a patent case was a case which required a "prolonged scientific examination," and consequently he remitted the action to the most proper tribunal for difficult scientific questions, "*the official referee.*" We are inclined to think that sect. 28 of the Patent, &c., Act, does away with this option. The words appear to read, "The Court may employ an assessor, and shall do so on the application of either party, and *shall* try the case; and the action *shall* be tried without a jury, &c."

Ord. XXXVI. rule 5 of the Rules of the Supreme Court, provides, "The Court or a judge may direct the trial, without a jury, of any cause, matter, or issue, requiring any prolonged examination of documents or accounts, or any scientific or local examination which cannot, in their or his opinion, conveniently be made with a jury;" and rule 6: "In any other cause or matter, upon the application of any party thereto, for a trial with a jury of the cause or matter, or any issue of fact, an order shall be made for a trial with a jury." These rules, together with the provisions of sect. 28 of the Patent Act, would show that the better opinion probably is that, unless a judge or the Court otherwise

b W. N. 1880, p. 28.

orders, the constitution of the Court shall be a judge sitting without a jury, and with or without an assessor.

The grounds of application for a trial by jury would be that the evidence shows a **conflict of testimony** in material parts, or that **grave questions of credibility** are likely to arise, or that a **charge of fraud** is made against either party.

Mr. Hindmarch, at p. 291 of his celebrated work, says: "Few causes require so much care and industry in preparing for trial as patent actions, in which very nice points of law and difficult questions of fact must often be decided between the parties; and it will frequently happen that a party will succeed or fail in obtaining a verdict according to the industry with which he has got up his case for trial. Properly to understand the questions raised in such actions and prepare the necessary proofs, a competent knowledge not only of law, but also of science in general and the useful arts, are essentially requisite."

It is no ground for **postponing the trial of an action for infringement** that a petition has been presented by the defendant or any other person under sect. 26 to revoke the patent.

We have seen that proceedings for revocation are similar to, and for the same purpose as, *scire facias* prior to the Act of 1883. In *Muntz* v. *Foster*(c), it had been held that the fact of a writ of *scire facias* being pending was no ground for staying the action for infringement. Tindal, C. J., said: "As a general rule, a plaintiff has a right to have his cause go on for trial according to the ordinary course of business. Special circumstances may exist upon which the Court may see fit to interfere; but the present does not appear to us to be a case in which we ought to interfere by staying the proceedings in the action."

(c) 2 Web. P. C. 93 (n.), 1 Dowl. & Low. 942.

The ground of this decision was that the plaintiff in the action for infringement, being defendant in the proceedings by *scire facias*, had not the conduct of those proceedings, and that the defendant in the action for infringement might delay them; but where in *Palleson* v. *Holland* (*d*), an action for infringement had been tried, and a rule nisi for a new trial had been obtained and argued, and it appeared that another action was pending in that Court for another infringement of the same patent, and that a *scire facias* had been sued out to repeal the patent, the Court suspended their judgment upon the rule for a new trial, and ordered the trial of the other action to be postponed until after the trial of the *scire facias*.

And where a verdict had already gone for the Crown on *scire facias*, but a new trial was pending, the plaintiff was not permitted to proceed to trial with his action for infringement until the rule for the new trial in *scire facias* had been disposed of (*e*).

In an action for infringement the plaintiff has the **right of beginning and of replying,** notwithstanding that the burden of proof may really be on the defendant, as, for instance, where the case principally turns upon questions of prior user or prior publication, which are introduced by the defendant. It sometimes happened that this privilege, particularly in cases of conflicting evidence, was of great value, and for the purpose of snatching it from the plaintiff the defendant did not wait for the plaintiff to commence his action, but commenced proceedings himself by *scire facias* to repeal the patent, so as to place himself in the position of plaintiff. But, by sect. 26, sub-sect. 7, of the Act of 1883, it is provided that in cases where it is sought to revoke a patent, " The defendant shall be entitled to begin and give evidence in support of the patent, and if the plaintiff gives evidence

d Hindmarch, 293.   *e* *Smith* v. *Hyton*, 6 M. & G. 251.

impeaching the validity of the patent, the defendant shall be entitled to reply."

The plaintiff must give evidence of the issues, which he is bound to prove. It is for him to support his patent and to establish its validity. He must prove his patent if the grant be denied. This is done by producing the patent itself, with the great seal—or, under the Act of 1883, the seal of the Patent Office—attached to it; sect. 12, sub-sect. 2, provides that, "A patent so sealed shall have the same effect as if it were sealed with the great seal of the United Kingdom"; or, under sect. 89, if it be not convenient or possible to produce the original, "Printed or written copies or extracts, purporting to be certified by the comptroller and sealed with the seal of the Patent Office, of or from patents, specifications, disclaimers, and other documents in the Patent Office, and of or from registers and other books kept there, shall be admitted in evidence in all Courts in her Majesty's dominions, and in all proceedings, without further proof or production of the originals."

If the plaintiff sues as assignee, or under any derivative title, and his title is denied, the entry from the register of patents may be proved in the manner suggested by the 89th section.

Under the 96th section, "a certificate purporting to be under the hand of the comptroller as to any entry, matter or thing which he is authorized by this Act, or any general rules made thereunder, to make or do, shall be primâ facie evidence of the entry having been made, and of the contents thereof, and of the matter or thing having been done or left undone."

For instance, if an entry in the register is denied by the defendant, he may prove its omission by a certificate under the 96th section.

If the fact of infringement is denied, the plaintiff must be ready with evidence that the defendant has made, used or sold the article or process, and any one of these acts will satisfy the allegation of infringement, whether the infringement was **intentional or not** (*f*). **Mere possession**, unaccompanied by user, does not amount to infringement (*g*). Evidence that the **defendant has sold** articles made by a patented process, or by a patented machine, will be sufficient (*h*). If the defendant has **imitated the plaintiff's process**, or substituted chemical or mechanical equivalents, he will have infringed the patent (*i*), and the plaintiff must be ready with expert and other evidence to satisfy the Court that the defendant has substantially imitated his process or article. It is an infringement to import and use or sell a patented article; although it is **no infringement to merely import** and no more (*k*). If an article, by its appearance or properties, can be distinguished as having been made by a patented process, and the defendant will not permit the plaintiff to see how it is made, Lord Ellenborough held, that a primâ facie case had been made out, which it was for the defendant to rebut (*l*). But the mere fact that there is a **similarity of appearance** between an article made by the patented process and the alleged infringement, is not sufficient: there must be reasonably satisfactory evidence that a similar article could not be produced in any other manner; that, in fact, it carries the footprint of the invention with it (*m*). It will be observed, that when **expert witnesses** are called for the purpose of proving infringement in this manner, they must be asked whether there is a similarity between the patented article and the alleged infringement, and also whether there is any other process, except the patented process,

---

(*f* *Stead* v. *Anderson*, 4 C. B. 806, and ante, p. 146.

g Ante, p. 163.

h) *Wright* v. *Hitchcock*, L. R., 5 Ex. 37.

i Ante, p. 155.

k) Ante, p. 163.

l *Huddart* v. *Grimshaw*, Davis, P. C. 288. See also *Betts* v. *Neilson*, L. R., 5 H. L. 11 and 12.

(*m*) See *Palmer* v. *Wagstaff*, 9 Ex. 494; 23 L. J., Ex. 217; 2 C. L. R. 1052; and *Davenport* v. *Richards*, 3 L. T. R., N. S. 504.

which will produce that similarity; but they cannot be asked their opinion as to whether or not there has been infringement. That is a question for the jury, or the Court in the absence of a jury (*n*).

The Court will consider the circumstances of the case, the behaviour of the witnesses and their credibility, when considering the question of infringement or no infringement.

In *Clark* v. *Adie* (*o*), Lord Blackburn said:—" Whenever a man knowing for the first time of an invention, either by seeing a machine at work or by reading a specification, proceeds to do what he never did before, and takes a part of the invention, it is always a very strong *argumentum ad hominem* to say: You are, by the very fact of taking this, making evidence against yourself that it was a new invention; otherwise, why did you take it? You are making evidence against yourself that at all events the part you took was new, or why did you take it? and whenever there is a case of theft or stealing knowingly, that observation ought to have some weight, although I think in practice it has more weight given to it than it ought to have. But where there is a case of an innocent infringement of property, by an unwitting use of this sort, that observation can have no weight against the party in the slightest degree, and I think it ought not to have any."

The burden of proving infringement is strictly on the plaintiff, and if he does not satisfactorily prove it there is no necessity of entering upon the defendant's case on other matters. The plaintiff must always give evidence, when the alleged infringement is the sale or use of an article, **that it was not made by himself or his agents** (*p*).

(*n*) Per Lord Wensleydale in *Seed* v. *Higgins*, 8 H. L. Cas. 550.

(*o*) L. R., 2 App. Cas. 337.
(*p*) *Betts* v. *Wilmott*, L. R., 6 Ch. 239.

When the defendant alleges that there is a **defect or insufficiency in the specification**, the burden of proving that there is no such defect is on the plaintiff.

We have seen (*q*) that it is for the jury to say whether a specification is **sufficient** or **intelligible** or not; it is for the Court to place a **construction** upon the language used in the specification. The plaintiff must therefore be prepared with evidence of an expert character as to the sufficiency of the specification; and in selecting this evidence the plaintiff cannot be better guided than by the judgment of Sir George Jessel in *Plimpton* v. *Malcolmson* (*r*): he must not select eminent engineers or celebrated chemists as the persons to whom the specification must be intelligible, but he must choose " ordinary workmen" in the particular branch of trade to which the invention refers—" not a careless man, but a careful man, though not possessed of that great scientific knowledge or power of invention which would enable him by himself unaided to supplement a defective description or correct an erroneous description." He may, of course, call eminent engineers, but their evidence can only be, " placing myself in the position of an ordinary workman I think it would or would not be intelligible or sufficient to me." If the specification be not sufficiently clear to be understood by an ordinary workman (a witness for the plaintiff), witnesses will not be allowed to be called to explain the intention of the patentees, and the plaintiffs will be non-suited (*s*).

Experiments conducted for the express purpose of manufacturing evidence, with a view to litigation, are to be looked at with distrust (*t*).

The plaintiff must, if the matter be put in issue, prove that the title, provisional specification and com-

(*q*) Ante, pp. 66 & 67.
(*r*) L. R., 3 Ch. D. 531.
(*s*) *Brooks* v. *Ripley*, 2 Lond. Jour. C. S. 35.
(*t*) *Young* v. *Fernie*, 4 Giff. 609.

plete specification, correspond and substantially describe the same invention (*u*).

If it is alleged by the defendant that the invention is illegal or useless, the burden of proof is on the plaintiff (*x*).

So the plaintiff must be prepared, if he intends to claim damages, and not an account, to prove the damage which he has sustained. If he has been in the habit of granting royalties, the amount of royalties to which he would have become entitled is the proper measure of his damages; as to the measure of damages in other cases, see *ante, pp.* 177 *and* 178.

When the **defendant pleads** that the grantee of the letters patent was **not the true and first inventor**, or **that the invention was not new**, it will be sufficient if the plaintiff gives some primâ facie evidence of novelty (*y*). It will be sufficient to call one or two persons acquainted practically with the trade to which the invention refers, to say that they never heard of it, or saw or heard of its having been put in practice or published before the date of the patent. Gibbs, C. J., said: "The first witness, a man of considerable experience, had never seen locks with the lips so perforated; *primâ facie* that is good evidence; but when the question is, whether this had existence previous to the patent, fifty witnesses proving that they never saw it before would be of no avail if one was called who had seen it and practised it" (*z*).

The plaintiff having given this *primâ facie* evidence, **the burden of proof** as to prior user or prior publication **is shifted to the defendant,** and if he would invalidate the patent he must prove his case.

We have previously discussed what amounts to prior

(*u*) Ante, pp. 55 et seq.
(*x*) Ante, p. 225.
(*y*) *Turner* v. *Winter*, 1 T. R. 606.

(*z*) *Manton* v. *Manton*, Davis, P. C. 350.

user and prior publication (*a*). The evidence which the defendant brings must be complete and satisfactory, and the question is one of fact.

If the defendant has succeeded in establishing a case against the plaintiff, the latter will be permitted, before the defendant sums up, **to adduce rebutting evidence.** In *Penn* v. *Jack and Others* (*b*), Sir W. Page-Wood, V.-C., said: " I think the plaintiff is entitled to adduce evidence, in reply, for the purpose of rebutting the case set up by the defendants; and for this reason, that it is quite impossible for him to know what is the nature of the evidence which is to be produced. The defendants, who contest the validity of the invention, have in effect put in a plea denying the novelty of the plaintiff's patent; and the affirmative of the issue thus raised in reality rests with the defendants, who are not obliged to give the names of their witnesses. How can the plaintiff possibly meet such a case until he hears the evidence for the defence, and knows what their witnesses will prove? I should be very sorry to have to put the parties to all the expense and delay of a new trial, which I should have to direct, if this evidence were excluded. Besides which, the witnesses are at hand and ready, and the sensible and obvious course is to examine them now. The practice at common law is stated in Taylor on Evidence; and it appears that where, as here, several issues are joined, the plaintiff may content himself with adducing evidence in support of those issues which he is bound to prove, reserving the right of rebutting his adversary's proofs, in the event of the defendant establishing a primâ facie case with respect to the issues which lie upon him. In support of this proposition, *Shaw* v. *Beck* (*c*) is cited, where Parke, B., used the following expression: ' But Abbott, C. J., laid down what appears to me to be a

---

a Ante, pp. 54 and 44.   (c) 8 Ex. 392.
(*b*) L. R., 2 Eq. at p. 317.

more reasonable rule, by holding that the defendant was bound to prove his plea, and that the plaintiff might answer it by additional evidence.' Other instances are also mentioned, all showing the wide discretion given to the judge in allowing evidence to be given by the plaintiff in reply. The plaintiff has put in his letters patent as formal evidence of his title. The defendants then plead want of novelty, and give, in proof of the issues thus raised by them, special evidence, which the plaintiff is entitled to rebut, by evidence, in reply. Regarding this case as one of an affirmative plea, the burden of proving which rests on the defendants, I feel bound to admit the evidence proposed to be given by the plaintiff in reply."

Although the plaintiff may, as of right, rebut the case made by the defendant, upon any issue which rests with the defendant, where the plaintiff has given such rebutting evidence, **the defendant will not be allowed to strengthen the case which he had made by adducing further evidence**; and this will apply with greater force when the defendant's counsel has summed up the evidence which has been offered (*d*).

At the hearing of the action, **no objection will be allowed, either to the particulars of objections, or to the particulars of breaches**, and any evidence will be received which they are wide enough to admit of. If there is any vagueness or insufficiency in the particulars, the party requiring further information must apply for it to a judge in chambers, within reasonable time before the trial of the action; but they will not be allowed to permit the opposite side to go to trial, and then to submit that, for want of sufficient particularity in the objection, the evidence is not admissible (*e*).

(*d*) *Penn* v. *Jack*, L. R., 2 Eq. at p. 318.

(*e*) *Neilson* v. *Harford*, 8 M. & W. 806; *Hall* v. *Bolland*, 1 H. & N. 134.

In *Sykes* v. *Howarth* (*f*), the plaintiff delivered particulars of breaches in May, 1878, which stated that the defendant had at divers times between the 29th of May, 1879, and the commencement of the action, infringed the plaintiff's patent by the manufacture, or sale, or use of fancy rollers, and in particular by fancy rollers manufactured and sold by or covered with cards, by the defendant, for Messrs. Shaw and Mr. Smith. In July, 1878, the statement of defence was delivered. It stated, "The defendant has made and sold to Messrs. Samuel Shaw and Co. and Mr. Charles Smith, in the particulars of breaches in this action respectivly mentioned, and to other persons, certain cards (in all six sets), which were all $2\frac{1}{2}$ inches in width;" and the defendant, in answer to interrogatories, disclosed the name of Hirst as one of the persons supplied with such sets of cards. Mr. Justice Fry admitted evidence in Hirst's case. He said: "The defendant did not apply for amended particulars, according to the case of *Hull* v. *Bolland* (*supra*). It appears to me I have to inquire what is the meaning of the particulars. I find that the case of Hirst is within the literal meaning of the particulars. If I had found that the case of Hirst was likely to create surprise, or likely to introduce any point not raised in Smith's or Shaw's case, I should probably have given an opportunity to the defendant to bring any fresh evidence." The learned judge would not have ruled that the plaintiff was prevented from giving the evidence in Hirst's case, but he would have allowed the defendant to rebut it.

These decisions must not be confused with a case where, for example, the particulars alleged infringement or prior user at London and Liverpool. In such a case no act of infringement or prior user would be admitted in evidence which did not occur at London or Liverpool, but if the words were London, Liverpool, or elsewhere,

(*f*) L. R., 12 Ch. D. 826.

then the evidence might extend to any part of the country, because any evidence would come within the strict meaning of the objections.

Upon the trial no evidence will be received in support of any issue which is not raised in the pleadings. In *Bovill* v. *Goodier* (*g*) it was held that an objection to the validity of a patent on the ground of the expiration of a foreign patent for the same invention, cannot be taken at the hearing of a suit to restrain the infringement of a patent unless it has been raised by the answer.

(*g*) L. R., 2 Eq. 195.

CHAPTER XI.

QUESTIONS FOR COURT AND JURY.

WE have seen that as a rule actions for the infringement of letters patent are directed to be tried before the Court without a jury. Still, under special circumstances, the parties, or either of them, may obtain an order to try before a jury. Under these circumstances it will still be material to consider what are the questions which the Court should leave to the jury, and which are left to the decision of the Court.

As to the specification. **The construction is for the Court** (*a*); and the rules of construction are similar to those which govern the construction of other documents (*b*). In *Hills* v. *Evans* (*c*); Lord Westbury said: " It is undoubtedly true, as a proposition of law, that the construction of a specification, as the construction of all other written instruments, belongs to the Court; but a specification of an invention contains most generally, if not always, some technical terms, some phrases of art, some processes, and requires generally the aid of the light derived from what are called surrounding circumstances. It is, therefore, an admitted rule of law that the explanation of the words or technical terms of art, the phrases used in commerce, and the proofs and results of the processes which are described (and in a chemical patent the ascertainment of chemical equivalents), that all these are matters of fact upon which evidence may be

---

a) Hills v. *Evans*, 31 L. J., Ch. 156; *Seed* v. *Higgins*, 8 H. L. Cas. 561; *Bovill* v. *Pimm*, 11 Ex. 710.

b) Simpson v. *Holliday*, 20 Newton's Lon. Jour. N. S. 105.

c, 31 L. J., Ch. 156.

given, contradictory testimony may be adduced, and upon which undoubtedly it is the province and the right of a jury to decide. But when these portions of a specification are abstracted and made the subject of evidence, and therefore brought within the province of the jury, the direction to be given to the jury with regard to the construction of the rest of the patent, which is conceived in ordinary language, must be a direction given only conditionally, that is to say, a direction as to the meaning of the patent upon the hypothesis or the basis of the jury arriving at a certain conclusion with regard to the meaning of those terms, the signification of those phrases, the truth of those processes, and the result of the technical procedure described in the specification. And so the rule is given by Parke, B., in delivering the judgment of the Court of Exchequer in the case, I think, of *Neilson* v. *Harford* (d). The language of the learned judge, which I adopt, is in these words: 'The construction of all written instruments belongs to the Court alone, whose duty it is to construe all such instruments as soon as the true meaning of the words in which they are couched and the surrounding circumstances, if any, have been ascertained as facts by the jury; and it is the duty of the jury to take the construction from the Court, either absolutely, if there be no words to be construed as words of art or phrases used in commerce, and no surrounding circumstances to be ascertained, or conditionally, when those words or circumstances are necessarily referred to them.' Now, adopting that as the rule in the comparison of two specifications, each of which is filled with terms of art and with the description of technical processes, the duty of the Court would be confined to this—to give the legal construction of such documents taken independently. But, after that duty is discharged, there would remain a most important function to be still

---

(d) 8 M. & W. 806.

performed, which is the comparison of the two instruments when they have received their legal exposition and interpretation; and as it is always a matter of evidence what external thing is indicated and denoted by any description, when the jury have been informed of the meaning of the description contained in each specification, the work of comparing the two, and ascertaining whether the words, as interpreted by the Court, contained in specification A, do or do not denote the same external matter as the words, as interpreted and explained by the Court, contained in specification B, is a matter of fact, and is, I conceive, a matter within the province of the jury, and not within the function of the Court."

Epitomising this elaborate judgment. When the language used is that which has an ordinary and legal meaning the question is, what has the man said? not what did he intend to say? and, therefore, the Court will place the legal meaning on his words. When the language used is that which has no ordinary legal meaning, or which under different circumstances may have two or more ordinary legal meanings, the question is, as a fact, with what meaning did the writer use the words or expressions which he has used? and that is a question which the Court should require the jury to solve. The matter could not be placed more lucidly than it is by Lord Westbury in the last dozen lines of the judgment which we have quoted.

It is for the jury to say whether the specification is **intelligible** (*m*) or not, and it is for the Court to direct the jury as to the class of persons to whom it must be intelligible (*n*).

It is for the jury to say whether the specification is **sufficient** or not, that is, whether it contains a sufficient description of the invention; but it is for the Court to

---

(*m*) *Neilson v. Harford*, 1 Web. P. C. 295.

(*n*) See cases cited at pp. 72 to 76 et seq.

inform the jury the degree of sufficiency which the law requires in specifications (*o*).

The novelty of the invention is a question for the jury. Questions of prior user or prior publication are always questions of fact, and it is for the jury to compare what has been done before and what is set up as being new, and to say whether or not they are identical. And so any document which is said to amount to prior publication must be construed by the Court, but it is for the jury to **compare it with the specification** and to say whether the described matter is the same or not (*p*).

The **utility of the invention is also for the jury**, subject to the directions of the Court as to the degree of utility which the law requires for the purpose of supporting the validity of a patent (*q*).

The question of infringement is for the jury. In *De la Rue* v. *Dickinson* (*r*), Campbell, C. J., said: "There may well be a case where the judge may and ought to take upon himself to say that the plaintiff has offered no evidence to be left to the jury to prove infringement, as if there were a patent for a chemical composition, and the evidence was that the defendant had constructed and used a machine for combing wool. But, if the evidence has a tendency to show that the defendant has used substantially the same means to obtain the same result as specified by the plaintiff, and scientific witnesses

(*o*) *Hill* v. *Thompson*, 1 Web. P. C. 235; *Bickford* v. *Skewes*, 1 Q. B. 938; *Neilson* v. *Harford*, 1 Web. P. C. 295; *Walton* v. *Bateman*, 1 Web. P. C. 621; *Beard* v. *Egerton*, 19 L. J., C. P. 38; *Wallington* v. *Dale*, 7 Ex. 888; *Parkes* v. *Stevens*, L. R., 8 Eq. 358, and L. R., 5 Ch. Ap. Cas. 56.

(*p*) *Cornish* v. *Keene*, 1 Web. P. C. 519; *Elliott* v. *Aston*, 1 Web.

P. C. 222; *Muntz* v. *Foster*, 2 Web. P. C. 107; *Spencer* v. *Jack*, 11 L. T. R., N. S. 242.

(*q*) *Hill* v. *Thompson*, 1 Web. P. C. 237; *Bloxam* v. *Elsee*, 1 C. & P. 565; *Cornish* v. *Keene*, 1 Web. P. C. 506; *Morgan* v. *Seaward*, 1 Web. P. C. 186; *Macnamara* v. *Hulse*, C. & M. 471.

(*r*) 7 E. & B. at p. 755.

have sworn that the defendant actually has used such means, the question becomes one of fact, mixed with law, which the judge is bound to submit to the jury."

In *Seed* v. *Higgins* (s), Lord Chelmsford in the House of Lords said: "What the defendant had done in any case was of course a question of fact, but whether, on proof of certain acts having been done by a defendant, the plaintiff had any case to go to a jury, was a question for the judge" (t).

(s) 30 L. J., Q. B. at p. 317.
(t) See also *Walton* v. *Potter*, 1 Web. P. C. 586; *Macnamara* v. *Hulse*, Car. & M. 471; *Newton* v. *Grand Junction Rail. Co.*, 5 Ex. 331; *Stevens* v. *Keating*, 2 Web. P. C. 191; *Sellers* v. *Dickinson*, 5 Ex. 323; *Curtis* v. *Platt*, 35 L. J., Ch. 852.

CHAPTER XII.

CERTIFICATES.

Sect. 31 of the Patents, &c., Act, 1883, is as follows:—
"In an action for infringement of a patent, the Court or a judge may **certify that the validity of the patent came in question,** and if the Court or a judge so certifies, then in any subsequent action for infringement, the plaintiff in that action, on obtaining a final order or judgment in his favour, shall have his full costs, charges and expenses as between solicitor and client, unless the Court or judge trying the action certifies that he ought not to have the same."

Similar provisions were contained in 5 & 6 Will. IV. c. 83, and also in the 43rd section of the Patent Law Amendment Act, 1883.

The object of these sections is to prevent patentees of important inventions being ruined by successive actions, which they are bound to bring to restrain infringements. Manufacturers banding themselves together to defeat a patentee's rights in this manner.

The Act of William IV. cited above gave the patentee a right to treble costs, but this was taken away by 5 & 6 Vict. c. 97, which gave him full costs; and now, as we have seen, costs as between solicitor and client are substituted for full costs.

To acquire the protection of the 31st section a certificate is requisite, and this should be applied for at the trial of the action, and the application must be made to the Court or judge who have tried the cause (*a*).

(*a*) *Gillet* v. *Green*, 7 M. & W. 347.

The Court have no power to order full costs upon the first trial in which the validity of the patent came in question, the words of the statute being "in any subsequent action for infringement" (b).

Where several simultaneous actions have been brought, and one of them has been made a test action and proceeded with to trial, upon a certificate being given in that action it will not operate upon the others (c).

An action was compromised at the trial by a verdict being entered for the plaintiff in the action for 40s. damages and costs, with all usual certificates. Subsequently, upon an ex parte application, the judge endorsed on the record a certificate that the record in a certain action, wherein Bovill was plaintiff and Keyworth was defendant, and the certificate thereon endorsed was given in evidence at the trial of this action (*Bovill* v. *Hadley*), it was held that this certificate was improperly granted, the record and certificate in the former action not having been given in evidence, and it not being under the circumstances a "usual certificate" within the contemplation of the parties (d). Upon the trial of the second action the record of the first action with the endorsement must be produced, but not before the verdict, in such a manner as to prejudice the second trial (e).

The certificate of the judge, which is granted for the purpose of affecting the costs in future cases, is one which cannot be given by consent. In obtaining this certificate **the plaintiff and the country are the parties, not the defendant**, and the judge is bound to protect the interests of the country and to see that the certificate is not given when the validity of the patent has not, in fact, been proved to the satisfaction of the Court; other-

---

(b) *Penn* v. *Bibby*, L. R., 3 Eq. 308.

(c) *Penn* v. *Fernie*, L. R., 3 Eq. 308.

(d) *Bovill* v. *Hadley*, 17 C. B., N. S. 435.

(e) *Newall* v. *Wilkins*, 17 L. T. R. 20.

wise, there is nothing to prevent collusive actions being merely brought for the purpose of obtaining this valuable privilege—a privilege which can be used as an enormous lever, preventing persons from incurring the risk of a conflict with the patentee (*f*).

We have seen that the object of this section is to prevent the patentee from being repeatedly harassed by the validity of his patent being called in question in succession of actions. It does not appear ever to have been decided whether, when in a second action the validity of the patent is not called in question, but there is a mere denial of infringement, the section applies. It is submitted that such a case was not within the contemplation of the legislature, and that the judge should direct only party and party costs whenever the validity of the patent is not called in question.

Sect. 29 of the Act of 1883, after providing for the delivery of particulars of breaches and objections, enacts: "(6) **On taxation of costs** regard shall be had to the particulars delivered by the plaintiff and by the defendant, and they respectively **shall not be allowed any costs** in respect of any particular delivered by them unless the same is certified by the Court or a judge to have been proven, or to have been reasonable and proper without regard to the general costs of the case."

The certificates granted under this section must not be confused with the certificate under sect. 31. The object of sect. 29 is to provide what costs shall be payable in the action itself, and the object of sect. 31 is to provide for the costs of future actions.

Care must be taken at the trial to ask the judge to certify as to each particular breach mentioned in the particulars of breaches, and as to each particular objection, and no costs of witnesses, or of, and incidental to,

---

(*f*) *Stocker* v. *Rodgers*, 1 C. & K. 99.

such breach or objection, as is not specially certified for, will be allowed (*g*).

If an action is not tried out, it is obvious that a difficulty may arise as to costs, since the parties have had no opportunity to prove or disprove their particulars. In *Greaves* v. *The Eastern Counties Railway Co.* (*h*) it was held that where the defendant had delivered particulars of objections, and just before trial the plaintiff had abandoned his action, thus giving the defendant no opportunity of proving or disproving his objections, the defendant was entitled to the costs of the objections and of the witnesses, for the act did not apply, except where the cause came on for trial. It will be observed, however, that there is a difference between the language of the 43rd sect. of the Patent Law Amendment Act, 1852, and the language of the 29th sect. sub-sect. (6) of the Patents, &c. Act, 1883. In the former case the words were: "Shall not be allowed any costs in respect of any particular unless certified by the *judge before whom the trial was had to have been proved.*" Under the latter statute: "Shall not be allowed any costs in respect of any particular delivered by them, unless the same is certified by the Court or a judge to have been proven, *or to have been reasonable and proper.*" It is submitted that the practice under the new act when the action has not been tried is to take out a summons before a judge at chambers for a certificate, on the ground that the particulars were reasonable and proper; such summons should be supported by an affidavit, alleging that the plaintiff or defendant had reasonable grounds for believing that he would at the trial have been able to prove the particulars in respect of which application is made; but a certificate so granted will not operate in a manner to entitle the plaintiff to costs as between solicitor and client in any subsequent action.

g Honibull v. *Bloomer,* 10 5 M. & W. 387. Exch. 538. See also *Losh* v. *Hague,* *h* 1 E. & E. 961.

We have seen that since the Judicature Acts, the Common Law Division and the Chancery Division can either of them grant full relief in an action for the infringement of a patent, **granting both an injunction and damages, or an account.** In olden times the Common Law Courts merely inquired into damages, and if less than 40s. was recovered a question arose as to whether or not County Court costs should not alone be allowed; but now in every patent case an injunction may be granted, and this removes the case from the operation of 30 & 31 Vict. c. 142, s. 5.

The Rules of the Supreme Court, 1883, provide for cases where the **higher scale and lower scale of costs** are to be allowed; and in future, notwithstanding that an injunction is granted, it will be necessary to ask the judge at the trial to certify for costs on the higher scale.

Order LXV. r. 8 provides: "In causes and matters commenced after these rules come into operation, solicitors shall be entitled to charge and be allowed the fees set forth in the column headed 'lower scale,' in Appendix N. in all causes and matters, and no higher fees shall be allowed in any case, except such as are by this order otherwise provided for; and in causes and matters pending at the time when these rules come into operation, to which the higher scale of costs previously in force was applicable, the same scale shall continue to be applied."

Rule 9.—"The fees set forth in the column headed 'higher scale' in Appendix N. may be allowed, either generally in any cause or matter, or as to the costs of any particular application made, or business done, in any cause or matter, if, on special grounds arising out of the nature and importance, or the difficulty or urgency of the case, the Court or a judge shall, at the trial or hearing, or further consideration of the cause or matter, or at the hearing of every application therein, whether the cause or matter shall or shall not be brought to trial or hearing, or to further consideration (as the case may be) so order; or if the taxing officer, under directions given to him for that purpose by the Court or a judge, shall think that such allowance ought to be made upon such special grounds as aforesaid."

Sect. 49 of the Judicature Act, 1873, provides that there shall be no appeal as to costs; but this was held not to apply where the costs were a matter of right, and not discretionary (*i*). Under the Rules of Court, which were in operation prior to the 24th October, 1883, the question of higher or lower scale was a matter of right (*k*). Hence, in *Re Terrell* (*l*), the Court of Appeal held that there was an appeal, but now it will be observed that the order is in the absolute discretion of the judge, and, therefore, it is submitted there is no appeal.

The **directors of a limited company**, whose servants have infringed a patent, **may be ordered to pay costs personally**. Sir W. Page-Wood, in *Betts* v. *De Vitre* (*m*), said : "Where there is a wilful act against the rights of a patentee, after he has obtained a verdict, and the certificate of a judge, that his title came in question, all the world must be taken to know that that was fairly and completely tried and disposed of, and, if they infringe the patent, they infringe it with a liability for costs." The reasoning of this decision is not quite clear, and it is submitted that, should the question arise again, the opinion of the Court of Appeal might be taken on the subject, regard being had to the case of *Denley* v. *Blore* (*n*).

Judgment having been recovered, minutes of judgment should be prepared. The minutes will be in accordance with one or other of the precedents given hereafter. We have drawn attention in previous pages to those

---

i *Turner* v. *Hancock*, C. A., 20 Ch. D. 303.

k Rules of S. C. Dec. 1875.

l L. R., 22 Ch. D. 173.

m 11 Jur., N. S. 11.

n 38 Lond. Jour. 224.

points which should be attended to in preparing these minutes. Care should be exercised when an account is directed to be taken that provision be made for the **payment of costs to the plaintiff up to and including the hearing,** otherwise the payment of all costs will be delayed until the final account has been taken, which in some cases has been known to amount to a delay of years.

CHAPTER XIII.

PRACTICE ON PETITION FOR REVOCATION.

All persons are not empowered to petition for revocation of a patent.

The parties who may petition are specified in sect. 26, sub-sect. 4 of the Patents Act, 1883.

The petition must be presented to the High Court of Justice.

A form of petition, applicable to such a case, is given hereafter (*a*).

Sub-sect. (5.) "The plaintiff must deliver with his petition particulars of the objections on which he means to rely, and no evidence shall, except by leave of the Court or a judge, be admitted in proof of any objection of which particulars are not so delivered."

The practice as to particulars is precisely similar to that in an action for infringement. It will, however, be observed that the judge has no power of certifying under sect. 31 that the validity of the patent came in question, nor will a certificate granted in a previous action for infringement affect the question of costs in proceedings for revocation, the words of sect. 31 being, " in any subsequent action for infringement."

Sect. 100 of the Judicature Act, defines "Pleading" as including any *petition* or summons, and also as including the statements, in writing, of the claims or demand of any plaintiff, and of the defence of any defendant thereto, and of the reply of the plaintiff to any counter-claim of a defendant.

Ord. XXXI. r. 1, of the Rules of the Supreme Court,

a Page 252.

gives power to the Court, or a judge, to permit interrogatories "*in any other cause or matter*," to be delivered by either party to the other. It is presumed that leave will be given to the respondent (called defendant in the Patent Act, 1883) to deliver interrogatories to the petitioner, and circumstances may arise when it would be just to permit the petitioner to examine the respondent. The rules as to interrogatories will be similar to those in an action for infringement.

The respondent having entered an appearance to the petition, the same will be set down for trial.

There does not appear to be any provision that the petition should be verified by affidavit, or that the respondent should deliver an answer.

The respondent should be careful that the **particulars of objections are sufficiently precise and accurate**, otherwise he may be taken by surprise at the hearing (*b*). He may apply for further and better particulars in the same manner as in an action for infringement; and under sect. 26, sub-sect. (6), " Particulars delivered may be, from time to time, amended by leave of the Court or a judge."

Sect. 28, sub-sect. (1), provides that the mode of trial of a petition for revocation shall be similar to that of an action for infringement.

Sect. 26, sub-sect. 7. " The defendant shall be entitled to begin and give evidence in support of the patent, and if the plaintiff gives evidence impeaching the validity of the patent, the defendant shall be entitled to reply."

The evidence which will be required of the respondent (defendant), in the first instance, will be very slight, and will be similar to that which he would give as to the validity of the patent were he plaintiff in an action for infringement (*c*). The petitioner will then have to prove

(*b*) Ante, p. 204. (*c*) Ante, p. 225.

the case he alleges in his petition and particulars, and the respondent has the right of reply. It is merely to preserve this right to reply, that the respondent is made practically plaintiff at the trial.

It is very doubtful whether sect. 29, sub-sect. (6), will be held to apply to petitions for revocation. Sub-sect. (1) of the same section, limiting, apparently, the operation of that section to actions for infringement, as distinguished from sect. 28, which deals with both actions for infringement and petitions for revocation.

CHAPTER XIV.

ACTION FOR INJUNCTION TO RESTRAIN THREATS.

SECT. 32 of the Patents Act, 1883, provides, "Where any person claiming to be the patentee of an invention, by circulars, advertisements, or otherwise, **threatens any other person** with any legal proceedings, or liability in respect of any alleged manufacture in sale or purchase of the invention, any person or persons aggrieved thereby may bring an action against him, and may obtain an injunction against the continuance of such threats, and may recover such damage (if any) as may have been sustained thereby, if the alleged manufacture, use, sale, or purchase, to which the threats related, *was not, in fact, an infringement of any legal rights of the person making such threats:* Provided that this section shall not apply if the person making such threats, with due diligence, commences and prosecutes an action for infringement of his patent."

This section gives the threatened party the power of testing the validity of the patent.

The words printed above in italics show that in defence to an action under the 32nd sect. the patentee may set up the validity of his patent and may choose to try the same as a defendant.

This is neither an action for infringement under sect. 29 nor a petition for revocation under sect. 26, and therefore the provisions as to particulars of objections do not apply. The provisions of the Rules of the Supreme Court, 1883, as to particulars do not appear to be available for the obtaining of particulars of objections in such a case, it being remembered that the patentee is defendant; that the cause of action is not to establish the patent but to restrain threats, and that the patentee himself has to set up his valid patent by way of substantive defence. The patentee is at such disadvantage in such form of action that it is to his interest forthwith to commence an action for infringement, and to apply for a stay of the action brought against him.

Forms of indorsement to writ, &c., under this section, are given hereafter.

It has been deemed advisable to limit the remarks in this work to such points of practice as pertain particularly to the law of patents. The general practice of the Courts has not been dealt with, and the practitioner is referred to the ordinary books of practice for such general information as he may require.

FORMS.

Indorsement on Writ.

1. *Action for Infringement.*

The plaintiff's claim is:—

1. For an injunction to restrain the defendant from infringing the plaintiff's patent, No. ——, and dated ——. Injunction.

2. For damages for the infringement of the said patent, or alternatively that an account may be taken of all the machines made in infringement of the said patent which have been manufactured, or sold, or let for hire, or used by or by the order, or for the use and profit, of the defendant, and also of the gains and profits made by the defendant by reason of such manufacture, sale, or letting for hire or use, and that the defendant may by a day to be appointed by the Court be ordered to pay to the plaintiff the amount of such gains and profits. Damages. Account.

3. That the defendant may be ordered upon oath to deliver up to the plaintiff, or break up, or otherwise render unfit for use, all machines or parts of machines made in infringement of the plaintiff's said patent, which are in the custody or power of the defendant, his servants, or agents. Order for destruction.

2. *Action to restrain Threats.*

The plaintiff's claim is:—

1. For an injunction restraining the defendant from, by circulars, advertisements, or otherwise, threatening to take legal or other proceedings against persons manufacturing, using, or selling an alleged invention of the defendants, to wit, ——. The said threats being to the prejudice of the plaintiff. Injunction.

2. For damages in respect of the injury sustained by the plaintiff by reason of the circulars, advertisements, or other threats of the defendant to take legal or other proceedings against persons manufacturing, using, or selling the said alleged invention.

3. Petition for the Revocation of a Patent.

In the High Court of Justice,
    Chancery [*or* Queen's Bench] Division.
    In the matter of Letters Patent granted to ———, of ———, dated ———, and numbered ———, and in the matter of the Patents, Designs, and Trade Marks Act, 1883, sect. 26.

To Her Majesty's High Court of Justice.

    The humble petition of Sir ———, Her Majesty's Attorney-General in England (*or* Ireland, *or* Lord Advocate in Scotland) (*or* other person authorized to petition by sect. 26, sub-sect. 4 of the Patents, &c. Act, 1883) (*a*).

Sheweth as follows:—

Grant.   1. Letters patent, dated the ———, 18—, have been granted to ———, for [*title of invention*]. The said letters patent were sealed on the ———.

Not first inventor.   2. On the said [*date of letters patent*], the said [*name of grantee*] was not the true and first inventor of the said invention.

Obtained in fraud of petitioner.   3. The said letters patent were obtained by the said [*name of grantee*], in fraud of the rights of your petitioner, who was the true and first inventor of such invention, [*or*, in fraud of the rights of J——— S———, who was the true and first inventor of the said invention. The said J——— S——— died on the ——— day of ———, intestate, and letters of administration of his estate were granted to your petitioner out of the Probate Division of this Honorable Court, on the ——— day of ———].

Invention not new.   4. The said invention was not at the time of the date of the said letters patent a new invention as to the public use and exercise thereof within this realm.

Had been used by petitioner.   5. Your petitioner (*or person under or through whom he claims an interest in any trade, business, or manufacture*) had prior to the date of the said letters patent publicly manufactured, used, or sold within this realm the alleged invention (or a part of the alleged invention, to wit, such part as relates to, &c., &c.), in respect of which such letters patent were granted as aforesaid.

Not subject matter for patent.   6. The said alleged invention was not any manner of new manufacture, the subject of letters patent and grant of privilege within sect. 6 of the Statute of Monopolies.

(*a*) If the petition be presented by any person under sect. 26, sub-sect. 4 (*c*), (d), or (*e*), the name and address, and description of petitioner must appear; if under (b), the fact of the authority of the Attorney-General must be stated. *Glazbrook* v. *Gillatt*, 9 Beav. 492.

Your petitioner humbly prays that the said letters patent may be revoked, or that such other order may be made in the premises as to this Honorable Court shall seem meet.

And your petitioner will ever pray.

It is intended to serve this petition on (b) ———, ———.

---

4. NOTICE OF MOTION FOR INTERLOCUTORY INJUNCTION.

In the High Court of Justice.

Chancery [or Queen's Bench] Division.

Between A. B. - - - - - - - Plaintiff,
and
C. D. - - - - - - - Defendant.

Take notice that this Honorable Court will be moved [*if short notice of motion*, by leave granted] on the ——— day of ———, or so soon thereafter as counsel can be heard by Mr. ———, of counsel for the above-named plaintiff, that an injunction may be awarded against the defendant to restrain the said defendant, his servants or agents until the trial of this action or further order from either directly or indirectly making, using, or putting in practice the invention described in the specification and drawings filed under the letters patent granted to the plaintiff [*or* assignor, *or* other predecessor in title of plaintiff], and numbered ———, or that such further order may be made in the premises as to the Court may seem meet.

---

5. AFFIDAVIT IN SUPPORT OF NOTICE OF MOTION.

[*Title as above.*]

I, ——— of ———, the above-named plaintiff, make oath and say,

1. Letters patent dated [———] were granted to me under   Grant. the seal of the Patent Office for an invention entitled "improvements, &c., &c.," for a period of fourteen years from the ——— day of ———.

2. At the time when the said letters patent were granted to   Novelty. me the said invention was new as to the public use and exercise thereof within this realm.

(b) Here insert the names and addresses of all persons who, either as original grantees or by assignment, are registered under sect. 23 of the Patent, &c. Act, 1883, as interested on the patent.

A copy of the petition must be served personally, unless an order has been obtained for substituted service. The original must be shown if demanded. An order may be obtained for service out of the jurisdiction; see Daniell's Chancery Practice.

First inventor.

3. I am the true and first inventor of the said invention [*or* John Smith or other predecessor in title of the plaintiff, was the true and first inventor of the said invention].

Utility.

4. The said invention is of great public utility.

5. [*State any particular facts, such as a previous action or long user, which have a tendency to cause a presumption of the validity of the patent.*]

Infringement.

6. On the ——— day of ——— the defendant infringed the plaintiff's said patent by manufacturing [selling *or* using], etc. (*c*).

7. [The articles sold by the defendant were not manufactured by me or by my licensees or agents.]

8. I believe that the defendant intends to continue the infringement of the said letters patent, whereby my trade is greatly injured; persons refusing to purchase the patented articles from me [*or* I am unable to grant licences, *or state any other grounds of special damage arising by reason of the continued infringement*].

---

6. INTERLOCUTORY ORDER TO RESTRAIN INFRINGEMENT OF PATENT.

Form 1.

Upon motion, &c. by counsel for the plaintiff, and upon hearing counsel for the defendant [*or* reading an affidavit of service of notice of this motion on the defendant ; *or, if moved ex parte before the defendant has appeared*, the writ of summons issued in this action on the ——— day of ———] [*enter affidavits in support and in opposition, if any*], and the plaintiff, by his counsel, undertaking to abide by any order this Court may make as to damages, in case this Court should hereafter be of opinion that the defendant shall have sustained any, by reason of this order, which the plaintiff ought to pay [*if so, and also undertaking to accept short notice of motion to dissolve the injunction hereby awarded*], let an injunction be awarded to restrain the defendant T., until further order, from manufacturing any tube expanders similar to the tube expander which has been purchased by the defendant B., as in the plaintiff's writ mentioned, or otherwise constructed so as to imitate or resemble the roller expanding tool described in the specification in the plaintiff's letters patent in the said writ mentioned, and to restrain the defendants T. and B., their agents, &c., from selling or offering for sale, or otherwise parting with the custody

Interlocutory injunction.

(*c*) Evidence should be adduced by supporting affidavits in case it is deemed that the defendant has infringed the patent. In *Moore* v. *Bennett*, 1880, M., No. 94, the evidence adduced was that of several persons who had purchased brushes, which, from their appearance, showed they had been made by the patented machine, from the defendant.

of any tube expanders, or parts of any tube expanders, which have been so manufactured by the said defendant T. Liberty to either party to apply to expedite the hearing (*d*).

Form 2.

On usual undertaking as to damages, let an injunction be awarded against the defendants S. and C., to restrain the said defendants, their servants, &c., until the trial of this action or further order, from either directly or indirectly making, using, or putting in practice the invention described in the specification and drawings filed under the letters patent, granted to N., dated the, &c., and numbered 2190, and now vested by assignment in the plaintiff, or any part thereof, except as to any skates made by the plaintiff, or his agents or agent (*e*). The same on terms.

---

7. INTERLOCUTORY INJUNCTION FOR INFRINGEMENT REFUSED ON TERMS.

Upon motion, &c. for injunction to restrain, &c., and the defendant, by his counsel, undertaking to keep an account of all moneys received or to be received by him, by reason of the sale or use of the parlour or roller skates in the writ mentioned, this Court does not think fit to make any order upon the said motion, but does order that the costs of the said motion be costs in the cause (*f*). Refusal on terms.

---

8. INSPECTION, NOTICE OF MOTION FOR.

[*Title as before.*]

Take notice, that this honourable Court will be moved [*if in the Chancery Division*, before his lordship, Mr. Justice ————], on the part of the plaintiff, that the plaintiff, his solicitors and agents, $\frac{\text{and}}{\text{or}}$ two scientific witnesses, to be named in the notice hereinafter mentioned, may be at liberty at all seasonable times, and as often as may be requisite, upon giving three days' previous notice in writing to the defendants' solicitors, to enter into and upon the business premises of the defendants, where the process of decorating or printing tin or metal plates is carried on by the defendants, as stated in the plaintiff's statement of claim in this action, and to inspect and examine there the whole of the process by which such printed and decorated tin and metal plates are manufactured by the defendants; and to take, on pay- Scientific witnesses.

(*d*) *Dudgeon* v. *Thompson*, M. R., 24th March, 1874, A. 723.
(*e*) *Plimpton* v. *Spiller*, M. R., 16th March, 1876, B. 424.
(*f*) *Plimpton* v. *Malcolmson*, M. R., 4th March, 1875, B. 421.

ing the reasonable charges of the defendants for the same, samples of such plates, and upon and during such inspection to make such observations as may be necessary and expedient for the purpose of obtaining full information and evidence of the mode by which such plates are manufactured by the defendants; and that the defendants may be ordered to permit the plaintiff, his solicitors and agents, and two persons to be named as aforesaid, to enter into and upon their said premises for the purposes aforesaid, and that the costs of this application may be costs in the action (*g*).

Take samples.

Costs.

9. INSPECTION, WHERE FOR A PROCESS AND TO TAKE SAMPLES.

[Title as above.]

[*Formal parts as above*] to enter in and upon the business premises of the defendants, where the manufacture of ——— is carried on by the defendants, as mentioned in the statement of claim in this action, and to inspect and examine there the machines used by the said defendants in the manufacture of ———, and the process by which ——— is manufactured by the said defendants, and that the said machines $_{\text{and}}^{\text{or}}$ process may be put to work upon such inspection, and that the plaintiff, his servants or agents, may be at liberty to take samples of the ——— made or to be made by the said machines or process, upon paying to the defendants their reasonable charges for the same.

Machines to be worked.

Samples.

10. INSPECTION, AND ORDER FOR DELIVERY BY DEFENDANT OF SAMPLES FOR ANALYSIS.

[Title as above.]

[*Formal parts as above*] may be at liberty, upon giving three days' previous notice in writing to the defendants' solicitors, to enter upon the defendants' premises, and to inspect the type there used by the said defendants in their printing processes, as mentioned in the statement of claim in this action; and that the defendant may be ordered to permit the plaintiff, his solicitors and agents, and one person to be named as aforesaid, to enter upon his premises for the purpose aforesaid, and that said defendant may be further ordered to deliver to the plaintiff a competent part of the said type so used, on payment of a fair

Samples for analysis.

(*g*) *Flower* v. *Lloyd*, 1876, A. 1254.

price for the same, and that the costs of this application may be costs in the action (*h*).

---

11. ORDER FOR INSPECTION OF DEFENDANTS' PROCESS BY EXPERTS.

Let I. and C., of, &c. be at liberty at all seasonable times, and as often as requisite, on giving three days' notice to the defendants, to enter into the business premises of the defendants where the process of decorating or printing tin and metal plates is carried on by the defendants, as stated in the plaintiff's statement of claim, and mentioned in the said affidavits, or some of them, and to inspect and examine there the whole of the process by which such printed and decorated tin (*i*) and metal plates are manufactured by the defendants, and to take, on paying the reasonable charges of the defendants for the same, samples of such plates, and upon and during such inspection to make such observations as may be necessary and expedient for the purpose of obtaining full information and evidence of the mode by which such plates are manufactured by the defendants (*k*).

Order for experts.

Full information.

(*h*) This was the notice of motion in *The Patent Type Founding Co.* v. *Walter*, reported at 5 H. & N. 192; 29 L. J., Ex. 207; 6 Jur., N. S. 103; 1 L. T. Rep., N. S. 382. The samples of type in this case were required for the purpose of analysis.

Notice of motion for inspection must be supported by affidavit; a fair *prima facie* case of validity and infringement must be made out. The order for inspection is frequently made upon the application for interlocutory injunction, and is sometimes made to include a cross order that the plaintiff shall permit the defendant to see and inspect the patented machine at work, and also to take samples. *Ames* v. *Kelsey*, 22 L. J., Q. B. 84. The affidavit should show that there is such property or machinery as is required to be inspected, that the inspection is necessary for the purpose of the action. *Shaw* v. *Bank of England*, 22 L. J., Ex. 26. It should also show what the patent is for, so that the Court or judge may see that there is necessity for the inspection. The order will not be granted on the plaintiff's application, unless the Court is satisfied that it is essential to enable him to prove his case. *Batley* v. *Kynock*, L. R., 19 Eq. 90; *Meadows* v. *Kirkmann*, 29 L. J., Ex. 205. In *The Singer Manufacturing Company* v. *Wilson*, 13 W. R. 560, the Court refused to give the plaintiff inspection of the defendant's stock before judgment, but ordered the defendant to verify by affidavit all the different kinds of sewing machines which he had sold since the last disclaimer entered by the plaintiff, and to produce one of each sort for inspection.

(*i*) No order will be made on this application for the inspection of books, for which a separate order must be obtained. *Vidi* v. *Smith*, 3 E. & B. 969.

(*k*) *Flower* v. *Lloyd*, C. A., 5th July, 1876, A. 1254.

T.

12. STATEMENT OF CLAIM.

In the High Court of Justice.
    Chancery [*or* Queen's Bench] Division.
        Between A. B. - - - - - Plaintiff.
                and
        C. D. - - - - - Defendant.

Statement of Claim.

Infringement. 1. The defendant has infringed the plaintiff's patent, numbered —, granted for the term of fourteen years from the ——— day of ———, for an invention entitled improvements in the manufacture of iron and steel.

First inventor. 2. The plaintiff was the first and true inventor of the said invention.

Injunction, damages, account. 3. The plaintiff claims an injunction to restrain the defendant from further infringement, and that accounts may be taken of the sales and profits made by the defendant by infringing the said letters patent [*or* in the alternative, £100 damages].

Particulars of breaches are delivered herewith.

[*Place of trial.*]
        Signed.
        Delivered the ——— day of ———, 18—.

---

13. PARTICULARS OF BREACHES.

In the High Court of Justice.
    Chancery [*or* Queen's Bench] Division.
        Between A. B. - - - - - - - Plaintiff,
                and
        C. D. - - - - - - - Defendant.

The following are the particulars of the breaches of the letters patent complained of in the statement of claim herein :—

Using. 1. The defendant on or about the ——— day of ——— at his factory at ———, in the county of ——— manufactured acetate of soda by the process and with the use of the machinery and appliances which form the subject matter of the plaintiff's patent.

Selling. 2. On the ——— day of ——— the defendant sold to John Smith of ———, one parcel containing ——— tons of acetate of soda manufactured by the defendant by the process and with the use of the machinery and appliances which form the subject matter of the plaintiff's patent.

3. On the ——— day of ——— the defendant sold, &c.
                Yours, &c.
                    X. Y.,
                Plaintiff's solicitor.

To Mr. E. F.
    Defendant's solicitor.

[*Formal parts as above.*]

1. The defendant, on or about the ——— day of ———, manufactured at his factory at ———, in the county of ———, sewing machines, which sewing machines were infringements of the plaintiff's patent. Making.

2. The defendant, on or about the ——— day of ——— at his shop at ———, in the county of ———, sold a sewing machine to ———, which sewing machine was an infringement of the plaintiff's patent. Selling.

3. The defendant, on or about the ——— day of ———, in his workshop at ———, in the county of ———, by himself, his servants or agents, used a sewing machine, which sewing machine was an infringement of the plaintiff's patent (*m*). Using.

(*Further and better particulars of breaches or objections obtained by summons, common form.*)

14. ORDER FOR DELIVERY OF FURTHER PARTICULARS OF BREACHES.

It is ordered that the plaintiffs within ——— days from the date of this order deliver to Messrs. ———, solicitors for the defendants, further and better particulars in writing of the breaches alleged to have been committed by the defendant, upon which the defendants intend to rely on the trial of the questions directed to be tried by the said order dated, &c., specifying by reference to the pages and lines the part of the plaintiffs' specification in respect of which such alleged breaches have been committed; and let the time within which the defendants are to deliver to the plaintiffs' solicitors particulars in writing of the objections to the letters patent in the plaintiffs writ mentioned, be enlarged until the twenty-first day after the delivery of such further and better particulars, costs of application to be costs in the cause (*n*). Pages and lines of specification.

15. STATEMENT OF DEFENCE.

In the High Court of Justice.
    Chancery [*Queen's Bench*] Division.
        Between A. B. - - - - - - - - Plaintiff,
                and
        C. D. - - - - - - - - - Defendant.
        Statement of Defence.

1. The defendant did not infringe the patent.
2. The invention was not new.

(*m*) In the case of a patent for a combination, or where there are several distinct claims, the particulars of breaches should specify what portion of the combination has been infringed, or as to which of the claims infringement is alleged.

(*n*) Lamb v. The *Nottingham Manufacturers' Company (Limited)*, M. R., 14th March, 1874, B. 776.

3. The plaintiff was not the first and true inventor.

4. The invention was not useful.

5. [*The denial of any other matter of fact affecting the validity of the patent.*]

6. The patent was not assigned to the plaintiff.

Particulars of objections are delivered herewith.

   Signed.
   Delivered the ——— day of ———, 18—.

---

16. PARTICULARS OF OBJECTIONS IN ACTIONS FOR INFRINGEMENT, AND ON PETITION FOR REVOCATION.

In the High Court of Justice.
 Chancery [*Queen's Bench*] Division.
   Between A. B. - - - - - - - Plaintiff,
       and
      C. D. - - - - - - - Defendant.

Take notice, that the defendant [*or petitioner*] will, on the trial of this cause, rely on the following objections to impeach the letters patent in the statement of claim [*or petition*] herein mentioned.

First inventor.
1. That the plaintiff [*or alleged inventor*] was not the first and true inventor of the said invention within this realm.

Subject-matter.
2. That the alleged invention was not subject-matter of a grant of letters patent, within the meaning of the 6th section of the Statute of Monopolies (that is, the act of the 21st year of King James 1, ch. 3).

Utility.
3. That the alleged invention was not useful to the public.

Insufficiency of specification.
4. That the specification of the said invention was not sufficient, and was unintelligible.

Novelty.
5. That the alleged invention was not a new invention as to the public use and exercise thereof within this realm.

Prior publication in specification.
6. That the alleged invention was published in a specification, dated the ——— day of ———, and numbered ———, and issued by Her Majesty's Commissioners of Patents prior to the date of the said letters patent.

Prior publication in book.
7. That the alleged invention was, prior to the date of the said letters patent, published in a book, which on the ——— day of ———, was in the British Museum Library and open for public inspection; the title of the said book was ———, and the pages of the said book particularly referred to are numbered ——— and ———.

Prior user.
8. That the alleged invention was used prior to the date of the said letters patent in the following manner, that is to say, by ———, at ———, on the ——— day of ———.

9. That a material part of the alleged invention, namely, that part which refers to ———, was not new at the date of the said letters patent, having been used by ———, at ———, on the ——— day of ———. *Part old.*

10. That the plaintiff does not sufficiently distinguish and point out in his specification which of the matters and things therein mentioned he claims to have invented, and which he does not claim to have invented, or admits to be old. *Combination not distinguished.*

11. The defendant will also rely, as examples of prior publication, upon the following specifications, filed with the Commissioners of Patents, and will object that the specification of the plaintiff's patent claims some of the matters thereby patented or specified, that is to say [*enumerate specifications*].

Yours, &c.,
L.
Defendant's Solicitor or Agent.

To Mr. A. B.,
Plaintiff's Solicitor.

---

17. Order for Delivery of Further Particulars of Objections.

Let the order dated 6th July, 1876, whereby it was ordered that the defendants should on or before the 20th July, 1876, deliver to the plaintiffs further and better particulars of objections, stating therein the names and addresses of the persons by whom, and the places where, and the dates at, and the manner in which the process of, &c., was known and publicly practised in England before the 8th March, 1864 [*date of letters patent*], and that in default thereof the words from, and after the words "in a dry state," in the 6th paragraph of the statement of defence, which had been delivered in this action, to the end of the said 6th paragraph, should be struck out; and in that case no evidence should be given by the defendants on the trial of this action of such prior publication, and that defendants should pay to the plaintiffs their costs of the application, to be taxed, &c., BE VARIED, and as varied be as follows:—Let the defendants on or before the ——— deliver to the plaintiffs further and better particulars of objections under the ——— paragraph of the statement of defence on which they mean to rely at the trial, stating therein the place or places at or in which, and in what manner, the process of printing upon tin or metal surfaces by direct impression by means of damp stones is alleged to have been used or published prior to the ——— day of ———, 1864 (*n*).

(*n*) *Flower* v. *Lloyd* (C. A.), 2nd August, 1876, A. 1528; 25 W. R. 17. Varying order of V.-C. B., 6th July, 1876, A. 1252.

18. Interrogatories.

Interrogatories may be delivered in the common form, subject to the Rules of 1883, by either party, notwithstanding the delivery of particulars. Enquiry may be made by the plaintiff as to the names and addresses of the persons by whom prior user is alleged to have been made as well as the places where the prior user has taken place (*o*).

---

19. Order for Reference under Sect. 57 of the Judicature Act, 1873.

[*Formal parts.*]

Upon hearing counsel for the plaintiff, and for the defendant [*or* This cause coming on for trial], It is ordered that the following questions

Novelty.
1. As to whether the invention, the subject of his letters patent of the ——— day of ———, was or was not, at the date of the said letters patent, new as to the public use and exercise thereof within this realm;

First inventor.
2. Whether the plaintiff was the true and first inventor of the said invention;

Sufficiency of specification.
3. Whether the specification of the said letters patent in the pleadings mentioned does or does not particularly describe the nature of the said invention, and in what manner the same is to be performed pursuant to the proviso in that behalf contained in the said letters patent;

Infringement.
4. Whether the defendant has, or has not, infringed the said letters patent, in or by any or either, and which of the apparatus manufactured by him, as in his statement of defence delivered in this action mentioned, or in any other manner;

Disclaimer
5. Whether the undisclaimed portions of the said alleged invention were used in the United Kingdom at the date of the said letters patent;

be referred, to be tried before one of the official referees [*or* a special referee], who shall have all the powers as to certifying and amending of a judge at nisi prius, and shall make his report of and concerning the matters ordered to be tried as aforesaid, pursuant to the statute; and it is further ordered that the said referee shall be at liberty, if he shall think fit, to examine the said parties to this action, and their respective witnesses upon oath or affirmation, and that the said parties do and shall produce before the said referee all books, deeds, papers, and writings in their or either of their custody or power relating to the matters ordered to be tried as aforesaid. And it is

---

(*o*) *Birch* v. *Mather*, 22 Ch. D. 629.

further ordered, that neither the plaintiff nor the defendant shall bring or prosecute any action against the said referee, or against each other of and concerning the matters ordered to be tried as aforesaid. And that if either party shall by affected delay, or otherwise, wilfully prevent the said referee from making his report, he or they shall pay such costs to the other as the said Court, or any judge thereof, shall think reasonable and just. And it is further ordered, that in the event of the said referee declining to act, or dying before he shall have made his report, the said parties may, or if they cannot agree, one of the judges of the said High Court may, upon application of either side, appoint a new referee.

20. Order for Trial of a Representative Case, for the purpose of determining the Question of Validity.

And the plaintiff, F., by his counsel, undertaking to be bound by the result of the trial hereinafter directed, and the said above-mentioned defendants, by their respective counsel, admitting that the letters patent in the pleadings mentioned are duly vested in the plaintiff, and consenting to be bound by the result of the trial hereinafter directed, and that the said trial shall be conducted by B., G., B. and W., four of the above-named defendants, on behalf of and as representing all the defendants in the said suit; let, by consent of all the said several defendants in the above-mentioned suits, the said defendants, B., G., B. and W., be the defendants in the said trial, and let the said defendants, B., G., B. and W., on or before the ——— day of ———, pursuant to the statute, deliver to the plaintiff their objections to the validity of the said patents; and let, by the consent of the plaintiff and the said defendants, the following question be tried before his lordship without a jury, that is to say, whether the patent in the pleadings mentioned, dated, &c., is a valid patent; and the plaintiff is to proceed to such trial on such day, &c. Adjourn the consideration of the costs on the several applications to the judge and to his lordship until after the said trial; and let all further proceedings in the above-mentioned causes be stayed until after the said trial, and any of the defendants in any suits commenced by the plaintiff with respect to infringement of the said patent are to be at liberty to apply to be made parties to this order (*p*). *Undertaking to be bound.* *Delivery of objections.* *Liberty to apply.*

(*p*) *Foxwell* v. *Bradbury*, &c., 80 other titles, L. C., 7th December, 1863, A. 2391; 4 D. J. S. 77.

21. FINAL JUDGMENT—RECITAL OF EVIDENCE—INJUNCTION—
INQUIRY AS TO DAMAGES—ORDER FOR DESTRUCTION—COSTS
AS BETWEEN SOLICITOR AND CLIENT—LIBERTY TO APPLY.

The following Order was settled by the late Master of the Rolls, Sir George Jessel, personally, in the case of Plimpton v. Spiller, reported L. R., 6 Ch. D. 412.

In the High Court of Justice.   1876. P. 69.
Chancery Division.

Thursday the 19th day of April, 1877.

Master of the Rolls.
Mr. Clowes, Reg.

Between J. L. P. - - - - - - - Plaintiff,
              and
    A. F. S., and T. C. - - - Defendants.

Evidence.

Certificate.

This action, coming on for trial the 11th and 12th days of April, 1877, and this day before this Court, in the presence of counsel for the plaintiff and the defendants, upon hearing an order, dated the 4th August, 1876, an affidavit of A. F. S., filed the 15th March, 1876; an affidavit of J. I., filed the 16th February, 1877, the bill, answers, orders, record for trial, and the certificate of the Master of the Rolls, the judge before whom the questions of fact were tried, that the validity of the letters patent of the 25th day of August, 1865, granted to A. V. N., and numbered 2190, hereinafter mentioned, came in question in the cause of P. v. M., 1875, P. 39, and upon hearing the said letters patent, and a certified printed copy of the specifications and drawings, filed under the said letters patent, and the indenture of assignment, dated the 10th day of January, 1866, and made between the said A. V. N., therein described, of the one part, and the plaintiff, J. L. P., of the other part, and registered in the Great Seal Patent Office on the day of the date thereof, the printed shorthand note of the evidence taken orally before this Court, on the trial of the said action of P. v. M., 1875, P. 39; of A. V. N., F. J. B., J. I., J. L. P., E. A. C., R. C. M., W. W. H. and E. J. C. W. and the exhibits marked 1, 2, and 4, then produced; the examination of H. J. A., W. B. P., W. G. A., A. F. S., J. I., T. M. W., G. B., C. P. B. S., E. E., W. S. M. and H. L., taken orally before this Court, on the 11th, 12th, and 19th days of April, 1877, and the exhibits marked: 1. 2. 4. A. B. C. D. E. F. G. H. I. L. M. N. O. P. E. E. 2. S. 1. S. 2. E. E. 1. E. E. 3. W. S. M. 1. W. 1. and W. 2. and the two catalogues and donation book produced to W. G. A., and the volume of the year 1863, of Jewitt's Book of Illustrations to the Report of the American Commissioners of Patent, and the "Scientific American" for the years 1863 and 1865; the records from the

Court of Bankruptcy of an assignment, dated the 11th August, 1865, by W. S. M., for the benefit of his creditors, and of a composition deed by the said W. S. M., in the year 1869, and what was alleged by counsel on both sides, and this Court being of opinion that the plaintiff has proved the breaches complained of, in the particulars of breaches delivered by him in this action, doth order that an injunction be awarded to restrain the defendants, their servants, agents, and workmen during the continuance of the letters patent, granted to A. V. N., dated the 25th day of August, 1865, and numbered 2190, and any extension of the term thereof, from using, or exercising, or causing or permitting to be used or exercised, the invention described in the hereinbefore mentioned specification and drawings, filed under the said letters patent, and from selling, letting for hire, or making any profitable use, or permitting the sale, letting for hire, or profitable use of any roller or runner skates not made by the plaintiff, or his licensees, and having applied thereto rollers or runners in manner described, and for the purposes mentioned in the said specification, or fitted with any apparatus for causing the skate to run in curved line, in the manner described in the said specification and drawings, or differing therefrom only colourably, and by the substitution of mere mechanical equivalents, and it is ordered that it be referred to the official referee in rotation, to inquire what sum of money is fit to be awarded to the plaintiff, to be paid by the defendants in respect of any damage sustained by the plaintiff up to the day of the date of this order, from the manufacture, sale, or letting for hire, of skates, being the same as the "Spiller" Skates, and "Wilson" Skates, in the pleadings in this action, and in the said order dated the 4th August, 1876, mentioned, or of any other skates made in infringement of the said letters patent, or otherwise from the sale, or use by the defendants of the said invention, or any apparatus in imitation of, or being only a colourable deviation from the said invention. And it is ordered, that the defendants, A. F. S. and T. C., do pay to the plaintiff, J. L. P., such sum of money as upon such inquiry shall be found fit, to be awarded to the plaintiff for such compensation as aforesaid, within twenty-one days after service of the official referee's report of the result of the said inquiry. And it is ordered, that the defendants, A. F. S. and T. C., do deliver up on oath to the plaintiff, or break up, or otherwise render unfit for use, all roller skates, or parts of roller skates so manufactured, or let for hire by, or by the order, or for the use of the defendants in infringements of the said letters patent as aforesaid, which are in the possession, custody, or power of the defendants, or either of them, or their, or either of their, servants or agents. And it is ordered, that the said defendants, A. F. S. and T. C., do pay to the plaintiff, J. L. P., his full costs, to be taxed by the taxing master as between solicitor and

[Marginal notes: Proof of breaches. Injunction. Mechanical equivalents. Enquiry as to damages. Payment of amount. Destruction. Full costs.]

client, including all costs, charges, and expenses. And any of the parties are to be at liberty to apply, as they may be advised.

Liberty to apply.

W. C.   Entered.
   G. L.

Registrar's Office, Entering Lib. B. Seal.

---

22. JUDGMENT FOR PERPETUAL INJUNCTION, UNDER THE PATENT LAW AMENDMENT ACT, 1852, RESTRAINING INFRINGEMENT OF PATENTED SKATES AFTER TRIAL WITHOUT JURY, WITH ACCOUNT OF SALES AND PROFITS, DISCOVERY, DELIVERY UP, OR DESTRUCTION.

Injunction. Let an injunction be awarded to restrain the defendant, his servants, &c., during the continuance of the said letters patent granted to N., dated &c., from using or exercising, or causing, or permitting to be used and exercised the invention described in the hereinbefore-mentioned specification and drawings of the said N., and from selling, letting for hire, or making any profitable use, or permitting the sale, letting for hire, or profitable use, of any roller or runner skates not made by the plaintiff or his licensees, and having applied thereto rollers or runners in manner described and for the purposes mentioned in the said specification, or fitted with any apparatus for causing the skate to run in a curved line in the manner described in the said specification and drawings, or differing therefrom only colourably and by the substitution of mere mechanical equivalents; and let an account be taken of all roller skates being the same as the skates sold by the defendant to G., as in the pleadings mentioned, or otherwise made in infringement of the said letters patent, which have been manufactured, or sold, or let for hire, by or by the order, or for the use or profit of the defendant, and also of the gains and profits made by the defendant by reason of such manufacture, sale, or letting for hire; and let the defendant within (seven) days after the service upon him of the chief clerk's certificate of the result of such account pay to the plaintiff the amount of such gains and profits, and let the defendant forthwith upon oath deliver to the plaintiff, or break up, or otherwise render unfit for use, all roller skates or parts of the roller skates so manufactured or let for hire, by or by the order or for the use of the defendants in infringement of the said letters patent as aforesaid, which are in the possession, custody, or power of the defendant or his servants or agents. Defendant to pay to plaintiff costs of suit (*y*).

Account of profits.
Destruction.
Ordinary costs.

(*y*) *Plimpton* v. *Malcolmson*, M. R., 28th January, 1876, B. 381.

23. JUDGMENT FOR PERPETUAL INJUNCTION UNDER THE PATENT LAW AMENDMENT ACT, 1852, RESTRAINING INFRINGEMENT AS TO PATENTED ARTICLES (PULLEYS) AFTER REFUSAL OF MOTION FOR NEW TRIAL AND FOR DELIVERY UP OF THE ARTICLES MADE BY DEFENDANT TO BE SPECIFIED BY AFFIDAVIT.

Let an injunction be awarded to restrain the defendant, S., during the continuance of the letters patent, and any extension of the term thereof, from using or exercising, &c., and from in any manner infringing the rights and privileges granted by the said letters patent; defendant within seven days to specify by affidavit what apparatus constructed or arranged according to the said invention and improvements, or only colourably differing from those described in the said specification and drawing, have been manufactured by or by the order or for the use of the said defendant as in the writ mentioned, and are in the possession, custody or power of the said defendant or his servants or agents; defendant within [seven] days after filing such affidavit to deliver up to the plaintiffs all such pulleys or apparatus (*r*). *Injunction.*

Delivery up of articles.

24. JUDGMENT FOR PERPETUAL INJUNCTION UNDER THE PATENT LAW AMENDMENT ACT, 1852, RESTRAINING INFRINGEMENT OF PATENT FOR MACHINERY AFTER TRIAL OF ISSUES BY A JURY—DISCOVERY—ACCOUNT OF PROFITS—CERTIFICATE FOR FULL COSTS.

And the parties having, on the ———— days of ————, proceeded to a trial of the questions of fact directed to be tried by the order dated, &c., before this court by a jury, when the jury found that [*findings for the plaintiff upon all the issues*]. And upon reading the letters patent, dated, &c., and the complete specification, dated, &c., in the writ respectively mentioned, an affidavit of the plaintiff's, &c. [*enter evidence*], this court doth order [*and*] decree [*and adjudge*] that an injunction be awarded to restrain the defendant, O., his agents, servants, &c., during the subsistence [*continuance*] of the plaintiff's letters patent in the writ mentioned, or any extension thereof, from manufacturing, or selling, or disposing of, or using any machine of the same construction as that supplied to him by the W. B. Co., in the said writ mentioned, or only colourably differing therefrom, or being an infringement of the plaintiff's said patent, and from in any way infringing the plaintiff's said patent; and it is ordered that the defendant, O., do, within [*seven*] days after service of this decree, make and file an affidavit stating what machines of the same construction as that supplied by him to the said W. B. Co., including such machines, are in his possession or power; and the plaintiffs are to be at liberty to inspect and mark the same for

Findings of jury.

Evidence.

Injunction.

Order to inspect and mark.

(*r*) *Tangye* v. *Scott*, V.-C. W., 12th February, 1866, B. 461.

Account.

Costs.

the purpose of identification. And it is ordered that an account be taken of the profits made by the defendant by making, using, selling, or disposing of the machines supplied by him to the said W. B. Co., or any other machine of the same construction therewith, or otherwise by an infringement of the plaintiff's patent. And it is ordered that the defendant, O., do, within one month after the date of the chief clerk's certificate, pay unto the plaintiffs, N. and C., what shall be certified to be the amount of such profits. Direction for certificate that the validity of the plaintiff's patent came in question. And it is ordered that the defendant, O., pay to the plaintiffs their costs of this cause up to and including this hearing, and their costs of the trial by jury of the questions of fact directed to be tried by the said order, dated, &c., including the costs of a special jury; such costs to be taxed, &c. Liberty to apply in chambers touching subsequent costs, and otherwise to apply as advised (s).

25. JUDGMENT FOR THE DEFENDANT.

[Formal parts as above.]

The action having on the ——— day of ——— been tried before Mr. Justice ——— [and a common or special jury of the county of ———, and the jury having found a verdict for the defendant on the issues] and the said Mr. Justice ——— having ordered that judgment be entered for the defendant on the issues [*certificate as to particulars of objections as in form*]: therefore it is adjudged that the plaintiff recover nothing against the defendant, and that the defendant recover against the plaintiff £———, for his costs of defence.

26. CERTIFICATES NECESSARY UNDER SECT. 29, SUB-SECT. 6, OF THE PATENTS, &C. ACT, 1883.

[Form of judgment for perpetual injunction, accounts of profits and damages as above.]

It is certified that the plaintiff has proved to the satisfaction of the Court the breaches mentioned in the particulars of breaches delivered by him, and numbered respectively 1, 2, 3, 4, and 5, and that the particulars numbered 6 and 7, were, under the circumstances of the case, reasonable and proper.

[Form of judgment for defendant as above.]

It is certified that the defendant has proved to the satisfaction of the Court the objections mentioned in the particulars of objections delivered by him, and numbered respectively 1, 2, 3, 4 and 5, and that the objections numbered 6 and 7 were, under the circumstances, reasonable and proper.

(s) *Needham* v. *Oxley*, V.-C. W., 24th June, 1863, B. 1395.

APPENDIX.

PATENTS, DESIGNS AND TRADE MARKS ACT, 1883.

46 & 47 VICT. c. 57.

An Act to amend and consolidate the Law relating to Patents for Inventions, Registration of Designs, and of Trade Marks.

[25th August, 1883.]

BE IT ENACTED by the Queen's most excellent Majesty, by and with the advice and consent of the lords spiritual and temporal, and commons, in this present Parliament assembled, and by the authority of the same, as follows:

PART I.—PRELIMINARY.

1. This act may be cited as the Patents, Designs, and Trade Marks Act, 1883. *Short title.*

2. This act is divided into parts, as follows:— *Division of act into parts.*
   PART I.—Preliminary.
   PART II.—Patents.
   PART III.—Designs.
   PART IV.—Trade Marks.
   PART V.—General.

3. This act, except where it is otherwise expressed, shall commence from and immediately after the 31st day of December, 1883. *Commencement of act.*

PART II.—PATENTS.

Application for and Grant of Patent.

4. (1) Any person, whether a British subject or not, may make an application for a patent. [*page 5*] *Persons entitled to apply for patent.*

   (2) Two or more persons may make a joint application for a patent, and a patent may be granted to them jointly. [*page 5*] *Joint application.*

5. (1) An application for a patent must be made in the form set forth in the first schedule to this act, or in such other form as may be from time to time prescribed; and must be left at, or sent by post to, the patent office in the prescribed manner. [*pages 5, 12, 52*] *Application and specification.*

   (2) An application must contain a declaration to the effect that the applicant is in possession of an invention, whereof he, or in the case of a joint application, one or more of the applicants, claims or claim to be *Declaration.*

the true and first inventor or inventors, and for which he or they desires or desire to obtain a patent; and must be accompanied by either a provisional or complete specification. [*pages 5, 52*]

Provisional specification.

(3) A provisional specification must describe the nature of the invention, and be accompanied by drawings, if required. [*pages 52, 59*]

Complete specification.

(4) A complete specification, whether left on application or subsequently, must particularly describe and ascertain the nature of the invention, and in what manner it is to be performed, and must be accompanied by drawings, if required. [*pages 53, 64 et seq.*]

Necessary contents of specification.

(5) A specification, whether provisional or complete, must commence with the title, and in the case of a complete specification must end with a distinct statement of the invention claimed. [*pages 53, 83*]

Reference of application to examiner.

6. The comptroller shall refer every application to an examiner, who shall ascertain and report to the comptroller whether the nature of the invention has been fairly described, and the application, specification, and drawings (if any) have been prepared in the prescribed manner, and the title sufficiently indicates the subject matter of the invention. [*pages 53, 59*]

Power for comptroller to refuse application or require amendment.

7. (1) If the examiner reports that the nature of the invention is not fairly described, or that the application, specification, or drawings has not or have not been prepared in the prescribed manner, or that the title does not sufficiently indicate the subject matter of the invention, the comptroller may require that the application, specification, or drawings be amended before he proceeds with the application. [*pages 53, 90*]

Appeal from comptroller.

(2) Where the comptroller requires an amendment, the applicant may appeal from his decision to the law officer.

Law officer may make order.

(3) The law officer shall, if required, hear the applicant and the comptroller, and may make an order determining whether and subject to what conditions, if any, the application shall be accepted.

Notice to be given to applicant.

(4) The comptroller shall, when an application has been accepted, give notice thereof to the applicant.

Where subsequent application before first sealed bears similar title, examiner to report to comptroller and give notice to applicants.

(5) If after an application has been made, but before a patent has been sealed, an application is made, accompanied by a specification bearing the same or a similar title, it shall be the duty of the examiner to report to the comptroller whether the specification appears to him to comprise the same invention; and, if he reports in the affirmative, the comptroller shall give notice to the applicants that he has so reported.

Comptroller determines whether applications are similar, and may refuse to seal second patent.

(6) Where the examiner reports in the affirmative, the comptroller may determine, subject to an appeal to the law officer, whether the invention comprised in both applications is the same, and if so he may refuse to seal a patent on the application of the second applicant.

Time for leaving complete specification.

8. (1) If the applicant does not leave a complete specification with his application, he may leave it at any subsequent time within nine months from the date of application. [*pages 53, 59*]

When specification deemed abandoned.

(2) Unless a complete specification is left within that time the application shall be deemed to be abandoned.

Comparison of provisional and complete specification.

9. (1) Where a complete specification is left after a provisional specification, the comptroller shall refer both specifications to an examiner for the purpose of ascertaining whether the complete specification has been prepared in the prescribed manner, and whether the invention particularly

described in the complete specification is substantially the same as that which is described in the provisional specification. [*pages 90, 92*]

(2) If the examiner reports that the conditions hereinbefore contained have not been complied with, the comptroller may refuse to accept the complete specification unless and until the same shall have been amended to his satisfaction; but any such refusal shall be subject to appeal to the law officer. [*page 55*] *Power of comptroller to refuse until amended.*

(3) The law officer shall, if required, hear the applicant and the comptroller, and may make an order determining whether and subject to what conditions, if any, the complete specification shall be accepted. [*pages 53, 90*] *Power of law officer.*

(4) Unless a complete specification is accepted within twelve months from the date of application, then (save in the case of an appeal having been lodged against the refusal to accept) the application shall, at the expiration of those twelve months, become void. *When specification void.*

(5) Reports of examiners shall not in any case be published or be open to public inspection, and shall not be liable to production or inspection in any legal proceeding, other than an appeal to the law officer under this act, unless the court or officer having power to order discovery in such legal proceeding shall certify that such production or inspection is desirable in the interests of justice, and ought to be allowed. *Reports of examiners to be private.*

10. On the acceptance of the complete specification the comptroller shall advertise the acceptance; and the application and specification or specifications with the drawings (if any) shall be open to public inspection. [*pages 54, 90*] *Advertisement on acceptance of complete specification.*

11. (1) Any person may at any time within two months from the date of the advertisement of the acceptance of a complete specification give notice at the patent office of opposition to the grant of the patent on the ground of the applicant having obtained the invention from him, or from a person of whom he is the legal representative, or on the ground that the invention has been patented in this country on an application of prior date, or on the ground of an examiner having reported to the comptroller that the specification appears to him to comprise the same invention as is comprised in a specification bearing the same or a similar title and accompanying a previous application, but on no other ground. [*page 99*] *Opposition to grant of patent. Time and grounds for.*

(2) Where such notice is given the comptroller shall give notice of the opposition to the applicant, and shall, on the expiration of those two months, after hearing the applicant and the person so giving notice, if desirous of being heard, decide on the case, but subject to appeal to the law officer. *After notice comptroller to decide.*

(3) The law officer shall, if required, hear the applicant and any person so giving notice and being, in the opinion of the law officer, entitled to be heard in opposition to the grant, and shall determine whether the grant ought or ought not to be made. *Or on appeal, law officer.*

(4) The law officer may, if he thinks fit, obtain the assistance of an expert, who shall be paid such remuneration as the law officer, with the consent of the treasury, shall appoint. *Who may obtain expert's assistance.*

12. (1) If there is no opposition, or, in case of opposition, if the determination is in favour of the grant of a patent, the comptroller shall cause a patent to be sealed with the seal of the patent office. [*pages 101, 102*] *Sealing of patent. When sealed.*

APPENDIX.

Great seal abolished for patents.	(2) A patent so sealed shall have the same effect as if it were sealed with the great seal of the united kingdom. [*page 225*]
Time for sealing.	(3) A patent shall be sealed as soon as may be, and not after the expiration of fifteen months from the date of application, except in the cases hereinafter mentioned, that is to say—
Exceptions to limit.	
(a) For legal proceedings.	(a) Where the sealing is delayed by an appeal to the law officer, or by opposition to the grant of the patent, the patent may be sealed at such time as the law officer may direct.
(b) When applicant dead.	(b) If the person making the application dies before the expiration of the fifteen months aforesaid, the patent may be granted to his legal representative and sealed at any time within twelve months after the death of the applicant.
Date of patent.	13. Every patent shall be dated and sealed as of the day of the application: provided that no proceedings shall be taken in respect of an infringement committed before the publication of the complete specification: provided also, that in case of more than one application for a patent for the same invention, the sealing of a patent on one of those applications shall not prevent the sealing of a patent on an earlier application.

Provisional Protection.

Provisional protection.	14. Where an application for a patent in respect of an invention has been accepted, the invention may during the period between the date of the application and the date of sealing such patent be used and published without prejudice to the patent to be granted for the same; and such protection from the consequences of use and publication is in this act referred to as provisional protection. [*page 17*]

Protection by Complete Specification.

Effect of acceptance of complete specification.	15. After the acceptance of a complete specification and until the date of sealing a patent in respect thereof, or the expiration of the time for sealing, the applicant shall have the like privileges and rights as if a patent for the invention had been sealed on the date of the acceptance of the complete specification: provided that an applicant shall not be entitled to institute any proceeding for infringement unless and until a patent for the invention has been granted to him. [*pages 64 et seq.*]

Patent.

Extent of patent.	16. Every patent when sealed shall have effect throughout the united kingdom and the Isle of Man. [*pages 102 et seq.*]
Term of patent.	17.—(1) The term limited in every patent for the duration thereof shall be fourteen years from its date.
Cesser on failure of payments.	(2) But every patent shall, notwithstanding anything therein or in this act, cease if the patentee fails to make the prescribed payments within the prescribed times.
Exception by application to comptroller.	(3) If, nevertheless, in any case, by accident, mistake or inadvertence, a patentee fails to make any prescribed payment within the prescribed time, he may apply to the comptroller for an enlargement of the time for making that payment.
Extension of time for	(4) Thereupon the comptroller shall, if satisfied that the failure has arisen from any of the above-mentioned causes, on receipt of the

PATENTS, DESIGNS, AND TRADE MARKS ACT, 1883.   273

prescribed fee for enlargement, not exceeding ten pounds, enlarge the time accordingly, subject to the following conditions : *(payment upon terms.)*
  (a) The time for making any payment shall not in any case be enlarged for more than three months. *(a) Period of extension.*
  (b) If any proceeding shall be taken in respect of an infringement of the patent committed after a failure to make any payment within the prescribed time, and before the enlargement thereof, the court before which the proceeding is proposed to be taken may, if it shall think fit, refuse to award or give any damages in respect of such infringement. *(b) Damages for infringement in the interval.*

Amendment of Specification.

18.—(1) An applicant or a patentee may, from time to time, by request in writing left at the patent office, seek leave to amend his specification, including drawings forming part thereof, by way of disclaimer, correction, or explanation, stating the nature of such amendment and his reasons for the same. [*pages 54, 92, 93, 101*] *Amendment of specification.*

(2) The request and the nature of such proposed amendment shall be advertised in the prescribed manner, and at any time within one month from its first advertisement any person may give notice at the patent office of opposition to the amendment. *Advertisement of amendment and notice of opposition to be given.*

(3) Where such notice is given the comptroller shall give notice of the opposition to the person making the request, and shall hear and decide the case subject to an appeal to the law officer. *Where notice given comptroller decides.*

(4) The law officer shall, if required, hear the person making the request and the person so giving notice, and being in the opinion of the law officer entitled to be heard in opposition to the request, and shall determine whether and subject to what conditions, if any, the amendment ought to be allowed. *Appeal to law officer.*

(5) Where no notice of opposition is given, or the person so giving notice does not appear, the comptroller shall determine whether and subject to what conditions, if any, the amendment ought to be allowed. *Where no notice comptroller determines conditions of amendment.*

(6) When leave to amend is refused by the comptroller, the person making the request may appeal from his decision to the law officer.

(7) The law officer shall, if required, hear the person making the request and the comptroller, and may make an order determining whether, and subject to what conditions, if any, the amendment ought to be allowed. *Appeal to law officer.*

(8) No amendment shall be allowed that would make the specification, as amended, claim an invention substantially larger than or substantially different from the invention claimed by the specification as it stood before amendment. *No amendment allowed so as to enlarge or alter materially specification.*

(9) Leave to amend shall be conclusive as to the right of the party to make the amendment allowed, except in case of fraud; and the amendment shall in all courts and for all purposes be deemed to form part of the specification. *Leave conclusive except in case of fraud; amendment forms part of specification.*

(10) The foregoing provisions of this section do not apply when and so long as any action for infringement or other legal proceeding in relation to a patent is pending. [*page 97*]

19.—(1) In an action for infringement of a patent, and in a proceeding for revocation of a patent, the court or a judge may at any time order that the patentee shall, subject to such terms as to costs and otherwise as the *Power to disclaim part of invention during action, &c.*

T.   T

court or a judge may impose, be at liberty to apply at the patent office for leave to amend his specification by way of disclaimer, and may direct that in the meantime the trial or hearing of the action shall be postponed. [*pages 94, 97*]

Restriction on recovery of damages.

20. Where an amendment by way of disclaimer, correction, or explanation, has been allowed under this act, no damages shall be given in any action in respect of the use of the invention before the disclaimer, correction or explanation, unless the patentee establishes to the satisfaction of the court, that his original claim was framed in good faith and with reasonable skill and knowledge. [*pages 94, 98*]

Advertisement of amendment.

21. Every amendment of a specification shall be advertised in the prescribed manner.

Compulsory Licenses.

Power for board of trade to order grant of licenses.

22. If on the petition of any person interested it is proved to the board of trade that by reason of the default of a patentee to grant licenses on reasonable terms— [*page 118*]
 (a) The patent is not being worked in the united kingdom; or
 (b) The reasonable requirements of the public with respect to the invention cannot be supplied; or
 (c) Any person is prevented from working or using to the best advantage an invention of which he is possessed,
the board may order the patentee to grant licenses on such terms as to the amount of royalties, security for payment, or otherwise, as the board, having regard to the nature of the invention and the circumstances of the case, may deem just, and any such order may be enforced by mandamus.

Register of Patents.

Register of patents. Where to be kept and contents.

23.—(1) There shall be kept at the patent office a book called the Register of Patents, wherein shall be entered the names and addresses of grantees of patents, notifications of assignments and of transmissions of patents, of licenses under patents, and of amendments, extensions, and revocations of patents, and such other matters affecting the validity or proprietorship of patents as may from time to time be prescribed. [*pages 20, 120*]

Is evidence.

(2) The register of patents shall be prima facie evidence of any matters by this act directed or authorized to be inserted therein.

Copies for filing.

(3) Copies of deeds, licenses, and any other documents affecting the proprietorship in any letters patent or in any license thereunder, must be supplied to the comptroller in the prescribed manner for filing in the patent office.

Fees.

Fees payable.

24.—(1) There shall be paid in respect of the several instruments described in the second schedule to this act, the fees in that schedule mentioned, and there shall likewise be paid, in respect of other matters under this part of the act, such fees as may be from time to time, with the sanction of the treasury, prescribed by the board of trade; and such fees shall be levied and paid to the account of her majesty's exchequer in such manner as the treasury may from time to time direct.

Power to reduce fees.

(2) The board of trade may from time to time, if they think fit, with the consent of the treasury, reduce any of those fees.

Extension of Term of Patent.

25.—(1) A patentee may, after advertising in manner directed by any rules made under this section his intention to do so, present a petition to her majesty in council, praying that his patent may be extended for a further term; but such petition must be presented at least six months before the time limited for the expiration of the patent. [*pages 123 et seq.*] Extension of term of patent on petition to Queen in council. When applied for.

(2) Any person may enter a caveat, addressed to the registrar of the council at the council office, against the extension. Entry of caveat.

(3) If her majesty shall be pleased to refer any such petition to the judicial committee of the privy council, the said committee shall proceed to consider the same, and the petitioner and any person who has entered a caveat shall be entitled to be heard by himself or by counsel on the petition. Privy Council jurisdiction.

(4) The judicial committee shall, in considering their decision, have regard to the nature and merits of the invention in relation to the public, to the profits made by the patentee as such, and to all the circumstances of the case. [*page 133*] Powers of judicial committee.

(5) If the judicial committee report that the patentee has been inadequately remunerated by his patent, it shall be lawful for her majesty in council to extend the term of the patent for a further term not exceeding seven, or in exceptional cases fourteen, years; or to order the grant of a new patent for the term therein mentioned, and containing any restrictions, conditions, and provisions that the judicial committee may think fit. On their report extension granted on conditions.

(6) It shall be lawful for her majesty in council to make, from time to time, rules of procedure and practice for regulating proceedings on such petitions, and subject thereto such proceedings shall be regulated according to the existing procedure and practice in patent matters of the judicial committee. [*page 131*] Power to make rules for such proceedings.

(7) The costs of all parties of and incident to such proceedings shall be in the discretion of the judicial committee; and the orders of the committee respecting costs shall be enforceable as if they were orders of a division of the high court of justice. Costs.

Revocation.

26.—(1) The proceeding by scire facias to repeal a patent is hereby abolished. [*pages 97, 100, 181, 223, 250*] Abolition of scire facias.

(2) Revocation of a patent may be obtained on petition to the court. Revocation of patent.

(3) Every ground on which a patent might, at the commencement of this act, be repealed by scire facias shall be available by way of defence to an action of infringement and shall also be a ground of revocation. How revocation obtained. Grounds of revocation.

(4) A petition for revocation of a patent may be presented by— Petition for revocation, who may present.
 (a) The attorney-general in England or Ireland, or the lord advocate in Scotland: [*pages 183, 184, 245*]
 (b) Any person authorized by the attorney-general in England or Ireland, or the lord advocate in Scotland:
 (c) Any person alleging that the patent was obtained in fraud of his rights, or of the rights of any person under or through whom he claims:
 (d) Any person alleging that he, or any person under or through whom he claims, was the true inventor of any invention included in the claim of the patentee:
 (e) Any person alleging that he, or any person under or through whom

he claims an interest in any trade, business, or manufacture, had publicly manufactured, used, or sold, within this realm, before the date of the patent, anything claimed by the patentee as his invention.

Plaintiff must deliver and be bound by particulars.

(5) The plaintiff must deliver with his petition particulars of the objections on which he means to rely, and no evidence shall, except by leave of the court or a judge, be admitted in proof of any objection of which particulars are not so delivered. [*page 246*]

Amendment of particulars.

(6) Particulars delivered may be from time to time amended by leave of the court or a judge. [*page 247*]

Patentee though defendant has privileges of plaintiff at trial.

(7) The defendant shall be entitled to begin, and give evidence in support of the patent, and if the plaintiff gives evidence impeaching the validity of the patent, the defendant shall be entitled to reply. [*pages 224, 247*]

Where patent revoked for fraud, first true inventor may obtain patent.

(8) Where a patent has been revoked on the ground of fraud, the comptroller may, on the application of the true inventor, made in accordance with the provisions of this act, grant to him a patent in lieu of and bearing the same date as the date of revocation of the patent so revoked, but the patent so granted shall cease on the expiration of the term for which the revoked patent was granted.

Crown.

Patent to bind crown.

27.—(1) A patent shall have to all intents the like effect as against her majesty the queen, her heirs and successors, as it has against a subject. [*pages 111, 159*]

Exceptions.

(2) But the officers or authorities administering any department of the service of the crown may, by themselves, their agents, contractors, or others, at any time after the application, use the invention for the services of the crown on terms to be before or after the use thereof agreed on, with the approval of the treasury, between those officers or authorities and the patentee, or, in default of such agreement, on such terms as may be settled by the treasury after hearing all parties interested.

Legal Proceedings.

Hearing with assessor.
By court.

28.—(1) In an action or proceeding for infringement or revocation of a patent, the court may, if it thinks fit, and shall, on the request of either of the parties to the proceeding, call in the aid of an assessor specially qualified, and try and hear the case wholly or partially with his assistance; the action shall be tried without a jury unless the court shall otherwise direct. [*pages 221, 247, 248*]

Court of appeal or privy council may sit with assessors.
Assessors' fees.

(2) The court of appeal or the judicial committee of the privy council may, if they see fit, in any proceeding before them respectively, call in the aid of an assessor as aforesaid.

(3) The remuneration, if any, to be paid to an assessor under this section shall be determined by the court or the court of appeal or judicial committee, as the case may be, and be paid in the same manner as the other expenses of the execution of this act.

Delivery of particulars of breaches.

29.—(1) In an action for infringement of a patent the plaintiff must deliver with his statement of claim, or by order of the court or the judge, at any subsequent time, particulars of the breaches complained of. [*pages 196, 221, 248, 250*]

(2) The defendant must deliver, with his statement of defence, or, by order of the court or a judge, at any subsequent time, particulars of any objections on which he relies in support thereof. [*page 201 et seq.*] — of objections.

(3) If the defendant disputes the validity of the patent, the particulars delivered by him must state on what grounds he disputes it, and if one of those grounds is want of novelty, must state the time and place of the previous publication or user alleged by him. [*page 260*] — Grounds must be stated.

(4) At the hearing no evidence shall, except by leave of the court or a judge, be admitted in proof of any alleged infringement or objection of which particulars are not so delivered. [*page 194*] — Evidence must not go beyond particulars.

(5) Particulars delivered may be, from time to time, amended, by leave of the court or a judge. [*page 194*] — Amendment.

(6) On taxation of costs, regard shall be had to the particulars delivered by the plaintiff and by the defendant; and they respectively shall not be allowed any costs in respect of any particular delivered by them, unless the same is certified by the court or a judge to have been proven, or to have been reasonable and proper, without regard to the general costs of the case. [*pages 241, 242, 248*] — Costs.

30. In an action for infringement of a patent, the court or a judge may, on the application of either party, make such order for an injunction, inspection, or account, and impose such terms, and give such directions respecting the same and the proceedings thereon as the court or a judge may see fit. [*page 216*] — Order for inspection, &c., in action.

31. In an action for infringement of a patent, the court or a judge may certify that the validity of the patent came in question; and if the court or a judge so certifies, then in any subsequent action for infringement, the plaintiff in that action, on obtaining a final order or judgment in his favour, shall have his full costs, charges, and expenses as between solicitor and client, unless the court or judge trying the action certifies that he ought not to have the same. [*pages 239, 241, 246*] — Certificate that validity questioned.

32. Where any person claiming to be the patentee of an invention, by circulars, advertisements, or otherwise, threatens any other person with any legal proceedings or liability in respect of any alleged manufacture, use, sale, or purchase of the invention, any person or persons aggrieved thereby may bring an action against him, and may obtain an injunction against the continuance of such threats, and may recover such damage (if any) as may have been sustained thereby, if the alleged manufacture, use, sale, or purchase to which the threats related was not, in fact, an infringement of any legal rights of the person making such threats: Provided that this section shall not apply if the person making such threats with due diligence commences and prosecutes an action for infringement of his patent. [*page 249*] — Remedy in case of groundless threats of legal proceedings.

Miscellaneous.

33. Every patent may be in the form in the first schedule to this act, and shall be granted for one invention only, but may contain more than one claim; but it shall not be competent for any person in an action or other proceeding, to take any objection to a patent on the ground that it comprises more than one invention. [*page 142*] — Patent for one invention only.

278   APPENDIX.

<table>
<tr><td>Patent on application of representative of deceased inventor.</td><td>34.—(1) If a person possessed of an invention dies without making application for a patent for the invention, application may be made by, and a patent for the invention granted to, his legal representative. [*pages 8, 112*]</td></tr>
<tr><td>Time and contents of application.</td><td>(2) Every such application must be made within six months of the decease of such person, and must contain a declaration by the legal representative that he believes such person to be the true and first inventor of the invention.</td></tr>
<tr><td>Patent to first inventor not invalidated by application in fraud of him.</td><td>35. A patent granted to the true and first inventor shall not be invalidated by an application in fraud of him, or by provisional protection obtained thereon, or by any use or publication of the invention subsequent to that fraudulent application during the period of provisional protection. [*page 16*]</td></tr>
<tr><td>Assignment for particular places.</td><td>36. A patentee may assign his patent for any place in or part of the united kingdom, or Isle of Man, as effectually as if the patent were originally granted to extend to that place, or part only. [*pages 114, 137, 142, 188*]</td></tr>
<tr><td>Loss or destruction of patent.</td><td>37. If a patent is lost or destroyed, or its non-production is accounted for to the satisfaction of the comptroller, the comptroller may, at any time, cause a duplicate thereof to be sealed.</td></tr>
<tr><td>Proceedings and costs before law officer.</td><td>38. The law officers may examine witnesses on oath, and administer oaths for that purpose under this part of this act, and may, from time to time, make, alter, and rescind rules regulating references and appeals to the law officers, and the practice and procedure before them under this part of this act; and in any proceeding before either of the law officers under this part of this act, the law officer may order costs to be paid by either party, and any such order may be made a rule of the court. [*pages 91, 98, 101.*]</td></tr>
<tr><td>Exhibition at industrial or international exhibition not to prejudice patent rights.</td><td>39. The exhibition of an invention at an industrial or international exhibition, certified as such by the board of trade, or the publication of any description of the invention during the period of the holding of the exhibition, or the use of the invention for the purpose of the exhibition in the place where the exhibition is held, or the use of the invention during the period of the holding of the exhibition by any person elsewhere, without the privity or consent of the inventor, shall not prejudice the right of the inventor or his legal personal representative to apply for and obtain provisional protection and a patent in respect of the invention or the validity of any patent granted on the application, provided that both the following conditions are complied with, namely,—</td></tr>
<tr><td>Conditions:
(a) Notice;
(b) Patent must be applied for.</td><td>(a) The exhibitor must, before exhibiting the invention, give the comptroller the prescribed notice of his intention to do so; and
(b) The application for a patent must be made before or within six months from the date of the opening of the exhibition.</td></tr>
<tr><td>Publication of illustrated journal, indexes, &c.</td><td>40.—(1) The comptroller shall cause to be issued periodically an illustrated journal of patented inventions, as well as reports of patent cases decided by courts of law, and any other information that the comptroller may deem generally useful or important.</td></tr>
<tr><td>Copies to be on sale.</td><td>(2) Provision shall be made by the comptroller for keeping on sale</td></tr>
</table>

copies of such journal, and also of all complete specifications of patents for the time being in force, with their accompanying drawings, if any.

(3) The comptroller shall continue, in such form as he may deem expedient, the indexes and abridgments of specifications hitherto published, and shall from time to time prepare and publish such other indexes, abridgments of specifications, catalogues and other works relating to inventions, as he may see fit. <small>Continuation of publication.</small>

41. The control and management of the existing patent museum and its contents shall, from and after the commencement of this act, be transferred to and vested in the department of science and art, subject to such directions as her majesty in council may see fit to give. <small>Patent museum.</small>

42. The department of science and art may at any time require a patentee to furnish them with a model of his invention on payment to the patentee of the cost of the manufacture of the model; the amount to be settled, in case of dispute, by the board of trade. <small>Power to require models on payment.</small>

43.—(1) A patent shall not prevent the use of an invention for the purposes of the navigation of a foreign vessel within the jurisdiction of any of her majesty's courts in the united kingdom, or Isle of Man, or the use of an invention in a foreign vessel within that jurisdiction, provided it is not used therein for or in connexion with the manufacture or preparation of anything intended to be sold in or exported from the united kingdom or Isle of Man. [*page 162*] <small>Foreign vessels in British waters.</small>

(2) But this section shall not extend to vessels of any foreign state of which the laws authorize subjects of such foreign state, having patents or like privileges for the exclusive use or· exercise of inventions within its territories, to prevent or interfere with the use of such inventions in British vessels while in the ports of such foreign state, or in the waters within the jurisdiction of its courts, where such inventions are not so used for the manufacture or preparation of anything intended to be sold in or exported from the territories of such foreign state. <small>Exception.</small>

44.—(1) The inventor of any improvement in instruments or munitions of war, his executors, administrators, or assigns (who are in this section comprised in the expression the inventor), may (either for or without valuable consideration) assign to her majesty's principal secretary of state for the war department (hereinafter referred to as the secretary of state), on behalf of her majesty, all the benefit of the invention and of any patent obtained or to be obtained for the same; and the secretary of state may be a party to the assignment. [*page 111*] <small>Assignment to secretary for war of certain inventions.</small>

(2) The assignment shall effectually vest the benefit of the invention and patent in the secretary of state for the time being on behalf of her majesty, and all covenants and agreements therein contained for keeping the invention secret and otherwise shall be valid and effectual (notwithstanding any want of valuable consideration), and may be enforced accordingly by the secretary of state for the time being. <small>Extent of assignment.</small>

(3) Where any such assignment has been made to the secretary of state, he may at any time before the application for a patent for the invention, or before publication of the specification or specifications, certify to the comptroller his opinion that, in the interest of the public service, the particulars of the invention and of the manner in which it is to be performed should be kept secret. <small>Power of secretary of state for war to keep invention secret on certifying that it is in public interest to do so.</small>

280 APPENDIX.

In which case specifications and documents are sealed up.

(4) If the secretary of state so certifies, the application and specification or specifications with the drawings (if any), and any amendment of the specification or specifications, and any copies of such documents and drawings, shall, instead of being left in the ordinary manner at the patent office, be delivered to the comptroller in a packet sealed by authority of the secretary of state.

For term of patent.

(5) Such packet shall, until the expiration of the term or extended term during which a patent for the invention may be in force, be kept sealed by the comptroller, and shall not be opened save under the authority of an order of the secretary of state, or of the law officers.

Delivery of packet under secretary of state's authority during term.

(6) Such sealed packet shall be delivered at any time during the continuance of the patent to any person authorized by writing under the hand of the secretary of state to receive the same, and shall if returned to the comptroller be again kept sealed by him.

At expiration.

(7) On the expiration of the term or extended term of the patent, such sealed packet shall be delivered to any person authorized by writing under the hand of the secretary of state to receive it.

Foregoing subsections to apply where patent applied for but specifications not published.

(8) Where the secretary of state certifies as aforesaid, after an application for a patent has been left at the patent office, but before the publication of the specification or specifications, the application, specification or specifications, with the drawings (if any), shall be forthwith placed in a packet sealed by authority of the comptroller, and such packet shall be subject to the foregoing provisions respecting a packet sealed by authority of the secretary of state.

Where certified by secretary of state no petition for revocation.

(9) No proceeding by petition or otherwise shall lie for revocation of a patent granted for an invention in relation to which the secretary of state has certified as aforesaid.

No copy of any secret specifications to be made public.

(10) No copy of any specification or other document or drawing by this section required to be placed in a sealed packet, shall in any manner whatever be published or open to the inspection of the public, but save as in this section otherwise directed, the provisions of this part of this act shall apply in respect of any such invention and patent as aforesaid.

Power of secretary of state to waive benefit of section.

(11) The secretary of state may, at any time by writing under his hand, waive the benefit of this section with respect to any particular invention, and the specifications, documents and drawings shall be thenceforth kept and dealt with in the ordinary way.

Communication to secretary of state for war not to be deemed publication.

(12) The communication of any invention for any improvement in instruments or munitions of war to the secretary of state, or to any person or persons authorized by him to investigate the same or the merits thereof, shall not, nor shall anything done for the purposes of the investigation, be deemed use or publication of such invention so as to prejudice the grant or validity of any patent for the same.

Existing Patents.

Provisions respecting existing patents.

45.—(1) The provisions of this act relating to applications for patents and proceedings thereon shall have effect in respect only of applications made after the commencement of this act.

(2) Every patent granted before the commencement of this act, or on an application then pending, shall remain unaffected by the provisions of this act relating to patents binding the crown, and to compulsory licenses. [*page 135*]

(3) In all other respects (including the amount and time of payment of fees) this act shall extend to all patents granted before the commencement of this act, or on applications then pending, in substitution for such enactments as would have applied thereto if this act had not been passed. [*page 135*]

(4) All instruments relating to patents granted before the commencement of this act required to be left or filed in the great seal patent office shall be deemed to be so left or filed if left or filed before or after the commencement of this act in the patent office. Documents left at great seal patent office deemed left at patent office on commencement of this act.

Definitions.

46. In and for the purposes of this act— Definitions of

" Patent " means letters patent for an invention : " Patent ;"

" Patentee " means the person for the time being entitled to the benefit of a patent : [*pages 5, 95*] " Patentee ;"

" Invention " means any manner of new manufacture the subject of letters patent and grant of privilege within sect. 6 of the Statute of Monopolies (that is, the act of the twenty-first year of the reign of King James the First, chapter 3, intituled, "An Act concerning monopolies and dispensations with penal laws and the forfeiture thereof"), and includes an alleged invention. [*pages 22, 119*] " Invention ;"

In Scotland " injunction " means " interdict." " Injunction " in Scotland.

PART III.—DESIGNS.

Registration of Designs.

47.—(1) The comptroller may, on application by or on behalf of any person claiming to be the proprietor of any new or original design not previously published in the united kingdom, register the design under this part of this act. Application for registration of designs.

(2) The application must be made in the form set forth in the first schedule to this act, or in such other form as may be from time to time prescribed, and must be left at, or sent by post to, the patent office in the prescribed manner. How made.

(3) The application must contain a statement of the nature of the design, and the class or classes of goods in which the applicant desires that the design be registered. Contents.

(4) The same design may be registered in more than one class. Classification

(5) In case of doubt as to the class in which a design ought to be registered, the comptroller may decide the question. Power of comptroller to classify.

(6) The comptroller may, if he thinks fit, refuse to register any design presented to him for registration, but any person aggrieved by any such refusal may appeal therefrom to the board of trade. Power to refuse registration.

(7) The board of trade shall, if required, hear the applicant and the comptroller, and may make an order determining whether, and subject to what conditions, if any, registration is to be permitted. Appeal to board of trade.

48.—(1) On application for registration of a design the applicant shall furnish to the comptroller the prescribed number of copies of drawings, photographs or tracings of the design sufficient, in the opinion of the comptroller, for enabling him to identify the design; or the applicant may, instead of such copies, furnish exact representations or specimens of the design. Drawings, &c., to be furnished on application.

Power of comptroller to refuse if not suitable.

(2) The comptroller may, if he thinks fit, refuse any drawing, photograph, tracing, representation or specimen which is not, in his opinion, suitable for the official records.

Certificate of registration. Copies.

49.— 1) The comptroller shall grant a certificate of registration to the proprietor of the design when registered.

(2) The comptroller may, in case of loss of the original certificate, or in any other case in which he deems it expedient, grant a copy or copies of the certificate.

Copyright in registered Designs.

Copyright on registration.

50.—(1) When a design is registered, the registered proprietor of the design shall, subject to the provisions of this act, have copyright in the design during five years from the date of registration.

(2) Before delivery on sale of any articles to which a registered design has been applied, the proprietor must (if exact representations or specimens were not furnished on the application for registration) furnish to the comptroller the prescribed number of exact representations or specimens of the design; and if he fails to do so, the comptroller may erase his name from the register, and thereupon his copyright in the design shall cease.

Marking registered designs.

51. Before delivery on sale of any articles to which a registered design has been applied, the proprietor of the design shall cause each such article to be marked with the prescribed mark, or with the prescribed word or words or figures, denoting that the design is registered; and if he fails to do so the copyright in the design shall cease, unless the proprietor shows that he took all proper steps to ensure the marking of the article.

Inspection of registered designs.

52.—(1) During the existence of copyright in a design, the design shall not be open to inspection except by the proprietor, or a person authorized in writing by the proprietor, or a person authorized by the comptroller or by the court, and furnishing such information as may enable the comptroller to identify the design, nor except in the presence of the comptroller, or of an officer acting under him, nor except on payment of the prescribed fee; and the person making the inspection shall not be entitled to take any copy of the design, or of any part thereof.

When copyright has ceased.

(2) When the copyright in a design has ceased, the design shall be open to inspection, and copies thereof may be taken by any person on payment of the prescribed fee.

Information as to existence of copyright.

53. On the request of any person producing a particular design, together with its mark of registration, or producing only its mark of registration, or furnishing such information as may enable the comptroller to identify the design, and on payment of the prescribed fee, it shall be the duty of the comptroller to inform such person whether the registration still exists in respect of such design, and if so, in respect of what class or classes of goods, and stating also the date of registration, and the name and address of the registered proprietor.

Foreign design.

54. If a registered design is used in manufacture in any foreign country, and is not used in this country within six months of its registration in this country, the copyright in the design shall cease.

Register of Designs.

55.—(1) There shall be kept at the patent office a book called the register of designs, wherein shall be entered the names and addresses of proprietors of registered designs, notifications of assignments and of transmissions of registered designs, and such other matters as may from time to time be prescribed. *[margin: Register of designs.]*

(2) The register of designs shall be primâ facie evidence of any matters by this act directed or authorized to be entered therein.

Fees.

56. There shall be paid in respect of applications and registration and other matters under this part of this act such fees as may be from time to time, with the sanction of the treasury, prescribed by the board of trade; and such fees shall be levied and paid to the account of her majesty's exchequer in such manner as the treasury shall from time to time direct. *[margin: Fees on registration, &c.]*

Industrial and International Exhibitions.

57. The exhibition at an industrial or international exhibition, certified as such by the board of trade, or the exhibition elsewhere during the period of the holding of the exhibition, without the privity or consent of the proprietor, of a design, or of any article to which a design is applied, or the publication, during the holding of any such exhibition, of a description of a design, shall not prevent the design from being registered, or invalidate the registration thereof, provided that both the following conditions are complied with, namely:— *[margin: Exhibition at Industrial or international exhibition not to prevent or invalidate registration.]*

(a) The exhibitor must, before exhibiting the design or article, or publishing a description of the design, give the comptroller the prescribed notice of his intention to do so; and *[margin: Conditions.]*

(b) The application for registration must be made before or within six months from the date of the opening of the exhibition.

Legal Proceedings.

58. During the existence of copyright in any design—

(a) It shall not be lawful for any person, without the licence or written consent of the registered proprietor, to apply such design or any fraudulent or obvious imitation thereof, in the class or classes of goods in which such design is registered, for purposes of sale to any article of manufacture or to any substance artificial or natural or partly artificial and partly natural; and *[margin: Penalty on piracy of registered design.]*

(b) It shall not be lawful for any person to publish or expose for sale any article of manufacture or any substance to which such design or any fraudulent or obvious imitation thereof shall have been so applied, knowing that the same has been so applied without the consent of the registered proprietor.

Any person who acts in contravention of this section shall be liable for every offence to forfeit a sum not exceeding fifty pounds to the registered proprietor of the design, who may recover such sum as a simple contract debt by action in any court of competent jurisdiction.

59. Notwithstanding the remedy given by this act for the recovery of such penalty as aforesaid, the registered proprietor of any design may (if he elects to do so) bring an action for the recovery of any damages arising from the application of any such design, or of any fraudulent or obvious *[margin: Action for damages.]*

imitation thereof for the purpose of sale, to any article of manufacture or substance, or from the publication, sale or exposure for sale by any person of any article or substance to which such design or any fraudulent or obvious imitation thereof shall have been so applied, such person knowing that the proprietor had not given his consent to such application.

Definitions.

60. In and for the purposes of this act—

Definition of "design."

"Design" means any design applicable to any article of manufacture, or to any substance artificial or natural, or partly artificial and partly natural, whether the design is applicable for the pattern, or for the shape or configuration, or for the ornament thereof, or for any two or more of such purposes, and by whatever means it is applicable, whether by printing, painting, embroidering, weaving, sewing, modelling, casting, embossing, engraving, staining, or any other means whatever, manual, mechanical, or chemical, separate or combined, not being a design for a sculpture, or other thing within the protection of the Sculpture Copyright Act of the year 1814 (54 Geo. 3, c. 56).

"Copyright."

"Copyright" means the exclusive right to apply a design to any article of manufacture or to any such substance as aforesaid in the class or classes in which the design is registered.

Definition of proprietor.

61. The author of any new and original design shall be considered the proprietor thereof, unless he executed the work on behalf of another person for a good or valuable consideration, in which case such person shall be considered the proprietor, and every person acquiring for a good or valuable consideration a new and original design, or the right to apply the same to any such article or substance as aforesaid, either exclusively of any other person or otherwise, and also every person on whom the property in such design or such right to the application thereof shall devolve, shall be considered the proprietor of the design in the respect in which the same may have been so acquired, and to that extent, but not otherwise.

PART IV.—TRADE MARKS.

Registration of Trade Marks.

Application for registration.

62.—1) The comptroller may, on application by or on behalf of any person claiming to be the proprietor of a trade mark, register the trade mark.

How made.

2) The application must be made in the form set forth in the first schedule to this act, or in such other form as may be from time to time prescribed, and must be left at, or sent by post to, the patent office in the prescribed manner.

Contents.

3) The application must be accompanied by the prescribed number of representations of the trade mark, and must state the particular goods or classes of goods in connexion with which the applicant desires the trade mark to be registered.

Power of comptroller to refuse.

4) The comptroller may, if he thinks fit, refuse to register a trade mark, but any such refusal shall be subject to appeal to the board of trade, who shall, if required, hear the applicant and the comptroller, and may make an order determining whether, and subject to what conditions, if any, registration is to be permitted.

(5) The board of trade may, however, if it appears expedient, refer the appeal to the court; and in that event the court shall have jurisdiction to hear and determine the appeal, and may make such order as aforesaid. *Appeal to board of trade.*

63. Where registration of a trade mark has not been or shall not be completed within twelve months from the date of the application, by reason of default on the part of the applicant, the application shall be deemed to be abandoned. *Limit of time for proceeding with application.*

64.—(1) For the purposes of this act, a trade mark must consist of or contain at least one of the following essential particulars: *Conditions of registration of trade mark. Must contain*
- (a) A name of an individual or firm printed, impressed, or woven in some particular and distinctive manner; or *(a) name.*
- (b) A written signature or copy of a written signature of the individual or firm applying for registration thereof as a trade mark; or *(b) signature.*
- (c) A distinctive device, mark, brand, heading, label, ticket, or fancy word or words not in common use. *(c) device.*

(2) There may be added to any one or more of these particulars any letters, words, or figures, or combination of letters, words, or figures, or any of them. *Combination of letters may be added.*

(3) Provided that any special and distinctive word or words, letter, figure, or combination of letters or figures, or of letters and figures used as a trade mark before the 13th day of August, 1875, may be registered as a trade mark under this part of this act. *Proviso protecting trade marks used before Act of 1875.*

65. A trade mark must be registered for particular goods or classes of goods. *Connexion of trade mark with goods.*

66. When a person claiming to be the proprietor of several trade marks which, while resembling each other in the material particulars thereof, yet differ in respect of (a) the statement of the goods for which they are respectively used or proposed to be used, or (b) statements of numbers, or (c) statements of price, or (d) statements of quality, or (e) statements of names of places, seeks to register such trade marks, they may be registered as a series in one registration. A series of trade marks shall be assignable and transmissible only as a whole, but for all other purposes each of the trade marks composing a series shall be deemed and treated as registered separately. *Registration of a series of marks.*

67. A trade mark may be registered in any colour, and such registration shall (subject to the provisions of this act) confer on the registered owner the exclusive right to use the same in that or any other colour. *Trade marks may be registered in any colour.*

68. Every application for registration of a trade mark under this part of this act shall as soon as may be after its receipt be advertised by the comptroller. *Advertisement of application.*

69.—(1) Any person may within two months of the first advertisement of the application, give notice in duplicate at the patent office of opposition to registration of the trade mark, and the comptroller shall send one copy of such notice to the applicant. *Opposition to registration. Notice of opposition.*

(2) Within two months after receipt of such notice, or such further time as the comptroller may allow, the applicant may send to the comp- *Counter statement of application.*

troller a counter statement in duplicate of the grounds on which he relies for his application, and if he does not do so, shall be deemed to have abandoned his application.

Notice to opposers and security for costs.

(3) If the applicant sends such counter statement, the comptroller shall furnish a copy thereof to the person who gave notice of opposition, and shall require him to give security in such manner and to such amount as the comptroller may require for such costs as may be awarded in respect of such opposition; and if such security is not given within fourteen days after such requirement was made, or such further time as the comptroller may allow, the opposition shall be deemed to be withdrawn.

Notice of security for costs.

(4) If the person who gave notice of opposition duly gives such security as aforesaid, the comptroller shall inform the applicant thereof in writing, and thereupon the case shall be deemed to stand for the determination of the court.

Assignment and transmission of trade mark.

70. A trade mark, when registered, shall be assigned and transmitted only in connexion with the goodwill of the business concerned in the particular goods or classes of goods for which it has been registered, and shall be determinable with that goodwill.

Conflicting claims to registration.

71. Where each of several persons claims to be registered as proprietor of the same trade mark, the comptroller may refuse to register any of them until their rights have been determined according to law, and the comptroller may himself submit or require the claimants to submit their rights to the court.

Restrictions on registration. No registration of identical marks.

72.—(1) Except where the court has decided that two or more persons are entitled to be registered as proprietors of the same trade mark, the comptroller shall not register in respect of the same goods or description of goods a trade mark identical with one already on the register with respect to such goods or description of goods.

Nor of very similar marks.

(2) The comptroller shall not register with respect to the same goods or description of goods a trade mark so nearly resembling a trade mark already on the register with respect to such goods or description of goods as to be calculated to deceive.

Further restriction on registration.

73. It shall not be lawful to register as part of or in combination with a trade mark any words the exclusive use of which would by reason of their being calculated to deceive or otherwise, be deemed disentitled to protection in a court of justice, or any scandalous design.

Addition to trade mark may be registered.
before 1875 Act;

74.—(1) Nothing in this act shall be construed to prevent the comptroller entering on the register in the prescribed manner, and subject to the prescribed conditions, as an addition to any trade mark—

(a) In the case of an application for registration of a trade mark used before the 13th day of August, 1875—

Any distinctive device, mark, brand, heading, label, ticket, letter, word, or figure, or combination of letters, words, or figures, though the same is common to the trade in the goods with respect to which the application is made;

under 1875 Act.

(b) In the case of an application for registration of a trade mark not used before the 13th day of August, 1875—

Any distinctive word or combination of words, though the same is common to the trade in the goods with respect to which the application is made;

(2) The applicant for entry of any such common particular or particulars must, however, disclaim in his application any right to the exclusive use of the same, and a copy of the disclaimer shall be entered on the register. *(Disclaimer.)*

(3) Any device, mark, brand, heading, label, ticket, letter, word, figure, or combination of letters, words, or figures, which was or were before the 13th day of August, 1875, publicly used by more than three persons on the same or a similar description of goods shall, for the purposes of this section, be deemed common to the trade in such goods. *(Marks used by more than three persons prior to 1875.)*

Effect of Registration.

75. Registration of a trade mark shall be deemed to be equivalent to public use of the trade mark. *(Registration equivalent to public use.)*

76. The registration of a person as proprietor of a trade mark shall be primâ facie evidence of his right to the exclusive use of the trade mark, and shall, after the expiration of five years from the date of the registration, be conclusive evidence of his right to the exclusive use of the trade mark, subject to the provisions of this act. *(Right of first proprietor to exclusive use of trade mark.)*

77. A person shall not be entitled to institute any proceeding to prevent or to recover damages for the infringement of a trade mark unless, in the case of a trade mark capable of being registered under this act, it has been registered in pursuance of this act, or of an enactment repealed by this act, or in the case of any other trade mark in use before the 13th of August, 1875, registration thereof under this part of this act, or of an enactment repealed by this act, has been refused. The comptroller may, on request, and on payment of the prescribed fee, grant a certificate that such registration has been refused. *(Restrictions on actions for infringement, and on defence to action in certain cases.)*

Register of Trade Marks.

78. There shall be kept at the patent office a book called the register of trade marks, wherein shall be entered the names and addresses of proprietors of registered trade marks, notifications of assignments and of transmissions of trade marks, and such other matters as may be from time to time prescribed. *(Register of trade marks.)*

79.—(1) At a time not being less than two months nor more than three months before the expiration of fourteen years from the date of the registration of a trade mark, the comptroller shall send notice to the registered proprietor that the trade mark will be removed from the register unless the proprietor pays to the comptroller before the expiration of such fourteen years (naming the date at which the same will expire) the prescribed fee; and if such fees be not previously paid, he shall at the expiration of one month from the date of the giving of the first notice send a second notice to the same effect. *(Removal of trade mark after fourteen years unless fee paid.)*

(2) If such fee be not paid before the expiration of such fourteen years the comptroller may, after the end of three months from the expiration of such fourteen years, remove the mark from the register, and so from time to time at the expiration of every period of fourteen years. *(Fees.)*

(3) If before the expiration of the said three months the registered proprietor pays the said fee together with the additional prescribed fee, the comptroller may, without removing such trade mark from the register, *(Time for payment.)*

accept the said fee as if it had been paid before the expiration of the said fourteen years.

Power of comptroller to restore trade mark.

(1) Where after the said three months a trade mark has been removed from the register for non-payment of the prescribed fee, the comptroller may, if satisfied that it is just so to do, restore such trade mark to the register on payment of the prescribed additional fee.

(5) Where a trade mark has been removed from the register for non-payment of the fee or otherwise, such trade mark shall nevertheless, for the purpose of any application for registration during the five years next after the date of such removal, be deemed to be a trade mark which is already registered.

Fees.

Fees for registration, &c.

80. There shall be paid in respect of applications and registration and other matters under this part of this act, such fees as may be from time to time, with the sanction of the treasury, prescribed by the board of trade; and such fees shall be levied and paid to the account of her majesty's exchequer in such manner as the treasury may from time to time direct.

Sheffield Marks.

Registration by cutlers' company of Sheffield marks.

81. With respect to the master, wardens, searchers, assistants, and commonalty of the company of cutlers in Hallamshire, in the county of York (in this act called the cutlers' company), and the marks or devices (in this act called Sheffield marks) assigned or registered by the master, wardens, searchers, and assistants of that company, the following provisions shall have effect:

Sheffield register.

1) The cutlers' company shall establish and keep at Sheffield a new register of trade marks (in this act called the Sheffield register):

Contents.

(2) The cutlers' company shall enter in the Sheffield register, in respect of cutlery, edge tools, or raw steel and the goods mentioned in the next sub-section, all the trade marks entered before the commencement of this act in respect of cutlery, edge tools, or raw steel and such goods in the register established under the Trade Marks Registration Act, 1875, belonging to persons carrying on business in Hallamshire, or within six miles thereof, and shall also enter in such register, in respect of the same goods, all the trade marks which shall have been assigned by the cutlers' company and actually used before the commencement of this act, but which have not been entered in the register established under the Trade Marks Registration Act, 1875.

To whom application made.

(3) An application for registration of a trade mark used on cutlery, edge tools, or on raw steel, or on goods made of steel, or of steel and iron combined, whether with or without a cutting edge, shall, if made after the commencement of this act by a person carrying on business in Hallamshire, or within six miles thereof, be made to the cutlers' company:

Notification of application.

(4) Every application so made to the cutlers' company shall be notified to the comptroller in the prescribed manner, and unless the comptroller, within the prescribed time, gives notice to the cutlers' company that he objects to the acceptance of the application, it shall be proceeded with by the cutlers' company in the prescribed manner:

(5) If the comptroller gives notice of objection as aforesaid, the application shall not be proceeded with by the cutlers' company, but any person aggrieved may appeal to the court. *Notice of objection.*

(6) Upon the registration of a trade mark in the Sheffield register, the cutlers' company shall give notice thereof to the comptroller, who shall thereupon enter the mark in the register of trade marks; and such registration shall bear date as of the day of application to the cutlers' company, and have the same effect as if the application had been made to the comptroller on that day: *Notification of entry of mark.*

(7) The provisions of this act, and of any general rules made under this act, with respect to application for registration in the register of trade marks, the effect of such registration, and the assignment and transmission of rights in a registered trade mark shall apply in the case of applications and registration in the Sheffield register; and notice of every entry made in the Sheffield register must be given to the comptroller by the cutlers' company, save and except that the provisions of this sub-section shall not prejudice or affect any life, estate, and interest of a widow of the holder of any Sheffield mark which may be in force in respect of such mark at the time when it shall be placed upon the Sheffield register: *Notice of entry in Sheffield register.*

(8) Where the comptroller receives from any person not carrying on business in Hallamshire or within six miles thereof an application for registration of a trade mark used on cutlery, edge tools, or on raw steel, or on goods made of steel, or of steel and iron combined, whether with or without a cutting edge, he shall in the prescribed manner notify the application and proceedings thereon to the cutlers' company: *Application from outside district.*

(9) At the expiration of five years from the commencement of this act the cutlers' company shall close the cutlers' register of corporate trade marks, and thereupon all marks entered therein shall, unless entered in the Sheffield register, be deemed to have been abandoned: *Close of register and expiry of trade marks therein.*

(10) A person may (notwithstanding anything in any act relating to the cutlers' company) be registered in the Sheffield register as proprietor of two or more trade marks: *Registry of more than one mark.*

(11) A body of persons, corporate or not corporate, may (notwithstanding anything in any act relating to the cutlers' company) be registered in the Sheffield register as proprietor of a trade mark or trade marks: *Bodies corporate or non-corporate may register.*

(12) Any person aggrieved by a decision of the cutlers' company in respect of anything done or omitted under this act may, in the prescribed manner, appeal to the comptroller, who shall have power to confirm, reverse or modify the decision, but the decision of the comptroller shall be subject to a further appeal to the court: *Appeal.*

(13) So much of the Cutlers' Company's Acts as applies to the summary punishment of persons counterfeiting Sheffield corporate marks, that is to say, the fifth section of the Cutlers' Company's Act of 1814, and the provisions in relation to the recovery and application of the penalty imposed by such last-mentioned section contained in the Cutlers' Company's Act of 1791, shall apply to any mark entered in the Sheffield register. *Application of Cutlers' Company's Acts.*

T   U

PART V.—GENERAL.

Patent Office and Proceedings thereat.

Patent office.

82.—(1) The treasury may provide for the purposes of this act an office with all requisite buildings and conveniences, which shall be called, and is in this act referred to as, the patent office.

(2) Until a new patent office is provided, the offices of the commissioners of patents for inventions and for the registration of designs and trade marks existing at the commencement of this act shall be the patent office within the meaning of this act.

Control.

(3) The patent office shall be under the immediate control of an officer called the comptroller general of patents, designs, and trade marks, who shall act under the superintendence and direction of the board of trade.

(4) Any act or thing directed to be done by or to the comptroller may, in his absence, be done by or to any officer for the time being in that behalf authorized by the board of trade.

Officers and clerks.

83.—(1) The board of trade may at any time after the passing of this act, and from time to time, subject to the approval of the treasury, appoint the comptroller-general of patents, designs, and trade marks, and so many examiners and other officers and clerks, with such designations and duties as the board of trade think fit, and may from time to time remove any of those officers and clerks.

Salaries.

(2) The salaries of those officers and clerks shall be appointed by the board of trade, with the concurrence of the treasury, and the same and the other expenses of the execution of this act shall be paid out of money provided by parliament.

Seal of patent office.

84. There shall be a seal for the patent office, and impressions thereof shall be judicially noticed and admitted in evidence. [*page 102*]

Trust not to be entered in registers.

85. There shall not be entered in any register kept under this act, or be receivable by the comptroller, any notice of any trust expressed, implied or constructive. [*pages 20, 121*]

Refusal to grant patent, &c., in certain cases.

86. The comptroller may refuse to grant a patent for an invention, or to register a design or trade mark, of which the use would, in his opinion, be contrary to law or morality. [*page 105*]

Entry of assignments and transmissions in registers.

87. Where a person becomes entitled by assignment, transmission, or other operation of law to a patent, or to the copyright in a registered design, or to a registered trade mark, the comptroller shall on request, and on proof of title to his satisfaction, cause the name of such person to be entered as proprietor of the patent, copyright in the design, or trade mark, in the register of patents, designs, or trade marks, as the case may be. The person for the time being entered in the register of patents, designs, or trade marks, as proprietor of a patent, copyright in a design or trade mark as the case may be, shall, subject to any rights appearing from such register to be vested in any other person, have power absolutely to assign, grant licenses as to, or otherwise deal with, the same and to give effectual receipts for any consideration for such assignment, license, or dealing. Provided that any equities in respect of such patent, design, or trade mark may be enforced in like manner as in respect of any other personal property. [*page 121*]

88. Every register kept under this act shall at all convenient times be open to the inspection of the public, subject to such regulations as may be prescribed; and certified copies, sealed with the seal of the patent office, of any entry in any such register shall be given to any person requiring the same on payment of the prescribed fee. [*page 121*] Inspection of and extracts from registers.

89. Printed or written copies or extracts, purporting to be certified by the comptroller and sealed with the seal of the patent office, of or from patents, specifications, disclaimers and other documents in the patent office, and of or from registers and other books kept there, shall be admitted in evidence in all courts in her majesty's dominions, and in all proceedings, without further proof or production of the originals. [*pages 121, 225*] Sealed copies to be received in evidence.

90.—(1) The court may on the application of any person aggrieved by the omission without sufficient cause of the name of any person from any register kept under this act, or by any entry made without sufficient cause in any such register, make such order for making, expunging, or varying the entry, as the court thinks fit; or the court may refuse the application; and in either case may make such order with respect to the costs of the proceedings as the court thinks fit. [*page 121*] Rectification of registers by court.

(2) The court may in any proceeding under this section decide any question that it may be necessary or expedient to decide for the rectification of a register, and may direct an issue to be tried for the decision of any question of fact, and may award damages to the party aggrieved. Powers of court to decide all necessary questions.

(3) Any order of the court rectifying a register shall direct that due notice of the rectification be given to the comptroller. Notice.

91. The comptroller may, on request in writing accompanied by the prescribed fee,— [*page 121*] Power for comptroller to correct clerical errors.
 (a) Correct any clerical error in or in connection with an application for a patent, or for registration of a design or trade mark; or
 (b) Correct any clerical error in the name, style or address of the registered proprietor of a patent, design, or trade mark;
 (c) Cancel the entry or part of the entry of a trade mark on the register: Provided that the applicant accompanies his request by a statutory declaration made by himself, stating his name, address, and calling, and that he is the person whose name appears on the register as the proprietor of the said trade mark.

92.—(1) The registered proprietor of any registered trade mark may apply to the court for leave to add to or alter such mark in any particular, not being an essential particular within the meaning of this act, and the court may refuse or grant leave on such terms as it may think fit. Alteration of registered mark.

(2) Notice of any intended application to the court under this section shall be given to the comptroller by the applicant; and the comptroller shall be entitled to be heard on the application. Notice to be given.

(3) If the court grants leave, the comptroller shall, on proof thereof and on payment of the prescribed fee, cause the register to be altered in conformity with the order of leave. Comptroller to alter in accordance with order.

93. If any person makes or causes to be made a false entry in any register kept under this act, or a writing falsely purporting to be a copy of an entry in any such register, or produces or tenders or causes to be produced or tendered in evidence any such writing, knowing the entry or writing to be false, he shall be guilty of a misdemeanor. Falsification of entries in registers.

292   APPENDIX.

Exercise of discretionary power by comptroller.

94. Where any discretionary power is by this act given to the comptroller, he shall not exercise that power adversely to the applicant for a patent, or for amendment of a specification, or for registration of a trade mark or design, without if so required within the prescribed time by the applicant giving the applicant an opportunity of being heard personally or by his agent. [*page 91*]

Power of comptroller to take directions of law officers.

95. The comptroller may, in any case of doubt or difficulty arising in the administration of any of the provisions of this act, apply to either of the law officers for directions in the matter.

Certificate of comptroller to be evidence.

96. A certificate purporting to be under the hand of the comptroller as to any entry, matter, or thing which he is authorized by this act, or any general rules made thereunder, to make or do, shall be primâ facie evidence of the entry having been made, and of the contents thereof, and of the matter or thing having been done or left undone. [*page 225*]

Applications and notices by post.

97. (1.) Any application, notice, or other document authorized or required to be left, made, or given at the patent office, or to the comptroller, or to any other person under this act, may be sent by a prepaid letter through the post; and if so sent shall be deemed to have been left, made, or given respectively at the time when the letter containing the same would be delivered in the ordinary course of post.

Proof.

(2.) In proving such service or sending, it shall be sufficient to prove that the letter was properly addressed and put into the post.

Provision as to days for leaving documents at office.

98. Whenever the last day fixed by this act, or by any rule for the time being in force, for leaving any document or paying any fee at the patent office shall fall on Christmas Day, Good Friday, or on a Saturday or Sunday, or any day observed as a holiday at the Bank of England, or any day observed as a day of public fast or thanksgiving, herein referred to as excluded days, it shall be lawful to leave such document, or to pay such fee, on the day next following such excluded day, or days if two or more of them occur consecutively.

Declaration by infant, lunatic, &c.

99. If any person is, by reason of infancy, lunacy, or other inability, incapable of making any declaration or doing anything required or permitted by this act or by any rules made under the authority of this act, then the guardian or committee (if any) of such incapable person, or if there be none, any person appointed by any court or judge possessing jurisdiction in respect of the property of incapable persons, upon the petition of any person on behalf of such incapable person, or of any other person interested in the making such declaration or doing such thing, may make such declaration or a declaration as nearly corresponding thereto as circumstances permit, and do such thing in the name and on behalf of such incapable person, and all acts done by such substitute shall be for the purposes of this act be as effectual as if done by the person for whom he is substituted. [*page 6*]

Transmission of certified printed copies of specifications, &c.

100. Copies of all specifications, drawings, and amendments left at the patent office after the commencement of this act, printed for and sealed with the seal of the patent office, shall be transmitted to the Edinburgh museum of science and art, and to the enrolments office of the chancery division in Ireland, and to the rolls office in the Isle of Man, within

twenty-one days after the same shall respectively have been accepted or allowed at the patent office; and certified copies of or extracts from any such documents shall be given to any person requiring the same on payment of the prescribed fee; and any such copy or extract shall be admitted in evidence in all courts in Scotland and Ireland and in the Isle of Man without further proof or production of the originals.

101.—(1) The board of trade may from time to time make such general rules and do such things as they think expedient, subject to the provisions of this act— [*page 119*]

(a) For regulating the practice of registration under this act :
(b) For classifying goods for the purposes of designs and trade marks :
(c) For making or requiring duplicates of specifications, amendments, drawings, and other documents :
(d) For securing and regulating the publishing and selling of copies, at such prices and in such manner as the board of trade think fit, of specifications, drawings, amendments, and other documents :
(e) For securing and regulating the making, printing, publishing, and selling of indexes to, and abridgments of, specifications and other documents in the patent office; and providing for the inspection of indexes and abridgments and other documents :
(f) For regulating (with the approval of the treasury) the presentation of copies of patent office publications to patentees and to public authorities, bodies, and institutions at home and abroad :
(g) Generally for regulating the business of the patent office, and all things by this act placed under the direction or control of the comptroller, or of the board of trade.

Power for board of trade to make general rules for classifying goods and regulating business of patent office.

(2) Any of the forms in the first schedule to this act may be altered or amended by rules made by the board as aforesaid.

Alteration of forms.

(3) General rules may be made under this section at any time after the passing of this act, but not so as to take effect before the commencement of this act, and shall (subject as hereinafter mentioned) be of the same effect as if they were contained in this act, and shall be judicially noticed.

General rules;

(4) Any rules made in pursuance of this section shall be laid before both houses of parliament, if parliament be in session at the time of making thereof, or, if not, then as soon as practicable after the beginning of the then next session of parliament, and they shall also be advertised twice in the official journal to be issued by the comptroller.

to be laid before parliament and advertised.

(5) If either house of parliament, within the next forty days after any rules have been so laid before such house, resolve that such rules or any of them ought to be annulled, the same shall after the date of such resolution be of no effect, without prejudice to the validity of anything done in the meantime under such rules or rule or to the making of any new rules or rule.

102. The comptroller shall, before the first day of June in every year, cause a report respecting the execution by or under him of this act to be laid before both houses of parliament, and therein shall include for the year to which each report relates all general rules made in that year under or for the purposes of this act, and an account of all fees, salaries, and allowances, and other money received and paid under this act.

Annual reports of comptroller.

International and Colonial Arrangements.

International arrangements for protection of inventions, designs, and trade marks.

103.—(1) If her majesty is pleased to make any arrangement with the government or governments of any foreign state or states for mutual protection of inventions, designs, and trade marks, or any of them, then any person who has applied for protection for any invention, design, or trade mark in any such state shall be entitled to a patent for his invention or to registration of his design or trade mark (as the case may be) under this act, in priority to other applicants; and such patent or registration shall have the same date as the date of the protection obtained in such foreign state. [*pages 185, 186*]

Time.

Provided that his application is made, in the case of a patent within seven months, and in the case of a design or trade mark within four months, from his applying for protection in the foreign state with which the arrangement is in force.

No protection prior to specification or registration.

Provided that nothing in this section contained shall entitle the patentee or proprietor of the design or trade mark to recover damages for infringements happening prior to the date of the actual acceptance of his complete specification, or the actual registration of his design or trade mark in this country, as the case may be.

Publication at or use in exhibition not to invalidate patent or trade mark.

2) The publication in the united kingdom or the Isle of Man, during the respective periods aforesaid, of any description of the invention, or the use therein during such periods of the invention, or the exhibition or use therein during such periods of the design, or the publication therein during such periods of a description or representation of the design, or the use therein during such periods of the trade mark, shall not invalidate the patent which may be granted for the invention, or the registration of the design or trade mark:

Application under this section to be made in same manner as ordinary application.

(3) The application for the grant of a patent, or the registration of a design, or the registration of a trade mark under this section, must be made in the same manner as an ordinary application under this act: Provided that, in the case of trade marks, any trade mark the registration of which has been duly applied for in the country of origin may be registered under this act:

Application of this section.

(4) The provisions of this section shall apply only in the case of those foreign states with respect to which her majesty shall from time to time by order in council declare them to be applicable, and so long only in the case of each state as the order in council shall continue in force with respect to that state.

Provision for colonies and India.

104.—1) Where it is made to appear to her majesty that the legislature of any British possession has made satisfactory provision for the protection of inventions, designs, and trade marks, patented or registered in this country, it shall be lawful for her majesty, from time to time, by order in council, to apply the provisions of the last preceding section, with such variations or additions, if any, as to her majesty in council may seem fit, to such British possession. [*pages 185, 186*]

Effect of order in council.

2) An order in council under this act shall, from a date to be mentioned for the purpose in the order, take effect as if its provisions had been contained in this act; but it shall be lawful for her majesty in council to revoke any order in council made under this act.

Offences.

105.—(1) Any person who represents that any article sold by him is a patented article, when no patent has been granted for the same, or describes any design or trade mark applied to any article sold by him as registered which is not so, shall be liable for every offence on summary conviction to a fine not exceeding five pounds. *[Penalty on falsely representing articles to be patented.]*

(2) A person shall be deemed, for the purposes of this enactment, to represent that an article is patented or a design or a trade mark is registered, if he sells the article with the word "patent," "patented," "registered," or any word or words expressing or implying that a patent or registration has been obtained for the article stamped, engraved, or impressed on, or otherwise applied to the article. *[Definition of false representation under this section.]*

106. Any person who, without the authority of her majesty, or any of the royal family, or of any government department, assumes or uses in connection with any trade, business, calling, or profession, the royal arms, or arms so nearly resembling the same as to be calculated to deceive, in such a manner as to be calculated to lead other persons to believe that he is carrying on his trade, business, calling, or profession by or under such authority as aforesaid, shall be liable on summary conviction to a fine not exceeding twenty pounds. *[Penalty on unauthorized assumption of royal arms.]*

Scotland; Ireland; &c.

107. In any action for infringement of a patent in Scotland the provisions of this act, with respect to calling in the aid of an assessor, shall apply, and the action shall be tried without a jury, unless the court shall otherwise direct, but otherwise nothing shall affect the jurisdiction and forms of process of the courts in Scotland in such an action or in any action or proceeding respecting a patent hitherto competent to those courts. *[Saving for courts in Scotland.]*

For the purposes of this section "court of appeal" shall mean any court to which such action is appealed. *[Definition of "court of appeal."]*

108. In Scotland any offence under this act declared to be punishable on summary conviction may be prosecuted in the sheriff court. *[Summary proceedings in Scotland.]*

109.—(1) Proceedings in Scotland for revocation of a patent shall be in the form of an action of reduction at the instance of the lord advocate, or at the instance of a party having interest with his concurrence, which concurrence may be given on just cause shown only. [*page 183*] *[Proceedings for revocation of patent in Scotland.]*

(2) Service of all writs and summonses in that action shall be made according to the forms and practice existing at the commencement of this act. *[Service in Scotland.]*

110. All parties shall, notwithstanding anything in this act, have in Ireland their remedies under or in respect of a patent as if the same had been granted to extend to Ireland only. [*page 184*] *[Reservation of remedies in Ireland.]*

111.—(1) The provisions of this act conferring a special jurisdiction on the court as defined by this act, shall not, except so far as the jurisdiction extends, affect the jurisdiction of any court in Scotland or Ireland in any proceedings relating to patents or to designs or to trade marks; and with reference to any such proceedings in Scotland, the term "the court" shall mean any lord ordinary of the court of session, and the *[General saving for jurisdiction of courts.]*

term "court of appeal" shall mean either division of the said court; and with reference to any such proceedings in Ireland, the terms "the court" and "the court of appeal" respectively mean the high court of justice in Ireland and her majesty's court of appeal in Ireland.

Rectification of register.

(2.) If any rectification of a register under this act is required in pursuance of any proceeding in a court in Scotland or Ireland, a copy of the order, decree, or other authority for the rectification, shall be served on the comptroller, and he shall rectify the register accordingly.

Isle of Man.
Jurisdiction of courts.

112. This act shall extend to the Isle of Man, and—

(1) Nothing in this act shall affect the jurisdiction of the courts in the Isle of Man, in proceedings for infringement or in any action or proceeding respecting a patent, design, or trade mark competent to those courts:

Punishments.

(2) The punishment for a misdemeanor under this act in the Isle of Man shall be imprisonment for any term not exceeding two years, with or without hard labour, and with or without a fine not exceeding one hundred pounds, at the discretion of the court;

Offences and penalties treated as in England under this act.

(3) Any offence under this act committed in the Isle of Man which would in England be punishable on summary conviction may be prosecuted, and any fine in respect thereof recovered at the instance of any person aggrieved, in the manner in which offences punishable on summary conviction may for the time being be prosecuted.

Repeal; Transitional Provisions; Savings.

Repeal and saving for past operation of repealed enactments, &c.
Exceptions.

113. The enactments described in the third schedule to this act are hereby repealed. But this repeal of enactments shall not—

(a) Affect the past operation of any of those enactments, or any patent or copyright or right to use a trade mark granted or acquired, or application pending, or appointment made, or compensation granted, or order or direction made or given, or right, privilege, obligation, or liability acquired, accrued, or incurred, or anything duly done or suffered under or by any of those enactments before or at the commencement of this act; or

(b) Interfere with the institution or prosecution of any action or proceeding, civil or criminal, in respect thereof, and any such proceeding may be carried on as if this act had not been passed; or

(c) Take away or abridge any protection or benefit in relation to any such action or proceeding.

Former registers to be deemed continued.

114.— 1 The registers of patents and of proprietors kept under any enactment repealed by this act shall respectively be deemed parts of the same book as the register of patents kept under this act.

(2 The registers of designs and of trade marks kept under any enactment repealed by this act shall respectively be deemed parts of the same book as the register of designs and the register of trade marks kept under this act.

Saving for existing rules.

115. All general rules made by the lord chancellor or by any other authority under any enactment repealed by this act, and in force at the commencement of this act, may at any time after the passing of this act be repealed, altered, or amended by the board of trade, as if they had been made by the board under this act, but so that no such repeal, altera-

tion, or amendment shall take effect before the commencement of this act; and, subject as aforesaid, such general rules shall, so far as they are consistent with and are not superseded by this act, continue in force as if they had been made by the board of trade under this act.

116. Nothing in this act shall take away, abridge, or prejudicially affect the prerogative of the crown in relation to the granting of any letters patent, or to the withholding of a grant thereof. *Saving for prerogative.*

General Definitions.

117.—(1) In and for the purposes of this act, unless the context otherwise requires,— *General definitions.*

"Person" includes a body corporate: *"Person."*

"The Court" means (subject to the provisions for Scotland, Ireland, and the Isle of Man) her majesty's high court of justice in England: *"Court."*
[*page 181*]

"Law officer" means her majesty's attorney-general or solicitor-general for England: *"Law officer."*

"The Treasury" means the commissioners of her majesty's treasury. *"Treasury."*

"Comptroller" means the comptroller general of patents, designs, and trade marks: *"Comptroller."*

"Prescribed" means prescribed by any of the schedules to this act, or by general rules under or within the meaning of this act: *"Prescribed."*

"British possession" means any territory or place situate within her majesty's dominions, and not being or forming part of the united kingdom, or of the Channel Islands, or of the Isle of Man, and all territories and places under one legislature, as hereinafter defined, are deemed to be one British possession for the purposes of this act: *"British possession."*

"Legislature" includes any person or persons who exercise legislative authority in the British possession; and where there are local legislatures as well as a central legislature, means the central legislature only. *"Legislature."*

In the application of this act to Ireland, "summary conviction" means a conviction under the Summary Jurisdiction Acts, that is to say, with reference to the Dublin metropolitan police district the acts regulating the duties of justices of the peace and of the police for such district, and elsewhere in Ireland the Petty Sessions (Ireland) Act, 1851, and any act amending it. *"Summary conviction" as applied to Ireland.*

SCHEDULES.

The First Schedule.

FORMS OF APPLICATION, &c.

Form A. Section 5.

FORM OF APPLICATION FOR PATENT.

£1 Stamp.

I, (*a*) *John Smith*, of 29, *Perry Street, Birmingham*, in the county of *Warwick*, *Engineer*, do solemnly and sincerely declare that I am in possession of an invention for (*b*) "*Improvements in Sewing Machines:*" that I am the true and first inventor thereof; and that the same is not in use by any other person or persons to the best of my knowledge and belief; and I humbly pray that a patent may be granted to me for the said invention.

(*a*) Here insert name, address and calling of inventor.
(*b*) Here insert title of invention.

And I make the above solemn declaration conscientiously believing the same to be true, and by virtue of the provisions of the Statutory Declarations Act, 1835.

(c) *John Smith.*

Declared at *Birmingham*, in the county of *Warwick*, this   day of   18 .
Before me,
(d) *James Adams, Justice of the Peace.*

NOTE.—Where the above declaration is made out of the united kingdom, the words "and by virtue of the Statutory Declarations Act, 1835," must be omitted; and the declaration must be made before a British consular officer, or where it is not reasonably practicable to make it before such officer, then before a public officer duly authorized in that behalf.

(c) Signature of inventor.
(d) Signature and title of the officer before whom the declaration is made.

FORM B.

FORM OF PROVISIONAL SPECIFICATION.

Improvements in Sewing Machines (a).

I, (b) *John Smith*, of 29, *Perry Street, Birmingham*, in the county of *Warwick, Engineer*, do hereby declare the nature of my invention for "*Improvements in Sewing Machines*," to be as follows (c) :—

(d) *John Smith.*

Dated this   day of   18 .

NOTE.—No stamp is required on this document.

(a) Here insert title, as in declaration.
(b) Here insert name, address, and calling of inventor, as in declaration.
(c) Here insert short description of invention.
(d) Signature of inventor.

FORM C.

£3 Stamp.

FORM OF COMPLETE SPECIFICATION.

Improvements in Sewing Machines (a).

I, b *John Smith*, of 29, *Perry Street, Birmingham*, in the county of *Warwick, Engineer*, do hereby declare the nature of my invention for "*Improvements in Sewing Machines*," and in what manner the same is to be performed, to be particularly described and ascertained in and by the following statement (c) :—

Having now particularly described and ascertained the nature of my said invention, and in what manner the same is to be performed, I declare that what I claim is (d)—
1.
2.
3. &c.

(e) *John Smith.*

Dated this   day of   18

(a) Here insert title as in declaration.
(b) Here insert name, address, and calling of inventor as in declaration.
(c) Here insert full description of invention.
(d) Here state distinctly the features of novelty claimed.
(e) Signature of inventor.

Form D.

Section 33.

Form of Patent.

VICTORIA, by the grace of God, of the united kingdom of Great Britain and Ireland, queen, defender of the faith: To all to whom these presents shall come greeting: [*pages 102, 103*] — The address.

Whereas *John Smith*, of 29, *Perry Street, Birmingham*, in the county of *Warwick*, engineer, hath by his solemn declaration represented unto us that he is in possession of an invention for "*Improvements in Sewing Machines*," that he is the true and first inventor thereof, and that the same is not in use by any other person to the best of his knowledge and belief: [*pages 103, 105*] — First recital.

And whereas the said inventor hath humbly prayed that we would be graciously pleased to grant unto him (hereinafter together with his executors, administrators, and assigns, or any of them, referred to as the said patentee) our royal letters patent for the sole use and advantage of his said invention: [*page 105*] — Second recital.

And whereas the said inventor hath by and in his complete specification particularly described the nature of his invention: [*page 105*] — Third recital.

And whereas we being willing to encourage all inventions which may be for the public good, are graciously pleased to condescend to his request: [*pages 105, 106*] — Fourth recital.

Know ye, therefore, that we, of our especial grace, certain knowledge, and mere motion, do by these presents, for us, our heirs and successors, give and grant unto the said patentee our especial license, full power, sole privilege, and authority, that the said patentee by himself, his agents or licensees, and no others, may at all times hereafter during the term of years herein mentioned, make, use, exercise, and vend the said invention within our united kingdom of Great Britain and Ireland and Isle of Man, in such manner as to him or them may seem meet, and that the said patentee shall have and enjoy the whole profit and advantage from time to time accruing by reason of the said invention, during the term of fourteen years from the date hereunder written of these presents: And to the end that the said patentee may have and enjoy the sole use and exercise, and the full benefit of the said invention, we do by these presents, for us, our heirs and successors, strictly command all our subjects whatsoever within our united kingdom of Great Britain and Ireland and the Isle of Man, that they do not at any time during the continuance of the said term of fourteen years, either directly or indirectly make use of or put in practice the said invention, or any part of the same, nor in anywise imitate the same, nor make or cause to be made any addition thereto or subtraction therefrom, whereby to pretend themselves the inventors thereof, without the consent, license, or agreement of the said patentee in writing under his hand and seal, on pain of incurring such penalties as may be justly inflicted on such offenders for their contempt of this our royal command, and of being answerable to the patentee according to law for his damages thereby occasioned: Provided that these our letters patent are on this condition, that, if at any time during the said term it be made to appear to us, our heirs and successors, or any six or more of our privy council, that this our grant is contrary to law, or prejudicial or inconvenient to our subjects in general, or that the said invention is not a new invention as to the public use and exercise thereof within our united kingdom of Great Britain and Ireland, and Isle of Man, or that the said patentee is not the first and true inventor thereof within this realm as aforesaid, these our letters patent shall forthwith determine, and be void to all intents and purposes, notwithstanding anything hereinbefore contained: Provided also, that if the said patentee shall not pay all fees by law required to be paid in respect of the grant of these letters patent, or in respect of any matter relating thereto at the time or times, and in manner for the time being by law provided; and also if the said patentee shall not supply or cause to be supplied, for our service all such articles of the said invention as may be required by the officers or commissioners administering any department of our service in such manner, at such times, and at and upon such reasonable prices and terms as shall be settled in manner for the time being by law provided, then, and in any of the said cases, these our letters patent, and all privileges and advantages whatever hereby granted shall determine and become void notwithstanding anything hereinbefore contained: Provided also, that nothing herein contained shall prevent the granting of licences in such manner and for such considerations as they may by law be granted: And lastly, we do by these presents for us, our heirs and successors, grant unto the said patentee that these our letters patent shall be construed in the most beneficial sense for the advantage of the said patentee. In witness whereof we have caused these our letters to be made patent this   18   and to be sealed as of the   18 . [*pages 106, 108, 109, 111*]

[Seal of Patent Office.]

— The grant.
— The prohibition.
— The conditions.
— The construction.

Section 47.

FORM E.

FORM OF APPLICATION FOR REGISTRATION OF DESIGN.

You are hereby requested to register the accompanying   day of   18 .
design, in class in the name of (*a*)   of
who claims to be the proprietor thereof, and to return the same to
Statement of nature of design
Registration fees enclosed £   ,,   *s.*
To the comptroller,
Patent Office, 25, Southampton Buildings, Chancery Lane, W.C.

(Signed)

(*a*) Here insert legibly the name and address of the individual or firm.

Section 62.

FORM F.

FORM OF APPLICATION FOR REGISTRATION OF TRADE MARK.

```
┌─────────────────────────────────────────────┐
│                                             │
│                                             │
│                                             │
│  (One representation to be fixed within     │
│   this square, and two others on separate   │
│   sheets of foolscap of same size.)         │
│                                             │
│                                             │
│                                             │
│  (Representations of a larger size may be   │
│   folded, but must be mounted upon linen    │
│   and affixed hereto.)                      │
│                                             │
│                                             │
└─────────────────────────────────────────────┘
```

You are hereby requested to register the accompanying trade mark, [*In class* – iron in bars, sheets, and plates; *in class* —steam engines and boilers; *and in class* —warming apparatus], in the name of (*a*)   , who claims to be the proprietor thereof.
Registration fees enclosed £   ,,   *s.*
To the comptroller,
Patent Office, 25, Southampton Buildings, Chancery Lane, W.C.

(Signed)

NOTE.—If the trade mark has been in use before August 13, 1875, state length of user.

(*a*) Here insert legibly the name, address, and business of the individual or firm.

Section 24.

THE SECOND SCHEDULE.

Fees on Instruments for obtaining Patents and Renewal.

	£ *s. d.*	£ *s. d.*
(a.) *Up to sealing.*		
On application for provisional protection	1 0 0	
On filing complete specification	3 0 0	
or		4 0 0
On filing complete specification with first application		4 0 0
(b.) *Further before end of four years from date of patent.*		
On certificate of renewal		50 0 0
(c.) *Further before end of seven years, or in the case of patents granted after the commencement of this act, before the end of eight years from date of patent.*		
On certificate of renewal		100 0 0

Or in lieu of the fees of £50 and £100 the following annual fees:—

					£	s.	d.
Before the expiration of the fourth year from the date of the patent					10	0	0
,,	,,	fifth	,,	,,	10	0	0
,,	,,	sixth	,,	,,	10	0	0
,,	,,	seventh	,,	,,	10	0	0
,,	,,	eighth	,,	,,	15	0	0
,,	,,	ninth	,,	,,	15	0	0
,,	,,	tenth	,,	,,	20	0	0
,,	,,	eleventh	,,	,,	20	0	0
,,	,,	twelfth	,,	,,	20	0	0
,,	,,	thirteenth	,,	,,	20	0	0

THE THIRD SCHEDULE.   Section 113.

Enactments Repealed.

21 James 1, c. 3 (1623).—The Statute of Monopolies. In part; namely, sections 10, 11 and 12.

5 & 6 Will. 4, c. 62 (1835) [In part].—The Statutory Declarations Act, 1835. In part; namely, section 11.

5 & 6 Will. 4, c. 83 (1835).—An act to amend the law touching letters patent for inventions.

2 & 3 Vict. c. 67 (1839).—An act to amend an act of the fifth and sixth years of the reign of king William the fourth, intituled "An Act to amend the law touching letters patent for inventions."

5 & 6 Vict. c. 100 (1842).—An act to consolidate and amend the laws relating to the copyright of designs for ornamenting articles of manufacture.

6 & 7 Vict. c. 65 (1843).—An act to amend the laws relating to the copyright of designs.

7 & 8 Vict. c. 69* (1844) [In part].—An act for amending an act passed in the fourth year of the reign of his late majesty, intituled "An act for the better administration of justice in his majesty's privy council, and to extend its jurisdiction and powers." In part; namely, sections 2 to 5, both included.

13 & 14 Vict. c. 104 (1850).—An act to extend and amend the acts relating to the copyright of designs.

15 & 16 Vict. c. 83 (1852).—The Patent Law Amendment Act, 1852.

16 & 17 Vict. c. 5 (1853).—An act to substitute stamp duties for fees on passing letters patent for inventions, and to provide for the purchase for the public use of certain indexes of specifications.

16 & 17 Vict. c. 115 (1853).—An act to amend certain provisions of the Patent Law Amendment Act, 1852, in respect of the transmission of certified copies of letters patent and specifications to certain offices in Edinburgh and Dublin, and otherwise to amend the said act.

21 & 22 Vict. c. 70 (1858).—An act to amend the act of the fifth and sixth years of her present majesty, to consolidate and amend the laws relating to the copyright of designs for ornamenting articles of manufacture.

22 Vict. c. 13 (1859).—An act to amend the law concerning patents for inventions with respect to inventions for improvements in instruments and munitions of war.

24 & 25 Vict. c. 73 (1861).—An act to amend the law relating to the copyright of designs.

28 & 29 Vict. c. 3 (1865).—The Industrial Exhibitions Act, 1865.

33 & 34 Vict. c. 27 (1870).—The Protection of Inventions Act, 1870.

33 & 34 Vict. c. 97 (1870).—The Stamp Act, 1870. In part; namely, section 65, and in the schedule the words and figures, "Certificate of the registration of a design . . £5 0 0. And see section 65."

38 & 39 Vict. c. 91 (1875).—The Trade Marks Registration Act, 1875.

38 & 39 Vict. c. 93 (1875).—The Copyright of Designs Act, 1875.

39 & 40 Vict. c. 33 (1876).—The Trade Marks Registration Amendment Act, 1876.

40 & 41 Vict. c. 37 (1877).—The Trade Marks Registration Extension Act, 1877.

43 & 44 Vict. c. 10 (1880).—The Great Seal Act, 1880. In part; namely, section 5.

45 & 46 Vict. c. 72 (1882).—The Revenue, Friendly Societies, and National Debt Act, 1882. In part; namely, section 16.

* *Note.*—Sects. 6 and 7 of this act are repealed by the Statute Law Revision No 2) Act, 1874.

PATENTS RULES, 1883.

By virtue of the provisions of the Patents, Designs, and Trade Marks Act, 1883, the Board of Trade do hereby make the following Rules:—

SHORT TITLE.

Short title. 1. These Rules may be cited as the Patents Rules, 1883.

COMMENCEMENT.

Commencement. 2. These Rules shall come into operation from and immediately after the 31st day of December, 1883.

INTERPRETATION.

Interpretation. 3. In the construction of these Rules, any words herein used defined by the said Act shall have the meanings thereby assigned to them respectively.

FEES.

Fees. 4. The fees to be paid under the above-mentioned Act, in addition to the fees mentioned in the Second Schedule thereto, so far as it relates to patents, shall be those specified in the list of fees in the First Schedule to these Rules.

FORMS.

Forms. 5. The Forms A., B. and C. in the First Schedule to the said
Alterations. Act shall be altered or amended by the substitution therefor respectively of the Forms A., A1., B. and C. in the Second Schedule hereto.

Application. 6. (1.) An application for a patent shall be made either in the Form A. or the Form A1. set forth in the Second Schedule hereto, as the case may be.

Specification. (2.) The Form B. in such Schedule of provisional specification and the Form C. of complete specification shall respectively be used.

Other forms. 3. The remaining forms set forth in such Schedule may, as far as they are applicable, be used in any proceedings under these Rules.

GENERAL.

Hours of business. 7. The Patent Office shall be open to the public every week-day during the hours of ten and four, except on the days and times following:—

 Christmas Day.
 Good Friday.
 The day observed as Her Majesty's birthday.
 The days observed as days of public fast or thanksgiving, or as holidays at the Bank of England.

8. An application for a patent must be signed by the applicant, but all other communications between the applicant and the comptroller and all attendances by the applicant upon the comptroller may be made by or through an agent duly authorised to the satisfaction of the comptroller, and if he so require resident in the United Kingdom. *Agency.*

9. The application shall be accompanied by a statement of an address to which all notices, requisitions, and communications of every kind may be made by the comptroller or by the Board of Trade, and such statement shall thereafter be binding upon the applicant unless and until a substituted statement of address shall be furnished by him to the comptroller. He may in any particular case require that the address mentioned in this Rule be in the United Kingdom. *Statement of address.*

10. All documents and copies of documents sent to or left at the Patent Office or otherwise furnished to the comptroller or to the Board of Trade shall be written or printed in large and legible characters in the English language upon strong wide ruled paper (on one side only), of a size of 13 inches by 8 inches, leaving a margin of two inches on the left-hand part thereof, and the signature of the applicants or agents thereto must be written in a large and legible hand. Duplicate documents shall at any time be left, if required by the comptroller. *Size, &c. of documents.*

11. Before exercising any discretionary power given to the comptroller by the said Act adversely to the applicant for a patent or for amendment of a specification, the comptroller shall give ten days' notice, or such longer notice as he may think fit, to the applicant of the time when he may be heard personally or by his agent before the comptroller. *Exercise of discretionary power by comptroller. Notice of hearing.*

12. Within five days from the date when such notice would be delivered in the ordinary course of post, or such longer time as the comptroller may appoint in such notice, the applicant shall notify to the comptroller whether or not he intends to be heard upon the matter. *Notice by applicant.*

13. Whether the applicant desires to be heard or not, the comptroller may at any time require him to submit a statement in writing within a time to be notified by the comptroller, or to attend before him and make oral explanations with respect to such matters as the comptroller may require. *Comptroller may require statement, &c.*

14. The decision or determination of the comptroller in the exercise of any such discretionary power as aforesaid shall be notified by him to the applicant, and any other person affected thereby. *Decision to be notified to parties.*

15. The term "applicant" in Rules 11, 12, and 13 shall include an applicant whose specification bears a title the same as or similar to that of the specification of a prior applicant, and has been reported on by the examiner. *Definition of "applicant."*

16. Such prior and second applicant respectively may attend the hearing of the question whether the invention comprised in both applications is the same, but neither party shall be at liberty to inspect the specification of the other. *Prior and second applicant may attend hearing.*

APPENDIX.

Industrial or international exhibitions.

17. Any person desirous of exhibiting an invention at an industrial or international exhibition, or of publishing any description of the invention during the period of the holding of the exhibition, or of using the invention for the purpose of the exhibition in the place where the exhibition is held, shall, after having obtained from the Board of Trade a certificate that the exhibition is an industrial or international one, give to the comptroller seven days' notice of his intention to exhibit, publish, or use the invention, as the case may be.

For the purpose of identifying the invention in the event of an application for a patent being subsequently made the applicant shall furnish to the comptroller a brief description of his invention accompanied, if necessary, by drawings, and such other information as the comptroller may in each case require.

Power of amendment, &c.

18. Any document for the amending of which no special provision is made by the said Act may be amended, and any irregularity in procedure, which in the opinion of the comptroller may be obviated without detriment to the interests of any person, may be corrected, if and on such terms as the comptroller may think fit.

Documents by post.

19. Any application, notice, or other document authorised or required to be left, made, or given at the Patent Office or to the comptroller or to any other person under these Rules may be sent by a prepaid letter through the post, and if so sent shall be deemed to have been left, made, or given respectively at the time when the letter containing the same would be delivered in the ordinary course of post.

In proving such service or sending it shall be sufficient to prove that the letter was properly addressed and put into the post.

Affidavits.

20. Affidavits may, except where otherwise prescribed by these Rules, be used as evidence in any proceedings thereunder when sworn to in any of the following ways, viz. :—

(1.) In the United Kingdom before any person authorised to administer oaths in the Supreme Court of Judicature or before a justice of the peace for the county or place where it is sworn or made.

(2.) In any place in the British dominions out of the United Kingdom before any court, judge, or justice of the peace or any person authorised to administer oaths there in any court.

(3.) In any place out of the British dominions before a British minister, or person exercising the functions of a British minister, or a British consul, vice-consul, or other person exercising the functions of a British consul, or a notary public, or before a judge or magistrate.

Statutory declarations.

21. Where any statutory declaration prescribed by these Rules, or used in any proceedings thereunder, is made out of the United Kingdom, the words, "and by virtue of the Statutory Declarations Act, 1835," must be omitted, and the declaration shall (unless the context otherwise requires) be made in the manner prescribed in Rule 20, sub-section 3.

APPLICATION WITH PROVISIONAL OR COMPLETE SPECIFICATION.

22. Applications for a patent sent by prepaid letter through the post shall, as far as may be practicable, be opened and numbered in the order in which the letters containing the same have been respectively delivered in the ordinary course of post. *Order of recording applications.*

Applications left at the Patent Office otherwise than through the post shall be in like manner numbered in the order of their receipt at the Patent Office.

23. Where a person making application for a patent includes therein by mistake, inadvertence, or otherwise, more than one invention, he may, after the refusal of the comptroller to accept such application, amend the same so as to apply to one invention only, and may make application for separate patents for each such invention accordingly. *Application for separate patents by way of amendment.*

Every such application shall bear the date of the first application, and shall, together therewith, be proceeded with in the manner prescribed by the said Act and by these Rules as if every such application had been originally made on that date for one invention only.

24. An application for a patent by the legal representative of a person who has died possessed of an invention shall be accompanied by an official copy of or extract from his will or the letters of administration granted of his estate and effects in proof of the applicant's title as such legal representative. *Application by representative of deceased inventor.*

25. On the acceptance of an application with a provisional or complete specification the comptroller shall give notice thereof to the applicant, and shall advertise such acceptance in the official journal of the Patent Office. *Notice and advertisement of acceptance.*

26. Upon the publication of such advertisement of acceptance in the case of an application with a complete specification, the application and specification or specifications with the drawings (if any) may be inspected at the Patent Office upon payment of the prescribed fee. *Inspection on acceptance of complete specification.*

APPLICATION ON COMMUNICATION FROM ABROAD.

27. An application for a patent for an invention communicated from abroad shall be made in the Form A 1 set forth in the Second Schedule hereto. *Communication from abroad.*

SIZES AND METHODS OF PREPARING DRAWINGS ACCOMPANYING PROVISIONAL OR COMPLETE SPECIFICATIONS.

28. The drawings accompanying provisional or complete specifications shall be made upon half-sheets or sheets of imperial drawing paper, to be within a border line of 19 inches by 12 inches, or 27 inches by 19 inches, with a margin of ½ an inch all round. *Size of drawings.*

29. A copy of the drawings will be required upon *rolled* imperial drawing paper or upon thin Bristol board of the same dimensions as the original drawing or drawings. All the lines must be absolutely black, Indian ink of the best quality to be used, and the same strength or colour of the ink maintained throughout the drawing. *Copies of drawings.*

Any shading must be in lines clearly and distinctly drawn and as open as is consistent with the required effect. Section lines should not be too closely drawn. No colour must be used for any purpose upon the copy of the drawings. All letters and figures of reference must be bold and distinct. The border line should be one fine line only. The drawings must not be folded, but must be delivered at the Patent Office either in a perfectly flat state or rolled upon a roller so as to be free from creases or breaks.*

30. Where a complete specification is left at the Patent Office after a provisional specification has been accepted the complete specification and drawing or drawings accompanying the same, as well as the copy thereof, must be prepared in accordance with Rules 10, 28, and 29.

ILLUSTRATED JOURNAL.

Additional drawing to be furnished.

31. Every applicant for the grant of a patent shall, in addition to the drawings to be furnished with his complete specification, furnish the comptroller with a drawing illustrative of the feature or features of novelty constituting his invention. Such drawing must be prepared in the manner prescribed for the copy of the original drawing or drawings accompanying the specification, but must not cover a space exceeding 16 square inches. The drawing must be accompanied by a concise explanatory statement on foolscap paper and legibly written or printed.

OPPOSITION TO GRANTS OF PATENTS.

Notice of opposition.

32. A notice of opposition to the grant of a patent shall state the ground or grounds on which the person giving such notice (hereinafter called the opponent) intends to oppose the grant, and shall be signed by him. Such notice shall state his address for service in the United Kingdom.

Copy for applicant.

33. On receipt of such notice a copy thereof shall be furnished by the comptroller to the applicant.

Particulars of prior patent.

34. Where the ground or one of the grounds of opposition is that the invention has been patented in this country on an application of prior date, the title, number, and date of the patent granted in such prior application shall be specified in the notice.

Opponent's evidence.

35. Within 14 days after the expiration of two months from the date of the advertisement of the acceptance of a complete specification, the opponent shall leave at the Patent Office statutory declarations in support of his opposition, and deliver to the applicant a list thereof.

Applicant's evidence.

Evidence in reply.

36. Within 14 days from the delivery of such list the applicant shall leave at the Patent Office statutory declarations in answer, and deliver to the opponent a list thereof, and within seven days from such delivery the opponent shall leave at the Patent Office his statutory declarations in reply, and deliver to the applicant a list thereof.

---

* As the drawings accompanying the provisional and complete specification respectively are copied at the Patent Office for publication by the process of photo-lithography, this rule must be strictly observed in order that correct copies may be made.

Such last-mentioned declarations shall be confined to matters strictly in reply.

Copies of the declarations mentioned in this and the last preceding Rule may be obtained either from the Patent Office or from the opposite party.

37. No further evidence shall be left on either side except by leave of the comptroller upon the written consent of the parties duly notified to him, or by special leave of the comptroller on application made to him for that purpose. *Closing of evidence.*

38. Either party making such application shall give notice thereof to the opposite party, who shall be entitled to oppose the application.

39. On the completion of the evidence the comptroller shall appoint a time for the hearing of the case, and shall give to the parties seven days' notice at the least of such appointment. *Notice of hearing.*

40. On the hearing of the case no opposition shall be allowed in respect of any ground not stated in the notice of opposition, and where the ground or one of the grounds is that the invention has been patented in this country on an application of prior date, the opposition shall not be allowed upon such ground unless the title, number, and date of the patent granted on such prior application shall have been duly specified in the notice of opposition. *Disallowance of opposition in certain cases.*

41. The decision of the comptroller in the case shall be notified by him to the parties. *Decision to be notified to parties.*

CERTIFICATES OF PAYMENT OR RENEWAL.

42. If a patentee intends at the expiration of the fourth or eighth year from the date of his patent to make the prescribed payment for keeping the same in force, he shall seven days at least before such expiration give notice to the comptroller of such intention, and shall, before the expiration of such fourth or eighth year, as the case may be, leave at the Patent Office a form of certificate of payment, duly stamped, subject as hereinafter provided, with the prescribed fee of 50*l*. or 100*l*., as the case may be. *Payment of fees of 50l. and 100l. for continuance of patent.*

43. In the case of patents granted before the commencement of the said Act, the above Rule shall be read as if the words "seventh year" were therein written instead of the words "eighth year." *As to patent granted before commencement of Act.*

44. If the patentee intends to pay annual fees in lieu of the above-mentioned fees of 50*l*. and 100*l*., he shall seven days at least before the expiration of the fourth and each succeeding year during the term of the patent, until and inclusive of the 13th year thereof, give notice to the comptroller of such intention, and shall, before the expiration of such respective periods as aforesaid, leave at the Patent Office a form of certificate of payment, duly stamped, with the fee prescribed to be paid at such periods respectively. *Payment of annual fees in lieu of 50l. and 100l.*

45. On due compliance with these Rules, and as soon as may be after such respective periods as aforesaid, or any enlargement thereof respectively duly granted, the comptroller shall give to the patentee a certificate that the prescribed payment has been duly made. *Certificate of payment.*

X 2

ENLARGEMENT OF TIME.

Enlargement of time for payments. 46. An application for an enlargement of the time for making a prescribed payment shall state in detail the circumstances in which the patentee by accident, mistake, or inadvertence has failed to make such payment, and the comptroller may require the patentee to substantiate by such proof as he may think necessary the allegations contained in the application for enlargement.

In other cases. 47. The time prescribed by these Rules for doing any act, or taking any proceedings thereunder, may be enlarged by the comptroller if he think fit, and upon such notice to other parties, and proceedings thereon, and upon such terms, as he may direct.

AMENDMENT OF SPECIFICATION.

Request for leave to amend. 48. A request for leave to amend a specification shall be signed by the applicant or patentee and accompanied by a copy of the original specification and drawings, showing in red ink the proposed amendment, and shall be advertised by publication of the request and the nature of the proposed amendment in the official journal of the Patent Office, and in such other manner (if any) as the comptroller may in each case direct.

Advertisement.

Notice of opposition. 49. A notice of opposition to the amendment shall state the ground or grounds on which the person giving such notice (hereinafter called the opponent) intends to oppose the amendment, and shall be signed by him. Such notice shall state his address for service in the United Kingdom.

Copy for the applicant. 50. On receipt of such notice a copy thereof shall be furnished by the comptroller to the applicant or patentee, as the case may be (hereinafter called the applicant).

Opponent's evidence. 51. Within 14 days after the expiration of one month from the first advertisement of the application for leave to amend, the opponent shall leave at the Patent Office statutory declarations in support of his opposition and deliver to the applicant a list thereof.

Further proceedings. 52. Upon such declarations being left, and such list being delivered, the provisions of Rules 36, 37, 38, and 39 shall apply to the case, and the further proceedings therein shall be regulated in accordance with such provisions as if they were here repeated.

Decision to be notified to parties. 53. The decision of the comptroller in the case shall be notified by him to the parties.

Requirements thereon. 54. Where leave to amend is given the applicant shall, if the comptroller so require, and within a time to be limited by him, leave at the Patent Office a new specification and drawings as amended, to be prepared in accordance with Rules 10, 28, and 29.

Leave by order of Court. 55. Where a request for leave to amend is made by or in pursuance of an order of the Court or a judge, an official or verified copy of the order shall be left with the request at the Patent Office.

Advertisement of amendment. 56. Every amendment of a specification shall be forthwith advertised by the comptroller in the official journal of the Patent

Compulsory Licenses.

57. A petition to the Board of Trade for an order upon a patentee to grant a license shall show clearly the nature of the petitioner's interest, and the ground or grounds upon which he claims to be entitled to relief, and shall state in detail the circumstances of the case, the terms upon which he asks that an order may be made, and the purport of such order. *Petition for compulsory grant of licenses.*

58. The petition and an examined copy thereof shall be left at the Patent Office, accompanied by the affidavits, or statutory declarations, and other documentary evidence (if any) tendered by the petitioner in proof of the alleged default of the patentee. *To be left with evidence at Patent Office.*

59. Upon perusing the petition and evidence, unless the Board of Trade shall be of opinion that the order should be at once refused, they may require the petitioner to attend before the comptroller, or other person or persons appointed by them, to receive his or their directions as to further proceedings upon the petition. *Directions as to further proceedings unless petition refused.*

60. If and when a *prima facie* case for relief has been made out to the satisfaction of the Board of Trade, the petitioner shall upon their requisition, and on or before a day to be named by them, deliver to the patentee copies of the petition and of the affidavits or statutory declarations and other documentary evidence (if any) tendered in support thereof. *Procedure. Petitioner's evidence.*

61. Within 14 days after the day of such delivery the patentee shall leave at the Patent Office his affidavits or statutory declarations in opposition to the petition, and deliver copies thereof to the petitioner. *Patentee's evidence.*

62. The petitioner within 14 days from such delivery shall leave at the Patent Office his affidavits, or statutory declarations in reply, and deliver copies thereof to the petitioner; such last-mentioned affidavits or declarations shall be confined to matters strictly in reply. *Evidence in reply.*

63. Subject to any further directions which the Board of Trade may give, the parties shall then be heard at such time, before such person or persons, in such manner, and in accordance with such procedure as the Board of Trade may, in the circumstances of the case, direct, but so that full opportunity shall be given to the patentee to show cause against the petition. *Further proceedings.*

Register of Patents.

64. Upon the sealing of a patent the comptroller shall cause to be entered in the register of patents the name, address, and description of the patentee as the grantee thereof, and the title of the invention. *Entry of grant.*

65. Where a person becomes entitled to a patent or to any share or interest therein, by assignment either throughout the United Kingdom and the Isle of Man, or for any place or places therein, or by transmission or other operation of law, a request for the *Request for entry of subsequent proprietorship.*

310 APPENDIX.

entry of his name in the register as such complete or partial proprietor of the patent, or of such share or interest therein, as the case may be, shall be addressed to the comptroller, and left at the Patent Office.

Signature of request.

66. Such request shall in the case of individuals be made and signed by the person requiring to be registered as proprietor, or by his agent duly authorized, to the satisfaction of the comptroller, and in the case of a body corporate by their agent authorized in like manner.

Particulars to be stated in request.

67. Every such request shall state the name, address, and description of the person claiming to be entitled to the patent, or to any share or interest therein, as the case may be (hereinafter called the claimant), and the particulars of the assignment, transmission, or other operation of law, by virtue of which he requires to be entered in the register as proprietor, so as to show the manner in which, and the person or persons to whom, the patent, or such share or interest therein as aforesaid, has been assigned or transmitted.

Production of documents of title and other proof.

68. Every assignment and every other document containing, giving effect to, or being evidence of, the transmission of a patent or affecting the proprietorship thereof as claimed by such request, except such documents as are matters of record, shall be produced to the comptroller, together with the request above prescribed, and such other proof of title as he may require for his satisfaction.

As to a document which is a matter of record, an official or certified copy thereof shall in like manner be produced to the comptroller.

Copies for Patent Office.

69. There shall also be left with the request an examined copy of the assignment or other document above required to be produced.

As to a document which is a matter of record, an official or certified copy shall be left with the request in lieu of an examined copy.

Body corporate.

70. A body corporate may be registered as proprietor by its corporate name.

Entry of orders of the Privy Council or of the Court.

71. Where an order has been made by her Majesty in Council for the extension of a patent for a further term or for the grant of a new patent, or where an order has been made by the Court for the revocation of a patent or the rectification of the register under section 90 of the said Act, or otherwise affecting the validity or proprietorship of the patent, the person in whose favour such order has been made shall forthwith leave at the Patent Office an office copy of such order. The register shall thereupon be rectified or the purport of such order shall otherwise be duly entered in the register, as the case may be.

Entry of payment of fees on issue of certificate.

72. Upon the issue of a certificate of payment under Rule 45, the comptroller shall cause to be entered in the Register of Patents a record of the amount and date of payment of the fee on such certificate.

73. If a patentee fails to make any prescribed payment within the prescribed time or any enlargement thereof duly granted, such failure shall be duly entered in the register. *Entry of failure to pay fees.*

74. An examined copy of every license granted under a patent shall be left at the Patent Office by the licensee, with a request that a notification thereof may be entered in the register. The licensee shall cause the accuracy of such copy to be certified as the comptroller may direct, and the original license shall at the same time be produced and left at the Patent Office if required for further verification. *Entry of licenses.*

75. The register of patents shall be open to the inspection of the public on every week day between the hours of ten and four, except on the days and at the times following:— *Hours of inspection of register.*
   (a) Christmas Day, Good Friday, the day observed as Her Majesty's birthday, days observed as days of public fast or thanksgiving, and days observed as holidays at the Bank of England; or
   (b) Days which may from time to time be notified by a placard posted in a conspicuous place at the Patent Office;
   (c) Times when the register is required for any purpose of official use.

76. Certified copies of any entry in the register, or certified copies of, or extracts from, patents, specifications, disclaimers, affidavits, statutory declarations, and other public documents in the Patent Office, or of or from registers and other books kept there, may be furnished by the comptroller on payment of the prescribed fee. *Certified copies of documents.*

POWER TO DISPENSE WITH EVIDENCE, &c.

77. Where, under these Rules, any person is required to do any act or thing, or to sign any document, or to make any declaration on behalf of himself or of any body corporate, or any document or evidence is required to be produced to or left with the comptroller, or at the Patent Office, and it is shown to the satisfaction of the comptroller that from any reasonable cause such person is unable to do such act or thing, or to sign such document, or make such declaration, or that such document or evidence cannot be produced or left as aforesaid, it shall be lawful for the comptroller, with the sanction of the Board of Trade, and upon the production of such other evidence, and subject to such terms as they may think fit, to dispense with any such act or thing, document, declaration, or evidence.

REPEAL.

78. All General Rules made by the Lord Chancellor, or by any other authority, under the Patent Law Amendment Acts, and in force on the 31st day of December 1883, shall be and they are hereby repealed as from that date, without prejudice, nevertheless, to any application then pending. *Repeal.*

Dated the 21st day of December 1883.

(Signed) J. CHAMBERLAIN,
President of the Board of Trade.

RULES REGULATING THE PRACTICE AND PROCEDURE ON APPEALS TO THE LAW OFFICERS.

I. When any person intends to appeal to the law officer from a decision of the comptroller in any case in which such appeal is given by the Act, he shall within 14 days from the date of the decision appealed against file in the Patent Office a notice of such his intention.

II. Such notice shall state the nature of the decision appealed against, and whether the appeal is from the whole, or part only, and if so, what part of such decision.

III. A copy of such notice of intention to appeal shall be sent by the party so intending to appeal to the law officers' clerk at room 549, Royal Courts of Justice, London; and when there has been an opposition before the comptroller, to the opponent or opponents; and when the comptroller has refused to seal a patent on the ground that a previous application for a patent for the same invention is pending, to the prior applicant.

IV. Upon notice of appeal being filed, the comptroller shall forthwith transmit to the law officers' clerk all the papers relating to the matter of the application in respect of which such appeal is made.

V. No appeal shall be entertained of which notice is not given within 14 days from the date of the decision appealed against, or such further time as the comptroller may allow, except by special leave upon application to the law officer.

VI. Seven days' notice, at least, of the time and place appointed for the hearing of any appeal, shall be given by the law officers' clerk, unless special leave be given by the law officer that any shorter notice be given.

VII. Such notice shall in all cases be given to the comptroller and the appellant; and, when there has been an opposition before the comptroller, to the opponent or opponents; and, when the comptroller has refused to seal a patent on the ground that an application for a patent for the same invention is pending, to the prior applicant.

VIII. The evidence used on appeal to the law officer shall be the same as that used at the hearing before the comptroller; and no further evidence shall be given, save as to matters which have occurred or come to the knowledge of either party, after the date of the decision appealed against, except with the leave of the law officer upon application for that purpose.

IX. The law officer shall, at the request of either party, order the attendance at the hearing on appeal, for the purpose of being cross-examined, of any person, who has made a declaration, in the matter to which the appeal relates, unless in the opinion of the law officer, there is good ground for not making such order.

X. Any person requiring the attendance of a witness for cross-examination shall tender to the witness whose attendance is required a reasonable sum for conduct money.

XI. Where the law officer orders that costs shall be paid by any party to another, he may fix the amount of such costs, and if he shall not think fit to fix the amount thereof, he shall direct by whom and in what manner the amount of such costs shall be ascertained.

XII. If any costs so ordered to be paid be not paid within fourteen days after the amount thereof has been so fixed or ascertained, or such shorter period as shall be directed by the law officer, the party to whom such costs are to be paid may apply to the law officer for an order for payment under the provisions of section 38 of the Act.

XIII. All documentary evidence required, or allowed by the law officer to be filed, shall be subject to the same regulations, in all respects, as apply to the procedure before the comptroller, and shall be filed in the Patent Office, unless the law officer shall order to the contrary.

XIV. Any notice or other document required to be given to the law officers' clerk, under these Rules, may be sent by a prepaid letter through the post.

HENRY JAMES, A.G.
FARRER HERSCHELL, S.G.

FIRST SCHEDULE.

List of Fees payable on and in connexion with Letters Patent.

Up to Sealing.

	£ s. d.	£ s. d.
1. On application for provisional protection	1 0 0	
2. On filing complete specification	3 0 0	
		4 0 0
or		
3. On filing complete specification with first application		4 0 0
4. On appeal from comptroller to law officer. By appellant		3 0 0
5. On notice of opposition to grant of patent. By opponent		0 10 0
6. On hearing by comptroller. By applicant and by opponent respectively		1 0 0
7. On application to amend specification:—		
Up to sealing. By applicant		1 10 0
8. After sealing. By patentee		3 0 0
9. On notice of opposition to amendment. By opponent		0 10 0
10. On hearing by comptroller. By applicant and by opponent respectively		1 0 0
11. On application to amend specification during action or proceeding. By patentee		3 0 0
12. On application to the Board of Trade for a compulsory license. By person applying		5 0 0
13. On opposition to grant of compulsory license. By patentee		5 0 0

		£	s.	d.
14.	On certificate of renewal:—			
	Before end of 4 years from date of patent	50	0	0
15.	Before end of 7 years, or in the case of patents granted under the "Patents, Designs, and Trade Marks Act, 1883," before the end of 8 years from date of patent	100	0	0
	or in lieu of the fees of 50*l.* and 100*l.*, the following annual fees:—			
16.	Before the expiration of the 4th year from the date of the patent	10	0	0
17.	,, ,, 5th ,, ,,	10	0	0
18.	,, ,, 6th ,, ,,	10	0	0
19.	,, ,, 7th ,, ,,	10	0	0
20.	,, ,, 8th ,, ,,	15	0	0
21.	,, ,, 9th ,, ,,	15	0	0
22.	,, ,, 10th ,, ,,	20	0	0
23.	,, ,, 11th ,, ,,	20	0	0
24.	,, ,, 12th ,, ,,	20	0	0
25.	,, ,, 13th ,, ,,	20	0	0
	On enlargement of time for payment of renewal fees:—			
26.	Not exceeding 1 month	3	0	0
27.	,, 2 months	7	0	0
28.	,, 3 months	10	0	0
29.	For every entry of an assignment, transmission, agreement, license or extension of patent	0	10	0
30.	For duplicate of letters patent . . . . . each	2	0	0
31.	On notice to comptroller of intended exhibition of a patent under section 39	0	10	0
32.	Search or inspection fee . . . . . each	0	1	0
33.	For office copies . . . . every 100 words (but never less than one shilling)	0	0	4
34.	,, of drawings, cost according to agreement.			
35.	For certifying office copies, MSS. or printed . . each	0	1	0
36.	On request to comptroller to correct a clerical error .	0	5	0
37.	For certificate of comptroller under section 96	0	5	0
38.	For altering address in register .	0	5	0

(Signed) J. CHAMBERLAIN,
President of the Board of Trade.

21st December 1883.

Approved:

(Signed) CHARLES C. COTES,
HERBERT J. GLADSTONE,
Lords Commissioners of
Her Majesty's Treasury.

4th December 1883.

PATENTS RULES, 1883.

THE SECOND SCHEDULE.
Forms.

		Page
A.—Form of Application for Patent		315
A1.— ,, ,, ,, Communicated from Abroad		316
B.— ,, Provisional Specification		316
C.— ,, Complete Specification		317
D.— ,, Opposition to Grant of Patent		317
E.— ,, Application for Hearing by Comptroller		318
F.— ,, ,, to amend Specification or Drawings		318
G.— ,, Opposition to Amendment of Specification or Drawings		318
H.— ,, Application for Compulsory Grant of License		319
H1.-- ,, Petition for Compulsory Grant of Licenses		319
I.— ,, Opposition to Compulsory Grant of License		320
J.— ,, Application for Certificate of Payment or Renewal		320
K.— ,, Application for Enlargement of Time for Payment of Renewal Fee		321
L.— ,, Request to enter Name upon the Register of Patents		321
M.— ,, Request to enter Notification of License in Register		322
N.— ,, Application for Duplicate of Letters Patent		322
O.— ,, Notice of intended Exhibition of Unpatented Invention		322
P.— ,, Request for Correction of Clerical Error		323
Q.— ,, Certificate of Comptroller		323
R.— ,, Notice for Alteration of an Address in Register		323
S.— ,, Application for Entry of Order of Privy Council in Register		324
T.— ,, Appeal to Law Officer		324

Patents, Designs, and Trade Marks Act, 1883.

[PATENT.]   Form A.

Application for Patent.

(*a*) ———, do solemnly and sincerely declare that ——— in possession of an invention for (*b*) ——— that ——— the true and first inventor thereof; and that the same is not in use by any other person or persons to the best of ——— knowledge and belief; and ——— humbly pray that a patent may be granted ——— for the said invention.

And ——— make the above solemn declaration conscientiously believing the same to be true, and by virtue of the provisions of the Statutory Declarations Act, 1835.

                                     (*c*) ———.
Declared at (*d*) ———, in the ———, this ——— day of ———, 18—.
                                   Before me (*e*) ———.
[Declared at (*d*) ———, in the ———, this ——— day of ———, 18—.
                                   Before me (*e*) ———.
                                                  (*f*).]

NOTE.—Where the above declaration is made out of the United Kingdom, the words "and by virtue of the Statutory Declarations Act, 1835," must be omitted, and the declaration must be made before a British Consular Officer, or, where it is not reasonably practicable to make it before such officer, then before a public officer duly authorised in that behalf.

(*a*) Here insert name, full address, and calling of applicant or applicants.
(*b*) Here insert title of invention.
(*c*) Signature of applicant or applicants.
(*d*) If declared by more than one applicant, and at different times or places, insert after "Declared" the words "by the above-named."
(*e*) Signature and title of the person before whom the declaration is made.
(*f*) If not required as in note (*d*), strike out part within brackets.

Patents, Designs, and Trade Marks Act, 1883.

[PATENT.]   FORM A1.

Application for Patent for Inventions Communicated from Abroad.

I (*a*) ———, of ———, in the county of ———, do solemnly and sincerely declare that I am in possession of an invention for (*b*) ———, which invention has been communicated to me from abroad by (*c*) ———, that I claim to be the true and first inventor thereof; and that the same is not in use within this realm by any other person or persons to the best of my knowledge and belief; and I humbly pray that a patent may be granted to me for the said invention.

And I make the above solemn declaration conscientiously believing the same to be true, and by virtue of the provisions of the Statutory Declarations Act, 1835.

(*d*) ———.

Declared at ———, in the county of ———, this ——— day of ———, 18—.

Before me, (*e*) ———.

NOTE.—Where the above declaration is made out of the United Kingdom the words, "and by virtue of the Statutory Declarations Act, 1835," must be omitted, and the declaration must be made before a British Consular Officer, or, where it is not reasonably practicable to make it before such officer, then before a public officer duly authorised in that behalf.

(*a*) Here insert name, full address, and calling of applicant.
(*b*) Here insert title of invention.
(*c*) Here insert name, address, and calling of communicant.
(*d*) Signature of applicant.
(*e*) Signature and title of the officer before whom the declaration is made.

To be issued with Form A or A1.

Patents, Designs, and Trade Marks Act, 1883.

FORM B.

Provisional Specification.

(To be furnished in Duplicate.)

(*a*) ———. (*b*) ———, do hereby declare the nature of said invention for to be as follows (*c*): ———.

NOTE.—No stamp is required on this document, which must form the commencement of the Provisional Specification; the continuation to be upon wide-ruled foolscap paper (but on one side only) with a margin of two inches on left hand of paper. The Provisional Specification and the "Duplicate" thereof must be signed by the applicant or his agent on the last sheet, the date being first inserted as follows:—

"Dated this ——— day of ———, 18—."

(*a*) Here insert title, as in declaration.
(*b*) Here insert name, full address, and calling of applicant or applicants, as in declaration.
(*c*) Here insert short description of invention.

Patents, Designs, and Trade Marks Act, 1883.

[PATENT.] FORM C.

Complete Specification.

(To be furnished in Duplicate—one unstamped.)

(*a*) ———. (*b*) ———, do hereby declare the nature of ——— invention for ——— and in what manner the same is to be performed, to be particularly described and ascertained in and by the following statement : (*c*) ———

NOTE.—This document must form the commencement of the complete Specification ; the continuation to be upon wide-ruled foolscap paper (but on one side only) with a margin of two inches on left hand of paper. The complete Specification and the "Duplicate" thereof must be signed by the applicant or his agent on the last sheet, the date being first inserted as follows :—
 "Dated this ——— day of ———, 18—."

(*a*) Here insert title, as in declaration.
(*b*) Here insert name, full address, and calling of applicant or applicants, as in declaration.
(*c*) Here insert full description of invention, *which must end with a distinct statement of claim or claims, in the following forms :*
 "Having now particularly described and ascertained the nature of my said invention, and in what manner the same is to be performed, I declare that what I claim is—
  "(1)
  "(2)
  "(3)   ."
Here state distinctly the features of novelty claimed.

———

Patents, Designs, and Trade Marks Act, 1883.

[PATENT.] FORM D.

Form of Opposition to grant of Patent.

[*To be accompanied by an unstamped copy.*]

*I ——— hereby give notice of my intention to oppose the grant of letters patent upon application No. ——— of ———, applied for by ——— upon the ground† ———.

(Signed)‡ ———.

To the Comptroller,
 Patent Office, 25, Southampton Buildings,
  Chancery Lane, London, W.C.

 * Here state name and full address.
 † Here state upon which of the grounds of opposition permitted by section 11 of the Act the grant is opposed.
 ‡ Here insert signature of opponent or agent.

Patents, Designs, and Trade Marks Act, 1883.

[PATENT.] FORM E.

Form of Application for Hearing by the Comptroller.

IN CASES OF REFUSAL TO ACCEPT, OPPOSITION, OR APPLICATIONS FOR AMENDMENTS, &c.

SIR,

———— of (a) ———— hereby apply to be heard in reference to ————
and request that I may receive due notice of the day fixed for the hearing.

Sir,
Your obedient Servant.

To the Comptroller,
Patent Office, 25, Southampton Buildings,
Chancery Lane, London, W.C.

(a) Here insert full address.

Patents, Designs, and Trade Marks Act, 1883.

[PATENT.] FORM F.

Form of Application for Amendment of Specification or Drawings.

* ———— seek leave to amend the specification of Letters Patent No.————
of 188—, as shown in red ink in the copy of the original specification
hereunto annexed ————.

My reasons for making this amendment are as follows † ————.
(Signed) ————.

To the Comptroller,
Patent Office, 25, Southampton Buildings,
Chancery Lane, London, W.C.

* Here state name and full address of applicant or patentee.
† Here state reasons for seeking amendment; and where the applicant is not the patentee, state what interest he possesses in the letters patent.

Patents, Designs, and Trade Marks Act, 1883.

[PATENT.] FORM G.

Form of Opposition to Amendment of Specification or Drawings.

[To be accompanied by an unstamped copy.]

* ———— hereby give notice of objection to the proposed amendment of
the specification or drawings of Letters Patent No.———— of 188— for the
following reason: † ————.
(Signed) ————.

To the Comptroller,
Patent Office, 25, Southampton Buildings,
Chancery Lane, London, W.C.

* Here state name and full address of opponent.
† Here state reason of opposition.

Patents, Designs, and Trade Marks Act, 1883.

[PATENT.] FORM II.

Form of Application for Compulsory Grant of License.

[*To be accompanied by an unstamped copy.*]

*—— hereby request you to bring to the notice of the Board of Trade the accompanying petition for the grant of a license to me by †——.
(Signed) ——.

NOTE.—The petition must clearly set forth the facts of the case and be accompanied by an examined copy thereof. *See* below.

To the Comptroller,
  Patent Office, 25, Southampton Buildings,
    Chancery Lane, London, W.C.

* Here state name and full address of applicant.
† Here state name and address of patentee, and number and date of his patent.

Patents, Designs, and Trade Marks Act, 1883.

FORM III.

Form of Petition for Compulsory Grant of Licenses.

To the LORDS of the COMMITTEE of PRIVY COUNCIL for TRADE.

THE PETITION of (*a*) —— of —— in the county of ——, being a person interested in the matter of this petition as hereinafter described:—

SHEWETH as follows :—

1. A patent dated —— No. —— was duly granted to —— for an invention of (*b*) ——.

2. The nature of my interest in the matter of this petition is as follows:—(*c*)

3. (*d*)

Having regard to the circumstances above stated, the petitioner alleges that by reason of the aforesaid default of the patentee to grant licenses on reasonable terms (*e*)

> Your petitioner therefore prays that an order may be made by the Board of Trade (*f*)
> or that the petitioner may have such other relief in the premises as the Board of Trade may deem just.

(*a*) Here insert name, full address, and description.
(*b*) Here insert title of invention.
(*c*) Here state fully the nature of petitioner's interest.
(*d*) Here state in detail the circumstances of the case under section 22 of the said Act, and show that it arises by reason of the default of the patentee to grant licenses on reasonable terms. The statement of the case should also show as far as possible that the terms of the proposed order are just and reasonable. The paragraphs should be numbered consecutively.
(*e*) Here state the ground or grounds on which relief is claimed in the language of section 22, sub-sections (*a*), (*b*), or (*c*), as the case may be.
(*f*) Here state the purport and effect of the proposed order and the terms as to the amount of royalties, security for payment, or otherwise, upon which the petitioner claims to be entitled to the relief in question.

Patents, Designs, and Trade Marks Act, 1883.

[PATENT.] FORM I.

Form of Opposition to Compulsory Grant of License.

* ——— hereby give notice of objection to the application of ——— for the compulsory grant of a license under Patent No. ——— of 188 .
(Signed) ———.

To the Comptroller,
  Patent Office, 25, Southampton Buildings,
    Chancery Lane, London, W.C.

* Here state name and full address.

Patents, Designs, and Trade Marks Act, 1883.

FORM J.

Application for Certificate of Payment or Renewal.

——— hereby transmit the fee prescribed for the continuation in force of ——— Patent No. ———, of 18 , for a further period of ———.
  Name* ———.
  Address ———.

To the Comptroller,
  Patent Office, 25, Southampton Buildings,
    Chancery Lane, London, W.C.

* Here insert name and full address of patentee or his agent.

Certificate of Payment or Renewal.

[PATENT.]

Letters Patent No. ——— of 188 .

——— 18 .

This is to certify that ——— did this ——— day of ——— 18 , make the prescribed payment of £——— in respect of a period of ——— from ———, and that by virtue of such payment the rights of ——— remain in force.*

(Seal.)

Patent Office, London.

* See section 17 of the Patents, Designs, and Trade Marks Act, 1883.

Patents, Designs, and Trade Marks Act, 1883.

[PATENT.] FORM K.

Form of Application for Enlargement of Time for Payment of Renewal Fee.

SIR,

I HEREBY apply for an enlargement of time for ——— month— in which to make the ——— payment of £——— upon my Patent, No. ——— of 188—.

I am,
Sir,
(a) ——— ———. Your obedient Servant,

To the Comptroller,
 Patent Office, 25, Southampton Buildings,
  Chancery Lane, London, W.C.

(a) Here insert full address to which receipt is to be sent.

Patents, Designs, and Trade Marks Act, 1883.

[PATENT.] FORM L.

Form of Request to enter Name upon the Register of Patents, and of Declarations in support thereof.

I (a), ——— hereby request that you will enter (b) ——— name (c) in the Register of Patents :—
(d) ——— claim to be entitled (e) ——— of the Patent No. ——— of 188—, granted to (f) ——— for (g) ——— by virtue of (h) ———.
And in proof whereof I transmit the accompanying (i) ——— with an examined copy thereof (j).

I am,
Sir,
Your obedient Servant,

To the Comptroller,
 Patent Office, 25, Southampton Buildings,
  Chancery Lane, London, W.C.

(a) Or We. Here insert name, full address, and description.
(b) My or our.
(c) Or names.
(d) I or We.
(e) Here insert the nature of the claim.
(f) Here give name and address, &c. of patentee or patentees.
(g) Here insert title of the invention.
(h) Here specify the particulars of such document, giving its date, and the parties to the same, and showing how the claim here made is substantiated.
(i) Here insert the nature of the document.
(j) Where any document which is a matter of record is required to be left, a certified or official copy in lieu of an examined copy must be left.

Patents, Designs, and Trade Marks Act, 1883.

[PATENT.] FORM M.

Form of Request to Enter Notification of License in the Register of Patents.

SIR,

I HEREBY transmit an examined copy of a license granted to me by ———, under Patent No. ——— of 188—, as well as the original license for verification, and I have to request that a notification thereof may be entered in the register.

I am,
Sir,

(a) —————. Your obedient Servant,

To the Comptroller,
    Patent Office, 25, Southampton Buildings,
        Chancery Lane, London, W.C.

(a) Here insert full address.

Patents, Designs, and Trade Marks Act, 1883.

[PATENT.] FORM N.

Application for Duplicate of Patent.

Date.

SIR,

I REGRET to have to inform you that the Letters Patent, dated *———, No. ———, granted to ———, for an invention of † ———, have been ‡ ———.

I beg therefore to apply for the issue of a duplicate of such Letters Patent.§

[Signature of Applicant.]

To the Comptroller,
    Patent Office, 25, Southampton Buildings,
        Chancery Lane, London, W.C.

* Here insert date, No., name, and full address of patentee.
† Here insert title of invention.
‡ Here insert the word "destroyed" or "lost," as the case may be.
§ Here state interest possessed by applicant in the letters patent.

Patents, Designs, and Trade Marks Act, 1883.

[PATENT.] FORM O.

Notice of Intended Exhibition of an Unpatented Invention.

* ——— hereby give notice of my intention to exhibit a ——— of ——— at the ——— Exhibition, which † ——— of ——— 18—, under the provisions of the Patents, Designs, and Trade Marks Act of 1883.

‡ ——— herewith enclose ———.

(Signed) ———.

To the Comptroller,
    Patent Office, 25, Southampton Buildings,
        Chancery Lane, London, W.C.

* Here state name and full address of applicant.
† State "opened" or "is to open."
‡ Insert brief description of invention, with drawings if necessary.

Patents, Designs, and Trade Marks Act, 1883.

[PATENT.] FORM P.

Form of Request for Correction of Clerical Error.

SIR,
I HEREBY request that the following clerical error (*a*) may be corrected in (*b*).

Signature ———
Full Address ———

To the Comptroller,
  Patent Office, 25, Southampton Buildings,
    Chancery Lane, London, W.C.

(*a*) Or errors.
(*b*) Here state whether in application, specification, or register.

Patents, Designs, and Trade Marks Act, 1883.

[PATENT.] FORM Q.

Certificate of Comptroller-General.

Patent Office,
London,
——— 188—.

I, ———, Comptroller-General of Patents, Designs, and Trade Marks, hereby certify

---

Patents, Designs, and Trade Marks Act, 1883.

[PATENT.] FORM R.

Form of Notice for Alteration of an Address in Register.

SIR,
  (*a*) ——— hereby request that ——— address now upon the Register may be altered as follows:—
  (*b*) ———————

———,
Sir,
Your obedient Servant,

To the Comptroller,
  Patent Office, 25, Southampton Buildings,
    Chancery Lane, London, W.C.

(*a*) Here state name or names and full address of applicant or applicants.
(*b*) Here insert full address.

Y 2

Patents, Designs, and Trade Marks Act, 1883.

[PATENT.] FORM S.

Form of Application for Entry of Order of Privy Council in Register.

(*a*)'—— hereby transmit an office copy of an Order in Council with reference to (*b*).

Sir,
Your obedient Servant,

To the Comptroller,
Patent Office, 25, Southampton Buildings,
Chancery Lane, London, W.C.

(*a*) Here state name and full address of applicant.
(*b*) Here state the purport of the order.

Patents, Designs, and Trade Marks Act, 1883.

[PATENT.] FORM T.

Form of Appeal to Law Officer.

I, (*a*) —— of (*a*) —— hereby give notice of my intention to appeal to the law officer from (*b*) —— of the Comptroller of the —— day of —— 188—, whereby he (*c*) —— No. (*d*) —— of the year 188— (*d*).

Signature ——
Date ——.

N.B.—This notice has to be sent to the Comptroller-General at the Patent Office, London, W.C., and a copy of same to the Law Officer's Clerk, at Room 549, Royal Courts of Justice, London.
21st December, 1883.

(*a*) Here insert name and full address of appellant.
(*b*) Here insert "the decision" or "that part of the decision," as the case may be.
(*c*) Here insert "refused [or allowed] application for patent," or "refused [or allowed] application for leave to amend patent," or otherwise, as the case may be.
(*d*) Insert number and year.

(Signed) J. CHAMBERLAIN,
President of the Board of Trade.

TRADE MARKS RULES.

By virtue of the provisions of the Patents, Designs, and Trade Marks Act, 1883, the Board of Trade do hereby make the following Rules :—

PRELIMINARY.

1. These Rules may be cited as the Trade Marks Rules, 1883, and shall come into operation from and immediately after the 31st day of December, 1883.

INTERPRETATION.

2. In the construction of these Rules any words herein used defined by the said Act shall have the meanings thereby assigned to them respectively. *Interpretation.*

FEES.

3. The fees to be paid in pursuance of the said Act, so far as it relates to trade marks, shall be the fees specified in the first schedule hereto. *Fees.*

FORMS.

4. The Form F. in the first schedule to the said Act shall be altered or amended by the substitution therefor of the Form F. in the second schedule to these Rules. *Forms.*

5.—(1) An application for registration of a trade mark shall be made in the Form F. in the second schedule to these Rules; (2) The remaining forms in such schedule may be used in all cases to which they are applicable.

CLASSIFICATION OF GOODS.

6. For the purposes of trade marks registration and of these Rules, goods are classified in the manner appearing in the third schedule hereto. *Classification of goods.*

If any doubt arises as to what class any particular description of goods belongs to, the doubt shall be determined by the comptroller.

APPLICATION FOR REGISTRATION.

7. An application for registration of a trade mark, if made by any firm or partnership, may be signed by some one or more members of such firm or partnership, as the case may be. *Application by firm.*

If the application be made by a body corporate, it may be signed by the secretary or other principal officer of such body corporate.

8. An application for registration and all other communications between the applicant and the comptroller may be made by or through an agent duly authorised to the satisfaction of the comptroller. *Agency.*

APPENDIX.

Acknowledgment of application.
9. On receipt of the application, the comptroller shall furnish the applicant with an acknowledgment thereof.

Contents of form of application.
10. Where application is made to register a trade mark which was used by the applicant or his predecessors in business before the 13th of August, 1875, the application shall contain a statement of the time during which and of the person by whom it has been so used in respect of the goods mentioned in the application.

Size, &c. of documents.
11. Subject to any other directions that may be given by the comptroller, all applications, notices, counter-statements, representations of marks, papers having representations affixed, or other documents required by the said Act or by these Rules to be left with or sent to the comptroller or to the Cutlers' Company, shall be upon foolscap paper of a size of 13 inches by 8 inches, and shall have on the left-hand part thereof a margin of not less than one inch and a-half.

Qualification of metal goods.
12. In the case of an application for the registration of a trade mark used on any metal goods, other than cutlery, edge tools, and raw steel, the applicant shall state in the specification of goods in the form of application of what metal or metals the goods in respect to which he applies are made.

Representations of trade mark.
13. Subject to any other directions that may be given by the comptroller, three representations of each trade mark, except in the case of marks applied for in classes 23 to 35 inclusive, must be supplied upon paper of the size aforesaid, and must be of a durable nature. One of such representations must be made upon or affixed to the form of application, the others upon separate half-sheets. In the case of trade marks exceeding the limits of the foolscap paper of the size aforesaid, such marks may be pasted and folded upon the sheets of foolscap.

In the case of marks applied for in classes 23 to 35 inclusive, the applicant shall supply four representations of each mark for each class.

Where a drawing or other representation or specimen cannot be given in manner aforesaid, a specimen or copy of the trade mark may be sent either of full size or on a reduced scale, and in such form as the comptroller may think most convenient.

The comptroller may, if dissatisfied with the representation of a trade mark, require a fresh representation, either before he proceeds with the application or before he registers the trade mark.

The comptroller may also, in exceptional cases, deposit in the Patent Office a specimen or copy of any trade mark which cannot conveniently be shown by a representation, and may refer thereto in the register in such manner as he may think fit.

Representations of a series of trade marks.
14. When an application relates to a series of trade marks differing from one another in respect of the particulars mentioned in section 66 of the said Act, a representation of each trade mark of the series shall be made or affixed upon the form of application and also upon each of the separate half-sheets of paper aforesaid.

Translation of foreign characters.
15. Wherever a mark consists of or includes words printed in other than Roman character, there shall be given at the foot or on the back of each representation a translation of such words, signed by the applicant or his agent.

16. Any application, statement, notice, or other document authorised or required to be left, made, or given at the Patent Office, or to the comptroller, or to any other person under these Rules, may be sent by a prepaid letter through the post, and if so sent shall be deemed to have been left, made, or given respectively at the time when the letter containing the same would be delivered in the ordinary course of post. *Mode of sending notices, &c.*

In proving such service or sending, it shall be sufficient to prove that the letter was properly addressed and put into the post.

EXERCISE OF DISCRETIONARY POWERS.

17. Before exercising any discretionary power given to the comptroller by the said Act adversely to the applicant for registration of a trade mark, the comptroller shall give him ten days' notice of the time when he may be heard personally or by his agent before the comptroller. *Hearing by comptroller.*

18. Within five days from the date when such notice would be delivered in the ordinary course of post, the applicant shall notify to the comptroller whether or not he intends to be heard upon the matter. *Notice of wish to be heard before comptroller.*

19. The decision of the comptroller in the exercise of any such discretionary power as aforesaid shall be notified to the applicant. *Notification of decision.*

APPEAL TO THE BOARD OF TRADE.

20. Where the comptroller refuses to register a trade mark, and the applicant intends to appeal to the Board of Trade from such refusal, he shall, within one month from the date of the decision appealed against, leave at the Patent Office, Trade Marks Branch, a notice of such his intention. *Appeal to Board of Trade.*

21. Such notice shall be accompanied by a statement of the grounds of appeal, and of the applicant's case in support thereof. *Statement of grounds of appeal.*

22. The applicant shall forthwith on leaving such notice send a copy thereof to the secretary of the Board of Trade, No. 7, Whitehall Gardens, London. *Copy of notice to Board of Trade.*

23. The Board of Trade may thereupon give such directions (if any) as they may think fit with respect to evidence, or otherwise, for the purpose of the hearing of the appeal by the Board of Trade, or for the purpose of their referring the appeal to the Court to hear and determine the same. *Directions by Board.*

24. Where the Board of Trade intend to hear the appeal, seven days' notice, or such shorter notice as the Board of Trade may in any particular case direct, of the time and place appointed for the hearing, shall be given to the comptroller and the applicant. *Notice of time of hearing.*

ADVERTISEMENT OF APPLICATION.

25. Every application shall be advertised by the comptroller in the official paper, during such times, and in such manner as the comptroller may direct. *Advertisement of application.*

If no representation of the trade mark be inserted in the official paper in connexion with the advertisement of an application, the comptroller shall refer in such advertisement to the place or places where a specimen or representation of the trade mark is deposited for exhibition.

Definition of official paper.

26. The official paper for the purposes of these Rules shall be some paper published under the direction of the Board of Trade, or such other paper as such Board may from time to time direct.

Means of advertising trade mark to be supplied to official paper.

27. For the purposes of such advertisement the applicant may be required to furnish a wood block or electrotype (or more than one, if necessary) of the trade mark, of such dimensions as may from time to time be directed by the comptroller, or with such other information or means of advertising the trade mark as may be required by the comptroller; and the comptroller, if dissatisfied with the block or electrotype furnished by the applicant or his agent, may require a fresh block or electrotype before proceeding with the advertisement.

Advertisement of series.

28. When an application relates to a series of trade marks differing from one another in respect of the particulars mentioned in section 66 of the said Act, the applicant may be required to furnish a wood block or electrotype (or more than one, if necessary) of any or of each of the trade marks constituting the series; and the comptroller may, if he thinks fit, insert with the advertisement of the application a statement of the manner in respect of which the several trade marks differ from one another.

OPPOSITION TO REGISTRATION.

Manner of bringing case before Court.

29.—(1.) Where a case stands for the determination of the Court, under the provisions of section 69 of the said Act, the comptroller shall require the applicant within one month, or such further time as the comptroller may allow, to issue a summons in the chambers of a judge of Her Majesty's High Court of Justice for an order that notwithstanding the opposition of which notice has been given the registration of the trade mark be proceeded with by the comptroller, or to take such other proceedings as may be proper and necessary for the determination of the case by the Court.

(2.) The applicant shall thereupon issue such summons, or take such other proceedings as aforesaid, within the period of one month above named, or such further time as the comptroller may allow, and shall also within the like period give notice thereof to the comptroller.

(3.) If the applicant shall fail to issue such summons, or to take such other proceedings, of which failure the non-receipt by the comptroller of the said notice shall be sufficient proof, the applicant shall be deemed to have abandoned his application.

Mode of giving notice that the matter has been brought before the Court.

(4.) Such notice to the comptroller shall be given by delivering at or sending to the Patent Office a copy of the summons or other initiatory proceeding bearing an endorsement of service signed by the applicant or his solicitor, or an endorsement of acceptance of service signed by the opponent or his solicitor.

Register of Trade Marks.

30. As soon as may be after the expiration of two months from the date of the first advertisement of the application, the comptroller shall, subject to any such summons or other proceeding as aforesaid and the determination of the Court thereon, if he is satisfied that the applicant is entitled to registration, and on payment of the prescribed fee, enter the name, address, and description of the applicant in the Register of Trade Marks as the registered proprietor of the trade mark in respect of the particular goods or classes of goods described in his application. *Time of registration of trade marks.*

31. In case of the death of any applicant for a trade mark after the date of his application, and before the trade mark applied for has been entered on the register, the comptroller, after the expiration of the prescribed period of advertisement, may, on being satisfied of the applicant's death, enter on the register, in place of the name of such deceased applicant, the name, address, and description of the person owning the goodwill of the business, if such ownership be proved to the satisfaction of the comptroller. *Where applicant dies before registration, the trade mark may be registered for successor to goodwill of business.*

32. Upon registering any trade mark the comptroller shall enter in the register the date on which the application for registration was received by the comptroller (which day shall be deemed to be the date of the registration) and such other particulars as he may think necessary. *Entries to be made in register.*

33. The comptroller shall send notice to the applicant of the registration of his trade mark, together with a reference to the advertisement of such trade mark in the official paper. *Notice of registration.*

34. Where a person becomes entitled to a registered trade mark by assignment, transmission, or other operation of law, a request for the entry of his name in the register as proprietor of the trade mark shall be addressed to the comptroller, and left at the Patent Office. *Request by subsequent proprietor.*

35. Such request shall in the case of an individual be made and signed by the person requiring to be registered as proprietor, and in the case of a firm or partnership by some one or more members of such firm or partnership, or in either case by his or their agent respectively duly authorised to the satisfaction of the comptroller, and in the case of a body corporate by their agent, authorised in like manner. *Signature of request.*

36. Every such request shall state the name, address, and description of the person claiming to be entitled to the trade mark (hereinafter called the claimant), and the particulars of the assignment, transmission, or other operation of law, by virtue of which he requires to be entered in the register as proprietor, so as to show the manner in which, and the person or persons to whom, the trade mark has been assigned or transmitted, and so as to show further that it has been so assigned or transmitted in connexion with the goodwill of the business concerned in the particular goods or classes of goods for which the trade mark has been registered. *Contents of request.*

37. Every such request shall be accompanied by a statutory declaration to be thereunder written, verifying the several statements *Declaration to accompany request.*

therein, and declaring that the particulars above described comprise every material fact and document affecting the proprietorship of the trade mark as claimed by such request.

Further proof of title if required.

38. The claimant shall furnish to the comptroller such other proof of title and of the existence and ownership of such goodwill as aforesaid as he may require for his satisfaction.

Body corporate.

39. A body corporate may be registered as proprietor by its corporate name.

Definition of applicant.

40. The term "applicant" in Rules 17, 18, and 19 shall include each of several persons claiming to be registered as proprietor of the same trade mark.

Comptroller may require statement from rival claimants.

41. Whether all of such persons so claiming require to be heard before the comptroller or not, he may, before exercising the discretion vested in him by section 71 of the said Act, require such persons, or any or either of them, to submit a statement in writing within a time to be notified by him, or to attend before him and make oral explanations with respect to such matters as the comptroller may require.

Submission to Court of conflicting claims.

42. Where each of several persons claims to be registered as proprietor of the same trade mark, and the comptroller refuses to register any of them until their rights have been determined according to law, the manner in which the rights of such claimants may be submitted to the Court by the comptroller or if the comptroller so require, by the claimants, shall, unless the Court otherwise order, be by a special case; and such special case shall be filed and proceeded with in like manner as any other special case submitted to the Court, or in such other manner as the Court may direct.

Settlement of special case.

43. Where the special case is to be submitted to the parties, it may be agreed to by them, or if they differ, may be settled by the comptroller on payment of the prescribed fees.

44. Where an order has been made by the Court in either of the following cases, viz.:—

(a) Allowing an appeal under section 62 of the said Act;

(b) Disallowing an opposition to registration under section 69; or,

(c) Under the provisions of sections 72, 90, or 92 of the said Act,

the person in whose favour such order has been made, or such one of them, if more than one, as the comptroller may direct, shall forthwith leave at the Patent Office an office copy of such order. The register shall thereupon be rectified or altered, or the purport of such order shall otherwise be duly entered in the register, as the case may be.

Removal of mark from register.

45. Where a trade mark has been removed from the register for non-payment of the prescribed fee or otherwise, under the provisions of section 79 of the said Act, the comptroller shall cause to be entered in the register a record of such removal, and the cause thereof.

TRADE MARKS RULES.

46. If the registered proprietor of a trade mark send to the comptroller, together with the prescribed fee, notice of an alteration in his address, the comptroller shall alter the register accordingly. <small>Alteration of address in register.</small>

47. Whenever an order is made by the Court for making, expunging, or varying an entry from or in the register, the comptroller shall, if he thinks that such rectification or variation should be made public, and at the expense of the person applying for the same, publish, by advertisement or otherwise, and in such manner as he thinks just, the circumstances attending the rectification or variation in the register. <small>Publication of rectification or variation of register.</small>

48. Whenever the registered proprietor of any trade mark intends to apply for the leave of the Court to add to or to alter such trade mark, under section 92 of the said Act, the notice to be given to the comptroller shall be given fourteen days at least before such application. If leave be granted on such application, the applicant shall forthwith supply to the comptroller such a number of representations of the trade mark, as altered, as he may deem sufficient. <small>Notice to comptroller of order of Court for alteration of trade mark under sect. 92 of Act.</small>

INSPECTION OF REGISTER.

49. The register of trade marks shall be open to the inspection of the public, on payment of the prescribed fee, on every week day between the hours of ten and four, except on the days and at the times following:— <small>Hours of inspection.</small>
   (a) Christmas Day, Good Friday, the day observed as Her Majesty's birthday, days observed as days of public fast or thanksgiving, and days observed as holidays at the Bank of England; or
   (b) Days which may from time to time be notified by a placard posted in a conspicuous place at the Patent Office;
   (c) Times when the register is required for any purpose of official use.

POWER TO DISPENSE WITH EVIDENCE.

50. Where under these Rules any person is required to do any act or thing, or to sign any document, or to make any declaration on behalf of himself or of any body corporate, or any document or evidence is required to be produced to or left with the comptroller, or at the Patent Office, and it is shown to the satisfaction of the comptroller that from any reasonable cause such person is unable to do such act or thing, or to sign such document, or make such declaration, or that such document or evidence cannot be produced or left as aforesaid, it shall be lawful for the comptroller, with the sanction of the Board of Trade, and upon the production of such other evidence, and subject to such terms as they may think fit, to dispense with any such act or thing, document, declaration, or evidence. <small>Dispensing with evidence.</small>

AMENDMENTS.

51. Any document or drawing or other representation of a trade mark for the amending of which no special provision is made by <small>Amendment of documents.</small>

the said Act, may be amended, and any irregularity in procedure which in the opinion of the comptroller may be obviated without detriment to the interests of any person, may be corrected, if the comptroller think fit, and on such terms as he may direct.

Enlargement of Time.

Comptroller may enlarge time.

52. The time prescribed by these Rules for doing any act, or taking any proceeding thereunder, may be enlarged by the comptroller, if he think fit, and upon such notice to other parties, and proceedings thereon, and upon such terms, as he may direct.

Cutlers' Company.

Sheffield applications in duplicate.

53. All applications to the Cutlers' Company for registration of a trade mark, under section 81 of the said Act, shall be in duplicate, accompanied by the prescribed fees and representations.

Notice to comptroller.

54. The Cutlers' Company shall, within seven days of the receipt by them of an application to register a trade mark, send the comptroller one copy of such application, by way of notice thereof, together with two representations of the mark for each class for which the applicant seeks registration.

Time within which comptroller may object to application made at Sheffield.

55.—(1. The time within which the comptroller shall give notice to the Cutlers' Company of any objection he may have to the acceptance of an application for registration made to the said company shall be one month from the date of the receipt by the comptroller of the notice from the said company of the making of the application.

Advertisement of application made at Sheffield.

2. If no such objection is made by the comptroller, the Cutlers' Company shall require the applicant to send the comptroller a wood block or electrotype as the comptroller may direct, and the comptroller shall if satisfied with such wood block or electrotype, advertise the application in the same manner as an application made to him at the Patent Office.

Manner of notifying to Cutlers' Company application received by comptroller.

3. The manner in which the comptroller shall notify to the Cutlers' Company an application and proceedings thereon made as mentioned in subsection 8 of section 81 of the said Act shall be by sending to the Cutlers' Company a copy of the official paper containing the application of which notice is required to be given, with a note distinguishing such application.

Similarity of proceedings at London and at Sheffield.

56. The provisions of these Rules as to forms, representations, the proceedings on opposition to registration, registration, and all subsequent proceedings shall, as far as the circumstances allow, apply to all applications to register made to the Cutlers' Company, and to all proceedings consequent thereon.

Certificates.

Certificate by comptroller.

57. The comptroller, when required for the purpose of any legal proceeding or other special purpose to give a certificate as to any entry, matter, or thing which he is authorised by the said Act or any of these Rules to make or do, may, on receipt of a request in writing, and on payment of the prescribed fee, give such certificate, and shall specify on the face of it the legal proceeding or other purpose for which such certificate is granted.

DECLARATIONS.

58. The statutory declarations required by the said Act and these Rules, or used in any proceedings thereunder, shall be made and subscribed as follows:— *(Manner in which, and persons before whom, declaration is to be taken.)*
- (a) In the United Kingdom, before any justice of the peace, or any commissioner or other officer authorised by law in any part of the United Kingdom to administer an oath for the purpose of any legal proceeding;
- (b) In any other part of Her Majesty's dominions, before any Court, judge, justice of the peace, or any officer authorised by law to administer an oath there for the purpose of a legal proceeding; and
- (c) If made out of Her Majesty's dominions, before a British minister, or person exercising the functions of a British minister, or a consul, vice-consul, or other person exercising the functions of a British consul, or a notary public, or before a judge or magistrate.

59. Any document purporting to have affixed, impressed, or subscribed thereto or thereon the seal or signature of any person hereby authorised to take such declaration in testimony of such declaration having been made and subscribed before him, may be admitted by the comptroller without proof of the genuineness of any such seal or signature, or of the official character of such person or his authority to take such declaration. *(Notice of seal of officer taking declaration to prove itself.)*

REPEAL.

60. All general rules as to the registration of trade marks heretofore made by the Lord Chancellor under the Trade Marks Registration Act, 1875, and in force on the 31st day of December, 1883, shall be, and they are hereby repealed, as from that date, without prejudice, nevertheless, to any proceeding which may have been taken under such Rules. *(Previous rules repealed.)*

J. CHAMBERLAIN,
President of the Board of Trade.

21st December, 1883.

SCHEDULES.

FIRST SCHEDULE.

Fees.	£	s.	d.
1. On application to register a trade mark for one or more articles included in one class	0	5	0
2. On appeal to Board of Trade on refusal of comptroller to register	1	0	0
3. For registration of a trade mark for one or more articles included in one class	1	0	0
4. For registering a series of trade marks, for every additional representation after the first in each class	0	5	0

		£	s.	d.
5. For entering notice of opposition, for each trade mark, whether in one or more classes		1	0	0
6. On application to register a subsequent proprietor in cases of assignment or transmission, the first mark		1	0	0
7. For every additional mark assigned or transmitted at the same time		0	2	0
8. For certificate of refusal to register a trade mark under section 77		1	0	0
9. For certificate of refusal at the same time for more than one trade mark, for each additional trade mark after the first		0	10	0
10. For continuance of mark at expiration of fourteen years		1	0	0
11. Additional fee where fee is paid within three months after expiration of fourteen years		0	10	0
12. Additional fee for restoration of trade mark where removed for nonpayment of fee		1	0	0
13. For altering address on the register, for every mark		0	5	0
14. For every entry in the register of a rectification thereof or an alteration therein, not otherwise charged		0	10	0
15. For cancelling the entry or part of the entry of a trade mark upon the register, on the application of the owner of such trade mark		0	5	0
16. On request to comptroller to correct a clerical error		0	5	0
17. For certificate of registration to be used in legal proceedings		0	10	0
18. For certificate of registration to be used for the purpose of obtaining registration in foreign countries		0	5	0
19. For copy of notification of registration		0	2	0
20. Settling a special case by comptroller		2	0	0
21. For inspecting register, for every quarter of an hour		0	1	0
22. For making a search amongst the classified representations of trade marks, for every quarter of an hour		0	1	0
23. For office copy of documents, for every 100 words (but never less than one shilling).		0	0	4
24. For certifying office copies, MS. or printed		0	1	0
25. For certificate of comptroller under section 96		0	5	0
26. In cases where a trade mark requires a greater space than two inches of the depth of the page of the *Trade Marks Journal*, for each additional inch or part of an inch		0	2	0
27. Manchester Trade Marks Office	-Same as above			
28. Sheffield Marks	-Same as above			
29. On appeal from Cutlers' Company, Sheffield, to comptroller		1	0	0

J. CHAMBERLAIN,
President of the Board of Trade.

Approved,
CHARLES C. COTES,
HERBERT J. GLADSTONE,
Lords Commissioners of
Her Majesty's Treasury.

4th December, 1883.

TRADE MARKS RULES.

SECOND SCHEDULE.

Forms.	Page
Form of Application for Registration	335
,, Additional Representation of Trade Mark	336
,, Appeal to Board of Trade	336
,, Transmission of Registration Fee	337
,, Notice of Opposition	337
,, Assignment of Trade Mark	337
,, Request for Certificate of Refusal	338
,, Notice of Application for Alteration of Address	338
,, Notice of Application for Rectification of Register	339
,, Application to Cancel Entry on Register	339
,, Declaration in support of Application to Cancel Entry	339
,, Request to Comptroller for Correction of Clerical Error	340
,, Request for Certificate of Registration for use in obtaining Registration Abroad	340
,, Request for Certificate of Registration for use in Legal Proceedings	341
,, Application for Settlement of a Special Case	341
,, General Certificate of Comptroller	341
,, Copy of Notification of Registration	342
,, Appeal from Cutlers' Company	342

Patents, Designs, and Trade Marks Act, 1883.

[TRADE MARKS.] F.

Application for Registration of Trade Mark.

> One representation to be fixed within this square, and two others to be sent on separate sheets of foolscap.
>
> Representations of a larger size may be folded, but must be mounted upon linen and affixed hereto.

You are hereby requested to register the accompanying Trade Mark in Class ———, in respect of (*a*) ——— in the name of (*b*) ——— who claims to be the proprietor thereof (*c*).

To the Comptroller,
    Patent Office, Trade Marks Branch,
      25, Southampton Buildings, London.   (Signed) ———(*d*)
Dated this ——— day of ———, 1883.

NOTE.—If the Trade Mark has been in use in respect of the goods since before August 13, 1875, state length of such user.

(*a*) Only goods contained *in one and the same class* should be set out here.
A separate application form is required *for each separate class*.
(*b*) Here insert legibly the full name, address, and business of the individual, firm, or company. In the case of an individual, add trading style (if any).
(*c*) Alter to "claim to be the proprietors thereof" in the case of a firm or company.
(*d*) To be signed by the applicant; or, in the case of a firm, by a partner, adding, "A member of the firm," or, in the case of a company, by the secretary or other principal officer, adding, "For the Company."
Or, *in any case*, an agent may sign, adding "Agent."

Patents, Designs, and Trade Marks Act, 1883.

G.

Additional Representation of Trade Mark, to accompany Application for Registration.

> One representation of the Trade Mark to be affixed within this square.
> It must correspond *exactly*, in all respects, with the representation affixed to the Application Form.
>
> Any representation of a larger size than foolscap may be folded, but must then be mounted upon linen and affixed hereto.

Two of these additional representations of the Trade Mark must accompany *each* form of application.
In the case of a Trade Mark claimed in one of the classes 23 to 35, three of these additional representations of the mark must accompany the form of application.

Patents, Designs, and Trade Marks Act, 1883.

[TRADE MARKS.] H.

Form of Appeal to Board of Trade on Refusal of Comptroller to Register a Trade Mark.

Sir,
 I HEREBY give notice of my intention to appeal against your decision upon my application to register a Trade Mark No. ——— in Class ——— for ———, and I beg to submit my case* for the decision of the Board of Trade.

        I am, Sir,
         Your obedient Servant,

To the Comptroller,
 Patent Office, Trade Marks Branch,
  25, Southampton Buildings,
   London.

---

* The statement of the case to be written upon foolscap paper (on one side only), with a margin of two inches on the left-hand side thereof.

Patents, Designs, and Trade Marks Act, 1883.

[TRADE MARKS.] I.

Fee for Registration of a Trade Mark.

SIR,

In reply to your request I hereby transmit the prescribed fee for the registration of the Trade Mark No. ———, in Class ———.

I am,
Sir,
Your obedient Servant,

To the Comptroller,
 Patent Office, Trade Marks Branch,
  25, Southampton Buildings,
   London.

Patents, Designs, and Trade Marks Act, 1883.

[TRADE MARKS.] J.

Notice of Opposition to Application for Registration.

[To be accompanied by an unstamped duplicate.]

In the matter of an Application, No. ———, by ———, of ———.

SIR,

Notice is hereby given that I ———, of ———, oppose the Registration of the Trade Mark advertised under the above number for Class ——— in the "Trade Marks Journal" of the ——— day of ——— 188—, No. ———, page ———.

The grounds of opposition are as follows :—

To the Comptroller,
 Patent Office, Trade Marks Branch,
  25, Southampton Buildings,
   London.

To be dated and signed at the end by the opponent or his solicitor.

Patents, Designs, and Trade Marks Act, 1883.

[TRADE MARKS.] K.

Request to Enter Name of subsequent Proprietor of Trade Mark upon the Register, with Declaration in support thereof.

I, (*a*) ——— hereby request that you will enter (*b*) ——— name (*c*) in the Register of Trade Marks as proprietor ——— of the Trade Mark No. ——— in Class ———.

(*d*) ——— entitled to the said trade mark and to the goodwill of the business concerned in the goods with respect to which the said trade mark is registered.

(*e*) ———.

And I do solemnly and sincerely declare that the above several statements are true, and the particulars above set out comprise every material fact and document affecting the proprietorship of the said trade mark as above claimed.

(*f*) And I make this solemn declaration, conscientiously believing the

T. Z

same to be true, and by virtue of the provisions of the Statutory Declarations Act, 1835.
Declared at ——— this ——— day of ——— 188—.

(g) ———.

Before me, ———
(h) ———.
To the Comptroller,
Patent Office, Trade Marks Branch,
25, Southampton Buildings, London.

(a) Or We.
Here insert name, full address, and description.
(b) My or our.
(c) Or names.
(d) I am, or We are.
(e) Here state whether trade mark transmitted by death, marriage, bankruptcy, or other operation of law, and if entitled by assignment state the particulars thereof, as, e.g. "by deed dated the ——— day of ——— 188—, made between so-and-so of the one part."
(f) This paragraph is not required when the declaration is made out of the United Kingdom.
(g) To be signed here by the person making the declaration.
(h) Signature and title of the authority before whom the declaration is made.

Patents, Designs, and Trade Marks Act, 1883.

[TRADE MARKS.] L.

Request for Certificate of Refusal to Register a Trade Mark in use before 13th August, 1875.

In the matter of an Application for registration of an old Trade Mark, No. ——— in Class ———.

SIR,—I, ———, of ———, the applicant in the above matter, hereby request you to furnish me with your certificate of refusal to register the said trade mark.

Dated this ——— day of ——— 188—.

* ———.

To the Comptroller,
Patent Office, Trade Marks Branch,
25, Southampton Buildings, London.

* Signature of applicant.

Patents, Designs, and Trade Marks Act, 1883.

[TRADE MARKS.] M.

Notice of Application for Alteration of Address on Register of Trade Marks.

In the matter of the Trade Mark, No. ———, registered in Class - .

SIR,—Notice is hereby given that I — of ——— the registered proprietor of the trade mark numbered as above, desire that my address on the Register of Trade Marks be altered to ———.

Dated this ——— day of ——— 188—.

* ———

To the Comptroller,
Patent Office, Trade Marks Branch,
25, Southampton Buildings, London.

* Signature of proprietor.

Patents, Designs, and Trade Marks Act, 1883.

[TRADE MARKS.]   N.

Notice of Application for Alteration or Rectification of Register of Trade Marks.

In the matter of the Trade Mark, No. ———, registered in Class ——— in the name of ———.

SIR,—Notice is hereby given, that by an order of the Court, made on the ——— day of ——— 188—, it was directed that the entry on the Register of Trade Marks, in respect of the trade mark numbered as above, should be rectified in the manner therein specified.

An office copy of the order of the Court is enclosed herewith.

Dated this ——— day of ——— 188—.   *———

To the Comptroller,
     Patent Office, Trade Marks Branch,
       25, Southampton Buildings, London.

* To be signed by the person interested or his agent.

Patents, Designs, and Trade Marks Act, 1883.

[TRADE MARK.]   O.

Form of Application by Proprietor of Registered Trade Mark to Cancel Entry on Register.

Trade Mark, No. ——— Class ——— advertised in "Trade Marks Journal," No. ———, page ———.

Name of registered proprietor or firm ———. Place of business ———.

I, the undersigned ———, of ——— [or I, the undersigned ———, a member of the firm of ———, of ———, on behalf of my said firm] ———, apply that the entry upon the Register of the Trade Marks in Class ——— of the Trade Mark No. ——— may be cancelled.

The ——— day of ——— 188—.

                       (Signed) ———.

This is the statement marked "O" referred to in the declaration of ———, made before me the ——— of ———, 188—.

Patents, Designs, and Trade Marks Act, 1883.

P.

Form of Declaration in Support of Application for Cancellation of Trade Mark by Owner.

I, ——— of ——— [or I, ———, a member of the firm of ———, of ———], do hereby solemnly and sincerely declare, to the best of my knowledge and belief, as follows:—

(1) The application signed by me, and dated the ——— day of ———, 188—, and marked with the letter "O," and shown to me at the time of making this declaration, is true.

(2) I am the person whose name appears on the Register of Trade Marks as the proprietor of the trade mark referred to in the said application marked with the letter "O."

[*or* My said firm is the firm whose name appears on the Register of Trade Marks as the proprietor of the trade mark referred to in the said application marked with the letter "O."

And I make this solemn declaration conscientiously believing the same to be true, and by virtue of the provisions of the Statutory Declarations Act, 1835.

(Signed) ———.

Declared at ——— this ———
day of ———, 188—.
Before me, ———

If the declaration be made before a commissioner to administer oaths it will require to be stamped with a 2s. 6d. impressed inland revenue stamp.

Patents, Designs, and Trade Marks Act, 1883.

[TRADE MARKS.] Q.

Form of Request for Correction of Clerical Error in regard to a Trade Mark.

SIR,

I hereby request that

To the Comptroller,
  Patent Office, Trade Marks Branch,
   25, Southampton Buildings,
    London.

Patents, Designs, and Trade Marks Act, 1883.

[TRADE MARKS.] R.

Request for Certificate of Registration of Trade Mark for use in obtaining Registration Abroad.

In the matter of the Trade Mark, No. ———, registered in Class ———, in the name of ———.

SIR,

I ———, of ———, the registered proprietor of the above Trade Mark hereby request you to furnish me with your certificate of registration for use in obtaining registration of the same in * ———

Dated this ——— day of ———, 188—.

† ———.

To the Comptroller,
  Patent Office, Trade Marks Branch,
   25, Southampton Buildings,
    London.

* Here state name of country in which registration is to be sought.
† Signature.

Patents, Designs, and Trade Marks Act, 1883.

[TRADE MARKS.]   S.

Request for Certificate of Registration of Trade Mark for use in Legal Proceedings.

In the matter of the Trade Mark, No. ———, registered in Class ———, in the name of ———.

SIR,

I, ———, of ———, the registered proprietor of the above Trade Mark hereby request you to furnish me with your certificate of registration for use in the following legal proceedings* ———.

Dated this ——— day of ———, 188—.

† ———.

To the Comptroller,
   Patent Office, Trade Marks Branch,
      25, Southampton Buildings,
         London.

* Here state exact title of legal proceedings.
† Signature.

Patents, Designs, and Trade Marks Act, 1883.

[TRADE MARKS.]   T.

Application for Settlement of a Special Case on application to Register a Trade Mark.

In the matter of the Application of ——— and of the Application of ———.

SIR,

Notice is hereby given that I, ———, of ———, and I, ———, are unable to agree upon the facts on which the opinion of the Court is to be taken, and that we request you to fix a day on which we may attend before you and obtain your finding on the matters of fact to be submitted to the Court as settled.

Dated this ——— day of ———, 188—.

*———.
*———.

To the Comptroller,
   Patent Office, Trade Marks Branch,
      25, Southampton Buildings,
         London.

* To be signed by both parties.

Patents, Designs, and Trade Marks Act, 1883.

[TRADE MARKS.]   U.

General Certificate of Comptroller-General as to Application for or Registration of a Trade Mark.

Patent Office, Trade Marks Branch,
      London,
      ——— 188—.

· I, ———, Comptroller-General of Patents, Designs, and Trade Marks, hereby certify

Patents, Designs, and Trade Marks Act, 1883.

[TRADE MARKS.] V.

Request for Copy of Official Notification of Registration of Trade Mark.

In the matter of the Trade Mark, No. ——, registered in Class ——.

SIR,—I, ——, of ——, the registered proprietor of the trade mark above named hereby request that you will furnish me with a copy of the official notification of the registration of the same.

* ——.

Dated this —— day of —— 188—.

To the Comptroller,
    Patent Office, Trade Marks Branch,
        25, Southampton Buildings, London.

* Signature.

Patents, Designs, and Trade Marks Act, 1883.

[TRADE MARKS.] W.

Form of Appeal from Cutlers' Company at Sheffield to Comptroller.

[To be accompanied by an unstamped duplicate.]

SIR,—I hereby give notice of appeal against the decision of the Cutlers' Company, of Sheffield, in regard to my application for registration of a Trade Mark, No. —— in Class —— for ——, and I beg to submit my case* for your decision accordingly.

† ——.

Dated this —— day of —— 188—.

To the Comptroller,
    Patent Office, Trade Marks Branch,
        25, Southampton Buildings, London.

* The statement of the case to be written upon foolscap paper (on one side only), with a margin of two inches on the left-hand side thereof.
† Signature.

THIRD SCHEDULE.

GENERAL NOTE.

Any wares made of mixed materials (for example, of both cotton and silk) shall be included in such one of the classes appropriated to those materials as the registrar may desire.

CLASSIFICATION OF GOODS.

Illustrations.

Note.—Goods are mentioned in this column by way of illustration, and not as an exhaustive list of the contents of a class.

CLASS 1.

Chemical substances used in manufactures, photography, or philosophical research, and anti-corrosives.

Such as—Acids, including vegetable acids; alkalies; artists' colours; pigments; mineral dyes.

Class 2.
Chemical substances used for agricultural, horticultural, veterinary, and sanitary purposes.

Illustrations.

Such as—Artificial manure; cattle medicines; deodorisers; vermin destroyers.

Class 3.
Chemical substances prepared for use in medicine and pharmacy.

Such as—Cod liver oil; medicated articles; patent medicines; plasters; rhubarb.

Class 4.
Raw or partly prepared vegetable, animal, and mineral substances used in manufactures, not included in other classes.

Such as—Resins; oils used in manufactures and not included in other classes; dyes, other than mineral; tanning substances; fibrous substances (*e.g.*, cotton, hemp, flax, jute); wool; silk; bristles; hair; feathers; cork; seeds; coal; coke; bone; sponge.

Class 5.
Unwrought and partly wrought metals used in manufacture.

Such as—Iron and steel, pig or cast; iron, rough; iron, bar and rail, including rails for railways; iron, bolt and rod; iron, sheet, and boiler and armour plates; iron, hoop; lead, pig; lead, rolled; lead, sheet; wire; copper; zinc; gold, in ingots.

Class 6.
Machinery of all kinds, and parts of machinery, except agricultural and horticultural machines included in Class 7.

Such as—Steam engines; boilers; pneumatic machines; hydraulic machines; locomotives; sewing machines; weighing machines; machine tools; mining machinery; fire engines.

Class 7.
Agricultural and horticultural machinery, and parts of such machinery.

Such as—Ploughs; drilling machines; reaping machines; thrashing machines; churns; cyder presses; chaff cutters.

Class 8.
Philosophical instruments, scientific instruments, and apparatus for useful purposes. Instruments and apparatus for teaching.

Such as — Mathematical instruments; gauges; logs; spectacles; educational appliances.

Class 9.
Musical instruments.

Class 10.
Horological instruments.

Class 11.
Instruments, apparatus, and contrivances, not medicated, for surgical or curative purposes, or in relation to the health of men or animals.

Such as—Bandages; friction gloves; lancets; fleams; enemas.

CLASS 12.
Cutlery and edge tools.

Illustrations.
Such as—Knives; forks; scissors; shears; files; saws.

CLASS 13.
Metal goods not included in other classes.

Such as—Anvils; keys; basins (metal); needles; hoes; shovels; corkscrews.

CLASS 14.
Goods of precious metals (including aluminium, nickel, Britannia metal, &c.) and jewellery, and imitations of such goods and jewellery.

Such as—Plate; clock cases and pencil cases of such metals; Sheffield and other plated goods; gilt and ormolu work.

CLASS 15.
Glass.

Such as—Window and plate glass; painted glass; glass mosaic; glass beads.

CLASS 16.
Porcelain and earthenware.

Such as—China; stoneware; terra cotta; statuary porcelain; tiles; bricks.

CLASS 17.
Manufactures from mineral and other substances for building or decoration.

Such as—Cement; plaster; imitation marble; asphalt.

CLASS 18.
Engineering, architectural, and building contrivances.

Such as—Diving apparatus; warming apparatus; ventilating apparatus; filtering apparatus; lighting contrivances; drainage contrivances; electric and pneumatic bells.

CLASS 19.
Arms, ammunition, and stores not included in Class 20.

Such as—Cannon; small-arms; fowling pieces; swords; shot and other projectiles; camp equipage; equipments.

CLASS 20.
Explosive substances.

Such as—Gunpowder; gun-cotton; dynamite; fog-signals; percussion caps; fireworks; cartridges.

CLASS 21.
Naval architectural contrivances and naval equipments not included in Classes 19 and 20.

Such as—Boats; anchors; chain cables; rigging.

CLASS 22.
Carriages.

Such as—Railway carriages; waggons; railway trucks; bicycles; bath chairs.

CLASS 23.
Cotton yarn and thread.

Such as—Sewing cotton on spools or reels; sewing cotton not on spools or reels; dyed cotton yarns.

TRADE MARKS RULES.   345

CLASS 24.
Cotton piece goods of all kinds.

Illustrations.
Such as—Cotton shirtings; long cloth.

CLASS 25.
Cotton goods not included in Classes 23, 24, or 38.

Such as—Cotton lace; cotton braids; cotton tapes.

CLASS 26.
Linen and hemp yarn and thread.

CLASS 27.
Linen and hemp piece goods.

CLASS 28.
Linen and hemp goods not included in Classes 26, 27, and 50.

CLASS 29.
Jute yarns and tissues, and other articles made of jute not included in Class 50.

CLASS 30.
Silk, spun, thrown, or sewing.

CLASS 31.
Silk piece goods.

CLASS 32.
Other silk goods not included in Classes 30 and 31.

CLASS 33.
Yarns of wool, worsted, or hair.

CLASS 34.
Cloths and stuffs of wool, worsted, or hair.

CLASS 35.
Woollen and worsted and hair goods not included in Classes 33 and 34.

CLASS 36.
Carpets, floor-cloth, and oil-cloth.

Such as—Drugget; mats and matting; rugs.

CLASS 37.
Leather, skins unwrought and wrought, and articles made of leather not included in other classes.

Such as—Saddlery; harness; whips; portmanteaus; furs.

CLASS 38.
Articles of clothing.

Such as—Hats of all kinds; caps and bonnets; hosiery; gloves; boots and shoes; other ready-made clothing.

APPENDIX.

CLASS 39.
Paper (except paper-hangings), stationery, and book-binding.

Illustrations.
Such as—Envelopes; sealing-wax; pens (except gold pens); ink; playing cards; blotting cases; copying presses.

CLASS 40.
Goods manufactured from india-rubber and gutta-percha not included in other classes.

CLASS 41.
Furniture and upholstery.

Such as—Paper hangings; papier-mâché; mirrors; mattresses.

CLASS 42.
Substances used as food, or as ingredients in food.

Such as—Cereals; pulses; olive oil; hops; malt; dried fruits; tea; sago; salt; sugar; preserved meats; confectionery; oil cakes; pickles; vinegar; beer clarifiers.

CLASS 43.
Fermented liquors and spirits.

Such as — Beer; cyder; wine; whisky; liquours.

CLASS 44.
Mineral and aërated waters, natural and artificial, including ginger-beer.

CLASS 45.
Tobacco, whether manufactured or unmanufactured.

CLASS 46.
Seeds for agricultural and horticultural purposes.

CLASS 47.
Candles, common soap, detergents; illuminating, heating, or lubricating oils; matches; and starch, blue, and other preparations for laundry purposes.

Such as—Washing powders; benzine collas.

CLASS 48.
Perfumery (including toilet articles, preparations for the teeth and hair, and perfumed soap).

CLASS 49.
Games of all kinds and sporting articles not included in other classes.

Such as—Billiard tables; roller skates; fishing nets and lines; toys.

CLASS 50.
Miscellaneous, including—
  (1) Goods manufactured from ivory, bone, or wood, not included in other classes.
  (2) Goods manufactured from straw or grass, not included in other classes.
  (3) Goods manufactured from animal and vegetable substances, not included in other classes.
  (4) Tobacco pipes.
  (5) Umbrellas, walking sticks, brushes and combs.
  (6) Furniture cream, plate powder.
  (7) Tarpaulins, tents, rick-cloths, rope, twine.
  (8) Buttons of all kinds, other than of precious metal or imitations thereof.
  (9) Packing and hose of all kinds.
  (10) Goods not included in the foregoing classes.

Illustrations.
Such as—Coopers' wares.

21st December, 1883.

J. CHAMBERLAIN,
President of the Board of Trade.

DESIGNS RULES.

By virtue of the provisions of the Patents, Designs, and Trade Marks Act, 1883, the Board of Trade do hereby make the following Rules:—

COMMENCEMENT.

1. These Rules may be cited as the Designs Rules, 1883, and shall come into operation from and immediately after the 31st day of December, 1883.

INTERPRETATION.

Interpretation. 2. In the construction of these Rules any words herein used defined by the said Act shall have the meanings thereby assigned to them respectively.

FEES.

Fees. 3. The fees to be paid under the said Act, so far as it relates to applications for and registration of designs, shall be the fees specified in the first schedule hereto.

FORMS.

Forms. 4. An application for the registration of a design shall be made in the Form E., in the second schedule hereto. The remaining forms in such schedule may be used in all cases to which they are applicable.

CLASSIFICATION OF GOODS.

Classification of goods. 5. For the purposes of the registration of designs and of these Rules, goods are classified in the manner appearing in the third schedule hereto.

APPLICATION FOR REGISTRATION.

Agents. 6. All communications between an applicant for the registration of a design and the comptroller or the Board of Trade, as the case may be, may be made by or through an agent duly authorized to the satisfaction of the comptroller.

Address of comptroller. 7. An application for the registration of a design shall, with the prescribed fee, be left at the Patent Office, Designs Branch, or be sent prepaid by post, addressed to the comptroller at the Patent Office, Designs Branch, 25, Southampton Buildings, Chancery Lane, London.

Size of papers. 8. An application for the registration of a design, and all drawings, sketches, photographs, or tracings of a design, and all other documents sent to or left at the Patent Office, Designs Branch, or otherwise furnished to the comptroller or to the Board of Trade, shall be written, printed, copied, or drawn upon strong wide-ruled foolscap paper (on one side only), of the size of 13 inches by 8 inches, leaving a margin of not less than one inch and a-half on the left-hand part thereof, and the signature of the applicants or agents thereto must be written in a large and legible hand.

The comptroller may in any particular case vary the requirements of this Rule as he may think fit.

9. An application for the registration of a design shall be accompanied by a sketch or drawing, or by three exactly similar drawings, photographs, or tracings of the design, or by three specimens of the design, and shall, in describing the nature of the design, state whether it is applicable for the pattern or for the shape or configuration of the design, and the means by which it is applicable. *Sketches and drawings. Nature of design.*

When sketches, drawings, or tracings are furnished, they must be fixed.

When the articles to which designs are applied are not of a kind which can be pasted into books, drawings, photographs, or tracings of such designs shall be furnished.

10. On receipt of an application for registration the comptroller shall send to the applicant an acknowledgment thereof. *Acknowledgment to applicant.*

11. If the comptroller determines to register a design, he shall as soon as may be send to the applicant a certificate of such registration in the prescribed form, sealed with the seal of the Patent Office. *Notice of registration.*

12. Any application, notice, or other document authorised or required to be left, made, or given at the Patent Office, or to the comptroller, or to any other person under these Rules, may be sent by a prepaid letter through the post, and if so sent shall be deemed to have been left, made, or given respectively at the time when the letter containing the same would be delivered in the ordinary course of post. *Applications may be sent by post.*

In proving such service or sending it shall be sufficient to prove that the letter was properly addressed and put into the post.

13. Before exercising any discretionary power given to the comptroller by the said Act adversely to an applicant for registration of a design the comptroller shall give him ten days notice of the time when he may be heard personally or by his agent before the comptroller. *Hearing by comptroller.*

14. Within five days from the date when such notice would be delivered in the ordinary course of post, the applicant shall notify to the comptroller whether or not he intends to be heard upon the matter. *Hearing by comptroller.*

15. The decision or determination of the comptroller in the exercise of any such discretionary power as aforesaid shall be notified to the applicant. *Notification of comptroller's decision.*

Appeal to the Board of Trade.

16. Where the comptroller refuses to register a design, and the applicant intends to appeal to the Board of Trade from such refusal, he shall, within one month from the date of the decision appealed against, leave at the Patent Office, Designs Branch, a notice of such his intention. *Notice of appeal to Board of Trade.*

Statement on appeal.	17. Such notice shall be accompanied by a statement of the grounds of appeal, and of the applicant's case in support thereof.
Notice to secretary of Board of Trade.	18. The applicant shall forthwith on leaving such notice send a copy thereof to the secretary of the Board of Trade, No. 7, Whitehall Gardens, London.
Directions by Board of Trade.	19. The Board of Trade may thereupon give such directions (if any) as they may think fit for the purpose of the hearing of the appeal for the Board of Trade.
Notice of time of hearing.	20. Seven days notice, or such shorter notice as the Board of Trade may in any particular case direct, of the time and place appointed for the hearing of the appeal shall be given to the comptroller and the applicant.

REGISTER OF DESIGNS.

Registering design.	21. Upon the sealing of a certificate of registration the comptroller shall cause to be entered in the register of designs the name, address, and description of the registered proprietor, and the date upon which the application for registration was received by the comptroller, which day shall be deemed to be the date of the registration.
Subsequent proprietors.	22. Where a person becomes entitled to the copyright in a registered design, or to any share or interest therein, by assignment, transmission, or other operation of law, or where a person acquires any right to apply the design either exclusively or otherwise, a request for the entry of his name in the register as such proprietor of the design, or as having acquired such right, as the case may be, (hereinafter called the claimant, shall be addressed to the comptroller, and left at the Patent Office, Designs Branch.
Signature to request.	23. Every such request shall, in the case of an individual, be made and signed by the person requiring to be registered as proprietor; and in the case of a firm or partnership, by some one or more members of such firm or partnership, or, in either case, by his or their agent respectively duly authorised to the satisfaction of the comptroller, and, in the case of a body corporate, by their agent authorised in like manner.
Particulars in request.	24. Every such request shall state the name, address, and description of the claimant, and the particulars of the assignment, transmission, or other operation of law by virtue of which the request is made, so as to show the manner in which and the person or persons to whom the design has been assigned or transmitted, or the person or persons who has or have acquired such right as aforesaid, as the case may be.
Statutory declaration with request.	25. Every such request shall be accompanied by a statutory declaration to be thereunder written verifying the several statements therein, and declaring that the particulars above described comprise every material fact and document affecting the proprietorship of the design or the right to apply the same, as the case may be, as claimed by such request.
Proof of title if required.	26. The claimant shall furnish to the comptroller such other proof of title as he may require for his satisfaction.

27. A body corporate may be registered as proprietor by its corporate name. *Corporate name.*

28. Where an order has been made by the Court, under section 90 of the said Act, the person in whose favour such order has been made shall forthwith leave at the Patent Office an office copy of such order. The register shall thereupon be rectified, or the purport of such order shall otherwise be duly entered in the register, as the case may be. *Notice of order of Court.*

Power to Dispense with Evidence.

29. Where under these Rules any person is required to do any act or thing, or to sign any document, or make any declaration on behalf of himself or of any body corporate, or any document or evidence is required to be produced to or left with the comptroller or at the Patent Office, and it is shown to the satisfaction of the comptroller that from any reasonable cause such person is unable to do such act or thing, or to sign such document, or make such declaration, or that such document or evidence cannot be produced or left as aforesaid, it shall be lawful for the comptroller, with the sanction of the Board of Trade, and upon the production of such other evidence and subject to such terms as they may think fit, to dispense with any such act or thing, document, declaration, or evidence. *Comptroller's discretion as to evidence.*

Amendments.

30. Any document, drawings, sketches, or tracings for the amending of which no special provision is made by the said Act, may be amended, and any irregularity in procedure which, in the opinion of the comptroller, may be obviated without detriment to the interests of any person may be corrected, if the comptroller think fit, and upon such terms as he may direct. *Amendments.*

Enlargement of Time.

31. The time prescribed by these Rules for doing any act or taking any proceeding thereunder may be enlarged by the comptroller, if he think fit, and upon such terms as he may direct. *Enlargement of time.*

Marking Goods.

32. Before the delivery on sale of any article to which a registered design has been applied, the proprietor of such design shall, if such article is included in any of the classes one to twelve in the third schedule hereto, cause each such article to be marked with the abbreviation "R^D" and the number appearing on the certificate of registration, and shall, if such article is included in the classes thirteen or fourteen in the third schedule hereto, cause each such article to be marked with the abbreviation "REG^D". *Registration mark.*

Inspection.

33. On such days and during such hours as the comptroller shall from time to time determine and notify by a placard posted at the Patent Office any person paying the prescribed fee may, on production of the number of any design of which the copyright has ceased, inspect such design, and any person paying the prescribed fee may take a copy or copies of such design. *Office hours.*

Certificate by Comptroller.

Certificate in legal proceeding.

34. Where a certificate is required for the purpose of any legal proceeding or other special purpose as to any entry, matter, or thing which the comptroller is authorised by the said Act or these Rules to make or do, the comptroller may, on a request in writing and on payment of the prescribed fee, give such certificate, which shall also specify on the face of it the purpose for which it has been requested as aforesaid.

Searches on Production of Sketch of Design.

Search.

35. The comptroller may, on receipt of the prescribed fee, make searches among the designs registered at the Patent Office after the commencement of the Act, and inform any person requesting him so to do whether a particular design produced by such person, and to be applied to goods in any particular class, is or is not identical with or an obvious imitation of any design applied to such goods and registered since the commencement of the Act.

Industrial and International Exhibitions.

Notice of exhibition.

36. Any person desirous of exhibiting a design, or any article to which a design has been applied, at an industrial or international exhibition, or of publishing a description of a design during the period of the holding of the exhibition, shall, after having obtained from the Board of Trade a certificate that the exhibition is an industrial or international one, give to the comptroller seven days notice in writing of his intention to exhibit the design or article, or to publish a description of the design, as the case may be.

For the purpose of identifying the design in the event of an application to register the same being subsequently made, the applicant shall furnish to the comptroller a brief description of the nature of the design, accompanied by a sketch or drawing thereof, and such other information as the comptroller may in each case require.

Repeal.

Repeal of previous Rules.

37. All general rules and regulations made by any authority under the Acts relating to the Copyright of Designs, and in force on the 31st December, 1883, shall be, and they are hereby repealed as from that date without prejudice nevertheless to any application then pending.

J. CHAMBERLAIN,
President of the Board of Trade.

21st December, 1883.

SCHEDULES.

FIRST SCHEDULE.

FEES.

		£	s.	d.
1. On application to register one design to be applied to single articles in each class except classes 13 and 14	-	0	10	0
2. On application to register one design to be applied to single articles in classes 13 and 14	-	0	1	0
3. On application to register one design to be applied to a set of articles for each class of registration	-	1	0	0
4. On notice of appeal to Board of Trade against refusal of comptroller to register	-	1	0	0
5. Copy of certificate of registration, each copy	-	0	1	0
6. On request for certificate of comptroller for legal proceedings or other special purpose	-	0	5	0
7. On request to enter name of subsequent proprietor		same as registration fee.		
8. On notice to comptroller of intended exhibition of an unregistered design	-	0	5	0
9. Inspection of design of which the copyright has expired, for each quarter of an hour	-	0	1	0
10. Copy of one such design	-	cost according to agreement.		
11. On request to correct clerical error	-	0	5	0
12. On request for search under section 53	-	0	5	0
13. On request to enter new address	-	0	5	0
14. For office copy, every 100 words	-	0	0	4
		(but never less than 1s.)		
15. For certifying office copies, MSS. or printed	-	0	1	0

NOTE.—The term "set" to include any number of articles ordinarily on sale together irrespective of the varieties of size and arrangement in which the particular design may be shown on each separate article.

J. CHAMBERLAIN,
President of the Board of Trade.

Approved,
    CHARLES C. COTES,
    HERBERT J. GLADSTONE,
        Lords Commissioners of Her Majesty's Treasury.

4th December, 1883.

APPENDIX.

SECOND SCHEDULE.

FORMS.

	Page
Form of Application to Register	354
,, Appeal to Board of Trade	354
,, Certificate of Registration	355
,, Application for Copy of Certificate of Registration	355
,, Request for Certificate for use in Legal Proceedings	355
,, Certificate for use in Legal Proceedings	356
,, Request to enter Name of Subsequent Proprietor	356
,, Notice of intending Exhibition of Unregistered Design	357
,, Request for Correction of Clerical Error or for entry of New Address	357

Patents, Designs, and Trade Marks Act, 1883.

[DESIGNS.]   E.

Application for Registration of Design in Classes———.

You are hereby requested to register the accompanying design in Class ———, in the name of (*a*) ———, of ———, who claims to be the proprietor thereof, and to return the same to ———.

Statement of nature of design (*b*)

                                                    (*c*)

                                  (Signed) ———

Dated the ——— day of ———, 188—.

To the *Comptroller*,
    Patent Office, Designs Branch,
        25, *Southampton Buildings*,
            Chancery Lane, London, W.C.

(*a*) Here insert legibly the name, address, and description of the individual or firm.
(*b*) Such as whether it is applicable for the pattern or for the shape.
(*c*) To be signed by the applicant.

Patents, Designs, and Trade Marks Act, 1883.

[DESIGNS.]   F.

Appeal to Board of Trade on Refusal of Comptroller to Register a Design.

[*To be accompanied by an unstamped copy.*]

SIR,—I hereby appeal against your decision upon my application to register ———, and beg to submit my case (*a*) for the decision of the the Board of Trade.

                I am, Sir, your obedient Servant,

The Comptroller,
    Patent Office, Designs Branch,
        25, *Southampton Buildings*,
            Chancery Lane, London, W.C.

(*a*) The statement of the case to be written upon foolscap paper (on one side only), with a margin of two inches on the left-hand side thereof.

Patents, Designs, and Trade Marks Act, 1883.

[SEAL OF PATENT OFFICE.] G.

Certificate of Registration of Design.

(R^D No. ———.)

Patent Office, Designs Branch,
25, Southampton Buildings,
Chancery Lane, London, W.C.

This is to certify that the design of which this is a copy was registered this ——— day of ——— 188—, in pursuance of the Patents, Designs, and Trade Marks Act, 1883, in respect of the application of such design to articles in Class ———, for which a copyright of five years is granted.

Patents, Designs, and Trade Marks Act, 1883.

[DESIGNS.] H.

Application for Copy of Certificate of Registration of Design.

Sir,—I hereby request you to furnish me with a Copy Certificate of Registration of Design No. ——— in Class ———.

(Signed) ———.

Dated the ——— day of ——— 188—.

To the Comptroller,
  Patent Office, Designs Branch,
    25, Southampton Buildings,
      Chancery Lane, London, W.C.

Patents, Designs, and Trade Marks Act, 1883.

[DESIGNS.] I.

Request for Certificate for use in Legal Proceedings.

Sir,—I hereby request you to send me for the purposes of use in the suit of (a) ——— a certificate that the design, of which a copy is herein enclosed, was (b) ———.

(Signed) ———
——— day of ——— 188—.

To the Comptroller,
  Patent Office, Designs Branch,
    25, Southampton Buildings,
      Chancery Lane, London, W.C.

(a) Here state the title of the legal proceeding or the other purpose for which the certificate is required.
(b) Here state the entry, matter, or thing which the writer wishes certified.

Patents, Designs, and Trade Marks Act, 1883.

J.

Certificate for use in Legal Proceedings.

In the matter of ———.

No. ———.

I, ———, Comptroller-General of Patents, Designs, and Trade Marks, hereby certify that ———.

Witness my hand and seal this ——— day of ——— 188—.

(Seal.)

Comptroller.

Patent Office, Designs Branch,
 25, Southampton Buildings, London.

Patents, Designs, and Trade Marks Act, 1883.

[DESIGNS.] K.

Request to enter Name of Subsequent Proprietor of Design, with Declaration in support thereof.

I, [*a*] ——— hereby request that you will enter [*b*] ——— name [*c*] ——— in the Register of Designs as proprietor ——— of the Design No. ——— in Class ———.

[*d*] ——— entitled as to the said Design ——— [*e*] ———.

[*f*] And I do solemnly and sincerely declare that the above several statements are true, and the particulars above set out comprise every material fact and document affecting the proprietorship of the said design as above claimed.

And I make this solemn declaration conscientiously believing the same to be true, and by virtue of the provisions of the Statutory Declarations Act, 1835.

[*g*] ———,

Declared at ——— this ——— day of ——— 188—.

Before me, ——— [*h*].

To the Comptroller,
 Patent Office, Designs Branch,
  25, Southampton Buildings,
   Chancery Lane, London, W.C.

[*a*] Or We.
Here insert name, full address, and description.
[*b*] My or our.
[*c*] Or names.
[*d*] I am, or We are.
[*e*] Here state whether design transmitted by death, marriage, bankruptcy, or other operation of law, and if entitled by assignment state the particulars thereof, as *e.g.*, "by deed dated the ——— day of ———, 188—, made between so-and-so of the one part."
[*f*] This paragraph is not required when the declaration is made out of the United Kingdom.
[*g*] To be signed here by the person making the declaration.
[*h*] Signature and title of the authority before whom the declaration is made.

Patents, Designs, and Trade Marks Act, 1883.

[DESIGNS.] L.

Notice of Intended Exhibition of an Unregistered Design.

(a) ——— hereby give notice of my intention to exhibit a ——— of ——— at the ——— Exhibition, which (b) ——— of ——— 188—, under the provisions of the Patents, Designs, and Trade Marks Act of 1883 (c) ——— herewith enclose a ———.

(Signed) ———.

Dated the ——— day of ——— 188—.

To the Comptroller,
 Patent Office, Designs Branch,
  25, Southampton Buildings,
   Chancery Lane, London, W.C.

(a) Here state name and address of applicant.
(b) State "opened" or "is to open."
(c) Insert brief description of design, with drawing.

———

Patents, Designs, and Trade Marks Act, 1883.

[DESIGNS.] M.

Request for Correction of Clerical Error or for Entry of New Address.

SIR,—I hereby request that

(Signed) ———.

Dated the ——— day of ——— 188—.

To the Comptroller,
 Patent Office, Designs Branch,
  25, Southampton Buildings,
   Chancery Lane, London, W.C.

———

THIRD SCHEDULE.

CLASSIFICATION OF ARTICLES OF MANUFACTURE AND SUBSTANCES.

Classes.
 1. Articles composed wholly or partly of metal, not included in Class 2.
 2. Jewellery.
 3. Articles composed wholly or partly of wood, bone, ivory, papier maché, or other solid substances not included in other classes.
 4. Articles composed wholly or partly of glass, earthenware or porcelain, bricks, tiles, or cement.
 5. Articles composed wholly or partly of paper (except hangings).
 6. Articles composed wholly or partly of leather, including bookbinding, of all materials.
 7. Paper hangings.
 8. Carpets and rugs in all materials, floorcloths, and oilcloths.
 9. Lace, hosiery.
 10. Millinery and wearing apparel, including boots and shoes.
 11. Ornamental needlework on muslin or other textile fabrics.
 12. Goods not included in other classes.
 13. Printed or woven designs on textile piece goods.
 14. Printed or woven designs on handkerchiefs and shawls.

J. CHAMBERLAIN,
President of the Board of Trade.

21st December, 1883.

APPENDIX.

RULES *to be observed in Proceedings before the* Judicial Committee of the Privy Council

Under the Act of the 5th and 6th Will. IV., intituled "An Act to amend the Law touching LETTERS PATENT FOR INVENTIONS" *(cap. 83).*

RULE I.

A party intending to apply by petition, under sect. 2 of the said act, shall give public notice by advertising in the London Gazette three times, and in three London papers, and three times in some country paper published in the town where or near to which he carries on any manufacture of anything made according to his specification, or near to or in which he resides, in case he carries on no such manufacture, or published in the county where he carries on such manufacture, or where he lives, in case there shall not be any paper published in such town, that he intends to petition his Majesty under the said section, and shall in such advertisements state the object of such petition, and give notice of the day on which he intends to apply for a time to be fixed for hearing the matter of his petition which day shall not be less than four weeks from the date of the publication of the last of the advertisements to be inserted in the London Gazette, and that on or before such day, notice must be given of any opposition intended to be made to the petition; and any person intending to oppose the said application, shall lodge notice to that effect at the Council Office, on or before such day so named in the said advertisements, and having lodged such notice shall be entitled to have from the petitioner four weeks' notice of the time appointed for the hearing.

RULE II.

A party intending to apply by petition, under sect. 4 of the said act, shall in the advertisements directed to be published by the said section, give notice of the day on which he intends to apply for a time to be fixed for hearing the matter of his petition which day shall not be less than four weeks from the date of the publication of the last of the advertisements to be inserted in the London Gazette, and that on or before such day caveats must be entered; and any person intending to enter a caveat shall enter the same at the Council Office, on or before such day so named in the said advertisements; and having entered such caveat, shall be entitled to have from the petitioner four weeks' notice of the time appointed for the hearing.

RULE III.

Petitions under sects. 2 and 4 of the said act must be presented within one week from the insertion of the last of the advertisements required to be published in the London Gazette.

Rule IV.

All petitions must be accompanied with affidavits of advertisements aving been inserted according to the provisions of sect. 4 of the said act, nd the 1st and 2nd of these rules, and the matters in such affidavits may e disputed by the parties opposing upon the hearing of the petitions.

Rule V.

All persons entering caveats under sect. 4 of the said act, and all parties to any former suit or action touching letters patent, in respect of which petitions shall have been presented under sect. 2 of the said act, and all persons lodging notices of opposition under the 1st of these rules, shall respectively be entitled to be served with copies of petitions presented under the said sections, and no application to fix a time for hearing shall be made without affidavit of such service.

Rule VI.

All parties served with petitions shall lodge at the Council Office, within a fortnight after such service, notice of the grounds of their objections to the granting of the prayers of such petitions.

Rule VII.

Parties may have copies of all papers lodged in respect of any application under the said act, at their own expense.

Rule VIII.

The registrar of the Privy Council, or other officer to whom it may be referred to tax the costs incurred in the matter of any petition presented under the said act, shall allow or disallow in his discretion all payments made to persons of science or skill examined as witnesses to matters of opinion chiefly.

Rule IX.

A party applying for an extension of a patent, under sect. 4 of the said act, must lodge at the Council Office six printed copies of the specification, and also four copies of the balance sheet of expenditure and receipts relating to the patent in question, which accounts are to be proved on oath before the lords of the committee at the hearing. In the event of the applicant's specification not having been printed, and if the expense of making six copies of any drawing therein contained or referred to would be considerable, the lodging of two copies only of such specification and drawing will be deemed sufficient.

All copies mentioned in this rule must be lodged not less than one week before the day fixed for hearing the application.

The Judicial Committee will hear the Attorney-General, or other counsel, on behalf of the Crown, against granting any application made under either the 2nd or 4th section of the said act, in case it shall be thought fit to oppose the same on such behalf.

INDEX.

ABANDONED, application for patent, 270.

ACCEPTANCE of complete specification, 99.

ACCIDENTAL discovery sufficient to support patent, 50.

ACCOUNTS,
    filing of, on application for extension of patent, 129.
    must be reasonable and precise, *ib.*, 132.
    when dispensed with, 131.
    of sales and profits, when allowed, 167, 179.
    not allowed when no profit made, 180.
    injunction granted on terms of keeping, 170.
    plaintiff must elect between damages and, 177, 187.
    of profits lost by competition, not allowed when license has been granted, 178.

ACTION for infringement. See *Infringement*.

ADDITION to known machine producing new result may be patented, 27.

ADDRESS,
    of letters patent, 102, 103.
    form of notice for alteration of, in register, 323.

ADMINISTRATORS. See *Executors*.

ADVANTAGES, claiming, 51.

ADVERTISEMENT,
    of amended specification, 93, 274, 308.
    of acceptance of specification, 99, 271.

AFFIDAVIT,
    not required on petition for revocation, 184.
    on motion for injunction, 191.
        what it must state, 192.
    after trial, 213.
    generally, 304.

AGENT,
    infringement by, 157.
    to sell, cannot maintain action for infringement, 189.
    discovery of name of, infringing after judgment, 213.
    application for patent by, 303.

AGREEMENT, fraudulent, will be set aside, 118.

362 INDEX.

ALIEN,
    may obtain patent, 5.
    liable for infringement, 144.

ALTERATION, memorandum of, 92.

AMBIGUITY,
    in specification, whether a question for jury, query, 71.
    latent, how explained, 120.

AMENDMENT. See *Specification*.
    of specification, 90, 273, 308.
    compulsory or voluntary, 90.
    report of examiner as to, necessary, *ib*.
    comptroller may require, *ib*.
    appeal to law officer, *ib*.
    power of, prior to Act, 92.
    duties of examiner as to, 91.
    compulsory, limited to matters of form, *ib*.
    by applicant or patentee, *ib*.
    now made at peril of inventor, 93.
    statutory declarations respecting, *ib*.
    must not enlarge the claim, 94, 96.
    disallowed in case of fraud, *ib*.
    when allowed after action brought, *ib*.
    must be by disclaimer, correction or explanation, 95.
    part of original specification, 97.
    reasons must be given for, 98.
    of particulars, 195, 196.
    upon terms, 206.
    generally, 301.
    form of, in case of clerical error, 323.

ANTICIPATION, 36, 148, 202. See *Prior User* and *Publication*.

APPARENT possession, doctrine of, does not affect patent right, 113.

APPEALS,
    to law officers, rules regulating, 312.
    form of, 324.

APPLICATION,
    for patent, 5, 269, 302.
    considered abandoned if specification not left within specified time, 270.
    what it must contain, 5.
    by infants and married women, 6.
    by first importer, whether now permissible, query, *ib*. 7.
    in fraud of inventor, 16.
    order of recording, 305.
    for separate patents by way of amendment, *ib*.
    by representative of deceased inventor, *ib*.
    on communication from abroad, *ib*.
    form of, 315.
        when communicated from abroad, 316.
        for hearing by comptroller, 318.
        for compulsory grant of license, 319.

ARCHITECT, when not liable for infringement, 144.

ASSESSORS, at trial of action, 221, 276.

INDEX.   363

ASSIGNEE,
    suing, 141.
    patent passes on bankruptcy to, 112.
    extension of patent to, 126.
    on what grounds, 127, 136.
    action by, of a portion, 141, 142, 188.
    as to action by local, query, 188.
    can restrain infringement within assigned area, 165.
    may sue in his own name, 188.

BALANCE SHEET must be lodged on application for extension, 131.

BANKRUPTCY of patentee, effect of, 112.

BOARD OF TRADE may grant licenses, 118.

BONA FIDES necessary in specification, 80, 82.

BREACHES, particulars of, 193, 194. See *Particulars*.

CAPITALIST may join inventor to obtain grant, 8.

CAVEAT, entry of, 123, 138.

CERTIFICATE,
    of comptroller, 225.
    of Court that validity of patent questioned, 239, 241.
    cannot be given by consent, 240.
    form of, 268, 323.
    of payment or renewal, 307.

CERTIFIED COPIES, 225, 310.

CLAIM,
    if too large, vitiates patent, 47.
    if advantages claimed are not new, does not vitiate patent, 51.
    general words, when admissible in, 69.
    must be distinct, 84.

CLERICAL ERRORS, 90, 323. See *Amendments*.

COLONIAL, arrangements as to patents, 186.

COLOURABLE IMITATION, 151.

COMBINATION, infringement of patent for a, 149, 153. See *Infringement*.
    elements of, may be used, 158.
    use of, patented in improved, 153.
    subject-matter of patent, 32, 86.
    though every part old, 33.
    must be claimed as such, 86, 151.

COMMUNICATION,
    from abroad, 20. See *Importer*.
    in England, 20.
    patent granted as for such communication, *ib*.

COMPANY, directors of, 144, 244. See *Directors*.

COMPOUND SUBSTANCE, discovery of, good ground for patent, 27.

COMPTROLLER,
    powers of, 270 *et seq.*
    may refuse to accept unamended specification, 90.
    determines when amendment allowable, 94.
    may refuse illegal patent, 105.
        no appeal from this decision, 106.
    notice of license given to, 121.
    may correct errors on register, *ib.*
    certificate of, as evidence, 225.
    form of application for hearing by, 318.

CONCEALMENT, in specification by patentee, 77—81.

CONDITIONS of grant, 109.

CONDONATION of infringement, 179.

CONFIRMATION abolished, 140.

CONSIDERATION,
    for grant, 8.
    merit, a part of, 11.
    how construed, 126.
    ingenuity, part of, 12.

CONSTRUCTION,
    of specification, when object old and means new, 32.
    of specification will be liberal, 68.
    as with other documents, 70, 234—236.
    of claims, 71.
    of grant most beneficial, 111.

CONTRACTOR,
    liable for infringement, 143, 157.
    with Crown, ditto, 159.

CO-OWNERS, action by, 188.

CORPORATION, may be registered as proprietor of patent, 310.

CORRECTION of specification, 95. See *Amendment.*

COSTS,
    of disclaimer, when allowed, 97.
    on application for leave to disclaim, 98.
    of extension of term, 124.
    of litigation on application for extension, 130.
    of entry of caveat, 138.
    on abandonment of petition for extension, *ib.*
    fixed sum in lieu of, *ib.*
    security for, by licensee using patentee's name, 143.
    discretion of court as to, 180.
    of abandoned defences, 200.
    of particulars allowed on certificate only, 201, 241.
    when particulars are amended, 206.
    of interrogatories, 215.
    between solicitor and client, when ordered, 239, 240.
    particulars considered on taxation of, 241.
    of abandoned action, 242.
    on higher or lower scale, 243.
    appeal as to, 244.
    when payable by directors personally, *ib.*
    up to hearing, 245.
    fees payable in connection with patents, 313.

INDEX. 365

CROWN,
    use of invention by servants of, 110, 159, 276.
    by contractor with, 159.
    liable for infringement, 110, 160.
    power of purchase by, 110.
    right of user without payment abolished, 111.
    terms of user by, *ib.*
    arrangements with other governments by, 185.

DAMAGES,
    when allowed after amendment, 95.
    when plaintiff entitled to, 177.
    measure of, in action for infringement, *ib.*, 178.
    where license granted, 178.
    against whom recoverable, *ib.*
    discovery in aid of, 179.
    do not depend on right to injunction, 180.
    plaintiff cannot claim account and, 187.
    must be proved when claimed, 229.
    forms of, 258.

DATE of patent, 272.

DECLARATION,
    what it must contain, 8, 269.
    must distinguish inventor and importer, 8.
    must be made by one of the applicants, *ib.*
    statutory, 304.

DEFAULT, particulars of wilful, 202.

DEFINITIONS of patent, patentee, invention, &c., 281. See *Sub titulis*.

DELAY,
    in practising invention, 133.
    in applying for injunction, 175.

DELIVERY up of infringing articles, 176.

DESCRIPTION,
    court will distinguish between claim and, 84.
    insufficient, in specification not fatal, 105.

DESTRUCTION,
    of infringing articles, 176.
    when ordered, *ib.*
    of patent, 278.

DETERMINATION, of patent for non-payment of fees, 110.

DEVOLUTION,
    of patent by assignment or operation of law, 112.
    absolute or limited, 113.
    assignment must be by deed, *ib.*
    by license under seal, *ib.*
    or verbal, 117.
    for any place, 114, 142.
    notice to comptroller on, 121.

DRAWINGS.
    do not limit claim as against specification, 72.
    size of, &c., 305, 306.

DUPLICATE form of application for patent, 322.

DURATION of patent, 106, 272.

ENLARGEMENT OF TIME,
    for payments, 308.
    in other cases, *ib.*
    form of application for, 321.

ENTRY of grant on register, 309.

EQUIVALENTS,
    mechanical or chemical, 155.
    description of, when necessary, 74.

ESTOPPEL,
    patentee estopped from questioning validity of patent assigned, 114, 117.
    except in case of fraud, *ib.*
    law as to, 115.
    by license not under seal, 116.
    of licensee, *ib.*
    as between partners, 117.

EVASION of patent, 153.

EVIDENCE,
    when receivable from petitioner, 132.
    power to dispense with, 311.

EXAMINER,
    may require amendment of specification, 90, 270.
    duties of, 91, 92.

EXCLUSIVE,
    right not extended by amendment, 95.
    license, 143. See *License.*

EXECUTORS AND ADMINISTRATORS,
    may sue, 113.
    property in patent passes to, 112.
    powers of, *ib.*
    when they may assign patent, 118.

EXHIBITION,
    of patent, when allowable, 278, 304.
    form of notice of intended, 322.

EXISTING patents, operation of Act on, 250.

EXPERIMENTS,
    cost of, allowed in application for extension, 130.
    with a view to discovery, 47.
    no infringement, 158.

EXPERT,
    may be called in by law officer, 100.
    inspection by, 257.

EXPLANATION of specification, 95. See *Amendment.*

INDEX.   367

EXPOSURE for sale, no infringement, 163.

EXTENSION,
    of term of patent, 272, 275.
    petition for, 123.
    when granted, and for how long, *ib.*
    former practice as to, 124, 125.
    evidence necessary to obtain, 126.
    granted to assignee, *ib.*
    accounts on application for, 129, 133.
        must be reasonable, 129.
    what costs allowed, 130.
    balance-sheet must be lodged, 131.
    grounds for refusing, 133, 134.
    inquiries on, *ib.*
    who may petition for, 136.
    whether granted to licensees, quære, 137.
    effect of, on assignments, *ib.*, 138.
    second, not granted, 139.

EXTENT of patent, 102, 199, 272.

EXTRANEOUS matter, when fatal in specification, 83.

FALSE suggestion avoids patent, 8, 21.

FEES, determination of patent for non-payment of, 110. See *Costs*.

FOREIGN,
    patents should be stated in petition for prolongation, 132.
    country, protection of patent in, 185.
    ship, use of patented invention by, 161, 162, 279.

FRAUD,
    no amendment allowed in case of, 94.
    no estoppel in case of, 114, 115.
    entry in register by, 122.
    particulars of, 209.
    must be accurately stated, *ib.*
    tried by jury, 223.

GRANT,
    of letters patent, 105.
    royal prerogative saved in, 106.
    creates property in invention, *ib.*
    form of prohibition in, 108.
    rights of crown limited in, 110, 111.
    construction of, beneficial, 111.

IGNORANCE of patent, no excuse for infringement, 146.

IMITATION,
    colourable, 151.
    of invention forbidden, 108, 154, 158.

IMPORTATION,
    mere, no infringement, 163.
    of invention formerly sufficient to support grant, 7.
    doubtful now, 7, 12, 109.

IMPORTED INVENTION, 17.
    patent for, at common law, 18.
    statutory provisions as to, *ib.*
    merit of, 126.

IMPROVEMENT,
    of manufacture, 25.
    by new process, *ib.*
    by alteration of known machine, 27.
    by new application of old invention, 28.
    by new combination, 33.

INDORSEMENT on writ, 251. See *Writ.*

INFANT may obtain patent, 6.

INFRINGEMENT,
    action for, 141, 187.
        statement of claim in, 193, 258.
        particulars of breaches in, 194, 195, 258.
        form of particulars, 258.
        further and better particulars, 195.
        defendant's objections to, 196. See *Particulars.*
        statement of defence in, 199.
        form of, 259.
        parties to, 141.
            as plaintiffs, *ib.*, 188.
                grantee or assignee, 141.
                of a portion or for a district, 142.
                joint owners, *ib.*
                trustee in bankruptcy, 143.
                executors and administrators, *ib.*
                licensee cannot maintain, 142.
                where agent for sale cannot maintain, 188, 189.
            as defendants, 143, 189.
                person physically using, 143.
                person threatening to infringe, 189, 193.
                contractors, 143, 157, 189.
                servants and agents, 143, 157.
                directors, 144.
                architect, *ib.*, 189.
                alien infringing in United Kingdom, 144.
    definition of, 145.
    prohibited by royal command, *ib.*
    a question for jury, 145, 227, 237.
    of invalid patent, no, 145.
    ignorance of patent immaterial, 146, 226.
    what amounts to, 148.
    where patent locally assigned, query, *ib.*
    of part of invention, *ib.*, 149.
    of patent for combination, 149.
    by other combination of same parts, 153.
    of substance of invention, 150, 155.
    by colourable imitation, 151, 158, 226.
    by evasion, 153.
    of patent for process, 152.
    by equivalents, 155, 226.
    sale of elements of combination, no, 158.
    experiments, no, *ib.*
    by crown and its servants, and contractors, 110, 159.

INFRINGEMENT—*continued.*
 by using, definition of, 160.
 what amounts to use in action for, *ib.*, 161.
 mere possession, no, 162, 226.
 by foreign or British ships, 161, 162.
 constructive, will not support action, 163.
 by selling, definition of, *ib.*
 mere purchases, exposure for sale, or importation, no, *ib.*, 226.
 actual sale, an, 165, 226.
 sale of patented article made abroad, an, 164.
 re-sale of article sold by patentee, no, 165.
 neglect to restrain, reason for not granting extension, 133.
 injunction, remedy by, 167, 190. See *Injunction.*
 damages for, 177. See *Damages.*
 by tacit permission, 179.
 defences to action for, 199, 203, 204.
 costs of abandoned defences, 200.
 defendant's particulars of objections, 201.
 form of, 260.
 trial of action for, 221. See *Trial.*
  before whom, 221, 223.
 grounds of postponement, 223, 224.
 forms in action for, 251.

INJUNCTION,
 remedy for infringement by, 167.
 interlocutory or perpetual, *ib.*
 when granted, 168, 169, 190, 191.
 usually upon terms, 170, 171, 190.
 against threats of action for infringement, 249, 277.
 alleged infringement to be strictly proved, 173.
 evidence of intention to infringe will support, 175.
 must be no delay in moving for, *ib.*
 falls with expiry of patent, 176.
 but not as to previously made articles, *ib.*
 mandatory, when granted, *ib.*
 master of Q. B. D. cannot grant, 191.
 dissolved if claim disagree with affidavits, 192.
 affidavits on motion for, *ib.*
 form of notice of motion for interlocutory, 253.
  of affidavit in support, *ib.*
  of refusal on terms, 255.

INSPECTION,
 power of Court to grant, 216, 277.
 object of Court in granting, 217.
 strong *primâ facie* necessary for, *ib.*
 mere similarity insufficient, 226.
 granted if essential, 218.
 samples may be ordered for, 219.
 mutual, when ordered, *ib.*
 application for, on motion or by summons, *ib.*
 form of notice of motion for, 255.
  of inspection of process, and to take samples, 256.
  of order for inspection of process by experts, 257.
 on acceptance of complete specification, 305.
 of register, 121.
  at what hours, 311.

T.   B B

INTELLIGIBILITY,
    of specification, 67.
    to skilled person, 72.

INTENTION of party infringing immaterial, 146, 147.

INTERLOCUTORY INJUNCTION, 167.
    forms of, 254. See *Injunction*.

INTERNATIONAL arrangements as to patents, 135.

INTERROGATORIES,
    may be administered, 196.
    must be relevant, 210.
    how far defendant must disclose secret process in, *ib.*
    some evidence of infringement necessary for delivery of, 211.
    differ from particulars, *ib.*
    fishing disallowed, 212.
    must be answered fully, *ib.*, 213.
    when permitted after trial, 213.
    by plaintiff and defendant differ, 214, 215, 247.
    costs of, 215.
    form of, 262.

INTRODUCER, first, 19.

INVALID patent, no infringement of, 145.

INVENTION,
    defined by Act, 3.
    what is an, 9.
    when already public property, 15.
    a new and useful, 22.
    of new article, *ib.*
    of new process, *ib.*
    novelty of, 34.
    a question of fact, 38.
    secret prior user of an, 36, 40.
    public prior user of an, *ib.*, 39.
    experiment, whether, 37.
    prior publication of an, 41.
    the whole must be new, 17.
    utility of, 48.
    claim of an, a question for court, 66.
    distinct statement of, necessary, 89.
    must not be enlarged by amendment of specification, 96.
    property in, created by grant, 106.
    infringement of part of, 149.
        of substance of, 151. See *Infringement*.
    importance of, how estimated, 128.

IRELAND, proceedings for revocation in, 184.

JOINT OWNERS, one of, may sue, 142.

JOURNAL,
    official advertisements in, 308.
    illustrative of invention, 306.

INDEX.

JUDGMENT,
    final, for plaintiff, forms of order of, 264—268.
    for defendant, 268.

JURY,
    questions for, 234, 235.
        infringement, 145.
        novelty, 37, 38.
        utility, 49.
    grounds of application for, 223.

KNOWN,
    material, application of, to new purpose, 28.
    instrument to ditto, *ib.*

LAW OFFICER,
    powers of, 270, 271.
    appeal to, 90. See *Appeals.*
    determines when specification may be amended, 94.
    cannot order applicant for disclaimer to pay costs, 98.

LEGAL personal representative, grant of patent to, 8. See *Executors.*

LICENSE,
    to use patent, should be under seal, 113.
    how far valid if not, *ib.*, 114.
    is not a deed, 114.
    a verbal, 117.
    differs from assignment, 118.
    compulsory, *ib.*, 274, 309.
    by whom granted, 118, 119.
    must be registered, 120.
    not assignable, 119.
    measure of damages after grant of, 178.
    an exclusive, 143.
    entry of, on register of patents, 311.
    form of application for compulsory grant of, 319.
        of opposition thereto, 320.
        of request to enter notification of license on register, 322.

LICENSEE,
    profits of, when considered, 131.
    whether extension granted to, query, 137.
    action for infringement not maintainable by ordinary, 142, 188.
    exclusive, may use patentee's name in action, 143.
    not exclusive user of patent in mere, 143.
    security for costs by exclusive, *ib.*

LOST patent, how supplied, 278.

MAKING,
    infringement by, 157.
    secret, by inventor before patent, 45.

MALA FIDES in specification, 83. See *Specification.*

MANDATORY orders only granted after trial, 176.

MANUFACTURE,
    what is a new, 22, 34.
    a new article, 22.
    a new process, *ib.*
    a principle not a, *ib.*
    construction of term a question of law, 37.

MANUFACTURER,
    distinguished from inventor, 9.
    profits of, distinguished from patentee's, 129.
    when considered in action for infringement, 177.

MARRIED women may obtain patent, 6.

MASTER liable for infringement by servant, 143.

MEMORANDUM of alteration, 92.

MERIT,
    not necessary in importer, 20.
    part of consideration, 49.

MISREPRESENTATION,
    in specification fatal, 77.
    particulars of, 202.

MISTAKE,
    in specification, 90.
    by including several inventions, 305. See *Amendment.*

MONOPOLIES, STATUTE of, 2.
    provisions of, 3.

MOTION for inspection, 219.

MUSEUM, PATENT, 279.

NON-USER,
    of patent, 127.
    ground for refusing extension, 133.

NOVELTY,
    want of, vitiates patent, 101.
    within the kingdom necessary, 109.
        whether this is so now, query, 109, 110.
    Privy Council will not inquire into, 127.

OBJECTIONS, particulars of, 201. See *Particulars.*

OFFICIAL
    referee, 222.
    journal, advertisement in, 305.

OLD. See *Known.*

OPPOSITION,
    to grant of patent, 99, 271, 306.
    grounds of, now available, *ib.*
    available prior to act, *ib.*
    notice of, by Comptroller, 100.
    patent sealed in absence of, 101.
    to amendment of specification, *ib.*
    notice of, 306.
    form of, to grant of patent, 317.

INDEX. 373

PART OF INVENTION,
    infringement of, 148, 149.
    when old, 43.

PARTICULARS,
    of objections, 182.
    of breaches, 193.
    form of, 258.
    of what they must consist, 194.
    must not be too general, 195, 204—206.
    effect of general words, when admitted, 205, 206.
    further and better, 205.
    form of order for delivery of further, 259, 261.
    where defendant has not objected to, 196.
    should distinguish process infringed, 197.
    in statement of defence, 201, 247.
    form of order for further, 261.
    when exceeding 3 folios, 202.
    on ground of prior user, *ib.*
    or publication, 20, 67.
    when names and addresses necessary in, 203, 207.
    amendment of, by defendant, 206.
    on what terms, *ib.*
    evidence of matters not disclosed in, 206.
    of objection that grantee not true inventor, 208.
    allegation of insufficiency of specification enough in, *ib.*
    differs from answers to interrogatives, 211.
    no objection allowed at trial to, 231, 232.

PARTIES to action for infringement, 141. See *Infringement.*

PARTNERS,
    estoppel of retiring, 117.
    plea of invalidity, when allowed, 118.

PATENTS,
    letters, to and by whom granted, 1, 6.
    conditions of grant, 3.
    form of application for, 5.
        what it must disclose, *ib.*
    whether granted to an importer doubtful, voided by false suggestion, 8.
    grant to joint applicants, *ib.*
    or to legal personal representative, *ib.*
    consideration for grant of, 8. See *Consideration.*
    determines on non-payment of fees, 110.

PENALTIES,
    mentioned in prohibition, 108.
    what they are, query, 109.

PERPETUAL injunction, 167. See *Injunction.*

PETITION,
    to Court substituted for *scire facias*, 97, 181.
    to extend term of patent, 123.
    by whom presented, 181, 183.
    for revocation, by whom presented, 246. See *Revocation.*
    forms, 252, 260.

PETITIONER,
    for extension, 136.
    may give evidence of profits, 132.

PHYSICAL user of invention, 143. See *Infringement.*

PORTION,
    action by assignee of, 141.
    application by assignee of, 151.

POSSESSION, mere, no infringement, 162.

POST, documents may be sent by, 304.

POSTPONEMENT of trial, 223, 224.

PRACTICE. See *Sub titulis ; Infringement ; Injunction ; Trial, &c.*

PREJUDICIAL concealment by patentee, 81.

PRESUMPTION in favour of patent with fair disclosure, 66.

PRINCIPLE,
    no invention can be claimed in a, 22, 155.
    method of applying a, 23, 25.

PRIOR USER,
    no longer ground of opposition, 99.
    confirmation of patent notwithstanding, 140.
    what amount of, invalidates patent, 148.
    objection on ground of, 202.
    evidence of, not disclosed in particulars of objection, 206.

PRIVY COUNCIL,
    power of, to avoid grant, 109.
    consideration of petition on entry of *caveat* by, 123.
    application for extension by, 125.
    will not inquire into novelty, 127.
    order as to rights of patentees abroad by, 186.
    form of application for entry on register of order of, 324.

PROCESS,
    infringement of patent for, 152.
    selling article made abroad by patented, 164.
    subject-matter of patent, 22, 26.

PROFITS,
    of patentee and manufacture, 179.
    how estimated, 130.
    by licensees must be added, 131.

PROHIBITION, in grant, 108, 145.

PROLONGATION of patent, 123 *et seq.* See *Extension.*

PROPERTY, right of, in infringing articles, 176.

PROTECTION,
    of patent abroad, 185.
    by complete specification, 272.
    provisional, 16.

PROVISIONAL,
    protection, 16.
        provisions of Act as to, 17, 272.
    specification, 59, 64, 270. See *Specification.*

PUBLIC use, 36.

INDEX. 375

PUBLICATION,
    prior, 41.
    in specification, book or newspaper, 44.
    book need not be sold, if exhibited for sale or open to inspection, *ib.*
    must contain sufficient description, *ib.*
    objections on ground of prior, 207.

PURCHASE, mere, of patented article no infringement, 163.

REBUTTING evidence by plaintiff, 230, 231.

RECITALS, must be four in number, 103.

REDUCTION, action of, in Scotland, 183.

REFEREE, official or special, 222.

REFERENCE, *form* of order for, 262.

REGISTER,
    of patents, 120, 274, 309 *et seq.*
    primâ facia evidence of matters therein, 121.
    no notice of trust receivable on, *ib.*
    inspection of, *ib.*
    comptroller may correct errors of, *ib.*
    fraudulent entry on, 122.
    entries of grant on, 309.
    orders affecting patents, to be entered, 310.
    including payment or non-payment of fees and licenses, *ib.*, 311.
    form of request to enter license on, 322.

RENEWAL of English after expiry of foreign patent, 128.

REPRESENTATIVE case, *form* of order for trial of, 263.

RESTRAINT of trade, covenant not to manufacture without patented invention not in, 120.

REVOCATION,
    provisions for, 100, 275.
    must be registered, 120.
    by petition, under the Act, 181.
    by whom presented, *ib.*
    proceedings for, resemble *scire facias*, 223.
    who may present petition for, 246.
    particulars of objection on, *ib.* See *Particulars.*
    form of petition for, 252.

RIVAL applicants, 16.

RULES,
    by whom made, 101, 124.
    Patent, 1883 ... 302 *et seq.*
    under 5 & 6 Will. 4, c. 83 ... 358 *et seq.*

SALE,
    infringement by, 163. See *Infringement.*
    by patentee carries right of free disposition, 165.

SAMPLES,
 of infringing article, when ordered to be delivered, 218.
 form of notice of motion to take, 256.
 of order for delivery of, *ib*.

SCIRE FACIAS, proceedings by, abolished, 97, 181—183.

SCOTLAND, action of reduction in, 183, 184.

SEAL,
 when affixed to patent, 101, 102, 271.
 of Patent Office, 102, 272.

SECRET,
 of trade, 107.
 no means of enforcing agreement to keep a trade, *ib*.
 if subject of intended patent, *secus*, *ib*.
 use, anticipation by, 36.

SERVANT infringing, 143, 157.

SHIPS,
 use of invention by foreign, 161, 162.
 by British, abroad, 162.

SPECIAL referee, 222.

SPECIFIC performance of agreement to assign, 118.

SPECIFICATION,
 provisions of Act as to, 52.
 title of, 55.
  requisites for, *ib*.
  title in old patents must contain claims, *ib*.
  must not be too general, *ib*.
  must correspond with invention, 56.
  vagueness of, fatal, 57.
  variance from, 58.
  must be consistent with invention, *ib*.
 Provisional,
  must describe nature of invention, 59.
  and agree with complete, 60, 64.
  its object, *ib*., 61, 62.
  distinguished from final, 63, 64.
  form of, 316.
 Complete,
  what it is, 64, 66, 270.
  a portion of the patent, 65.
  should make fair disclosure, 66, 77.
  must be intelligible and sufficient, 64, 67, 228.
  and *bonâ fide*, 80.
  to whom intelligible, 72, 75.
  must not claim too much, 72.
  will be fairly construed, *ib*., 228.
  one document with title, 68.
  use of general words in claim of, 69, 70.
  must distinguish new from old, 70, 71.
  ambiguity in, *ib*.
  drawings in, how used, 72.
  old apparatus need not be described in, 73.
  error curable in, 74.
  sufficiency, a question for jury, 66, 236.

SPECIFICATION—*continued.*
    Complete—continued.
        what constitutes sufficiency, 75.
        intelligibility, novelty, and utility, 236.
        degrees of sufficiency required, 76, 79.
        suppression or false suggestion fatal in, 77, 80, 82.
        must be read in relation to existing knowledge, 78.
        general rule as to sufficiency, 79.
        unnecessary and misleading details fatal, 83.
        must contain a distinct claim, 84, 89.
            and not too large, 84.
        disclaimer of what is old, 85.
        improvements in old processes must be so claimed, 86.
        combination of old parts ditto, *ib.*
        form of, 317.
            of amendment, 318. See *Amendment.*
        allegation of insufficiency of, in action, 208, 209.
        construction of, for Court, 234.

STATEMENT,
    of claim, 193.
    form of, 258.
    of defence, 199. See *Infringement, action for.*

STATUTE,
    of monopolies its origin, 2.
    declares common law, *ib.*
    creates no right, 3.

SUBJECT-MATTER of patent must not be illegal or immoral, 105.

SUBSTANCE,
    new subject-matter of patent, 23.
    of invention, infringement of, 150.

SUBTRACTION from known machine, 27.

SUFFICIENCY,
    of specification, 64.
    question for jury, 66.
    what is, 75.

SUGGESTIONS,
    by one person to another, 11.
    in book or publication, 42.
    in recitals must not be false, 103—105.

SUMMONS,
    for amendment of particulars, 206.
    for inspection, 219.
    for certificate of costs, 242.

SUPPRESSION of information by patentee, 77—81.

TAXATION of costs, 241. See *Costs.*

THREATS of bringing action, 249, 277. See *Injunction.*

TITLE,
    one document with specification, 68.
    how construed, *ib.*
    of specification. See *Specification.*

TRADE MARK, how distinguished from patent, 106.

TRIAL,
    of action for infringement, 221.
    constitution of Court, *ib.*, 222.
    postponing, 223.
    right of opening and replying at, 224.
    issues on plaintiff at, 225, 228, 229.
    when plaintiff may produce rebutting evidence, 230, 231.
    defendant cannot produce further evidence, 231.
    no objection to particulars allowed at, *ib.*

TRUST,
    not receivable on register, 20, 121.
    particulars of breach of, 202.

TRUSTEE in bankruptcy may sue, 143, 188.

UNDUE INFLUENCE, particulars of, 202.

USE,
    what constitutes infringement by, 160, 161. See *Infringement*.
    of foreign invention does not invalidate patent, 186.
    objection on ground of prior, 202.

UTILITY,
    of invention, 48.
    substantial improvement constitutes, 50.
    Privy Council will not inquire into, 127.
    presumption by non-user against, *ib.*

VERBAL license by patentee, 117.

WAIVER of forfeiture by licensor, 120.

WAR, patents for munitions of, 279 *et seq.*

WORKMAN,
    assisting master, 10, 13.
    invention by, 10.

WRIT,
    form of indorsement on, 251.
    in action for infringement, *ib.*
    to restrain threatened infringement, *ib.* See *Infringement, Action for.*